THE S

THE SERIAL KILLERS

A Study in the Psychology of Violence

**Colin Wilson and
Donald Seaman**

This revised edition first published in Great Britain in 1992 by
True Crime
an imprint of Virgin Publishing Ltd
332 Ladbroke Grove
London W10 5AH
Reprinted 1992 (three times), 1993

Copyright © 1990, 1992 Colin Wilson and Donald Seaman

**Cataloguing in Publication Data
available from the British Library**

ISBN 0 86369 615 5

Typeset by Medcalf Type Ltd, Bicester, Oxon.
Set in Times.

Printed and bound in Great Britain by
Cox & Wyman Ltd, Reading, Berks.

Analytical Table of Contents

Hazlewood and Douglas on serial killers. The Boston Strangler. Formation of the Behavioral Science Unit at Quantico. Psychological profiling. The NCAVC (National Centre for the Analysis of Violent Crime).

Monster of the Andes'. Daniel Barbosa. Henry Lee
Lucas. Leonard Lake and Charles Ng.

Why have serial killers appeared at this point in
history? The overcrowded rat theory. The increase in
the 'Emperor Syndrome'. Marxism and murder.
Renwick Williams, the eighteenth century 'Monster'.
Lyons, the California Panty Bandit. The actual
number of serial murders. Computerisation of
fingerprinting. Solutions to the problem?

Illustrations

(Unless otherwise indicated, all photographs are reproduced courtesy of Associated Press.)

Acknowledgements

The authors wish to place on record their gratitude to the FBI for invaluable help and guidance, freely given at all times, during research for this book in the United States; and especially for permission to visit the National Centre for the Analysis of Violent Crime (NCAVC) at Quantico, Virginia — the first such visit by any British publisher. Thanks are due to FBI Director William S. Sessions; also the Assistant Director Milt Ahlerich, and Supervisory Special Agent Stephen Markardt, of the FBI Office of Public Affairs, US Department of Justice, for arranging the visit to Quantico, and later providing research facilities at the FBI J. Edgar Hoover headquarters building in Washington, DC.

We also wish to thank FBI Behavioural Science Unit Chief John Henry Campbell, at Quantico; Supervisory Special Agent Alan E. Burgess, Unit Chief of the Behavioural Science Unit (Investigative Support Wing) and Administrator of the NCAVC, and Supervisory Special Agent John E. Douglas, Criminal Investigative Analysis Programme Manager, for research facilities made available there; VICAP (the Violent Criminal Apprehension Programme) analyst Kenneth A. Hanfland, and social psychologist Dr Roland Reboussin, Ph.D., both of BSIS; Supervisory Special Agent Robert R. ('Roy') Hazelwood, Programme Manager/Training Programme, Behavioural Science Unit (Instruction and Research); and Dr David Icove, Ph.D., P.E., Senior Systems Analyst of the NCAVC, for their individual specialist help.

Both authors owe a major debt of gratitude to Candice Skrapec, one of America's leading experts on serial killers, for her help in establishing contact with the Behavioural Science Unit at Quantico, as well as providing much invaluable information. We also wish to thank the many friends who have provided press cuttings and information on serial killers, particularly June O'Shea; Stephen Spickard; Denis Stacy; Brian Marriner; Ian Kimber; and the late John Dunning.

In addition we wish to thank Dr David Canter, and Dr Anne Davies, the Principal Scientific Officer of the Metropolitan Police Forensic Science Laboratory.

Finally, the authors are indebted to a number of distinguished journalists, all of whom contributed in their specialist ways to aiding research in England and/or America. Those in Washington, DC, include Ross Mark, the White House correspondent of the *Daily Express*; bureau chief Ian Brodie and reporter Hugh Davies of the *Daily Telegraph*; and Ralph Stow, public relations officer for the AMOCO Corporation; and in London James Nicoll, former Foreign Editor of the *Daily Express*; Derek Stark (Travel Manager) and Frank Robson (former Air Correspondent of the *Daily Express*); Brian McConnell, QGM, author and veteran crime reporter of the *Daily Mirror*; Melvin Harris; Peter Johnson, author and *Sunday Times* journalist; and Ronald Gerelli, former *Daily Express* photographer.

Introduction

This book is about the psychology of the serial killer. It is not intended to be a comprehensive history of serial murder — that would require a far longer volume — but an attempt to understand the complex mechanisms that lead to a 'habit of killing'. So although there has been an attempt to offer at least some brief account of the most notorious serial murderers of the twentieth century, there are many omissions: for example, Adolf Seefeld, Peter Manuel, William MacDonald, Herb Mullin and Randall Woodfield. On the other hand, considerable space is devoted to some criminals who do not, strictly speaking, qualify as serial killers: notably Hiroko Nagata, Cameron Hooker, and Gary Heidnik. The reason, which will become clear from the text itself, is that these people enable us to understand an important facet of the psychology of the serial killer. This understanding, which has emerged over the course of the past decade, amounts to a minor revolution in the science of criminology. Now it is possible to state that, with the researches of the FBI Behavioural Science Unit, and of similar groups that are following their example in other countries, we are at last in a position to understand some of the answers to one of the most disturbing riddles of the twentieth century.

One

A Short History of Sex Crime

Since the early 1980s, American law enforcement agencies have become aware of the emergence of an alarming new phenomenon, the serial killer.

This recognition came about, it seems, through analysis of the steep rise in sex crime and 'motiveless murder'. Ever since the 1960s, 'multiple murder' had been on the increase. The 'Manson Family' had killed at least nine people. Vaughn Greenwood, the 'Skidrow Slasher' of Los Angeles, killed nine homeless vagrants. Necrophile Ed Kemper killed ten, including his grandparents and mother. Paranoid schizophrenic Herb Mullin killed thirteen. Dean Corll, the homosexual murderer of Houston, Texas, killed twenty-seven boys. John Wayne Gacy of Chicago admitted to killing thirty-two boys. Patrick Kearney, the 'Trash Bag Murderer' of Los Angeles, killed twenty-eight men. William Bonin, the 'Freeway Killer', killed a minimum of twenty-two young men. The 'Hillside Stranglers', Kenneth Bianchi and Angelo Buono, raped and killed a dozen girls. Ted Bundy killed twenty-three. Randall Woodfield, the 'I.5 Killer', murdered forty-four. The South American sex killer Pedro Lopez, 'the Monster of the Andes', admitted to killing three hundred and sixty pre-pubescent girls. In 1983, a derelict named Henry Lee Lucas made headlines in America when he also confessed to killing three hundred and sixty people, mostly women.

All this raised a disturbing possibility: that perhaps a fairly small number of killers were responsible for the rise in sex crime and motiveless murder. ('Motiveless murders' had risen from 8.5% in 1976 to 22.1% in 1984.) America is a large country, and many killers roam from state to state, moving on before police have a chance to catch up with them. Twenty-two-year-old Steven Judy, who murdered a mother and her three children in 1979, admitted before his execution that he had 'left a string' of murdered women across America. The family of Sherman

1

McCrary – three men and two women – travelled from Texas to California, robbing drug stores and restaurants, and also abducting waitresses and shop assistants, whose violated bodies were left in lonely places. For this kind of killer, murder becomes a habit and an addiction. Henry Lee Lucas told police: 'I was bitter at the world . . . Killing someone is just like walking outdoors.' It also became clear that such killers murder out of some fierce inner compulsion, and that after the crime, experience a sense of relief and a 'cooling-off period'. Then, like the craving for a drug, the compulsion builds up again, until it is time to go in search of another victim. It was this type of murderer for whom the police coined the term 'serial killer'. One police officer suggested that there could be as many as thirty-five serial killers at large in America, and that the number could be increasing at the rate of one a month. More recent estimates have been as high as five hundred.

What has caused this epidemic of mass murder? One thing at least is clear: that it is part of a pattern that has emerged since the Second World War. In order to understand it, we need to go much further back to the beginning of the 'age of the sex crime'.

The emerging pattern first became clear (to Colin Wilson) in the late 1950s when he was engaged in compiling *An Encyclopedia of Murder* with Patricia Pitman: 'The purpose was to try to provide a standard work that would include all the "classic" murders of the past few centuries and serve as a reference book for crime writers and policemen. Pat Pitman chose to deal with domestic murders and poisoning cases, while I wrote about mass murderers like Landru, Haigh and Christie.

'I was soon struck by an interesting recognition: that sex crime was not, as I had always supposed, as old as history, but was a fairly recent phenomenon. It was true that soldiers had always committed rape in wartime, and that sadists like Tiberius, Ivan the Terrible, Vlad the Impaler and Gilles de Rais certainly qualify as sex criminals; but in our modern sense of the word – that is, a man who commits rape because his sexual desires tend to run out of control – sex murder makes its first unambiguous appearance in the late nineteenth century. The Jack the Ripper murders of 1888 and the murders of the French "disemboweller" Joseph Vacher in the 1890s are among the first recorded examples. Some of the most famous sex crimes of the century occurred after the First World War: these included the murders of the "Düsseldorf Vampire" Peter Kürten, of America's "Gorilla Murderer" Earle Nelson, of the child killer Albert Fish, and the extraordinary crimes of the Hungarian Sylvestre Matushka, who experienced orgasm as he blew up trains.

'Were there no sex killers before the late nineteenth century? As far as I have been able to determine, the answer is no. At first I was inclined to believe that a French peasant named Martin Dumollard was an exception. In the 1850s he lured a number of servant girls seeking work into lonely places, then murdered them and buried the bodies; but the records reveal that his motive was to steal their belongings, and there is no evidence of sexual assault. For most working-class people of the period — and this included the "criminal class" — life was hard, and when they committed murder, it was for money, not sex.'

What then caused the 'age of the sex crime'? One reason was certainly the nineteenth-century attitude to sex, the kind of prudery that made Victorian housewives conceal table legs with a long tablecloth in case the mere thought of legs caused young ladies to blush. In earlier centuries, sex was treated with healthy frankness. As soon as the Victorians started to regard it as a shameful secret, it began to exercise the fascination of the forbidden. The rise of pornography dates from the 1820s; there were indecent books before that, but their purpose was to satirise the clergy, and they were usually about priests seducing nuns and penitents. Then, in the 1820s, there emerged books with titles like *The Lustful Turk* and *The Ladies' Telltale*, about virgins being kidnapped and raped by Mediterranean pirates and little girls being seduced by the butler.

If we wish to trace it to its beginnings, it could be argued that the age of the sex crime begins in the year 1791, with the publication of a novel called *Justine, or The Misfortunes of Virtue*, by Alphonse Donatien de Sade. The Marquis de Sade is the patron saint of pornography and sex crime. Contrary to the general impression, Sade never killed anyone; his most reprehensible exploit was making small cuts in a prostitute's skin and pouring hot wax into them. For a number of similar misdemeanours, he was thrown into prison at the age of thirty-

3

seven, and stayed there for thirteen years, until the time of the French Revolution. For a man of Sade's imperious temperament, prison must have been unimaginable torment. For three years he was plunged into transports of despair and self-pity. Then he began to recover and to direct his hatred and resentment into literary channels. Resentment mingled with frustrated eroticism to produce works of almost insane cruelty. His favourite fantasy was of some virtuous, innocent girl who falls into the hands of a wicked libertine and is flogged, raped and tortured. His most characteristic work is a huge novel called *The 120 Days of Sodom*, a long sexual daydream about four libertines – including a bishop and a Lord Chief Justice – who retire to a château and set out to indulge every possible kind of sexual perversion. Brothel madames tell stories about their most debauched clients, stimulating the libertines to rape, flog and torture a small band of young men and women who have been procured for their pleasure. Yet, oddly enough, Sade is never pornographic in the modern sense of the word; there are no gloating descriptions of sexual acts. His real desire is to scream defiance at the Church and State; he loves to show judges abusing their authority, and monks and nuns engaged in debauchery and corrupting children. His descriptions of torture are anything but sexually stimulating; even devotees of pornography find them repetitive and nauseating.

Sade was far more than a mere advocate of torture and murder; he regarded himself as the first truly honest philosopher in the history of human thought. The so-called 'great philosophers' he regarded as liars and lackeys. All animals, he says, seek pleasure as the greatest good; the body was obviously made for pleasure, expecially sexual pleasure. Then why do we not spend our lives seeking pleasure? Because it would not suit our rulers. They try to persuade us that unselfishness, hard work and self-sacrifice are virtues, and that there is a God in heaven who will judge us for our misdeeds. This is untrue; there is no God, and if we were not such slaves, we would throw off our shackles and devote our lives to the pursuit of ecstasy. Would this not lead us into doing harm to others? Of course it would, says Sade. Why not? Animals devour one another; that is the law of Nature. *The only truly honest attitude to human existence is one of total selfishness.* The truly courageous man chooses crime rather than virtue, for he knows that virtue was invented by our rulers to keep us in subjugation. Kings and popes know better; they spend their lives in every kind of debauchery . . .

Sade was released from prison in 1789, and for a time scraped a living as a playwright. (He was never, even in his youth, a rich man, and the fierce underlying resentment of his works owes a great deal to poverty.) Then he was arrested again for publishing filthy books, and spent the rest of his life in an asylum, where he died in 1816. His works began to enjoy a certain vogue in England, and his obsession with 'the forbidden' gave rise to the first truly pornographic novels of the 1820s: works whose purpose was not to denounce the Church and the legal profession, but merely to serve as an aid to masturbation — what one French writer called 'books that one reads with one hand'. It is significant that many of these early pornographic works are about the seduction of children and schoolgirls. In the Victorian age, prostitutes were cheap; in fact, few working-class girls would have turned down the offer of five shillings — a week's wages — in exchange for half an hour in a rented room. In the circumstances, rape of adult women would have been superfluous; this is why most sex crimes were committed against children — children were still 'forbidden'.

There was one Victorian gentleman who devoted his whole life to the pursuit of sexual pleasure, and whose career may be regarded as highly instructive in the present context. In his anonymous autobiography, *My Secret Life*, he simply calls himself Walter, and his identity remains a mystery. He describes how his sexual education began at the age of twelve, when he lifted his baby sister's nightdress. In his mid-teens he succeeded in pushing a servant girl on the bed and taking her virginity. From then on, Walter devoted his life to sex. He spent hours of every day peering through cracks in bedroom doors, watching servant girls undress or using the chamberpot. With his cousin Fred he spent days in a basement which had a grating through which he could peer up the skirts of women who walked overhead.

What emerges most clearly from his eleven-volume autobiography — published at his own expense in the 1890s — is that his craving for sex was not a desire to give and receive mutual satisfaction, but an expression of the *will to power*. In the second volume he describes picking up a middle-aged woman and a ten-year-old girl in Vauxhall Gardens, and having intercourse with the child, standing in front of a mirror, 'holding her like a baby, her hands round my neck, she whining that I was hurting her . . .' He adds: 'I longed to hurt her, to make her cry with the pain my tool caused her, I would have made her bleed if I could.' The same attitude emerges again and again in his descriptions of intercourse: 'In the next instant . . . I was up the howling little bitch.' 'Her cry of pain gave me pleasure, and fetched me.'

My Secret Life affords an important insight into the mind of the Marquis de Sade. The normal reader finds it difficult to understand how sexual gratification can be associated with pain and violence: with the gouging out of eyes or the mutilation of genitals. 'Walter' was no sadist, yet his craving for women was basically a desire to violate them. Sade had always enjoyed flogging and being flogged. Incarcerated in a damp cell, with only his imagination to keep him company, the daydreams of flogging and violation turned into daydreams of murder, torture and mutilation. The human imagination has this curious power to *amplify* our desires. Yet it is important to note that, even when released from prison, de Sade made no attempt to put these fantasies into practice. He had already exhausted them by writing them down. In the same way, 'Walter's' sadism never developed beyond a desire to cause pain in the act of penetration, because he had an endless supply of women with whom he could act out his fantasies. The essence of sadism lies in frustration. As William Blake put it: 'He who desires but acts not breeds a pestilence.'

Most of 'Walter's' early encounters with teenage whores took place in the 1840s, when the streets were full of starving women and children for whom five shillings meant the difference between life and death. By the 1880s all this had begun to change. The Public Health Act and the Artisans' Dwellings Act of 1875 had made an attempt to grapple with disease and poverty. When H.G. Wells came to London as a student in 1884, his cousin Isobel – whom he later married – worked as a retoucher of photographs in Regent Street, and many of

6

his fellow students were women. The typewriter had been invented in the 1860s, and businessmen soon discovered that women made better typists than men. Drapers' shops were now full of women counter assistants. All of which meant that — although there were still plenty of prostitutes on the streets — there was now a whole new class of 'unavailable' women to excite the concupiscence of men like 'Walter'. The result was that, in the last decades of the nineteenth century, rape of adult women became far more common, and sex crime — in our modern sense of the word — made its appearance. In 1867, a clerk named Frederick Baker lured a little girl named Fanny Adams away from her companions in Alton, Hampshire, and literally tore her to pieces. In 1871, a French butcher named Eusebius Pieydagnelle killed six young women with a knife, experiencing orgasm as he stabbed them. (He has a claim to be the first serial killer.) In Italy in the same year, Vincent Verzeni was charged with a number of sex crimes including two murders — he experienced orgasm in the act of strangulation. In Boston, USA, in 1873, a bell-ringer named Thomas Piper murdered and raped three women, then lured a five-year-old girl into the belfry and battered her to death with a cricket bat; he was interrupted before the assault could be completed, and hanged in 1876. In 1874, a fourteen-year-old sadist named Jesse Pomeroy was charged with the sex murders of a boy and a girl in Boston and sentenced to life imprisonment. In 1880, twenty-year-old Louis Menesclou lured a five-year-old girl into his room in Paris and killed her, keeping the body under his mattress overnight; when he tried to burn her entrails he was betrayed by the black smoke. He wrote in his notebook: 'I saw her, I took her.'

Crimes like these were regarded as the solitary aberrations of madmen, and scarcely came to the attention of the general public. The crimes of an American mass murderer named Herman Webster Mudgett, alias Henry Howard Holmes, should be noted as an exception. Holmes began as a confidence trickster, and in the late 1880s he built himself a large house in a Chicago suburb that would become known as 'Murder Castle'. When Holmes was arrested in 1894 for involvement in a swindle, police soon came to suspect that he was responsible for the murder of an associate named Pitezel, and three of Pitezel's children. Further investigation revealed that Holmes had murdered a number of ex-mistresses, as well as

7

women who had declined to become his mistress. Moreover, as Holmes himself confessed, killing had finally become an addiction which, he believed, had turned him into a monster. The total number of his murders is believed to be twenty-seven, and they qualify him as America's first serial killer. He was hanged in 1896.

It was the crimes of Jack the Ripper though – which will be further discussed in the next chapter – that achieved worldwide notoriety and made the police aware that they were confronted by a new type of problem: a killer who struck *at random*. The murders took place in the Whitechapel area of London between 31 August 1888 and 9 November 1888. The first victim, a prostitute named Mary Ann Nicholls, was found in the early hours of the morning with her throat cut; in the mortuary, it was discovered that she had also been disembowelled. The next victim, another prostitute named Annie Chapman, was found spreadeagled in the backyard of a slum dwelling, also disembowelled; the contents of her pockets had been laid around her in a curiously ritualistic manner – a characteristic that has been found to be typical of many 'serial killers'. The two murders produced nationwide shock and outrage – nothing of the sort had been known before – and this was increased when, on the morning of 30 September 1888, the killer committed two murders in one night. A letter signed 'Jack the Ripper', boasting of the 'double event', was sent to the Central News Agency within hours of the murders. When the biggest police operation in London's history failed to catch the murderer, there was unprecedented public hysteria. As if in response to the sensation he was causing, the Ripper's next murder was the most gruesome so far. A twenty-four-year-old prostitute named Mary Jeanette Kelly was killed and disembowelled in her room; the mutilations that followed must have taken several hours. Then the murders ceased – the most widely held theories being that the killer had committed suicide or was confined in a mental home. From the point of view of the general public, the most alarming thing about the murders was that the killer seemed to be able to strike with impunity, and that the police seemed to be completely helpless.

The French police found themselves confronting the same frustrations in the mid-1890s when a travelling killer who became known as 'the Disemboweller of the south-east' raped and mutilated eleven victims, including three boys. (It is interesting to observe that many sex criminals have been tramps or wandering journeymen; it is as if the lack of domestic security produced an exaggerated and unnatural form of the sex needs.) He was finally caught – after three years – when he attacked a powerfully-built peasant woman, whose husband and children heard her screams. He proved to be twenty-eight-year-old Joseph Vacher, an ex-soldier who had spent some time in an asylum after attempting suicide. The lesson of the case was that Vacher had been able to kill with impunity for three years, although his description – a tramp with a suppurating right eye and paralysed cheek – had been circulated to every policeman in south-east France.

The failure was doubly humiliating because France was now celebrated throughout the civilised world as the home of scientific crime detection. As early as 1814, the great doctor Mathieu Orfila had written the first treatise on poisons, revealing how they could be detected in the body; but for many years, other branches of crime detection had remained crude and inefficient. Throughout the nineteenth century, police had been pursuing more or less hit-or-miss methods of detecting criminals, relying on informers and policemen who knew the underworld. The chief virtue of a detective was simply immense patience – the ability, for example, to look through half the hotel registers in Paris in search of the name of a wanted man. All that changed in 1883 when a young clerk named Alphonse Bertillon invented a new method of identifying criminals by taking a whole series of measurements – of their heads, arms, legs, etc. These were then classified under the head measurements, and it became possible for the police to check within minutes whether a man arrested for some minor offence was a wanted murderer or footpad. 'Bertillonage' was soon in use in every major city in the world. The science of identification also achieved a new precision. In 1889, a doctor named Alexandre Lacassagne solved a particularly baffling murder when he identified an unknown corpse by removing all the flesh from the bones and revealing that the man had suffered from a tubercular infection of the right leg which had deformed his knee. Once the corpse had been identified, it was relatively simple to trace the murderers, a couple named Michel Eyraud and Gabrielle Bompard.

The next great advance occurred in England, where Sir Francis Galton realised that no two persons have the same

9

fingerprints. The first case to be solved by a fingerprint occurred in a small town in Argentina in 1892; a young mother named Francisca Rojas had murdered her two children and tried to put the blame on a peasant called Velasquez; an intelligent police chief named Alvarez observed a bloody fingerprint on the door, and established that it belonged to Francisca; she then confessed that she had been hoping to persuade a young lover to marry her, but that her 'illegitimate brats' stood in the way . . . When fingerprinting was introduced at Scotland Yard in 1902, it was so successful that Bertillon's more complicated system was quickly abandoned. All over the world, 'bertillonage' was quickly replaced by the new fingerprint system.*

It was at this point, when science seemed to be transforming the craft of the manhunter, that killers like Jack the Ripper and Joseph Vacher made a mockery of all attempts to catch them. A well-known cartoon published at the time of the Ripper murders showed policemen blundering around with blindfolds over their eyes. Scientific crime detection depended on finding some *link* between the crime and the criminal. If a rich old dowager was poisoned, compiling a list of suspects was easy; the police merely had to find out who would benefit in her will, and which of these had access to poison. But the sex killer struck at random and, unless he left some clue behind, there was nothing to link him to the victim.

One important advance offered hope of a partial solution. In 1901, a young Viennese doctor, Paul Uhlenhuth, discovered a method for testing whether a bloodstain was animal or human. Blood is made up of red cells and a colourless liquid called serum. Uhlenhuth discovered that if a rabbit is injected with chicken blood, its serum develops a 'resistance' to chicken blood. And if a drop of chicken blood is then dropped into a test tube containing serum from the rabbit, the serum turns cloudy. It was obvious that the same method could be used to detect human blood, for when an animal is injected with human blood, its serum will then turn cloudy if a drop of

* For a more detailed account of the history of crime detection, see *Written in Blood: A History of Forensic Detection*, Colin Wilson, 1989.

human blood — or even a few drops of dried blood in a salt solution — is introduced into it. In 1901, Uhlenhuth used his method to help convict a sadistic killer of children. Ludwig Tessnow was a carpenter, and in 1898 he had been a suspect when two little girls were killed and dismembered in a village near Osnabrück. Tessnow had insisted that brown stains on his clothes were wood dye, and the police believed him. When, three years later, two young brothers were killed in the same manner — literally torn to pieces — on the island of Rügen, Tessnow was again a suspect; again he insisted that stains on his clothing were of wood dye. The police sent his clothes to Uhlenhuth, who was able to show that some stains were of human blood, and that others were of sheep's blood (Tessnow was also suspected of disembowelling sheep). He was executed in 1904.

Tessnow had been living in the areas where the murders took place; but if he had been a tramp, like Vacher, he might never have been caught. This may not have been apparent in 1902, but as the rate of sex crime began steadily to rise in the second decade of the twentieth century, it became increasingly obvious. If a sex criminal observed a reasonable degree of caution, there was nothing to stop him from going on for years. In Cinkota, near Budapest, a plumber named Bela Kiss killed at least a dozen women between 1912 and 1914, storing most of the bodies in oil drums; he had been conscripted into the army by the time someone found the corpses in his cottage, and he was never caught. In Hanover soon after the First World War, a homosexual butcher named Fritz Haarmann killed about fifty youths, and disposed of their bodies by selling them for meat. Georg Grossmann, a Berlin pedlar, killed an unknown number of girls during the same period, and also sold them for meat. (When police burst into his flat in 1921, they found the trussed-up carcase of a girl lying on the bed, ready for butchering.) Karl Denke, a Munsterberg landlord, made a habit of butchering strangers, and eating their flesh; when he was arrested in 1924, police found the pickled remains of thirty bodies, and Denke admitted that he had been eating nothing but human flesh for three years. These four killers escaped notice because they killed their victims on their own premises. All were undoubtedly motivated by sex.

Sex killers who moved around were equally elusive. Between 1910 and 1934, an itinerant carpenter named Albert Fish tortured and killed an unknown number of children — he

11

confessed to four hundred — and was finally caught only because he was careless enough to put a letter describing one of the murders in an envelope that could be traced. During 1926 and 1927, a travelling rapist and murderer killed twenty-two women in America and Canada, starting in San Francisco and ending in Winnipeg, and in the meantime travelling as far east as Philadelphia. Most of the victims were landladies who advertised rooms to rent, and their naked bodies were usually found in the room they were offering. For a long time the police were not even aware of what the killer looked like, but eventually a woman to whom he had sold some jewellery — taken from a victim — was able to describe him as a polite young man with a simian mouth and jaw. The police eventually caught up with Earle Nelson, the 'Gorilla Murderer', simply because he was unable to stop killing, and left a well-defined trail of corpses behind him. In Düsseldorf during 1929, an unknown sadist attacked men, women and children, stabbing them or knocking them unconscious with a hammer. Eight victims were killed; many others were stabbed or beaten unconscious. The killer, Peter Kürten, was eventually caught when one of his rape victims led police to his flat. In Cleveland, Ohio, in the mid-1930s, a killer who became known as the 'Mad Butcher of Kingsbury Run' killed and dismembered a dozen men and women, mostly derelicts and prostitutes; in two cases, two victims were killed at the same time and the dismembered parts of the bodies mixed together. The murders ceased in 1938, and the 'Cleveland Torso Killer' was never caught.

Yet in spite of the notoriety achieved by these mass murderers, sex crime remained at a fairly low level during the 1930s. It accelerated during the Second World War — partly because the anarchic social atmosphere produced a loss of inhibition, partly because soldiers were deprived of their usual sexual outlet. By 1946, sex crime had doubled in England from its pre-war level. In large American cities, it had quadrupled by 1956. Even in Japan, where sex crime was still rare, a laundry worker — and employee of the American army — named Yoshio Kodaira raped and murdered ten girls in Tokyo between May 1945 and August 1946. He had made the mistake of giving his last victim his name and address when he offered her a job in his laundry, and she had left it with her parents; Kodaira was hanged in October 1949.

* * *

By the time I began compiling *An Encyclopedia of Murder* in 1959, a strange new type of crime was beginning to emerge – 'the motiveless crime'. In April 1959, a bachelor named Norman Smith, who lived alone in his caravan in Florida, watched a television programme called 'The Sniper', then took a pistol, and went out with the intention of shooting someone – anyone. The victim happened to be a Mrs Hazel Woodard, who was killed as she sat watching television. Colin commented: 'Apparently he killed out of boredom,' and compared it with the case of Nathan Leopold and Richard Loeb, the two wealthy Chicago students who decided to commit a murder simply as a 'challenge'. In May 1924 they chose at random a fourteen-year-old boy named Bobbie Franks and battered him to death with a chisel. They were caught because Leopold lost his glasses at the site where the body was dumped. The strange motivation – or lack of it – led journalists to label the murder 'the crime of the century'. In June 1949, a pretty nineteen-year-old brunette named Ruth Steinhagen checked into the Edgewater Beach hotel in Chicago, and sent a note to a man whom she had adored from afar for two years: baseball player Eddie Waitkus, the unmarried first baseman of the Phillies; she asked if she could see him briefly to tell him something of great importance. In her room, she pointed a rifle at him and shot him dead. Asked why she did it, she explained that she 'wanted the thrill of murdering him'. By the late 1950s, such crimes were ceasing to be unusual. In July 1958, a man named Norman Foose stopped his jeep in the town of Cuba, New Mexico, and with a rifle shot dead two children as they stood beside their mother; when caught, he explained that he wanted to do something about the population explosion. In February 1959, a pretty blonde named Penny Bjorkland accepted a lift from a man she knew slightly, and shot him dead with a revolver; traced through the bullet, she explained that she was curious to see if she could commit a murder and not have it on her conscience.

During the 1960s, there was a perceptible rise in such crimes. In 1960, a young German named Klaus Gosmann knocked on the door of a flat he had chosen at random, and shot dead the man who opened the door, as well as his fiancée, who was standing behind him. Then he turned and walked away. He committed four more 'random' murders before he was caught. In November 1966, an eighteen-year-old student named Robert

Smith walked into a beauty parlour in Mesa, Arizona, ordered five women and two children to lie down on the floor, and shot them all in the back of the head. Both Gosmann and Smith were highly intelligent, regarded by their professors as good students. Yet apparently both suffered from a sense of boredom, of unreality. Smith's explanation of his motive provides the vital clue to this new type of murder. 'I wanted to become known, to get myself a name.' He felt that killing seven people would ensure that his name appeared in newspapers around the world. The 'motiveless murderer' who began to emerge in the late 1950s was usually suffering from a kind of ego-starvation, a desire to be 'recognised'. In short, such murders are not committed out of sexual frustration, but out of a frustrated craving for 'self-esteem'.

This seemed to provide an interesting clue to what was going on. In the 1940s, the American psychologist Abraham Maslow had suggested an interesting theory of human motivation, which he called the 'hierarchy of needs'. Maslow pointed out that if a man is starving to death, his basic need is for food; he imagines that if he could have two square meals a day he would be completely happy. If he achieves this aim, then a new level of need emerges — for security, a roof over his head; every tramp dreams of retiring to a country cottage. If he achieves this too, then the next level emerges: for love, for sex, for emotional satisfaction. If this level is achieved, then yet another level emerges: for self-esteem, the satisfaction of the need to be liked and respected.

These four 'levels' could be clearly seen in the history of criminality over the past two centuries. In the eighteenth century there was so much poverty and starvation that most crime was committed out of a simple need for survival — Maslow's first level. By the mid-nineteenth century, the most notorious crimes are domestic murders that take place in respectable middle-class homes, and the motive is a desire to preserve domestic security. Towards the end of the century, Maslow's third level emerges: sex crime. In the mid-twentieth century, the fourth level — self-esteem — becomes a motive for murder. It is as if society is passing through the same stages as the individual; and since society is composed of individuals, this may be less absurd than it sounds.

Now obviously, no murder can be genuinely without motive; when we label a crime motiveless we are simply admitting that it cannot be classified under the usual headings. When we drum our fingers impatiently on the tabletop, the action seems to have no motive, but a zoologist would say that it is a 'displacement activity', and that it is due to frustration. In the same way, Robert Smith's murders in the Arizona beauty parlour were not truly motiveless; they were an expression of boredom and *resentment*. This leads to the recognition that resentment can be detected in the majority of motiveless crimes. This resentment is often totally paranoid in character − like the desire to 'do something about the population explosion' that drove Norman Foose to shoot two children. A more recent example occurred near Santa Cruz, California, when a 'dropout' with an obsession about the environment murdered a whole family. On 19 October 1970 the house of Dr Victor Ohta, an eye surgeon, was seen to be on fire. Firemen discovered five bodies in the swimming pool − those of Dr Ohta, his wife and two children, and his secretary Dorothy Cadwallader. Under the windscreen wiper of his Rolls-Royce was a note that declared that 'today World War III will begin', and that anyone who misused the environment would from now on suffer the penalty of death. 'Materialism must die or mankind must stop.' It was signed: 'Knight of Wands − Knight of Pentacles − Knight of Cups − Knight of Swords' − these being cards in the Tarot pack. The surgeon's estate car had been driven into a railway tunnel, obviously in the hope of causing a serious accident, but a slow-moving goods train had pushed it out of the way.

In nearby woods there was a colony of 'hippies', and one of these told the police about a twenty-four-year-old car mechanic named John Linley Frazier who had recently deserted his wife and moved into a shack near the village of Felton; it was approached by a kind of drawbridge across a deep ditch, and Frazier apparently drew this up every night. He had told other hippies that he had burgled the Ohtas' house on an earlier occasion, and that they were 'too materialistic' and ought to be killed. Frazier was taken in for questioning, and his fingerprints on the Rolls-Royce established his guilt beyond all doubt. The evidence indicated that he had planned the murders several days in advance, and he was sentenced to death. It also became clear at the trial that there was no foundation for his charge that the Ohtas were destroying the environment − they had taken care to leave the woodland

15

around their house untouched. Nor could Ohta be accused of materialism – he helped finance a local hospital and often gave free treatment to those who could not afford his fees. The murders were based upon the same kind of paranoid resentment that had led Charles Manson to write 'Death to pigs' in blood on the bedroom wall of one victim.

Does not the use of a term like 'paranoid resentment' indicate that such a killer should be regarded as insane, and therefore not responsible for his actions? There are certain cases where this is obviously true – as when the killer suffers from delusions or hears imaginary voices; but it is difficult to draw an exact dividing line between paranoia and a resentment based on self-pity and envy. When Judge Ronald George, who tried the case of the Hillside Stranglers of Los Angeles, Kenneth Bianchi and Angelo Buono, was asked whether such acts did not prove them insane, he replied: 'Why should we call someone insane because he or she chooses not to conform to our standards of civilised behaviour?' This seems to apply to the majority of 'motiveless murders' since the 1950s, as well as to many acts of political violence, as will be seen.

There is an additional complication to be taken into account. In the case of the Ohta killings, there was no evidence of sexual assault. But many 'motiveless murders' involve rape or other forms of sexual violence. At first this sounds like a contradiction in terms until we recall that most 'motiveless murders' involve boredom and resentment. The murder of Bobbie Franks is a case in point. Leopold and Loeb had originally meant to kidnap a girl and rape her. Yet even if they had done so, the murder would still be classified as a motiveless crime, since the motive was not sex, but a desire to prove themselves 'supermen'. The determining factor has to be the psychology of the killers.

This can also be seen in the case of multiple killer Carl Panzram, executed in 1930. When Panzram was arrested for housebreaking in Washington, DC in 1928, no-one suspected that he was a murderer. For many years he had been known in many American prisons as the toughest troublemaker they had ever encountered – in one prison he had burned down the workshop and wrecked the kitchen with an axe. When guards discovered a loosened bar in his cell, Panzram received a brutal beating and was suspended from the ceiling by his wrists. A young guard named Henry Lesser was shocked, and sent Panzram a dollar by a 'trusty'. At first Panzram thought it was a joke; when he realised that it was a gesture of sympathy, his eyes filled with tears. He told Lesser that if he could get him a pencil and paper, he would write him his life story. The result was one of the most extraordinary documents in the annals of criminality. Born on a mid-western farm of Prussian immigrant parents, Panzram had been in trouble from an early age. His father had deserted the family and life was hard. Carl envied more well-to-do boys at school and, when he burgled the house of a neighbour, was sent to reform school. Always tough and rebellious, he was repeatedly beaten, and the more he was beaten, the more he dreamed of revenge. Hitching a lift on a freight train, he was sodomised by four hoboes. From then on, he frequently inflicted sodomy — at gunpoint — on people he disliked. His sense of injustice drove him to a frenzy of resentment. This in turn finally drove him to murder. He stole a yacht, then lured sailors aboard and raped and killed them. In Africa, working for an oil company, he sodomised and murdered a black child, and shot six negroes in the back 'for fun'. Back in America, he continued to rape and kill male children, bringing his total of murders up to twenty.

When Henry Lesser asked him: 'What's your racket?', Panzram smiled and replied: 'I reform people.' When Lesser asked how, he replied: 'By killing them.' He liked to describe himself as 'the man who goes around doing good'. He meant that he regarded life as so vile that to murder someone was to do him a favour. He explained in his autobiography that he felt that the guilt for his murders would somehow be visited on the people who had done him harm. This is a typical example of the strange upside-down logic of the 'motiveless' killer: when he kills, he feels he is somehow taking revenge on 'society' — unaware that there is no such thing as 'society', only individuals.

In Leavenworth Jail — where he had been sentenced to twenty-five years on the basis of his confession — Panzram murdered a foreman with an iron bar and was sentenced to death. When the Society for the Abolition of Capital Punishment tried to intervene, he told them not to waste their time. 'I look forward to death as a real pleasure . . .' His wish was granted on 5 September 1930.

The same 'suicidal' urge can be seen in many mass murderers and serial killers. In his book *Compulsive Killers*, the psychiatrist Elliott Leyton speaks of 'the serial killer whose murders provide both revenge and a lifelong *celebrity career*, and the mass killer who no longer wishes to live, and whose murders constitute his *suicide note*'. The 'resentment killer' feels that he is killing with a definite aim: to prove to himself that he is not a weakling and a loser, to take revenge on society, and so on. He soon realises that killing brings him no closer to his objective; in fact, it leaves him with a curious sense of meaninglessness and emptiness – and the knowledge that he has placed himself beyond the bounds of normal society. The result may be suicide, or an act of carelessness that invites arrest. Panzram challenged the jury to sentence him to death, declaring: 'If I live I'll execute some more of you.' Steve Judy, the rapist killer already mentioned, told the jury: 'You'd better put me to death. Because next time it might be one of you, or your daughter.' Harvey Glatman, a Los Angeles photographer who raped and murdered three girls, asked his public defender to request the death penalty. Gary Gilmore, who committed two pointless murders in the course of robbery in 1976, begged the jury to sentence him to death, and died by firing squad in January 1977.

The element of resentment can clearly be seen in one of the most widely publicised cases of the 1960s, the 'Moors murders' (which will be discussed more fully in Chapter 5). Like Carl Panzram, Ian Brady, the illegitimate son of a Glasgow waitress, became a burglar at the age of eleven because he envied the well-to-do boys in the 'posh' school to which he had been sent by the local authorities. After several years on probation and a period in reform school, he discovered the ideas of the Marquis de Sade, and became enthusiastic about Sade's 'philosophy of selfishness'. He began to daydream about 'the perfect crime'; but it was not until he met an eighteen-year-old typist, Myra Hindley, who became completely infatuated with him, that he began seriously to consider putting the dreams into practice. Between 1963 and 1965, with Myra Hindley's help, he raped and murdered five children. Myra was completely dominated by Brady, and it seems to have been this heady sense of power over another person – Brady had

18

always been a loner — that led, eighteen months after they became lovers, to the first murder, that of sixteen-year-old Pauline Reade. It was in planning his fifth murder, that of a seventeen-year-old homosexual named Edward Evans, that he made the mistake that led to his arrest. He had become friendly with Myra's brother-in-law, sixteen-year-old David Smith. Brady had already converted Myra from Catholicism to atheism and Nazism. David Smith proved an equally apt pupil, writing in his journal: 'Rape is not a crime, it is a state of mind. Murder is a hobby and a supreme pleasure.' 'God is a superstition, a cancer that eats into the brain.' 'People are like maggots, small, blind and worthless.' However, when he witnessed Brady murdering Edward Evans with an axe, he suddenly understood the gap between the theory and practice of sadism, and telephoned the police.

The result was the murder trial whose impact on the British public can only be compared with that of the Jack the Ripper case nearly seventy years earlier. Before Brady and Hindley had murdered ten-year-old Lesley Ann Downey, they had taken pornographic photographs, then made a tape recording of her screams and pleas for mercy, which they concluded with some lively music. Played in court, it created a sense of unbelief and shock. The novelist Pamela Hansford Johnson, who, together with her husband C.P. Snow, attended the trial, found that it had the quality of a nightmare. She records that one of the most frightening things about the accused was their sheer ordinariness. They seemed unaware of the enormity of what they had done. She goes on to cite other recent crimes of brutality and vandalism, and the strange 'affectlessness' of the perpetrators — the plea: 'I was bored.'

Yet in assuming that Brady's murders were committed out of boredom, she is overlooking the real motive. Detective Chief Superintendent Peter Topping, in his book on the case, quotes Myra Hindley: 'She felt he enjoyed the perverse sense of power that his physical superiority over children gave him . . .' And in fact, the Moors murder case is about power rather than about sex. And the craving for power springs, in turn, out of resentment. In this respect, at least, Brady is not unlike the majority of human beings — the need for self-esteem is common to everyone. Ernest Becker analyses it in his book *The Denial of Death*: 'We are all hopelessly absorbed with ourselves . . . In childhood we see the struggle for self-esteem at its least disguised . . . His whole organism shouts the claims of his natural narcissism.' And this does not apply merely to spoilt children. 'It is too all-absorbing and relentless to be an aberration, it expresses the heart of the creature: the desire to stand out, to be *the* one in creation . . . he must desperately justify himself as an object of primary value in the universe; he must stand out, be a hero, make the biggest contribution to world life, show that he *counts* more than anyone else.' When this 'urge to heroism' and self-assertion is frustrated, it turns into resentment. And in Brady's case, as with so many other serial killers, the resentment turned to murder.

Four years later, a Los Angeles jury found themselves baffled as they listened to the evidence against Charles Manson and three of his female 'disciples', Susan Atkins, Patricia Krenwinkel and Leslie van Houten, accused of involvement in the death of nine people, including film star Sharon Tate. There was a slightly insane air about the whole trial, and it was the weird logic of Manson's supporters that created the mad atmosphere. Like Hitler after his unsuccessful *putsch* of 1923, he seemed determined to turn it into a trial of his accusers. 'You make your children what they are . . . These children — everything they have done, they have done for the love of their brothers.' Asked if she thought that killing nine people was unimportant, Susan Atkins countered by asking if the killing of thousands of people with napalm was important, apparently arguing that two blacks make a white. Yet in private, reported the prosecutor, Vincent Bugliosi, Manson had allegedly confessed to thirty-five murders.

It is tempting to dismiss all this as the confused rhetoric of drug addicts. Yet it is worth studying more closely because it is so typical of the self-justification of the serial killer. What Manson was really implying was that the laws of an unjust society deserve to be broken, and that in doing this, criminal violence is justified. Even if we accept his argument, it is difficult to see how his victims were responsible for the injustice. His attitude is based on self-pity; he told the psychiatrist Joel Norris that he saw himself as the 'ultimate victim of society'. Manson played guitar and wrote songs, and he believed that he deserved to be as successful as Bob Dylan or the Beatles. His reasoning seemed to be that since he was not successful, then someone must be to blame, and someone deserved to suffer. Carl Panzram had written: 'Before I left [home] I looked around and figured that one of our neighbours who was rich and had a nice home full of nice things, he had too much and I had too little.' And punishment only made him dream of getting his own back. 'Then I began to think that I would have my revenge . . . If I couldn't injure those who had injured me, then I would injure someone else.' This is what Jean Paul Sartre has called 'magical thinking' – which means thinking with the emotions rather than reason. And it inevitably leads to absurd results. An old joke tells of an Arab in the desert who asked another Arab why he was carrying an umbrella. 'I bought it in England. If you want it to rain you leave it at home.' In 1959 a labourer named Patrick Byrne, who had raped and then decapitated a girl in a Birmingham hostel, told the police: 'I was trying to get my own back [on women] for causing my nervous tension through sex.' But then none of us is free of this tendency to irrationality. Is there anyone in the world who doesn't swear when he stubs his toe, or feel victimised when a traffic light changes to red just before he arrives?

Sartre himself was not free from the tendency to magical thinking; his leftism was based on a lifelong detestation of the bourgeoisie (the class to which his own family belonged), and he once declared that true political progress lies in the attempt of the coloured races to free themselves through violence. In fact, much of the extreme leftism that Sartre espoused has its roots in the kind of negative thinking that we have observed in Panzram, Brady and Manson. (The same, of course, applies to many extreme right-wing groups, such as the American Weathermen or the Italian Ordine Nero.) When we analyse the thought process that leads to crime, we see that it involves looking around for someone on whom we can *lay the blame*. What Panzram, Manson, Sartre, Karl Marx and the majority of serial killers in this book have in common is that they lay the blame on 'society'. And what these people also have in common is that they have blinded themselves to the idea that they themselves might be partly to blame for their problems.

The nearest Japanese equivalent to the Manson case involved members of a group who called themselves the United Red Army Faction, the *Rengo Sigikun*, an organisation formed in

1969 by radical students. Nine members of the Red Army Faction were responsible for hijacking a Japanese Air Lines jet on 31 March 1970 and were released in North Korea. After a raid on a Mooka gunshop in February 1971, members of the group escaped with large quantities of arms. Later that year, thirty-seven policemen were injured in a bomb explosion while trying to control a demonstration in the Meiji Park in Tokyo. In the autumn, the wife of a police official died when she opened a parcel bomb that arrived through the mail. In both cases, the suspects were Tsuneo Mori, leader of the Red Army Faction, and Hiroko Nagata.

In February 1972, police searching empty holiday residences in the area of Mount Kasha, Gumma province, found finger-prints of a wanted radical in a cottage at the foot of the mountain. While police watched the cottage from hiding, a van containing five young people was spotted in the nearby town of Matsuida. Two were captured; the other three escaped into the mountains. The following day, an army of police with tracker dogs combed the area. Suddenly an armed man ran out of the bushes and tried to stab a policeman; a woman came to the man's aid as he struggled. When finally subdued, they proved to be Tsuneo Mori, the twenty-seven-year-old leader of the Red Army Faction, and Hiroko Nagata. The operation also seems to have flushed out six more revolutionaries — four men and two women — who went into a shop in the railway station of Karuiwaza, Nagano — a holiday resort — to buy cigarettes. Their smell and the state of their clothes led the woman behind the counter to suspect that they had been sleeping rough, and she told the station manager, who notified the police. The radicals fled to an empty villa, taking hostage the wife of the caretaker, and it was soon surrounded by police. After a ten-day siege and the death of two policemen the radicals surrendered. The youngest of the captives was a sixteen-year-old youth.

Meanwhile, Tsuneo Mori had confessed to the police that his group had murdered twelve of their own members during the time they had been in hiding on Mount Kasho. Following his instructions, police unearthed three decomposing corpses in a cedar forest — one man and two women, one of whom was eight months pregnant. Medical examination revealed that the cause of death was freezing in sub-zero temperatures; all three had been bound and left in the open to die. The women proved to be members of another radical organisation which had merged with the Red Army Faction – the Chukyo Anti-Japan-US Security Pact. Nine more bodies were eventually discovered, bringing the total to three women and nine men. Police searching for the corpses in the mountains admitted that their efficiency had been improved during the previous year when they had searched for the eight victims of a sex maniac called Kiyoshi Okubo in the same area; they had learned to tell a grave by the colour of the earth.

What gradually emerged was that Tsuneo Mori was not the one who was mainly responsible for the murders. The person who had inspired them had been Hiroko Nagata. Mori was a weak character, who felt that he had to maintain his leadership through harshness; he spent much of the interrogation in tears. Hiroko Nagata, a pharmaceutical graduate, was altogether stronger. But her inferiority complex about her unattractive appearance had turned to murderous paranoia in the freezing winter hideout where the thirty Red Army members hid for three months. (They frequently made long treks in the moonlight, staggering with exhaustion, to other empty cabins; Mori urged them on by reminding them that Mao Tse Tung had suffered worse things during the Long March.) A woman member who escaped told of candlelight discussions of points of Marxist doctrine, ending with demands for ruthless 'self-criticism'. All this led to harsh punishments, and to a series of 'loyalty purges' rather like the Stalin purges of the thirties. One twenty-two-year-old youth – the founder of the Chukyo group – was beaten, then stabbed to death by his two younger brothers, who were ordered to carry out the murder to prove their loyalty. A woman who escaped – leaving her three-month-old baby behind – had watched her husband stabbed to death but had not dared to protest in case she was killed too. It had been Hiroko Nagata who had led the discussions, often losing her temper and becoming hysterical. She liked to tell other members of the group that they were too materialistic. It was Nagata, too, who had ordered that the hair of the three dead women should be cropped close to the skull as a punishment; one of them had been tied up naked and confined in a narrow space below the floor, another tied to a pillar for several days until she died. Her crime was wearing earrings.

In prison and under interrogation, Hiroko Nagata at first

23

remained arrogant, ordering the investigators around, demanding coffee, turning her back on them. But as police pointed out the various mistakes that had led to her arrest, she suddenly admitted: 'We've been licked'; thereafter she began combing her hair, which until then she had kept in a 'revolutionary' state of untidiness.

In January 1973, Tsuneo Mori hanged himself in prison. Hiroko Nagata was sentenced to life imprisonment.

In retrospect, the most incomprehensible thing about the murders is that the other members of the group permitted them. This may be due partly to the natural obedience to authority that characterises the Japanese (one of the survivors described how all used to listen, with averted eyes, as Mori and Nagata harangued them). But it also seems clear that the group were totally dominated by their leaders, just as the Manson family was dominated by its father figure, and Myra Hindley by Ian Brady. In effect, they were brainwashed – and this again seems to be a phenomenon that is often associated with revolutionary movements. When heiress Patty Hearst was kidnapped at gunpoint by a group calling itself the Symbionese Liberation Army on 5 February 1974, it was as a 'capitalist' hostage; the 'Army's' motto was 'Death to the Fascist insect that preys upon the life of the people'. After her father had distributed two million dollars' worth of food to the poor – on the orders of the 'Army' – Patty Hearst sent her parents a tape stating that she had been converted to the revolutionary ideology, and denouncing the food distribution as a sham; shortly afterwards she took part in the armed robbery of a bank. In May, the 'Army's' Los Angeles hideout was surrounded by police; in the battle and the fire that followed, the leaders of the movement were killed. Yet Patty Hearst continued 'on the run' with the remaining members of the gang until her arrest in September 1975. Her trial led to a sentence of seven years' imprisonment but she was released on probation after eight months and quickly returned to the non-revolutionary views of her early days.

In the Red Army Faction case, perhaps the most striking thing is the degeneration of Tsuneo Mori and Hiroko Nagata as they realised that they possessed absolute power over their followers. For Hiroko Nagata at any rate, murder became a pleasure. This is again something that can be observed in the majority of serial killers. Killing and inflicting torture become an addiction. Yet perhaps this is hardly surprising when we consider that de Sade's attitude towards society is also 'revolutionary', and that there is a definite link between his political views and his 'sadism'. He takes it for granted that all authority is unutterably corrupt, and bases his philosophy of murder and torture on this completely negative attitude. Since the masters are vile, and the slaves little better than maggots, both deserve utter contempt. In Nagata and Mori, the same attitude led to torture and executions. In other Marxist revolutionary groups it has often led to a kind of ruthlessness that springs out of paranoia — as when, on 21 June 1977, Italian 'Red Army' terrorists burst into the room where Remo Cacciafesta, dean of Rome University's School of Economics, was lecturing, and shot him in the legs, shouting that he was teaching his students to adapt to a fundamentally immoral society. The common denominator of political revolutionaries and serial killers is resentment and 'magical thinking'.

What is responsible for this increase in 'magical thinking' that has led to the increase in serial murder and political violence? In 1935, the philosopher Edmund Husserl suggested a link between political brutality — of Hitler, Stalin, Mussolini — and the gradual decay of faith in rational certainty that had occurred over the past two centuries. His argument was less far-fetched than it sounds. For practical purposes, the philosophy of revolution can be traced back to 1762, the year Rousseau's *Social Contract* appeared, with its famous opening sentence: 'Man is born free, and everywhere he is in chains.' The corollary was that he is *not* free because various wicked authorities have entered into a conspiracy to deprive him of his freedom. Rousseau was weak and neurotic, and he urgently wanted to find somewhere to lay the blame for his own unhappiness. So he created the myth that there was once a golden age when all men lived together in perfect harmony, and that this came to an end because a few evil men seized power and enslaved the rest. It followed, of course, that the answer to the problem was for the oppressed to strike off their chains and overthrow the oppressors. His philosophy, as developed by Marx, has eventually come to dominate half the globe, until it is a part of the air we breathe. We take it for

25

granted that all right-thinking young people hold strong views about social justice, and to regard 'protest' with favour and authority with disfavour. We even take it for granted that most people hate the police. The tendency to 'look for somewhere to lay the blame' has become a part of our intellecutal inheritance, and it is impossible to understand the psychology of the serial killer without taking it into account.

In practice, the kind of violence typified by the Red Army Faction — and the kind of irrationality that seemed to lie behind it — produced a powerful backlash. There was a general feeling that people who are willing to commit murder for their political ideology are dangerous cranks who have no place in a civilised society. Groups like the Japanese Red Army, the Italian Red Brigades, the Baader-Meinhof gang and the Symbionese Liberation Army were hunted down with the full approval of the public. The suicides of Ulrike Meinhof and Andreas Baader in 1977 seemed to symbolise the end of an epoch. By the mid-1980s, Mikhail Gorbachev's policies of *glasnost* and *perestroika* had made the politics of violent revolution seem oddly irrelevant. Yet it was at about this point, when a new age of reason seemed to have dawned in politics, that the general public became aware of the emergence of the serial killer.

In England, it was the case of the 'Yorkshire Ripper' that brought a general awareness of the problems of tracking down a random killer. It was appropriate that the press should have labelled him the Yorkshire Ripper, for he was the most notorious serial killer in Great Britain since the days of Jack the Ripper. The first three attacks occurred in the second half of 1975. Two women were knocked unconscious by hammer blows dealt from behind; in the first case, the attacker had raised her dress and was about to plunge the knife into her stomach when he was interrupted and ran away; in the second, he made slashes on the woman's buttocks with a hacksaw blade. The third victim, a prostitute, was knocked unconscious with the hammer, then stabbed to death. She was the first of thirteen murder victims over the course of the next five years. Some were prostitutes; some were simply women or girls who happened to be out walking in the dark. In most cases, the victim was stabbed and slashed repeatedly in the area of the stomach and vagina, although the killer stopped short of actual disembowelment.

By early 1978, the hunt for the Yorkshire Ripper had become the biggest police operation ever mounted in Britain. Yet the problem facing the police – as in all such cases – was the sheer number of suspects. In the early years of the twentieth century the great criminologist Edmond Locard had stated the basic tenet of forensic detection: 'Every contact leaves a trace'; but in the case of a random killer, the 'traces' left behind are useless, since they afford no clue to his identity. The police had to hunt the Yorkshire Ripper with the 'needle-in-the-haystack' method – checking thousands of remote possibilities. In this case, the numberplates of all cars seen regularly in red-light districts were noted, and the drivers interviewed. When one murdered prostitute was found to be in possession of a new £5 note, the police traced the batch of notes from the bank to twenty-three factories in Bradford, whose employees they interviewed. These included T. & W.H. Clark (Holdings) Ltd, an engineering transport firm, and among those they interviewed was a bearded, powerfully-built young man named Peter Sutcliffe; but they were satisfied with his alibi. In the following year Sutcliffe was again questioned because his car had been seen seven times in a red-light district, but he was believed when he said that he had to drive through it on his way to work. The car registration numbers had been fed into the police computer at Hendon; but the names of suspects interviewed were not fed into a computer. So the constable who talked to Sutcliffe about his car numberplate had no idea that he had also been interviewed in connection with the £5 note. It *had* been noted in reports at the Leeds police headquarters, but a huge backlog meant that these had not yet been processed – after all, 150,000 people had been interviewed and 27,000 houses searched. So Peter Sutcliffe was enabled to go on killing for two more years. When further investigation of the £5 note reduced the number of firms who might have received it from twenty-three to three, Sutcliffe was questioned yet again, and his workmates began jokingly to call him Jack the Ripper. In fact, when Sutcliffe was interviewed this time, he was wearing the boots he had worn when murdering his tenth victim, a nineteen-year-old clerk named Josephine Whitaker; the police had taken a mould of the imprint, but the police who questioned him did not think to look at his feet.

After the thirteenth murder — of a student named Jacqueline Hill — the police decided to set up an advisory team of experts to study the murders all over again. These went to examine all the murder sites and used a computer to estimate their 'centre of gravity'. This led then to the conclusion that the killer lived in Bradford rather than Leeds, where many of the murders had taken place. The next obvious step was to interview again every suspect who lived in Bradford — especially those who had already been interviewed in connection with the £5 note. Since the clues now included three sets of tyre tracks and three sets of footprints, it seems certain that this latest investigation would have identified Peter Sutcliffe as the Yorkshire Ripper. In fact, he was caught before that could happen. On 2 January 1981 two policemen on a routine patrol of the red-light district of Sheffield stopped their car to question a couple in a parked Rover. The man identified himself as Peter Williams; a check on the car with the police computer at Hendon revealed that it had a false numberplate. Taken in for questioning, Sutcliffe soon admitted his identity. In the Ripper Incident Room at Leeds, it was noted that the size of his shoes corresponded to the imprints found by three bodies. The constable who had arrested him recalled that he had requested permission to urinate before accompanying the police. His colleague, Sergeant Robert Ring, returned to the spot — an oil storage tank — and found a knife and a hammer. Faced with this evidence, Peter Sutcliffe finally confessed to being the Yorkshire Ripper. The initial motive of the attacks had been a brooding resentment about a prostitute who had cheated him of £10, which had become (in the illogical manner of serial killers) a desire to punish all prostitutes. After a while, violence had become an addiction, and he attacked any woman he saw walking alone after dark. In May 1981 he was sentenced to life imprisonment, and subsequently removed to Broadmoor, a secure hospital for the criminally insane.

The Yorkshire Ripper case taught the police an important lesson. If suspects, like car number plates, had been fed into a computer, Sutcliffe would probably have been taken in for questioning in 1978 — when he was wearing the boots whose imprint was found beside Josephine Whitaker — and three lives would have been saved. A computer would have had no problem storing 150,000 suspects and 22,000 statements.

Yet even with the aid of a computer, the task of tracking down a random serial killer like Sutcliffe would have been enormous. It could only display such details as the methods of known sex offenders, and the names of suspects who had been interviewed more than once. In their next major investigation of a serial killer, the Surrey police began with a list of 4,900 sex offenders — which, as it happened, contained the name of the man they were seeking. The 'Railway Rapist' began to operate in 1982; at this stage two men were involved in sexual attacks on five women on or near railway stations. By 1984 one of the men had begun to operate alone. He threatened his victims with a knife, tied their hands, and raped them with a great deal of violence. Twenty-seven such attacks occurred in 1984 and 1985. In January 1986, the body of nineteen-year-old Alison Day was found in the River Lea; she had vanished seventeen days earlier on her way to meet her boyfriend. She had been raped and strangled. In April 1986, fifteen-year-old Maartje Tamboezer, daughter of a Dutch oil executive, was accosted as she took a short cut through woods near Horsley, and dragged off the footpath; she was also raped and strangled. Her attacker was evidently aware of the most recent advance in forensic detection, 'genetic fingerprinting', by which a suspect can be identified from the distinctive pattern in the DNA of his body cells. The killer had stuffed a burning paper handkerchief into her vagina. A man who had been seen running for a train soon after the murder was believed to be the rapist, and two million train tickets were examined in an attempt to find one with his fingerprints.

A month later, a twenty-nine-year-old secretary named Anne Lock disappeared on her way home from work; her body was found ten weeks later. Again, an attempt had been made to destroy sperm traces by burning.

It was at this point that the police forces involved in the investigation decided to link computers; the result was the list of 4,900 sex offenders, soon reduced to 1,999. At number 1,594 was a man called John Duffy, charged with raping his ex-wife and attacking her lover with a knife. The computers showed that he had also been arrested on suspicion of loitering near a railway station. (Since the blood group of the Anne Lock strangler had been the same as that of the 'Railway Rapist',

29

police had been keeping a watch on railway stations.) Duffy was called in for questioning, and his similarity to the 'Railway Rapist' noted. (Duffy was small, ginger-haired and pockmarked.) When the police tried to conduct a second interview, Duffy was in hospital suffering from amnesia, alleging that he had been beaten up by muggers. The hospital authorities declined to allow him to be interviewed. Since he was only one of two thousand suspects, the police did not persist.

At this point, the investigation team decided that an 'expert' might be able to help. They asked Dr David Canter, a professor of psychology at the University of Surrey, to review all the evidence. Using techniques similar to those used by the Yorkshire Ripper team – studying the locations of the attacks – he concluded that the 'centre of gravity' lay in the North London area, and that the rapist probably lived within three miles of Finchley Road. He also concluded that he had been a semi-skilled worker, and that his relationship with his wife had been a stormy one. When Canter's analysis was matched up against the remaining suspects, the computer immediately threw up the name of John Duffy, who lived in Kilburn. Police kept him under surveillance until they decided that they could no longer take the risk of leaving him at liberty – another schoolgirl had been raped with typical violence since Duffy was committed to hospital – and arrested him. When a fellow martial arts enthusiast admitted that Duffy had persuaded him to beat him up so he could claim loss of memory, the police were certain that he was the man they were seeking. Five of rape victims picked him out at an identity parade, and string found in the home of his parents proved to be identical with that which had been used to tie Maartje Tamboezer's wrists. When forensic scientists matched fibres from Alison Day's sheepskin coat to fibres found on one of Duffy's sweaters, the final link in the chain of evidence was established; although he continued to refuse to admit or deny his guilt, John Duffy was sentenced to life imprisonment.

Dr David Canter has described the techniques he used to pinpoint where the railway rapist lived:*

'Many environmental psychology studies have demonstrated that people form particular mental maps of the places they

* *New Society*, 4 March 1988

30

use. Each person creates a unique representation of the place in which he lives, with its own particular distortions. In the case of John Duffy, journalists recognised his preference for committing crimes near railway lines to the extent that they dubbed him the "Railway Rapist". What neither they nor the police appreciated was that this characteristic was likely to be part of his way of thinking about the layout of London, and so was a clue to his own particular mental map. It could therefore be used to see where the psychological focus of this map was and so specify the area in which he lived.'

By the time John Duffy was arrested in 1985, the techniques of 'psychological profiling' had alredy been in use in America for a decade, and the use of the computer had also been recognised as a vital part of the method. A retired Los Angeles detective named Pierce Brooks had pointed out that many serial killers remained unapprehended because they moved from state to state, and that before the state police realised they had a multiple killer on their hands, he had moved on. The answer obviously lay in linking up the computers of individual states, and feeding the information into a central computer. Brooks's programme was labelled VICAP — the Violent Criminal Apprehension Programme — and the FBI Academy at Quantico, Virginia, was chosen as the centre for the new crimefighting team. VICAP proved to be the first major step towards the solution of the problem of the random sex killer.

Two

Profile of a Serial Killer

U p to the time this book went to press, no defendant facing charges of multiple murder in any British court had ever been described in proceedings as a 'serial killer', or his alleged crimes as 'serial murder'. No such classification obtains either in British legal terminology or, indeed, in everyday conversation.

Even now, despite increasing use of the term in media reports, it is doubtful if one layman in a hundred in Britain knows what distinguishes the serial killer from all other multiple murderers. That is certainly not because none are to be found in the annals of British crime; on the contrary. The reason is that their identification and acceptance as a unique species of murderer is new, so new that outside the United States – the country worst affected by these most dangerous of all killers – the civilised world is only just waking up to the threat they pose to society.

Paradoxically, the man generally regarded as *the* archetypal serial killer is also the world's most notorious murderer: Jack the Ripper. 'The Ripper' – the only name by which we know him, for he was never caught – stalked and mutilated his victims in the gas-lit alleys of London's East End more than one hundred years ago. How many women he killed during that brief reign of autumn terror in 1888 is uncertain. Four, perhaps five; by no means an exceptional tally in the context of the violent 1980s, yet nonetheless a series of murders which continue to excite worldwide interest – fascination, even – both because of their savagery, and persistent conjecture as to the identity of the Ripper and his fate.

While his identity may never now be satisfactorily established, modern criminal profiling techniques enable us to discern a clearly identifiable pattern in the five Ripper murders. Their significant behavioural thread lies not so much in the *modus operandi* which governed all five homicides — the 'pick-up', followed by the slitting of the victim's throat — as in the post-mortem mutilation which accompanied four of the murders (the Ripper was disturbed during the course of the other one).

Such a ritual, sexually sadistic trait is a hallmark of a certain kind of serial killer. The *modus operandi* may vary over time; it is chosen basically because it is practical — and because it works. Changes may be introduced should some flaw emerge (perhaps during the early murders, which do not always proceed to plan), or even deliberately to try to confuse the investigating police. The ritual aspect of the crime, however — which is conceived of fantasy, and endlessly rehearsed in the offender's mind before he kills for the first time — is his 'signature', his mark; and it is principally this 'signature' which enables a series of crimes to be linked through behavioural analysis.

The most advanced, *systematic* profiling technique in use today — the Criminal Investigative Analysis Programme, devised and developed by agents of the FBI's Behavioural Science Unit at Quantico, Virginia — is based on the tenet that behaviour reflects personality. Thus, expert crime scene interpretation (based on police and medical reports, photographic and forensic evidence, etc.), translated into identifiable behavioural characteristics, enables the FBI analyst to profile the *type* of offender responsible — as distinct from the individual. Such detailed behavioural analysis is not a theoretical aid to criminal investigation: it works. It is used every day by FBI analysts at Quantico, and is especially effective when dealing with apparently 'motiveless' murders (i.e. where there is no apparent connection between murderer and victim). The same behavioural analysis technique is used to combat a variety of offences, notably serial murder but also in cases involving abduction, rape, arson, drug trafficking and certain planned terrorist crimes, such as hijacking and hostage-taking. The scope for expansion would appear to be almost limitless, given time for research; meantime its greatest immediate value in the United States lies in aiding local law enforcement agencies in the tracking down and arrest of serial offenders.

*　　*　　*

No violent criminal instils a greater sense of fear and outrage among the community than the serial killer. The sadistic nature of his crimes, especially in the relatively rare cases involving torture and/or mutilation, inevitably attracts maximum publicity; while public alarm is further heightened by an awareness that – unlike most other murderers – many serial killers deliberately target total strangers as their victims. The net result is a vicious circle of ever-increasing fear and publicity as each new murder is discovered, all of it combining to add significantly to existing pressures on the police concerned. However, thwarted from the outset by a lack of clues to the murderer's identity (a situation aggravated by the apparent absence of any connection between assailant and victims), the investigation may drag on for years in the face of mounting criticism and even hostility. (One recent example in Britain involved the six-year-long hunt for Peter Sutcliffe, alias the Yorkshire Ripper, who killed thirteen women before he was caught in 1981 – and then during a routine police patrol check, as mentioned in Chapter 1.)

Man's quest for a composite profile of 'the murderer' is not new. Pioneering work in the eighteenth century, using physiognomy (the art of judging character by facial features), and phrenology (the study of cranial bumps and ridges, *vis-à-vis* the development of mental faculties), failed to reveal significant common physical similarities. A more recent, twentieth-century theory held that chromosomal imbalance (caused by the presence of an additional male, or 'Y', chromosome in the genes), increased the probability of violent criminal behaviour. This supposition, however, was challenged when Richard Speck – the American multiple murderer who killed eight nurses in one night in 1966, and who was thought to suffer from such an imbalance – was found on examination to have *no* extra chromosome. Subsequent research showed that most males with such an imbalance display no abnormally violent behaviour. The FBI profilers (or analysts, as they are officially called) use behavioural traits commonly identified in convicted, sexually-oriented murderers as their analytical mainstay; and that this technique stands the test of time is clearly borne out by scrutiny of the 1888 Ripper murders.

All the five Ripper murders were obviously sexually motivated. All five victims were the same *type* of person, i.e. prostitutes. All were actively soliciting in the same general 'red-light' area on the nights they met their deaths. Four of the murders – those of Mary Ann Nicholls, Annie Chapman, Catherine Eddowes, and Mary Jane Kelly – were plainly ritualistic, with post-mortem mutilation. Nicholls was disembowelled. So was Chapman. But, unlike Nicholls (whose robust stays precluded mutilation above the level of the diaphragm), Chapman's uterus was cut out and removed, her entrails severed from their mesenteric attachments and left draped symbolically over one shoulder. Eddowes was similarly mutilated, except that in her case the left kidney was removed with the uterus. Following that murder a letter from someone, claiming to be the killer, referred to anthropophagy (cannibalism), viz. '(the kidney) tasted very nise [*sic*]'.

Mary Jane Kelly, the last of the Ripper's victims and the only one found dead in her room, suffered the most bizarre mutilation. On this one unhurried occasion when, having changed his *modus operandi,* he ran less risk of being disturbed, the Ripper's mutilation of the body was more elaborate than hitherto. The room measured only twelve feet square, so that every detail loomed large. Kelly's throat was cut so deep she was all but decapitated, drenching sheets and palliasse in blood. She was dressed only in her chemise. The rest of her clothes were found folded on a chair, while other items of female clothing – including a skirt and hat – had been burned in the grate, apparently to provide light for the ritual mutilation.

The Ripper cut off the wretched woman's nose and both breasts, and – as if they were trophies – displayed them on the bedside table, together with strips of flesh carved from her thighs. Her forehead was flayed, the abdomen ripped open, her uterus and liver cut out. The uterus had vanished: the liver was left for the police to find, neatly positioned between Mary Jane Kelly's feet. In a final, symbolic gesture the Ripper had taken one of the woman's hands and thrust it deep inside her gaping belly.

Only Elizabeth ('Long Liz') Stride – the first of his two victims to die on 30 September 1888 (hence the night of the 'double event') – was spared mutilation. This was not from any sense of compassion on the Ripper's part, but strictly to save his own skin. Bruises found on Stride's shoulders and collarbone indicated where he grabbed hold of her before dragging her to the ground. A single sweep of his knife was enough to sever her windpipe (all five of his victims died in this way, with their throats slit right to left). On this occasion, however, as he knelt to rip open Stride's abdomen, he was disturbed and forced to flee — possibly by the approach of a horse and cart, whose driver (a steward in a nearby working men's club) first discovered the still warm corpse.

The Ripper wasted little time in stalking a replacement prostitute victim. Within the hour, and only a half-mile away in Mitre Square, Aldgate, he accosted and murdered street-walker Catherine Eddowes — who ironically had just been released from Commercial Street police station. In the words of Constable Watkins, the 'peeler' who found her body, the crime scene revealed by his bull's-eye lantern resembled nothing so much as 'the slaughter of a pig in market'. A curious feature of this murder was that the Ripper placed part of the intestine between her left arm and body.

Pathologist Dr F. Gordon Brown commented that the abdominal cuts had 'probably been made by one kneeling between the middle of the body', and said there had been little or no bleeding since they were inflicted after death. However, Kate Eddowes had also sustained multiple facial wounds (one of which severed the tip of her nose), while the gash in her throat ran almost from ear to ear. 'All the vessels in the left side of the neck were severed,' said Dr Brown, 'and all the deeper structures in the throat were divided down to the backbone. Both the left carotid artery and jugular vein were opened, death being caused by haemorrhage from the cut artery.'

Such an attack would undoubtedly have left bloodstains on the Ripper's hands, cuffs, some outer clothing and, very probably, his boots (elastic-sided boots were widely worn in 1888). He evidently paused afterwards to wash his hands in a sink in the passage north of the Square; the bloodstained water was still visible when Major Smith, the acting City Police Commissioner, arrived on the scene. The Ripper's disciplined conduct in the wake of his earlier street murders indicates a calculated awareness of the risks he ran. Each mutilation, carried out at the murder scene, was a 'high risk' situation, and he made off fast afterwards with his body-part souvenirs. If that was an obvious precaution to take, his ability always to make his way apparently unnoticed though ill-lit streets and alleyways — burdened by the urgent need of a wash at very least, and most likely a change of clothing — speaks of methodical advance planning on the Ripper's part.

Furthermore, on the night of 30 September 1888, his awareness of the hue and cry certain to follow the discovery earlier of Stride's body half a mile away would have been doubly acute: this was a time when Ripper-mania was at its height in dockland London. And yet – on this one occasion when the ritual mutilation had been denied him – he now took an even greater risk by remaining in the same general area *and* committing a second murder within the hour. Not content with that, he also made time to sever and remove the coveted body parts from this second victim before attempting to flee: no easy task in any circumstances, on that darkened strip of pavement where Eddowes was murdered. As Doctor Brown revealed at the inquest, 'The left kidney was completely cut out and taken away. The renal artery was cut through three-quarters of an inch . . . the membrane over the uterus was cut through and the womb extracted, leaving a stump of about three-quarters of an inch. The rest of the womb was absent – taken completely away from the body, together with some of the ligaments . . .'

The conclusion must be that the ritual was of supreme importance to the Ripper. More than that, it was a clamorous, overpowering need, a *compulsion*, which overruled all other considerations that night – personal safety included. Such criminal characteristics were so rarely encountered in the late nineteenth century as to be wholly incomprehensible to the average police officer, no matter how experienced. Outside the fictional world of Sherlock Holmes or Sergeant Cuff, most investigative thinking then was directed towards far more elementary criminal motivation.

Thanks to the FBI's criminal investigative technique – based on the behavioural analysis of violent crime – the clues which abound in those 1888 murders point clear as a signpost to the type of person responsible. The main traits so far identified, i.e. the repetitive, sadistic nature of the crimes; the targeting on each occasion of an identical kind of 'stranger' victim (a prostitute), with all five murdered in the one general area; and the evident planning behind the murders, from attack to escape, stamp the Ripper unmistakably as a serial killer.

The same research has also established that the serial killer is to a large degree sexually motivated, and often decides in advance on the type of victim he intends to target (as opposed to specific individuals); so that the crime may be a true 'stranger murder' in all respects. ('Stranger murder' is a term often used by the American press to describe serial killing.) Since the selective process must turn on the psyche of the murderer concerned, it follows that the range of possible serial murder victims will encompass the whole spectrum of society; from the youngest infant to the aged and infirm, and from the wholly respectable to the brazenly disreputable.

Although his victim may be a random choice, the serial killer may nonetheless have planned the murder with considerable care. Once decided on the type of person he intends to kill, he will possibly stake out a specific locale: a shopping precinct, perhaps, or a school playground, an old folks' home, a singles bar, a lonely bus stop — or busy main road even, if hitchhikers are his target — to await or cruise for those victims of opportunity likely to be encountered there. Moreover, before he launches his first attack he is likely to have methodically reconnoitred the locale — his way in and way out, nearby traffic lights, roundabouts, one-way streets, any factor likely to impede his getaway in an emergency — until satisfied he has a practical escape route available. Such a precaution will be doubly important if the serial killer intends to abduct his victim and dispose of the body elsewhere.

Given obvious changes in traffic conditions, the same characteristics may plainly be seen in the Ripper's behaviour one hundred years ago. Prostitutes were the type of people he elected to murder, and Whitechapel was the locale he staked out for victims of opportunity. That he knew his way well through those gas-lit alleys is self-evident; no matter how close the hue and cry, he got clean away each time without once being stopped for questioning. Over the years, a number of theories have been expounded as to why the Ripper murdered (women) prostitutes only. Sexual motivation aside, the most popular has always been that he was some kind of moral avenger: a man who dealt out rough justice to all whores, because one had infected him (or some close relative) with syphilis. On the other hand his twentieth-century counterpart Peter Sutcliffe, alias 'The Yorkshire Ripper', who murdered thirteen women over six years on the assumption all were prostitutes, claimed that a voice from the grave told him that he had a God-given mission to do so. Sutcliffe had in fact once worked briefly as a grave-digger: however, his plea was rejected by the trial court as a ruse to try to obtain a lenient sentence.

The simplest and perhaps most likely explanation may be that prostitutes have always presented an easy, and even obvious target for the sexually-motivated killer. They symbolise carnality; they actively invite an approach, often touting for custom; and no potential 'high risk' victim ever risks injury or death more readily than by entering the nearest dark alleyway with a total stranger. Because of widespread poverty, and the influx of workless Irish and East Europeans into Britain in the late nineteenth century, the Ripper's chosen killing ground at Whitechapel was notorious for prostitution. He could guarantee to find victims of opportunity there on every foray he made: whores were as thick on the ground in the East End at night as were the fleas in their doss-house bedding.

Hindsight apart, contemporary written evidence exists which appears to confirm that the Ripper had targeted whores as his intended victims *before* he committed at least three of the five murders attributed to him. In a letter, thought to be genuine, to the Central News Agency in London and post-marked 27 September 1888 (i.e. three days before the 'double event', and six weeks before the murder of Mary Jane Kelly), the writer – who signed himself 'Jack the Ripper', thus coining the immortal nickname – declared: 'I am down on whores and shan't quit ripping them till I do get bucked'.

This trait, of first choosing a *type* of victim to murder and then staking out a likely locale in which to trawl for them, can be identified time and again in the behaviour of modern serial killers. Dennis Nilsen, the thirty-seven-year-old homosexual British civil servant and serial killer, prowled the 'gay' bars of Soho for four years between 1979 and 1983 looking for homeless, vulnerable youths. His *modus operandi* was to ply each 'pick-up' with drink, offer him a bed and then strangle him with his tie as he slept. Next morning he would either secrete the body beneath the floorboards of his home in Muswell Hill, north London, or dismember it and dispose of the pieces elsewhere. Each murder left Nilsen ephemerally replete but wholly unmoved, like a spider despatching a fly. He described his reaction after he deposited victim number ten (and third corpse to be dealt with in this way) under the floorboards. 'That was it. Floorboards back. Carpets replaced. And back to work at Denmark Street' (the offices of the Manpower Services Commission). Sheer carelessness in disposal of body parts led directly to Nilsen's arrest. His practice was

39

to boil the severed heads, or burn them with the trunk and limbs on bonfires and flush the lesser remains down the toilet. Instead he blocked the drains – and was caught.

Peter Sutcliffe, the 'Yorkshire Ripper', scoured the red-light districts of Bradford, Leeds, Sheffield and elsewhere during a six-year search for victims prior to his arrest in 1981. Like Jack, he targeted prostitutes: and in that period he intercepted thirteen 'victims of opportunity' – by no means all of whom were streetwalkers – and killed them all with exceptional violence. His compulsive urge to murder whores led him to presume that every woman he encountered in those areas where he lay in wait was a prostitute: in fact, five of the thirteen were respectable passers-by. All were subjected to the same degree of violence, and most of the bodies were mutilated after death.

On one occasion Sutcliffe returned to the murder scene days after the attack, and further mutilated the still-undiscovered body by attempting to sever the head with a hacksaw. To return to the scene of the crime is a common behavioural characteristic in certain serial killers. They do so for a variety of reasons: to check on the progress (if any) made by the police, to relive the fantasy which inspired the murder, and to commit acts of further mutilation and/or necrophilia.

Prime importance is placed by FBI analysts on the role of fantasy in serial murder. Detailed, ongoing research shows that some convicted serial killers enact violent fantasies – including acts of murder – in their minds at seven and eight years of age, occasionally even earlier. These aggressive daydreams continue to develop and expand through adolescence into manhood, the age when their violent dreams are usually first translated into the physical act of killing. (Some serial killers commit murder in their teens. In the next chapter we discuss one youth who committed four murders by the age of fifteen: pp. 129–31, The Profilers.)

Serial killers are almost invariably found to have experienced environmental problems in their early years. In many cases they stem from a broken home in which the parents are divorced or separated, a home with a weak or absent father-figure and dominant female, sometimes a home-life marked by a lack of consistent discipline. As policemen and probation officers have long known, the psychological damage resulting from such a deprived or miserable childhood all too often manifests itself in a number of recognisably aggressive traits. They include defiance of authority, theft, persistent lying, acts of wilful destruction, arson, cruelty to animals and other children; with such symptoms accompanied by long periods of daydreaming (or fantasising) — that ever-available trapdoor leading into a private, make-believe world where the unhappy young can shape their revenge on society for all ill-treatment, real or imagined.

In the context of serial murder, the triad of youthful behaviour most frequently seen as indicative of violence ahead is: *enuresis* (bed wetting) beyond the age of twelve (although analysts also recognise that there may be several different reasons for this). Next is *arson* — sometimes committed by children as young as five or six. Its long-term significance lies in the type of arson offence. A 'disorganised' young arsonist is likely to cause smaller fires and least monetary damage. In contrast the 'organised' arsonist — the one who thinks things through — usually starts his fires from the outset in occupied buildings. His intention is to hurt people, as well as to inflict maximum monetary damage.

The ultimate state of the behavioural triad is *cruelty*, to animals and other people. 'We're not talking here about kicking the dog,' said one analyst. 'We're talking about throwing puppies on to bonfires or tying firecrackers to the cat, that kind of behaviour. One serial killer talks about "Tying a cherry-bomb to the cat's leg, lighting it — and blowing the cat's leg off. Made a lot of one-legged cats." ' This trait can be seen in children on both sides of the Atlantic who grew up to be serial killers. Moors murderer Ian Brady won a childhood reputation as an embryo psychopath who threw cats from tenement windows in the Glasgow Gorbals. When Ed Kemper, the Californian serial killer, was thirteen he cut the family cat into pieces with his Scout's knife.

'The next step is aggression against people. He chooses animals first because animals can scream, they show fear, they bleed, they do all those things we do — but they're not *people*. This time, it's projection. Now he's getting even with society.' Hostility to society is one of the hallmarks of the adult serial killer. Some express it in the murders they commit, others express it in words. We know that the man calling himself Jack the Ripper wrote 'I am down on whores and shan't quit ripping them till I do get buckled'. When actress Sharon Tate begged the Manson 'Family' gang to spare her for the sake of her unborn child, Tex Watson, Susan Atkins and Patricia Krenwinkel responded by stabbing her sixteen times, inflicting several wounds after her death. Finally Atkins dipped a towel in the actress's blood and wrote 'Pig' on her living-room door. Dennis Nilsen — a heavy drinker — clearly felt this need to 'get even' with society in each murder he committed — including those he could barely remember next morning. While awaiting trial, he wrote from jail to the police who had questioned him: 'God only knows what thoughts go through my mind when it is captive within a destructive binge. Maybe the cunning, stalking killer instinct is the only single concentration released from a mind which in that state knows no morality . . . There is no disputing the fact that I am a violent killer under certain circumstances. It amazes me that I have no tears for these victims. I have no tears for myself or those bereaved by my actions. Am I a wicked person, constantly under pressure, who just cannot cope with it, who escapes to reap revenge against society through a haze of a bottle of spirits?'

The same detailed behavioural research which first indentified the importance of fantasy in the evolution of the serial killer also examined the part played by pornography. Between 1979 and 1983 agents from the FBI's Behavioural Science Unit conducted an in-depth psychological study of thirty-six convicted, incarcerated sex murderers held in United States prisons nationwide. Of those thirty-six murderers, twenty-five were serial killers: the other eleven were either 'spree' killers (a detailed classification of murderers appears in the next chapter), or single or double sex murderers. Nearly half of those who co-operated with the FBI analysts (43%) were found to have been sexually abused in childhood, one third (32%) during adolescence, and a slightly larger percentage (37%) over the age of eighteen. Perhaps unsurprisingly, most admitted to 'sexual problems' as adults. More importantly in the context of pornography, nearly seventy per cent said they felt 'sexually incompetent' (as adults), and relied heavily on visual stimuli

– with a large majority rating pornography as the most effective stimulus.

Pornography is seen by analysts of the Behavioural Science Unit as a factor which fuels the serial killer's violent fantasy, rather than as a cause of the murders he commits. In particular they condemn the 'bondage' type pornography – so frequently portrayed on the cover of American detective magazines – as the sex stimulus most likely to fuel, say, the Bundy-type murderer's fantasies.

'That is what appeals most to the sexual sadist. To see a woman who is bound, or restrained in some way with a gag round her mouth, looking terrified as someone threatens her with a knife or a gun. That *is* their fantasy: to dominate and control, to inflict pain and suffering on the victim. To see this portrayed on the cover of the magazine may fuel that fantasy – but it's not the *cause* of the murder (he commits). Such killers have these desires, they have this violent tendency within them, and that's why they're attracted to this type of pornography. We find the sexual sadist and the really violent offender more drawn to this type of pornography than what one might call "classical" pornography, with its explicit sexual content. What the sexual sadist looks for is dominance, control over the victim, and that's what he sees in this kind of magazine cover. Bundy may have blamed pornography for his "sick obsessions" but that kind of statement is typical of the serial killer. He *always* blames someone – or something – else for what he's done; he is not to blame, it's never his fault.'

Although the original survey of the thirty-six murderers was completed in 1983, the practice of interviewing convicted offenders by FBI analysts is a valued, ongoing process. No inducement of any kind is offered to the prisoners concerned – some of whom may be on Death Row, awaiting the outcome of their appeals – in return for their co-operation. Furthermore, no visitor may carry weapons inside prison for obvious security reasons, with the result that the lone FBI agents who carried out those pioneer interviews ran considerably personal risk in questioning convicted, violent murderers who literally had nothing to lose, no matter how they reacted. That practice ceased after one agent – who conducted a solitary interview with a serial killer weighing close on three hundred pounds (more than twenty-one stone) and standing six feet nine inches tall – rang three times in fifteen minutes without response when attempting to alert the prison staff that the interview was over. The serial killer (FBI agents do not identify violent offenders who co-operate in Behaviour Research Interviews) whose crimes included the decapitation of most of his victims, was fully aware of the interviewer's dilemma. 'I could screw your head off and place it on the table to greet the guard,' he said. The agent bluffed his way through until the warder arrived, and was not harmed; but today all FBI agents work in pairs when interviewing violent offenders in jail.

Such interviews may last from four to seven hours. One agent talks with the prisoner, while his colleague monitors the conversation. Even so the authorities recognise that there must always be some element of risk involved. Some penal institutions require signed waivers ruling out negotiation in the event of hostage-taking, and/or to release the state from responsibility should death or injury result from the interview. While neither analyst nor offender may claim to enjoy the experience, it can prove beneficial to both parties – if for vastly different reasons. Some murderers who have admitted their crimes find relief in talking freely about them. Others feel flattered to be included in a work of reference. Not a few try to impress the interviewer with their innocence. For the analyst it is a unique opportunity to meet face to face with an offender whose violent, sometimes bizarre crimes are a matter of record: a rare chance to probe the psyche of the *kind* of serial murderer he may encounter time and again in the investigative years ahead.

With most serial killers except 'medical serial killers' (see pp. 50–6), their individual libido is mirrored in the kind of victim they mark down for murder. The heterosexual targets females, homosexuals prey on fellow 'gays' and the bisexual serial killer makes no distinction between male and female victims. Ted Bundy, a heterosexual and former law student at the University of Washington in Seattle, was a handsome and intelligent undergraduate who enjoyed normal sexual relationships with a number of female students before he turned Peeping Tom and, ultimately, one of the worst serial killers in United States criminal history.

At first, whenever opportunity occurred during the four years in which he was an active serial killer (he spent half the time in custody, but twice escaped), Bundy scoured university campuses, student rooming houses and youth hostels searching for 'look-alike', attractive female victims. His *modus operandi* was to use guile, plus his undoubted surface charm, to lure them to a waiting car. The car was almost always stolen; in a sudden Jekyll-and-Hyde switch of character he would club them over the head, abduct and drive them to some lonely spot, then rape and sexually abuse his victims before strangling them and dumping their bodies like so much refuse. 'Throwaways', he called them contemptuously.

After his second escape from custody in 1977, Bundy deteriorated into a drunken, disorganised 'blitz' type of serial killer. While he continued to target female students, he now attacked them in a wild 'overkill' fashion after breaking in to their quarters. On the night of his penultimate attack in January 1978, he broke into a student rooming house in Tallahassee, Florida, and battered four girls unconscious. One he raped and strangled. He sexually abused another, who died on her way to hospital. A third girl suffered a fractured skull, and the fourth a broken jaw. Bundy fled. Three weeks later he murdered again, and for the last time. His victim was a twelve-year-old schoolgirl whom he abducted, strangled and sexually violated. He was arrested shortly afterwards – not for her murder (the child's body was not found for a month) – but for firing on a traffic policeman who gave chase while Bundy was driving a stolen car. Bundy, who was using an assumed name, was identified in custody (the FBI had profiled him) and later charged with the three Florida murders only. He was tried and found guilty, and – after a decade of highly-publicised and largely self-conducted appeals – Ted Bundy was executed in 1989.

Negro drug pusher, burglar, rapist and heterosexual serial killer Carlton Gary, alias 'The Stocking Strangler' of Columbus, Georgia, assaulted, raped and strangled five elderly white women in Columbus in the late 1970s. His victims were all complete strangers who lived alone, and whose homes Gary broke into in the exclusively white Wynnton district of the city. A sixth white woman of seventy-eight, whom Gary raped when he broke into her Wynnton home immediately preceding the fifth murder, escaped death only because she fought him off long enough to sound a burglar alarm and summon the police. Gary escaped, and the murders ceased abruptly in February 1978. Although a native of Columbus, Gary had moved east in the mid-1970s. After escaping from a New York state prison in 1977, he returned to Columbus and committed the Wynnton murders. At that time he was not a suspect; then in 1979 – a year after the Wynnton murders had ceased – he was arrested elsewhere in Georgia on unrelated charges. After interrogation he was charged with three of the Wynnton stranglings, together with associated counts of rape and burglary. In 1986 he was tried, found guilty and sentenced to death in the electric chair. Gary, now thirty-seven, is on Death Row awaiting the outcome of appeals which may not be decided until the early 1990s.

One *racial* criminal behaviour characteristic links the Carlton Gary homicides in Columbus, Georgia, with nine serial murders committed in New York City in 1974 by Calvin Jackson – another heterosexual negro ex-convict – and a series of at least seven murders, committed a decade later and more than four thousand miles away in Stockwell, South London, by the bisexual British serial killer Kenneth Erskine.

By early summer in New York in 1974, five women – mostly elderly – had been found dead in their rooms over a period of two years in the run-down Park Plaza Hotel at 50 West 77th Street. Foul play was not suspected. All were thought to have died either from acute alcoholism or (in one case) asphyxia, that might have been self-induced. Then Yetta Vishnefsky, who was seventy-nine, was found dead in Room 605. This time no pathologist was needed to establish the cause of death. She had been bound with her own stockings, and knifed in the back: the post-mortem examination revealed that she had been raped. Shortly afterwards Kate Lewinsohn, who was sixty-five, was found dead in Room 221 with a fractured skull. She, too, had been raped. And on 8 June Winifred Miller was found burned to death in her bed in Room 406.

While the police investigation into those three murders was continuing, a ninth victim – sixty-nine-year-old Mrs Pauline

Spanierman — was found by a maid, battered to death in her room in the adjacent twelve-storey apartment house at 40 West 77th Street. On this occasion there was a suspect; a black man, weighing about one hundred and forty pounds (ten stone) and five feet seven inches tall, who had been seen making his way down the fire escape at the Park Plaza at half-past three that morning, approximately the time that Mrs Spanierman was murdered. The precise description led the police to Calvin Jackson, an ex-convict and former drug addict, who worked at the Park Plaza as a porter — and shared a room there with a woman named Bernice Myers.

Jackson (who, it transpired, was also wanted for questioning in connection with a series of murders in Buffalo, New York State) confessed to the nine Park Plaza killings and stood trial in 1976. Psychiatrist Dr Emilia Salanga, one of a group of mental specialists who considered Jackson to be unfit to plead, told the court '[Jackson] told me he enjoys killing. He said it was like sex, and that he had sex with his victims sometimes before and sometimes after he killed them. He believes that his body and mind were being controlled, and he told me he had thought of seeking out a priest. He thought he was the Devil, and he wanted himself exorcised.'

His confession, which was tape-recorded, appeared to tell a different story: of a man determined to kill a certain type of woman, with rape a secondary motive. 'When I came in the room, she was scared and offered me some sex. I guess that was in hopes I might leave, that I'd be satisfied just to have sex with her.' And with another victim: 'I lied to her. I told her I was not going to kill her. Then I strangled her with my hands. I made sure she was dead by forcing her face down into a pillow . . . I think one sock might have been burned off when I started the fire in the bed.' After first returning to the courtroom for a ruling on the definition of 'intentional murder', the jury returned a verdict of guilty; and on 6 July 1976 Jackson was sent down for four terms of life imprisonment.

Kenneth Erskine, who was born of mixed West Indian and Scottish parentage, was dubbed 'The Stockwell Strangler' by the British press after he terrorised the South London district of that name for four months in 1986. Between early April and late July that year he strangled at least seven old-age pensioners — four men and three women, aged from sixty-

47

seven to ninety-four − and sodomised five of them in the process. Erskine, who was described by counsel as 'a killer who enjoyed killing', was believed by police to have murdered two other elderly victims during the same period, but no charges were preferred through lack of evidence.

Erskine, a slim coffee-coloured man of twenty-four (but said to have a mental age of only eleven), targeted old folk exclusively. His *modus operandi* was to break in to their flats with great stealth − in one case he squeezed in through the cat-flap − and surprise his victims in their sleep. He would then clamp one hand over their mouths and strangle them slowly with the other, by alternately increasing and lessening the pressure on their throats. By offering (and promptly denying) his old, terrified victims the long-drawn-out hope of life, Erskine heightened the erotic pleasure he derived from the act of murder. He invariably tidied up the room afterwards, tucking his naked victims neatly into bed with the sheets drawn up to their chins. Because of their age and inability to resist strongly, the bruising on their throats was usually too slight to be obvious to the naked eye. Hence, his first victim − whose body was examined both by a doctor and a policeman − was wrongly thought to have died in her sleep and was shortly to be cremated when a relative noticed that the television set was missing. (As with the Carlton Gary murders in Columbus, Georgia, and the Calvin Jackson homicides in New York City, robbery was Erskine's secondary motive.)

The identifiable racial behaviour link that stamped his crimes − like those of Gary and Jackson − as the work of a coloured man was his sexual assault of the elderly; it is the only sex crime that blacks commit more often than whites. No-one knows why − it is a statistic established by years of patient criminal behaviour research. Interestingly, the same behavioural research shows that most serial killers are young, male, and white − again there seems no logical reason why − and most serial killers, regardless of colour, commit their first murder between the ages of twenty-five and thirty.

One of the earliest known bisexual serial killers was Joseph Vacher, an ex-army corporal sometimes referred to as 'The French Ripper' and a near contemporary. Vacher murdered eleven people in the countryside around Belley, in south-east France (some forty miles from Lyons), between 1894 and 1897, when he was arrested and later guillotined. His victims were mostly farm workers. Seven were females, whose ages ranged from sixteen to fifty-eight; the four males were all youths of fourteen to sixteen. The murders ceased for a period of six months in 1896 when Vacher served a brief prison sentence (for vagrancy), and resumed almost immediately on his release.

Vacher carried a set of knives with him as well as a cudgel, which bore the legend '*Mary of Lourdes: who does good, finds good*'. He stabbed, raped and disembowelled the females, and sodomised and castrated each of the youths. Several of the bodies bore the imprints of his teeth. He was caught when he attacked a powerfully-built peasant woman, who fought him off until her family came to the rescue. Vacher, who was then aged twenty-eight, was a former mental patient who had recently been discharged as 'cured'. At his trial he claimed that his 'madness' dated back to a bite from a rabid dog years earlier. However, he was found guilty of the murder of a shepherd boy (his final victim) and executed on New Year's Eve, 1897.

Although serial killers are mostly male, women serial killers have always been with us. Two of the earliest-known pre-date Jack the Ripper. Bavarian solicitor's widow Anna Zwanziger was sentenced to death in 1809 for the murder of two women and a child. Sentence was carried out two years later. Hélène Jegard, a Breton peasant, was executed in 1852 for the murder of twenty-three people, including her sister. Both killers were arsenic poisoners. As if the need to kill was an addiction, Zwanziger told the judge it would have been impossible for her to cease poisoning others and described the virulent poison as her 'truest friend'.

In the 1960s a number of young female serial killers were found guilty of multiple murder. In Britain in 1966 Myra Hindley and her lover, Ian Brady – the so-called 'Moors Murderers' – were jointly charged with three murders, two of them of children aged ten and twelve respectively. Brady, a self-confessed disciple of de Sade, was found guilty of all three murders: Hindley guilty of two, and of being an accessory to the third. Such was the sense of public outrage it was known as 'the trial of the century'. The trial judge described the pair of them as 'sadistic killers of the utmost depravity'.

In August 1969, four young American women serial killers — Susan Atkins, Lynette 'Squeaky' Fromme, Patricia Krenwinkel and Leslie van Houten, all members of the notorious Manson 'Family' gang — took an active part in two apparently 'motiveless' murders which stunned Los Angeles. In the first, film star Sharon Tate (then eight months pregnant), three of her friends and a delivery boy were either knifed repeatedly or shot dead. Two days later, husband and wife Leno and Rosemary LaBianca were first tortured and then stabbed to death. Rosemary LaBianca suffered forty-one knife wounds, her husband twelve — plus fourteen 'puncture' wounds from a large, double-pronged meat fork. The victims in both sets of murders were complete strangers to the Manson gang. All four women 'Family' members were sentenced to death — sentences which were commuted to life imprisonment in 1972, after the California Supreme Court voted to abolish the death penalty for murder.

A newly-identified sub-species of serial murderer has emerged with increasing frequency in today's welfare-oriented society, often in institutions caring for the elderly and infirm — the *medical* serial killer. This type of multiple murderer may be male or female, and although clearly less violent than, say, the Manson 'Family' women or the male, Ripper-style ritual murderers, these self-styled 'mercy killers' consistently claim large numbers of victims before they are apprehended.

In November 1981, a heavily-moustachioed Los Angeles male night nurse named Robert Diaz — then aged forty-two, a man who had always wanted to be a doctor but felt he was too old for medical school — was arrested and charged with the murder of twelve patients by injecting them with massive doses of Lidocaine, a powerful heart drug. It was a case which aroused nationwide concern in the United States. In April of that year, a deputy coroner in San Bernadino County, Los Angeles, received an anonymous telephone call from a woman who said nineteen mystery deaths had occurred in two weeks at the Community Hospital of the Valleys, near Perris. Police enquiries showed there had been eleven deaths at Perris, and one other at nearby Banning Hospital between 29 March and 25 April 1981. The twelve were all hospital patients, aged between fifty-two and ninety-five; and all had died suddenly after complaining of dizzy spells or seizures, and were found to have high blood acidity and an unusual blueish tinge to their skin from the waist up.

The first break in the investigation came after a doctor at the Perris hospital reported the disappearance of confidential papers relating to patients in the intensive care unit. Suspicion fell on Diaz; a warrant was obtained, and although the search of his home failed to reveal any papers, police found two vials of Lidocaine, a syringe and some morphine. Diaz's explantion was that nursing staff often pocketed part-used vials of medicine and later found they had taken them home in error.

Subsequent enquiries showed that supplies of Lidocaine, stored at Perris and re-submitted to the Chicago manufacturers for tests, in some cases contained an unusually low drug content; while in at least one other instance a vial was found to have a far higher Lidocaine content than that stipulated on the label. On 23 November 1981 Diaz was arrested and charged with the twelve murders. District Attorney Thomas Hollenhurst said the charges followed a number of exhumations, and a study of hospital records, which showed a 'common plan and design' in the twelve deaths. All had occurred at hospitals where Diaz was working at the time. The victims died either during the shift he worked on (usually between 1am and 4am) or shortly before 7am, when he went off duty: 'There almost appeared to be a time for dying.' He also said Diaz had been on duty on ten of the shifts in which patients had died over a twelve-day period.

Diaz responded by filing a multimillion dollar suit against the Riverside County authorities, in which he alleged defamation of character and violation of civil rights. His trial for murder, however, went ahead in March 1984. Some witnesses testified that Diaz — who liked to 'play doctor' — sometimes predicted the death of patients whose condition appeared stable; and die they did. Other nurses said they had seen him flitting from room to room 'like a butterfly' late at night, administering injections which had not been prescribed by a doctor. Diaz himself denied injecting any patient with a fatal overdose of Lidocaine, although he admitted he sometimes took on the role of doctor in emergencies 'because the doctors on duty did absolutely nothing'.

Robert Diaz was born in Gary, Indiana, one of a family of thirteen children. He joined the United States Marines when he was eighteen, but deserted and was subsequently discharged as unsuitable. He lived in a fantasy world and liked to be called 'Dr Diaz' when only a nursing student. He told some of his fellow students he had lived an earlier life, in the body of an ancient Egyptian king; with others he purported to be a descendant of 'El Cid' — real name Rodrigo Diaz, the Spanish knight and folk-hero who defeated the Moors in the eleventh century. His motive for murdering the twelve patients seemed obscure, although prosecutor Patrick Magers said Diaz committed the crimes 'for his own amusement and entertainment' while playing doctor. On 30 March 1984 he was found guilty of all twelve murders, and sentenced to die in the gas chamber.

In March 1983 Dr Arnfinn Nesset was found guilty of murdering twenty-two elderly patients under his care at the Orkdal Valley nursing home in central Norway. The doctor — a mild-looking, bespectacled man of forty-six — killed them all in three years by injecting curacit into their veins. Curacit is a derivative of curare, the vegetable poison which South American Indian tribes paint on the tips of their arrows to kill animals and enemies. (It paralyses the motor nerves, including those in the respiratory system, to cause swift but agonising death.)

How many unsuspecting elderly patients Dr Nesset murdered in this way is uncertain. He himself told police during the preliminary investigation 'I've killed so many I'm unable to remember them all'. At one stage it was thought possible he might have been responsible for as many as sixty-two suspicious patient deaths, dating back to 1962 and the first of three such institutions where he had worked. In the event, no post-mortem examinations were made because of the difficulty in tracing curacit in the human body with the passage of time; so, once Dr Nesset retracted his alleged confession and the trial began, he was charged only with the twenty-five murders the prosecution felt it could prove.

The patients involved — fourteen women, eleven men — were aged between sixty-seven and ninety-four. It took the clerk of the court a quarter of an hour to read the lengthy indictment. No fewer than 150 witnesses were called, yet a curious feature of the prosecution case was that none had actually *seen* Nesset administer a lethal injection. (A number had seen him alone with patients shortly before they died, and evidence of injection by hypodermic syringe was found on their arms.) The murder enquiry was started when a woman reporter on a local newspaper became suspicious about the deaths at Orkdal Valley nursing home, after receiving a tip-off that Dr Nesset had ordered large amounts of curacit. Nesset, who pleaded not guilty to all charges, was found guilty of twenty-two murders and one attempted murder; it took the jury three days to arrive at its multiple verdict. He was also found guilty of five charges of forgery and embezzlement (worth altogether about £1200 sterling, or 2000 US dollars), although this was not suggested as a motive for the killings.

No clear motive was established, despite a lengthy police investigation. The prosecution claimed that under early interrogation, Nesset had suggested a variety of motives – mercy killing, pleasure, 'schizophrenia coupled with self-assertion', and a morbid need to kill. Four psychiatrists who examined the doctor found him sane and accountable for his actions when administering the poison, but said his emotional development had been 'disturbed'. They considered that Nesset, who was an illegitimate child, felt unwanted and isolated in the tightly-knit rural community on Norway's west coast where he grew up. They said this left him with a marked inferiority complex, and aggressive tendencies which were liable to 'erupt' in certain circumstances. However, the three judges who heard the case sentenced Nesset to twenty-one years' imprisonment – the maximum for murder under Norwegian law – and up to ten years' preventive detention. The twenty-two murders of which he was found guilty were sufficient to make the doctor the record mass killer in Scandinavian crime history.

In Cincinnati, Ohio, in 1987 nursing attendant Donald Harvey – a dark-haired, handsome man of thirty-five – was sentenced to three consecutive terms of life imprisonment after pleading guilty to the murder of twenty-four people in four years. Most of them were elderly patients at the Daniel Drake memorial hospital in the city, where he worked at the time of his arrest.

Harvey, who was described in press reports as an 'avowed' homosexual, was born in a quiet rural community in Kentucky.

There was nothing in his ordinary, family background to suggest unhappiness or deprivation in childhood. His parents were regular Sunday churchgoers who worked hard all year, farming tobacco. His teacher remembered Harvey as a 'very attractive child' who got on well with everyone. Reactions were much the same when he went to work in Cincinnati as a young man; at first all his nursing staff colleagues thought him a gentle, cheerful person incapable of harming anyone.

In fact Harvey led a double life for at least four years in Cincinnati. Outwardly he was a pleasant young man ready to do anyone a good turn: the man no-one knew was a mass murderer who 'talked about killing so matter-of-factly you'd think he was talking about going to the chemist, or ordering a sandwich'. He committed his first murder in 1983. On 10 April that year he baked a pie for elderly, ailing Helen Metzger who lived in the flat upstairs and relied upon good-neighbour Harvey for many favours. She thought it a typical kindness – but the pie was laced with arsenic, and she died (presumably in agony) soon afterwards. Murder was not suspected.

During the early 1980s a young man (who knew nothing of Harvey's double life) moved in to share the apartment. Whether Harvey saw the young man's parents as a challenge to his own domination of their son is not known; however, he later confessed to murdering the father, and attempting to murder the mother, by giving them meals poisoned with arsenic. Again there was no suspicion of foul play. According to Hamilton County prosecutor Arthur Ney at Harvey's trial, the Kentucky killer also administered arsenic occasionally to his young flatmate, never enough to kill him, deliberately, but because '(Harvey) just wanted to see him suffer from time to time'.

In 1985 Harvey was suspected of stealing body tissues from the Veterans Administration medical centre in Cincinnati, where he had worked since 1976 as a mortuary attendant. No charges were brought: instead he was allowed to 'resign' – and promptly joined the Daniel Drake memorial hospital as a nursing orderly. As always he made a good first impression. Even his quips 'I got another one today', whenever a patient died in the ward where he was working – something which happened with increasing frequency over the next two years – were accepted as in-jokes for a time: by the time they aroused suspicion, a total of twenty-one patients had been murdered.

On Harvey's own admission some were poisoned with cyanide, rat poison, arsenic and even hepatitis germs. He suffocated others by drawing a plastic bag over their heads, or injected air into their veins to cause blood clots ending in heart failure. In March 1987 a post-mortem on a patient named John Powell, who died suddenly following admission to the Daniel Drake hospital after a road accident, revealed traces of cyanide poison. Harvey, who refused to take a lie-detector test, later confessed to the one murder. When a local television station reported that staff at the hospital were concerned about other 'mystery' deaths there, he confessed to twenty-four murders (including those of twenty-one patients). Thanks to plea-bargaining, however, he evaded the death sentence. Although a list of the twenty-four names was found behind a picture in Harvey's flat, the victims themselves were buried after first being embalmed — which meant no traces of poison were likely to be found. Furthermore, there was no eye-witness evidence against him: so that without the confession, the case might have collapsed. Even so, prosecutor Arthur Ney left the court in no doubt as to his views: 'He's no mercy killer, and he's not insane. He killed because he *liked* killing.' That view was supported by Cincinnati psychologist Dr Walt Lippert, who said 'We expect our killers to look like Frankenstein, [but] it's all about power. Donald Harvey could hurt these people — watch them die — and they couldn't do a thing.'

In 1989 nursing sister Michaela Roeder was charged at Wuppertal, West Germany, with the murder of seventeen patients by injection with Catapresan, a drug which affects high blood pressure. Public prosecutor Karl-Hermann Majorowsky accused her of playing 'mistress of life or death' over patients in the intensive care unit of St Peter's Hospital in Wuppertal-Barmen, by her random selection of who should live or die. Twenty-eight bodies were exhumed after a nurse claimed to have seen Sister Roeder injecting a cancer patient with Catapresan. Seventeen of the corpses were found to contain traces of the drug. Newspaper reports said that even before suspicion was first aroused, Sister Roeder — who denied the murder charges — had been nicknamed 'The Angel of Death' by her colleagues, because of the high death rate in the ward. She was alleged by police to have admitted involvement in six deaths 'because she could not bear to see patients suffer unnecessarily'.

On 10 April 1989 Dr Alois Stacher — head of Vienna's hospital system — told a press conference that four women nurses working at the Lainz Hospital had been charged with the multiple murder of patients aged between seventy-three and eighty-two, and a warrant issued for the arrest of a fifth nurse. He said the 'bloody murders', allegedly committed at intervals since 1983, totalled at least forty-nine — probably the largest number of 'series murders' in European history. When first interrogated, said Dr Stacher, the nurses claimed the deaths were 'mercy killings'. He disagreed: 'These nurses enjoyed killing, because it gave them an extraordinary power over life and death. They killed patients who had become a nuisance to them, who had angered them or who posed a special problem.'

The killing rate rose from one patient every three months to one a month and continued virtually unnoticed — until a chance remark by an off-duty nurse to a ward doctor was reported to Dr Stacher, who immediately called in the police. The nurses were alleged to have changed their *modus operandi* from time to time, to avoid rousing suspicion. The method most frequently used was to drown patients by forcing water down their throats whilst holding their nostrils closed. 'This is a painful death which leaves virtually no trace,' said Dr Stacher. 'Water in the lungs of an elderly person is considered quite normal.' The nurse named as leader of the death group was said to have confessed personally to murdering twenty-two patients in this way. Other methods allegedly included injection of insulin, glucose and sleeping drugs. None of the accused had been brought to trial when this book went to press.

One twentieth-century poisoner who appeared to be a straight throwback to the Anna Zwanziger type of serial killer (she regarded arsenic as her 'truest friend') was Englishman Graham Young. Young, who was born in 1947, yearned obsessively for publicity. His mother died when he was only a few months old, and the solitary, intelligent child grew into an adolescent odd-man-out who disliked society generally and, perversely, transferred his admiration to Hitler and the Nazis. Another of his early heroes was Dr William Palmer, the English multiple murderer who poisoned his creditors and probably his wife, his mother-in-law, and four of his children before he was hanged in the 1850s.

Graham Young began experimenting with poison in 1961 – when he was fourteen – by administering small doses of antimony tartrate to his family. His elder sister Winifred suffered considerably from what she thought to be a permanently upset stomach. In April 1962 Graham Young's stepmother died. When his father, who was also ill and growing steadily weaker, was taken to hospital the doctors diagnosed arsenic poisoning. Fifteen-year-old Graham Young was outraged. His comment 'How ridiculous not to be able to tell the difference between arsenic and antimony poisoning' aroused immediate suspicion, and he was soon arrested. Vials of antimony tartrate were found on him and he was sent to Broadmoor, the asylum for criminal lunatics. While he was incarcerated there a fellow inmate died of poisoning, in mysterious circumstances.

Young was released after nine years, in February 1971. Far from being cured, his compulsion to carry on poisoning was undiminished. A few weeks after he took a job with a photographic firm at Bovingdon in Hertfordshire, head storekeeper Bob Egle began to suffer pains in the back and stomach. Mr Egle died in July 1971. Very soon so many of the staff were suffering from stomach upsets that the term 'Bovingdon bug' became common parlance. In October the same year another storekeeper, Fred Biggs, fell ill. On 31 October Graham Young noted in his diary 'I have administered a fatal dose of the special compound to F'. Mr Biggs died three weeks after he was admitted to hospital, cause unknown. In November 1971 two more Bovingdon employees complained of stomach upsets, 'pins and needles' in their feet and found their hair was falling out. Finally a team of doctors was called in to try to identify the deadly 'Bovingdon bug'; whereupon Graham Young, a newcomer to the firm who was forever trying to impress by his knowledge, astonished Dr Robert Hynd, the presiding Medical Officer of Health, by asking if the 'bug' symptoms were consistent with thallium poisoning. (Thallium, or Tl, is a metallic element found in flue dust resulting from the manufacture of sulphuric acid, and causes gradual paralysis of the nervous system.)

Such a question naturally aroused suspicion, and Scotland Yard was asked if Young had a criminal record. When his

Broadmoor background became known he was arrested on suspicion of murder. A subsequent search revealed his diary, complete with incriminating entries. At first Young claimed they were notes intended for a novel; but when he was found to have thallium in his possession (intended as a suicide potion if he were caught) he confessed to murdering both storekeepers, and was imprisoned for life. His sister Winifred, who had suffered for so long at his hands, told of her brother's 'craving for publicity, and notice' in her book, *Obsessive Poisoner*. She also said he spoke of loneliness and feelings of depression when he called on her shortly before his arrest (he referred to himself as 'Your friendly neighbourhood Frankenstein'). When she suggested he should mix more with other people, Young replied, 'Nothing like that can help . . . You see, there's a terrible coldness inside me.'

A number of serial killers express similar longings to be *important*. Some, mistaking fame for notoriety, hope to win acclaim by evading arrest while continuing to commit murder galore. Many genuinely believe they cannot be caught, like Jack the Ripper, and even if mistaken are quick to voice their surprise. Kenneth Erskine, alias The Stockwell Strangler, told the police who arrested him, 'I wanted to be famous . . . I thought you were never going to catch me'. After he was jailed for the last time, Ted Bundy expected authors Stephen G. Michaud and Hugh Aynesworth to write their book* not about his crimes, but about *him*: Bundy, the celebrity. Michaud overcame the problem by persuading him to speculate on 'the nature of a person capable of doing what Bundy had been accused of doing' – which the killer happily did.

Paul John Knowles, a young, red-headed American ex-convict who had spent half his adult life in jail, was a rapist and serial killer who murdered at least eighteen people in the four months before he was arrested for the last time, in November 1974. He was then twenty-eight. Sandy Fawkes, a visiting British woman journalist who by chance met Knowles before he was arrested and covered the courtroom hearing (see pp. 276–82), recognised this longing to be somebody in Knowles' evident pride on being interviewed by the press. 'He was having his hour of glory . . . He was already being referred

---

The Only Living Witness, New York: Linden Press/Simon & Schuster, 1983.

to as the most heinous killer in history.' His hour of glory, as it transpired, was no more than that – almost literally. As Knowles was being transferred the next day to a maximum-security jail, he succeeded in picking the lock on his handcuffs and tried to steal the escorting sheriff's gun. FBI agent Ron Angel, however, was quicker on the draw – and shot Knowles dead.

Regardless of the *type* of serial killer concerned, case histories show that most prefer to work alone. There are a number of instances of convicted serial killers working in pairs, but these are a minority group and usually consist of dominant leader and accomplice. As with the loners, serial killers who work in pairs are usually male: the man-woman team, while not unknown, is rare. A serial killer 'pack' is rarest of all; these too usually have a dominant leader (like Manson). The alleged Lainz Hospital medical 'pack' is unique, in that all its five first-reported members were female. The eight members of the Manson gang convicted of the 1969 murders comprised four of each sex: pack leader Manson, Bruce Davis, Clem Grogan and Charles 'Tex' Watson, plus females Susan Atkins, Patricia Krenwinkel, Lynette 'Squeaky' Fromme and Leslie van Houten. No charges were brought against the other two women member of the 'Family' – Mary Brunner and Linda Kasabian – who turned state evidence. On the premise that more than two serial killers constitutes a 'pack', the Texan homosexual murderer Dean Corll and his two accomplices, teenagers Elmer Wayne Henley and David Owen Brooks, rate among the more notorious. Together they took part in the torture, homosexual rape and murder of some twenty-seven youths in the 1970s. Finally, after Corll ordered Henley to rape and kill a girl of fifteen while Corll sodomised and murdered a male teenager, Henley refused and shot Corll instead. He and Brooks were later imprisoned for life for their part in the previous murders.

Almost all known instances of serial killers working in pairs have occurred in the United States. They include Patrick Kearney and David Hill, alias 'The Trashbag Killers', who murdered thirty homosexuals in Southern California in the late 1970s and put their bodies out for collection in bags, as if they were normal household refuse. Ex-convicts Henry Lee Lucas and Ottis Toole were arrested in Texas in 1983 after a string of murders, of which Lucas was found guilty of eleven. How many Lucas alone may have committed can only be guesswork: he killed for the first time at fifteen, and was fifty-one when finally arrested in 1983. Whilst in custody he 'confessed' to more than three hundred murders, but withdrew the 'confession' later. (In any event it was worthless: like so many serial killers, Lucas was found to be a compulsive liar.)

Also in the 1980s Vietnam veteran Leonard Lake and his accomplice, Charles Ng, abducted three women and kept them as their 'sex slaves' in a specially-built torture chamber beneath their cabin near Wisleyville, in Calaveras County, California. The three women were murdered when their captors finally tired of them, as were the two young children abducted with their 'sex slave' mothers. Seven adult males who were subsequently lured to the cabin were also murdered, robbed and buried there.

Two murderers who formed a rare 'mixed' pair of serial killers were British − Ian Brady and his mistress Myra Hindley, alias 'The Moors Murderers'. In 1966 they were jointly charged with three murders, two of them the murders of children aged ten and twelve respectively. A unique feature of their trial was that Brady and Hindley stood in a dock protected by bullet-proof glass, lest an attempt be made on their lives (there was widespread public outrage over the child murders). Discreetly, the police described the screen as a 'draught excluder'. Brady was found guilty of all three murders, Hindley of two, and of being an accessory to the third. For both, the timing of the trial was all-important: the death penalty for murder had been abolished just two months earlier.

The numbers of victims murdered by some lone serial killers are occasionally so large that the normal mind reels. The grim numerical record is thought to be held by a thirty-one-year-old Ecuadoran peasant, Pedro Alonzo Lopez. Lopez targeted young, pre-pubescent girls. Four makeshift graves were disturbed in April 1980 when a river overflowed its banks near Ambato (south of the capital Quito, in central Ecuador), and the bodies floated free to raise the alarm. Lopez was arrested shortly afterwards as he tried unsuccessfully to abduct a girl of eleven. He later confessed to killing 'about' three hundred and fifty, during the two previous years. In 1986 – again in Ecuador, this time in Quito itself – a transient Colombian serial killer named Daniel Camargo Barbosa confessed to murdering seventy-two girls a year earlier, and was jailed for sixteen years (reportedly the maximum penalty under the law).

When set against such leviathan totals, the numbers of victims regularly attributed to lone serial killers elsewhere sound almost respectably few. In fact, they serve only to underline how dangerous the species is. Ted Bundy admitted to twenty-three murders before he was executed in 1989 in 'Old Sparky' – criminalese for the electric chair in the state penitentiary at Starke, in Florida. Most police investigators believe Bundy was 'good' for half as many again, probably thirty-four murders. John Wayne Gacy, the homosexual serial killer from Chicago, was sentenced to life imprisonment in 1980 for strangling thirty-three youths. Charles Manson, who was sentenced to death (later commuted to life imprisonment) for nine murders committed in the summer of 1969, privately admitted to thirty-five. When he first heard this Deputy District Attorney Vincent Bugliosi, who prosecuted Manson and his 'Family', reckoned such a total to be 'sick boasting': with hindsight, however, he came to think Manson guilty of understatement.

In the 1980s, the official Soviet news agency Tass reported the pending trial of a man in Vitebsk, Byelorussia (or 'White Russia', some three hundred and fifty miles west of Moscow), charged with murdering thirty-three women. The Tass report was a rare admission, which served to underline the shock effect of multiple murder in communist Russia which, in the days before *glasnost*, censored virtually every public reference to violent crime in the USSR. The numbers of victims known to have been murdered by convicted British and European serial killers tend to be lower than those of their American or Russian counterparts, if equally alarming in the context of lower national average homicide rates. Vacher, the French Ripper, murdered fourteen people. Peter Sutcliffe, the Yorkshire Ripper, took thirteen lives. Peter Kürten, the Monster of Düsseldorf, who terrorised the Rhineland in the late 1920s (and is regarded by many as second only to the Ripper himself in terms of sexually sadistic brutality), was executed for nine murders, although he was probably guilty of more. Kenneth Erskine, the Stockwell Strangler, was convicted of seven murders. Irish-born John Duffy, ex-railwayman and long-term rapist turned serial killer, stood trial at the Old Bailey in 1988 charged with three murders, multiple rape and other offences. Duffy was found guilty of two of the murders, and five cases of rape: the judge described him as a 'predatory animal', and sentenced him to seven terms of life imprisonment.

There are few set rules governing the criminal behaviour of all serial killers. Most commit murder — and will continue to commit murder again and again, for as long as they remain free — whenever a compulsive urge, an uncontainable frenzy temporarily dormant within them, suddenly erupts and boils over. From that moment on the serial killer becomes every whit as lethal as a hired assassin, bent on killing his targeted victim (usually a total stranger) as soon as opportunity presents itself. Whatever potential risk may be involved is unlikely to serve as a deterrent. For many serial killers the risk will have been calculated when devising their *modus operandi*; for others, the greater an element of risk incurred, the greater the 'high' they attain from the act of killing.

Once in the thrall of this frenzy, the pent-up desires now unleashed will be every bit as compelling, say, as the drug addict's need of a 'fix'. The difference is that this need can be assuaged only by murder, all too often the murder of a complete stranger; a *type* of person known only to the killer himself, since both the type of victim and the way in which he or she will be put to death will have been conceived in fantasy, perhaps years before they meet. Not until the fantasy-inspired murder has run its course — possibly including violent assault, abduction, rape, torture and/or mutilation — will the frenzy abate, and a 'cooling-off' period set in.

What causes this indeterminate, emotional metamorphosis is uncertain. It may be remorse, or self-disgust even, once the enormity of the offence is fully realised. Or it may simply be a passing surfeit of murder and mayhem, with their inevitable inner tensions. Whatever its mainspring, this unique, emotional break in the murder cycle sets the serial killer apart from all other multiple murderers. Dr James Dobson, the American psychologist who spoke at length with Ted Bundy on the eve of Bundy's execution in 1989, was told by Bundy that he felt remorse only once – after the abduction, rape and murder of his first victim, student Lynda Ann Healy. 'Then the sex frenzy overcame him, and he killed again: and as each crime passed, he became de-sensitised.'

The 'triggering factor' which drives the serial killer to commit murder is almost endless in its variety, yet in the context of the violence of the crime often such a trivial thing. The type of victim he kills is always in the mind: conceived in fantasy, possibly years beforehand and uneasily dormant since. The serial murderer himself is often an 'under-achiever', an intelligent person (not an Einstein, but still of obvious promise); yet for some reason the potential has never been realised. Now, say, he has been sacked. To his mind, it will always be unfairly; and all the deep-seated hostility he harbours against society now erupts. He seeks out his symbolic victim – and kills. Another serial killer may have a 'dominant female' stress problem. After a blazing row with his wife/partner/mother he storms out, has a few drinks (or takes drugs), and ends up murdering a 'stranger' victim of opportunity: the classic transferred-aggression syndrome. Ed Kemper, an unmarried Californian serial killer, lived – and quarrelled incessantly with – his divorced, dominant mother. His practice was to behead, and later sexually assault, pretty students (the type of girl his mother told him he would never be able to date). After one row too many, Kemper turned on his mother – and decapitated her. With some serial killers, the triggering factor may be partly self-induced. Bundy, for example, blamed pornography for feeding his 'sick obsessions'. Medical serial killers, on the other hand, crave the ultimate power (over life and death); and once tasted, their need of it becomes addictive.

No matter what emotion may spark off – or terminate – the unique 'cooling-off' period, its duration can vary considerably in the same serial killer, from one murder to the next: from an hour, say, to a day, a week, months possibly and even years. We see this clearly in the irregular timing of the sixteen murders committed (to date) by the unknown criminal, thought to be Europe's longest 'working' serial killer but known only as 'The Monster of Florence'. *Il Mostro*, a Peeping Tom who haunts lovers' lanes and holiday camping

63

sites near the Tuscan capital in late summer and autumn, pounces on young couples as they embrace – usually in a parked car or caravan. His *modus operandi* is to play voyeur before shooting them dead – always the man first – with his .22 automatic pistol. He then mutilates the woman, Ripper-style, by disembowelling her; and finally – as if determined to emulate the Ripper in every way – he taunts his police pursuers by posting a body-part, taken from the woman victim, to the magistrate directing murder enquiries.

Il Mostro carried out his first double-murder in 1968. The next seven 'double events' followed in 1974, 1981 (in that year he struck twice, claiming four lives), 1982, 1983, 1984 and 1985. Thus there was a gap of six years between his first and second attacks, seven years between the second and third, only ten weeks between the third and fourth, with the rest occurring at regular annual intervals – until 1985. Because of the duration of his first two 'cooling-off' periods, there is no reason to suppose the Monster has yet done with killing. So, to this day, special precautions are taken each summer and autumn by the Florence police. This same, inexplicable variation in the duration of the cooling-off period may perhaps account for the erratic timing of the four undisturbed Ripper murders in 1888: 31 August (Mary Nichols), 8 September (Annie Chapman), 30 September (Kate Eddowes, the second victim in the 'double event'),and 9 November (Mary Jane Kelly).

Sexually sadistic serial killers like the Ripper, Vacher, Sutcliffe, Kemper and Il Mostro, etc., who torture and/or mutilate their victims, form a minority sub-species of serial killer known as 'lust murderers'. The sheer brutality of their crimes makes them the most feared of all sex murderers. In 1950, author and criminologist Dr J. Paul de River said of them in his book, *Crime and the Sexual Psychopath*, 'The lust murderer usually, after killing his victim, tortures, cuts, maims or slashes the victim in the regions on or about the genitalia, rectum, breast in the female, and about the neck, throat and buttocks, as usually these parts contain sexual significance to him and serve as sexual stimulus.'

Thirty years later, two senior special agents from the

Behavioural Science Unit of the FBI at Quantico — Robert R. ('Roy') Hazelwood and John E. Douglas — put the lust killer under their joint behavioural microscope. Both agents were already vastly experienced in the ways of the serial killer, and are recognised today as authorities on criminal profiling. They describe lust murder as: 'One of the most heinous crimes committed by man. While not a common occurrence, it is one which frightens and arouses the public as does no other crime . . . It is the authors' contention that the lust murder is unique, and is distinguished from the sadistic homicide by the involvement of a mutilating attack or displacement of the breasts, rectum or genitals. Further, while there are always exceptions, basically two types of individuals commit the lust murder . . . the Organised Nonsocial and Disorganised Asocial personalities.'

Briefly, they define the *organised nonsocial* lust killer as an egocentric who dislikes people generally, yet is adept at posing as an outwardly warm person for as long as may be needed to gain his own ends. Behind the façade lies a cunning methodical killer who is very much aware of the impact his sort of murder will have on society — and commits it for precisely that reason, to shock and offend. Usually he 'lives some distance from the crime scene and will cruise, looking for a victim'. Like his disorganised, fellow lust killer he 'harbours similar feelings of hostility (to society) but . . . overtly expresses it through aggressive and seemingly senseless acts. Typically, he begins to demonstrate his hostility as he passes through puberty and into adolescence. He would be described as a troublemaker and a manipulator of people, concerned only for himself. It is the nonsocial's aim to get even with society and inflict pain and punishment upon others.'

In contrast, the *disorganised asocial* lust killer is a loner. 'He experiences difficulty in negotiating interpersonal relationships and consequently feels rejected and lonely. He lacks the cunning of the nonsocial type, and commits the crime in a more frenzied and less methodical manner. The crime is likely to be committed in close proximity to his residence or place of employment, where he feels secure and more at ease . . . Family and associates would describe him as a nice, quiet person who keeps himself to himself, but who never quite realised his potential. During adolescence he may have engaged

65

in voyeuristic activities or the theft of feminine clothing. Such activities serve as a substitute for his inability to approach women sexually in a mature and confident manner.'

Evidence unwittingly revealed by the scene of the crime – such as the location of the body, the presence or absence of the murder weapon, and probable sequence in which the various criminal acts were performed – may also provide clues to the type of lust killer at work. 'Typically, the asocial type leaves the body at the scene of death, and while the location is not open to the casual observer there has been no attempt to conceal the body. Conversely, the nonsocial type commits the murder in a secluded or isolated location, and may later transport it to an area where it is likely to be found. While there is no conscious intent to be arrested, the nonsocial type wants the excitement derived from the publicity about the body's discovery and its impact on the victim's community.'

By identifying the sequence of the criminal acts committed in a number of such murders – some obvious to the trained, naked eye, others revealed by the pathologist's report – the two FBI authors established that lust killers usually murder their victims 'shortly following abduction or attack . . . If however there is physical or medical evidence indicating that the victim was subjected to torture or mutilation prior to death, this factor indicates that the perpetrator is the nonsocial rather than the asocial type.'

The two agents also found that few lust killers use a gun to murder their victims. Firearms generally are too impersonal a weapon for such sexually sadistic murderers. To attain the 'high' they seek in the fulfilment of their violent, fantasy-inspired homicides, most prefer to use their hands more directly when despatching their victims. 'Most frequently death results from strangulation, blunt force, or the use of a sharp, pointed instrument . . . The asocial type is more prone to use a weapon of opportunity and may leave it at the scene, while the nonsocial type may carry the murder weapon with him and take it when departing the scene. Therefore the murderer's choice of weapon and its proximity to the scene can be greatly significant to the investigation.'

Even a superficial study of lust murders committed in countries thousands of miles from the United States – and in some instances, committed a century ago – reveals numerous behavioural characteristics similar to those noted by the two FBI authors in their survey. Jack the Ripper slit the throats of his five victims, and disembowelled four of them with a sharp, pointed long-bladed knife which he took with him on every foray into the streets of Whitechapel. (He did not leave the knife at any murder scene, nor was it found by the police. Its detailed description comes from pathologists, who gave evidence at the subsequent inquests.) Joseph Vacher carried a whole set of knives with him, plus a cudgel, throughout the three years he was 'working' in south-eastern France. They were recovered after his arrest. Similarly Peter Sutcliffe used two knives and 'blunt force' (in his case, a ball-headed hammer) to murder his victims. Thanks to the alertness of the uniformed police sergeant who arrested Sutcliffe on suspicion, both knives and the hammer were recovered next day.

Because he targets two victims simultaneously, even Italy's unknown 'Monster of Florence' − one of the few lust killers known to use a gun when committing the murder − may be seen as an exception who proves the rule. *Il Mostro* uses his .22 pistol to eliminate the main threat (the male victim) at the outset; he then turns it on the female to silence her before she can raise the alarm. Having thus established control over the situation, he then attends to the principal task − the ritual 'signature' mutilation − by using a sharp knife to disembowel the female and remove selected body parts. Californian lust killer Ed Kemper's *modus operandi* in the early 1970s was similar in certain respects. Because he targeted two female students at a time, he carried a gun to shoot them dead before transporting the bodies for mutilation (when he used a hunting knife, which he called 'The General').

Latterday British serial killers (as distinct from lust killers) Dennis Nilsen, Kenneth Erskine, and John Duffy also strangled their victims. So did John Reginald Halliday Christie, London's notorious 'Monster of 10 Rillington Place', in the 1950s; but none mutilated their victims. Erskine and Christie used their bare hands: although Christie, who was a necrophiliac, had first to ply his prostitute victims with drink, and finally render them insensible with coal-gas inhalation before he was physically capable of rape-strangulation. Perhaps coincidentally, the civil servant serial killer Dennis Nilsen used his tie to throttle his victims. John Duffy, once regarded as a comparatively 'non-vicious' rapist — only to become a singularly vicious killer — used a stick and length of string (or an article of clothing taken from the victim) to form a tourniquet, and so exert immense pressure round the murder victim's throat.

Among the many theories about Jack the Ripper's lifestyle, perhaps the most widely accepted was that he was a doctor. This stemmed largely from the premise that such precise mutilation, carried out in the dark and aimed at the removal of selected organs from a human body, necessarily required specialist skills which could only be acquired in medical school. While never discounting the possibility, no FBI criminal profiler at Quantico would accept that supposition *per se*. Although such murders remain comparatively rare, research shows that twentieth-century lust killers with no medical training whatsoever sometimes decapitate their victims, and/or remove arms, legs, feet, hands, breasts, buttocks, genitals, etc. in the course of their fantasy-inspired murders. They do so not necessarily to destroy the victim symbolically (though that may apply to some): often the intention is to retain certain body parts, for much the same reason as the big-game hunter mounts the head and antlers taken from his prey, and the lepidopterist pins rare, dead butterflies to his board — as trophies of the chase.

A few serial killers collect bodies. Christie stripped some of his victims naked, and stored them in his kitchen cupboard (in his case as sexual partners as well as trophies: evidence of sexual intercourse was found in all (three) cupboard corpses). Robert Hansen, the Alaskan baker and big-game enthusiast who hunted his naked prostitute victims through the snow before shooting them dead, was a trophy hunter. As a married man with a family, it would have been impossible for him to store human 'trophies' at home alongside the elk antlers and bearskins adorning the gun room. Instead, he stole items of paste jewellery from his victims — and hid them in his loft, so that he could relive his fantasy-inspired murders at will.

Jewellery — usually rings, brooches, bracelets and earrings

– are commonly taken by serial killers from their victims as 'souvenirs', regardless of monetary value; as with Hansen, the motive is gratification. Others collect footwear and clothing, fetish items mostly such as stiletto-heeled shoes, nylon stockings, suspender belts, brassieres and panties. When Scotland Yard detectives searched John Christie's house in Rillington Place shortly before they arrested him in 1953, they discovered some of the more bizarre 'souvenirs' collected by any serial murderer – four sets of pubic hair, neatly waxed, stored in an otherwise empty pipe-tobacco tin. The sets were never matched to any of the bodies found on the premises.

Some serial killers take video films and/or still pictures of their victims, dead and alive, as 'souvenirs' (see Harvey Glatman, pp. 149–52). Police in California in the 1980s found pornographic 'snuff' videos made by Leonard Lake and Charles Ng as they tortured and abused their three abducted 'sex slaves' at Wisleyville (see p. 60). Other serial killers tape-record the screams and pleas for mercy uttered by their victims; these, too, are stored and kept for subsequent gratification at will. On Boxing Day 1964, the 'Moors Murderers' Ian Brady and Myra Hindley tape-recorded the cries of ten-year-old Lesley Ann Downey, as they stripped the child and forced her to pose for pornographic pictures shortly before they murdered her. The recording, which was taped to the background music of Christmas carols, was played to the jury at the Moors Murderers' trial two years later. Although they denied torturing the child, the judge said in his summing-up: 'One will never forget how the recording started with that fantastic screaming from the girl. What was happening before that screaming, and a woman's and a child's voice only were being heard?'

As well as the torture and mutilation of their victims, and the theft of jewellery or clothing as souvenirs, some serial killers also practise anthropophagy. This is not a recent phenomenon; there were written indications of cannibalism following the murder of Kate Eddowes in 1888 (see p. 35), and there have been a number of known cases during the present century. In the early 1920s Karl Denke, who ran a boarding house in Munsterberg, Silesia, murdered at least thirty of his male and female lodgers. With rare Teutonic attention to detail he then entered their names, deadweight, and date of death in a ledger before pickling the choice cuts in brine, and eating them. Denke committed suicide shortly after his arrest in 1921, by hanging himself with his braces.

Joachim Kroll, alias 'The Ruhr Hunter', murdered some fourteen people over a period of seventeen years before his arrest at Duisburg, in West Germany, in 1976. Most were women. Kroll, a small, balding man who sported tinted glasses, ate the flesh of five of his younger female victims; three teenagers and two children, aged four and five. He was caught eventually, not by any feat of investigative skill but because, like Dennis Nilsen (see p. 40), Kroll blocked the drains. He had a meal of human flesh and vegetables cooking on the stove as police entered his apartment. Possibly the most notorious known flesh eater in sex-crime history was the New York painter and decorator, Albert Fish. Fish was a true sadist. Six years after abducting and murdering a girl of ten, he wrote an anonymous letter to the child's mother, admitting the murder, saying 'how sweet the flesh tasted, roasted in the oven'. As if by poetic justice, a design on the envelope betrayed Fish's whereabouts, and he was caught in 1934 by a dedicated policeman from the city's Missing Persons Bureau, who put off retirement for two years to get his man. Fish, by then a man of sixty-four, confessed to the murder of some four hundred children over the preceding quarter-century. Unfortunately Fish – like Henry Lee Lucas (see p. 60) and most serial killers – was a compulsive liar; but although his overall confession was suspect he was thought to be responsible for 'dozens' of child murders, and was executed by electric chair in 1934. One behavioural characteristic he confirmed was that while mutilation of their victims is common to both categories of lust killer, anthropophagy is indicative of asocial involvement.

Special agents Hazelwood and Douglas also established that one of the oldest crime fiction chestnuts – that the murderer returns to the scene of the crime, like a moth to a candle – is true of both types of lust killer, 'albeit for different reasons . . . While the asocial type may return to engage in further mutilation or to relive the experience, the nonsocial type returns to determine if the body has been discovered and to check on the progress of the investigation.' So compelling is the urge of the non-social killer to check on police progress that some frequent the bars used by off-duty detectives, either to eavesdrop or even intrude on their converstion on some pretext. Ed Kemper (see p. 63) was almost a 'regular' at his local police haunts. Another serial killer 'returned to the scene after it had been examined by police laboratory technicians and deposited articles of clothing worn by the victim on the day she died. In both of two other cases, the killer visited the cemetery site . . . and left articles belonging to the victim on her grave. Such actions appear to further his "will to power", or desire to control.'

One major riddle bequeathed by Jack the Ripper was *why* did he cease killing so abruptly after his ritual mutilation of Mary Jane Kelly — victim number five — on the night of 8 November 1888? The two most widely accepted theories are that either he fled the country to avoid arrest, or that he committed suicide. The first seems unlikely, for a variety of reasons. Despite claims to the contrary, Scotland Yard patently did not have the remotest clue to his identity; it is a case which remains unsolved after more than one hundred years. Furthermore, while murderers of every kind frequently leave a particular area to avoid arrest, statistics show that 'working' serial killers rarely cease killing of their own volition — and certainly not because they change location. The reverse, in fact, is often the case: serial killers change location to avoid arrest in order to carry on killing.

Ted Bundy is one recent notorious example. Following the hue and cry which attended his first eight murders in 1974, Bundy moved from Washington (state) to Utah, and later from Utah to Colorado, killing afresh each time; and after he excaped from jail a second time and moved to Florida, so the murders began again. Earle Nelson, alias 'The Gorilla Killer' of the 1920s, murdered twenty-two people (mostly landladies) between February 1926 and June 1927. He was on the move all the time, from California to Oregon, down to Iowa, across to New York state, back to Illinois and across into Canada — where he was caught, and hanged, in 1928. Because it pays serial killers in the United States to be transient (driving from one state into another, which will have separate jurisdiction, automatically lessens the chances of arrest), FBI analysts at Quantico now use computer links via Washington to monitor cases geographically (see p. 122). Had the Ripper felt constrained to quit England in November 1888 for fear of arrest – because of the hue and cry – he would still have been unlikely to be able to resist killing again: homicide is the serial killer's *raison d'être*. Furthermore, in an era when the 'signature' ritual mutilation of a victim was so rare as to bring him lasting notoriety, it is logical to assume that any new spate of ritual mutilation murders – no matter where they occurred – would inevitably have attracted massive publicity.

Suicide is indeed a possibility, although perhaps less likely than may be supposed. Modern research shows us that serial killers rarely take their own lives; one possible reason being that the majority tend to 'externalise' (i.e. to blame others – not excluding the victim – for their crimes) rather than admit responsibility themselves. We have evidence of that from statements made by convicted offenders. Alaskan serial killer Robert Hansen told the investigating police he would never have harmed his victims had they not been prostitutes. 'I'm not saying I hate all women, I don't. I'd do everything in my power, any way, shape or form for [a good woman] and to see no harm ever came to her, but I guess prostitutes are women I'm putting down as lower than myself . . . It's like it was a game, they had to pitch the ball before I could bat.' Ed Kemper, the giant Californian who decapitated his mother (whom he abhorred), blamed her for the murders of his several female student victims. 'Those girls are dead because of the way that mother raised her son,' he would say, as if he himself were another person. After beheading his mother, he cut out her larynx (a symbolic gesture, to signify that she could never nag him again), and threw it in the garbage disposal machine. When he switched on, the machine malfunctioned and the larynx flew up out again. 'Even when she was dead, she was still bitching at me,' Kemper complained. 'I *couldn't* get her to shut up!'

The lone exception to the 'externalisation' thought process is sometimes found – in the ranks of the lust killer, a category of serial killer which certainly includes Jack the Ripper. However, in their 1980 survey (see p. 64) FBI agents Hazelwood and Douglas say 'Seldom does the lust killer come from an environment of love and understanding. It is more likely that he was an abused or neglected child who experienced a great deal of conflict in his early life and was unable to develop and use adequate coping devices. Had he been able to do so, he would have withstood the stresses placed upon him and developed normally in early childhood . . . These stresses, frustrations and subsequent anxieties, along with the inability to cope with them, may lead the individual to withdraw from the society which he perceives as hostile and threatening.

'Through this internalisation process, he becomes secluded and isolated from others and may eventually select suicide as an alternative to a life of loneliness and frustration. The authors have designated this reaction to life as disorganised asocial.' Whether the Ripper belonged to this category is unclear. Perversely, he exhibited certain behavioural characteristics which could fit both types of lust killer. For example the location of the bodies (all left where they were murdered), clear evidence of post-mortem mutilation, and the indication of anthropophagy which followed the murder of Kate Eddowes, all point to the *disorganised asocial* type. Similarly, the absence of clues at the scene of the crime (notably the Ripper's removal of the murder weapon), and subsequent letters to the Central News Agency (as if to involve himself in the investigation), suggest the more calculating *organised non-social* type.

In itself, this is not unusual: FBI analysts at Quantico frequently encounter serial killers who display 'mixed' organised and disorganised characteristics. By carefully weighing *all* the available evidence — police report, results of forensic tests, pathologist's report, crime scene photographs, etc. — they still produce an accurate profile of the type of offender responsible. Pathologists' reports aside, little else of analytical value is available today on the Jack the Ripper murders, for nineteenth-century police investigators had no specialised technique for analysing such apparently 'motiveless' murders.

Ongoing, modern research suggests there could well be a third, entirely feasible explanation for the abrupt cessation of the Victorian serial murders; that the Ripper may have been arrested and jailed for some unrelated offence after murdering Mary Jane Kelly in November 1988, and thus removed from society involuntarily. This is frequently found to be the case in the United States whenever a series of violent crimes (rape as well as murder) ceases abruptly, without the arrest and conviction of the person or persons responsible. For example, the 'Boston Strangler' committed the first of his thirteen murders on 14 June 1962. His victim was Anna Slesers, a fifty-five-year-old seamstress. Victim number thirteen died on 4 January 1964. She was Mary Sullivan, a student of nineteen who was working her way through night school. Her murder reduced the city of Boston to near panic, as the police searched in vain for the unknown killer and the manhunt entered its third calendar year. Then in February 1965 a man named Albert DeSalvo – detained at the time in a Boston mental institution, awaiting trial on charges not immediately connected with the murder inquiries – began boasting incessantly to other inmates about his sexual exploits. Among his captive audience was George Nassar, a schizophrenic who himself faced charges of first-degree murder.

It suddenly dawned on Nassar that DeSalvo was Boston's most wanted man. He told his lawyer, the remarkable F. Lee Bailey, who also represented DeSalvo after he confessed to being the Strangler. Ironically, when DeSalvo was jailed for life in 1967, he *was* removed from society permanently: within six years he was stabbed to death by an unknown fellow prisoner. (See Albert DeSalvo, alias the Boston Strangler pp. 206–18).

Similarly the Manson gang was arrested in the autumn of 1969 only after 'Family' member Susan Atkins – by then in custody on an unrelated charge – told a cellmate about her involvement in the Sharon Tate murders. The Hollywood murders were front-page news, the information immensely valuable to any remand prisoner hoping to bargain for her release; and as soon as it filtered back to the Los Angeles police department, Susan Atkins' accomplices were quickly rounded up and the whole gang brought to trial.

Many serial killers habitually commit offences other than homicide – Carlton Gary was also a burglar, Ted Bundy a car thief, Robert Hansen an obsessional shoplifter. As a result, when a run of violent serial crimes ends suddenly without the arrest of a suspect, the investigating law enforcement officers in the United States do not automatically regard suicide as a likely reason. Statistics show that such offenders are usually: *one*, in custody for some unrelated offence, or *two*, have left the area because the publicity generated by their murders has made them increasingly nervous of arrest. When this happens, the move will probably have been planned to avoid arousing suspicion — by changing jobs, perhaps, or joining the armed forces. Should a cycle of similar violent crimes suddenly start up elsewhere, they will — once reported to the FBI at Quantico — be automatically linked to the previous offences by VICAP (see pp. 119–22), the Violent Criminal Apprehension Programme databank. If no such new outbreak is reported, the analysts may then examine a third possibility; that the suspect has died, either from accident, natural causes — or suicide.

Although the 1980s was the decade in which murder and the serial murderer came very much to the fore, violent crime of every kind had been on the increase in the United States for years beforehand. A general rise in crimes of violence in the United States started circa 1963, and with it a sea change in traditional American habits also manifested itself. Increasingly over the next two decades, and especially in the big cities, it became the accepted practice for many people never to open their doors to callers without first vetting them — either by voice identification, or via a closed-circuit television screen. In some areas — in Hollywood for example, following the Manson gang murders — the more affluent took to hiring private guards and/or dog handlers to provide additional security; but no matter what precautions were adopted, the national violent crime graph continued inexorably to rise.

By 1980, the country faced the worst crisis in its criminal history. A floodtide of violence — rape, arson, aggravated assault, armed robbery, abduction and street mugging — reached record levels, and there was no sign of abatement. Above all 1980 was a year of murder galore. Special agent Roger L. Depue, then head of the FBI Behavioural Science Unit's training and research wing at Quantico (and later Administrator of the newly-formed National Centre for the Analysis of Violent Crime), painted a grim word picture of America's entry into the 1980s. 'More than 20,000 people were being murdered per year as we entered the new decade. The year 1980 itself became a record year, with more than 23,000 people becoming victims of homicide. It was unprecedented mayhem. The rates for other serious violent crimes such as aggravated assault, forcible rape, and robbery were equally disturbing. Predatory stranger-to-stranger violent crime was increasing steadily, while the number of cases cleared by arrest were decreasing. It was a downward spiral. Something had to be done.'

The record total of 23,000-plus murders in 1980 meant that the homicide rate in the United States had more than doubled since the graph began its upward climb in 1963. It represented an average rate of 63 murders a day, 440 each week, 1,900 per month – an orgy of homicide which tarnished the national image abroad, as well as arousing fear and anger at home. In contrast the sum total of murders committed in 1980 in Britain – with a population numbering roughly one quarter that of the United States – was 549.

There was no mistaking America's reaction. Public outrage and alarm, which had risen hand-in-hand with each successive upward surge in lawlessness, came to a head. Now the Administration was compelled to find some way of applying the brakes; nothing less would suffice. Lois Haight Herrington, who chaired the President's Task Force on Victims of Crime, minced no words when delivering her report to the White House. 'Something insidious has happened in America: crime has made victims of us all. Awareness of its danger affects the way we think, where we live, where we go, what we buy, how we raise our children, and the quality of our lives as we age. The spectre of violent crime and the knowledge that, without warning, any person can be attacked or crippled, robbed, or killed, lurks at the fringes of consciousness. Every citizen of this country is more impoverished, less free, more fearful, and less safe because of the ever present threat of the criminal. Rather than alter a system that has proven itself incapable of dealing with crime, society has altered itself.'

Clearly it had; America was in danger of becoming a fortress society. Fortunately, new techniques to help combat violent crime – particularly the apparently 'motiveless' murders which were consistently making the headlines – had already been devised and successfully employed by agents from the FBI's Behavioural Science Unit at Quantico, Virginia. In essence, these men were 'reading' the crime scene for behavioural clues which would enable them to profile the *type* of offender responsible (as distinct from the individual). Another way in which the new method differed from traditional 'psychological profiling' was that this technique of criminal analysis — which combined behavioural clues deduced from crime scene evidence, statistical probability, and the intuitive judgement which comes to the investigator from years of experience — offered a *systematic* approach to crime investigation, as opposed to guidance based on the professional assessment of a psychologist or psychiatrist.

The idea sprang from hours of two-way discussion between Behavioural Science Unit instructors and 'students' (many of whom were experienced police officers) attending specialist training courses at the FBI Academy at Quantico. Then as now, informal exchanges about bizarre or unusual homicides confronting 'students' in their home areas were constantly encouraged. In time the instructors — who alone provided the continuity — were able to say to new classes: 'We traded ideas recently on a similar case with another class — and they've since made an arrest.' The lessons learned would then be passed on, and contact maintained. As other arrests followed, and more and more common behavioural traits began to emerge, so the FBI instructors reversed the process — and began to translate crime scene evidence, backed by police reports, autopsy findings and so on — into positive behavioural characteristics, which enabled them to build a profile of the type of offender responsible for apparently 'motiveless' crimes.

One important early accomplishment was their ability to identify murderers as either 'organised' or 'disorganised' offenders. In itself it provided an immediate, easy to picture, lead to the type of criminal involved: basically, the organised serial killer *plans* his crimes, whereas the disorganised type is more of an opportunist. The opportunist is more likely, for instance, to murder his victim with the nearest weapon to hand — a stone, say — while the organised killer usually carries the murder weapon with him (knife, gun, length of rope), plus the restraints he intends to use (gag, handcuffs, etc.). Early investigations produced failure as well as success. The problem was that the fledgling law enforcement-designed technique of profiling sex killers by organised and disorganised classification depended over-heavily on investigative experience (and often, intuition): further guidelines from within the same behavioural concept were urgently needed.

To this end a second important, related step was taken in

the late 1970s to extend the scope of this new profiling technique. FBI agents from the Behavioural Science Unit, together with other agents specially trained for the task, began carrying out a survey of thirty-six convicted sex murderers held in jails throughout the United States. Of these, twenty-five were serial killers. The rest were either single, double or 'spree' (see next chapter for homicide classification) killers. Twenty-four were organised murderers, twelve disorganised. It was the first time in any country that such a survey – and on this scale – had been conducted. Given the co-operation of the convicted men (some of whom were on Death Row, see pp. 43–4) the potential value of the information available, in terms of criminal behaviour analysis, was immeasurable.

Each FBI interviewer possessed detailed knowledge of the offender's serial murders and criminal record overall, from courtroom transcripts, police records, prison, probationary and psychiatric reports. Every scrap of information on the victims' background and lifestyle was also collated. What the prison interviews afforded was a unique opportunity to match established facts with the offender's eye-witness account of all that transpired before, during and after each murder he had committed. The quest for common behavioural characteristics in both the organised and disorganised types of serial killer included questions about childhood and adolescence – the all-important 'rearing environment' which had shaped them, first into children who tortured pets or set fire to houses, and finally into adults who committed fantasy-inspired serial murder. Only such men – some awaiting almost certain execution – could reveal the thinking behind their selection of the 'stranger' victims (or types of stranger victim) they targeted, often abducted, almost invariably physically and sexually assaulted, and sometimes tortured before murdering. Only they possessed first-hand experience of the compulsive frenzy (or 'voices') which drove them to perform each 'signed' mutilation of their victims' bodies; or could describe the various phases they passed through in the course of each bizarre murder, and describe the various stratagems they adopted to evade detection and arrest for so long.

By any investigative standards, here was priceless material for analysis. The FBI does not disclose the names of the murderers who took part. However, the information they volunteered was sufficient to form an encyclopaedic databank guide to future behavioural analysis; a guide which is continually being reviewed and extended as new material flows in. (So successful was the original survey that prison interviews of convicted serial killers is now an ongoing process.) Even before it was fully completed — in 1983 — enough had been learned to ensure that no time was wasted when US Attorney General William French Smith called on all the agencies of the Justice Department for urgent recommendations on how best to contain and reduce the record 1980 violent crime figures.

In November 1982, following a meeting between members of the Criminal Personality Research Project advisory board (who had instituted the thirty-six killer survey) and other specialists, the bold concept of a single National Centre for the Analysis of Violent Crime, or NCAVC, was put forward. That proposal was unanimously adopted seven months later by a conference of all the interested parties, held at the Sam Houston University's Centre for Criminal Justice in Huntsville, Texas. The delegates further agreed that the NCAVC should be founded at the FBI Academy in Quantico, and run by the agents of the elite Behavioural Science Unit. President Reagan then formally announced its establishment on 21 June 1984 when he gave it the primary mission of 'identifying and tracking repeat killers'.

The NCAVC was never envisaged as a replacement for traditional crime *investigation* by local law enforcement agencies: there is no substitute for prompt, on-the-spot investigation by trained police officers. The need for a national centre arose because of the continuing rise in violent crime throughout the United States, a situation worsened by the ease with which transient serial offenders — killers, kidnappers, rapists and arsonists alike — could remain at large, simply by crossing the state lines in a country served by numerous independent jurisdictions. The NCAVC sees its proper role as a clearing house-cum-resource centre in the combined national fight against all violent criminals.

That said, the NCAVC is some clearing house. Standards of entry into the FBI are uniformly high, and only agents of exceptional calibre are recruited into the specialist Behavioural Science Unit. Most of its supervisory special agents (or SSAs) hold at least a Master's degree. The NCAVC uses the latest advancements in computer engineering to combat serial violent crime nationwide, including VICAP (the Violent Criminal Apprehension Programme) and PROFILER (another world first: a robot, rule-based expert system programmed to profile serial murderers), both of which are discussed in detail in the next chapter. Research on new projects is continuous — the Behavioural Science Unit has long been known as law enforcement's 'Think Tank' in the United States — and no great vision is required to anticipate the further advances which will be made in the coming decade. Here, surely, is the blueprint crime-fighting centre for every advanced nation in the twenty-first century.

Three

The Profilers

Over the years, the name of one man more than any other — James A. Brussel, M.D. — has become synonymous with the art of psychological profiling. In the mid-1950s this spare, pipe-smoking American psychiatrist, with the *forte* voice and fund of knowledge concerning errant mankind, profiled the then unknown 'Mad Bomber' of New York with quite superlative accuracy — right down to the way he would wear the jacket of his double-breasted suit: buttoned. This was after just one meeting with the investigating city police, who had had the Mad Bomber on their 'wanted' list for sixteen years. James Brussel was that good. Small wonder the press dubbed him 'The Sherlock Holmes of the Couch'.

For many years no-one knew why the Mad Bomber had declared his one-man war on Consolidated Edison, the firm which supplies New York with electric light. The campaign began on 16 November 1940 when a home-made metal pipe bomb was found on a windowsill at the Consolidated Edison plant on West 64th Street. It failed to explode, but a note wrapped round it left no-one in doubt as to the bomb-maker's intention. 'CON EDISON CROOKS — THIS IS FOR YOU', it said. There were no tell-tale fingerprints. In those days, no-one made telephone calls claiming responsibility. Moreover, there was a real war being fought in Europe, where cities were being razed by bombs; so, perhaps understandably, the discovery of one, dud, home-made, explosive device in Manhattan failed to make a line in the papers. The same lack of publicity attended a second unexploded pipe bomb, found in the street a few blocks from Consolidated Edison headquarters on the corner of Irving Place and 14th Street a year later. Within another three months, America herself was at war.

Somewhat magnanimously the unknown bomb-maker wrote

81

to New York city police headquarters, pledging a truce for the duration. As with all his letters it was hand-printed in neat, capital letters, and signed with the initials 'FP'. He used hyphens instead of commas and full stops, and old-fashioned phrases ('dastardly deeds' was his favourite). 'I WILL MAKE NO MORE BOMBS FOR THE DURATION OF THE WAR – MY PATRIOTIC FEELINGS HAVE MADE ME DECIDE THIS – LATER I WILL BRING THE CON EDISON TO JUSTICE – THEY WILL PAY FOR THEIR DASTARDLY DEEDS – FP'[.]

The 'Mad Bomber', as he was later dubbed by the press, kept his word. World War Two was long over before the first bomb exploded, on 24 April 1950. It wrecked the phone booth in which it was planted, outside the New York Public Library on Fifth Avenue; by chance, there were no casualties. Over the next six years he planted bombs in subway lockers, phone booths or holes cut in cinema seats from Broadway to Brooklyn – fifty-four altogether by his count by March 1956. A number of people were injured: again by chance, only a handful seriously. Part of a letter sent by 'FP' that month to the *New York Herald Tribune* warned 'THESE BOMBINGS WILL CONTINUE UNTIL CON EDISON IS BROUGHT TO JUSTICE – MY LIFE IS DEDICATED TO THIS TASK'[.]

On 2 December 1956 he struck again. His most powerful device to date exploded in the Paramount cinema in Brooklyn injuring seven of the audience, three seriously. On Boxing Day the *Journal-American* published an open letter calling on the Mad Bomber to give himself up, while offering him space to air his grievances. He rejected the appeal by return of post: 'PLACING MYSELF IN CUSTODY WOULD BE STUPID – DO NOT INSULT MY INTELLIGENCE', but clearly welcomed the publicity, by declaring another bombing truce until mid-January 1957. He also listed the fourteen devices he had planted in 1956, several of which had not been discovered. A police search uncovered eight. Five were dummies. The rest were armed, but for technical reasons had failed to explode.

Still the police did not know where to look, or for whom. Then by responding to a second open letter in the *Journal-American* on 10 January 1957, the Mad Bomber inadvertently revealed the first clues to his identity. 'I WAS INJURED ON A JOB AT CONSOLIDATED EDISON PLANT – AS A RESULT I AM ADJUDGED TOTALLY AND

PERMANENTLY DISABLED – I DID NOT RECEIVE ANY AID OF ANY KIND FROM COMPANY – THAT I DID NOT PAY MYSELF – WHILE FIGHTING FOR MY LIFE – SECTION 28 CAME UP'[.] Section 28 of the New York State Compensation Law requires legal claims to be submitted within two years of injury. An immediate search of Consolidated Edison files failed to unearth the complaint which could identify the Mad Bomber. A third appeal by the newspaper, asking for further details of his injuries, failed to elicit a quick response. As the search went on, the police asked Dr Brussel to help them by profiling the unknown wanted man.

While the police had not consulted him before in a criminal investigation, James Brussel was no stranger to the world of the criminally insane. Although in private practice, he was also assistant commissioner of the New York State's mental health department. He had formerly been assistant director of a mental hospital. During World War Two he had served in the US army as a senior neuropsychiatrist, and was recalled in the Korean war as head of the Neuropsychiatric Centre at El Paso, Texas. He knew of the Mad Bomber, of course, from the newspapers. He now listened to the police version, studied photographs of the unexploded bombs and read through a host of letters inked in neat, capital letters. In his loud voice he then delivered the psychological profile which has since become legend.

The Mad Bomber's sex? Dr Brussel assumed him to be a man: most bombers are. That was to prove correct, as did his professional diagnosis that the offender's marathon resentment of Con-Edison, for offences real or imagined – plus his total disregard for the lives of others when settling old scores – to be the conduct of a man suffering from acute persecution mania: a paranoiac. Correction. A *middle-aged* paranoiac. Why? Because paranoia usually reaches a dangerous stage in patients in their mid-thirties, and this bombing campaign dated back to 1940. Elementary, my dear Watson.

To James Brussel, the bundle of letters on his desk, each one meticulously printed in neat, inked capitals to justify the mayhem it portended, denoted a neat, formally polite, yet hugely dangerous, mad author. To his psychiatrist's eye the flowing shape of the 'w's, with their pointed tips, represented token female breasts. Experience had taught him the Oedipus-complex was not uncommon among paranoiacs. He had

83

learned from the police how the Mad Bomber cut holes in cinema seats to plant his bombs. Was this, he wondered, the explanation for the bombing campaign – a sexual problem, sparked off by real or imagined resentment of *male* authority in the shape of Consolidated Edison management?

Dr Brussel was wrong there. Events showed it to be a straight grudge vendetta with no sexual overtones. In most other respects his profiling was inspired. He was certain of one thing; the Mad Bomber was not homosexual. Brussel saw him as a brooding, solitary person of average height and 'athletic' build (this last a statistical characteristic of most paranoiacs) who either lived alone or was looked after by some older, unmarried female relative – an aunt perhaps, or a sister. (The police found he lived with two doting, older unmarried sisters.) The stilted phraseology suggested either an immigrant American or – given his age – one born of immigrant parents who learned the new English language from Victorian-era books. Brussel decided he was a first-generation American of Slav descent (Slav because he chose bombs as his weapon), which in turn suggested he might also be a Roman Catholic. Remarkably, the police found Dr Brussel right on all counts. The Mad Bomber was born in Waterbury, Connecticut, in 1903 of Polish immigrant stock. Furthermore, he attended mass every Sunday up to the time of his arrest.

In his protest letters, the Mad Bomber constantly complained of a 'serious' illness resulting from injuries caused by an accident at work – date unknown, but clearly pre-1940. Wearing his hat as a qualified medical practitioner, James Brussel narrowed the list of probable illnesses to three – cancer, tuberculosis and heart disease. He thought, wrongly, it had to be heart disease. Why? Cancer would almost certainly have killed him by 1957, and tuberculosis could be successfully treated. A feasible deduction – yet on this one day when he seemed almost clairvoyant, Dr Brussel overlooked the one behavioural characteristic he knew better than most: that all paranoiacs think they know far more than mere doctors, and so rarely consult them voluntarily. Subsequent, obligatory medical examination showed the Mad Bomber to be suffering from TB.

But that is to carp. In almost every other respect his proved to be a near-perfect profile of the unknown, dangerous criminal who had terrified New York for more than a decade. All the police lacked was a name — and that was soon forthcoming. A Consolidated Edison secretary traced the missing file, and handed it to them. The cover was labelled 'Metesky, George'. Inside was his 1930 address in Waterbury, Connecticut. (He had since moved to a different street, but was quickly located.) There was also a letter from Mr Metesky, complaining about the company's 'dastardly deeds', while his personnel slip showed him to be a Roman Catholic. For good measure the *Journal-American*'s third open letter had reaped dividends too. A hand-printed letter, signed 'FP', listed the date of his accident at work as 5 September 1931. It matched the date in the firm's file — the last shred of evidence needed to identify Metesky as the Mad Bomber.

He was dressed in pyjamas when the police called, since it was after midnight: none the less he addressed them with formal courtesy. 'You think I'm the Mad Bomber, don't you?' he said, but did not admit to it: he volunteered the information that 'FP' stood for 'Fair Play', but little more. When the police discovered his bomb factory (complete with bomb parts, lathe and metal tubing) in the garage behind the house, they allowed Metesky time to dress before leading him away. As his two sisters watched and wept, the 'Mad Bomber' left with shoes a-gleam, his hair neatly brushed, sporting a collar and tie beneath his blue, double-breasted suit — buttoned, naturally: exactly as the Sherlock Holmes of the Couch had pictured him, days earlier.*

By combining identifiable behavioural characteristics with statistical probability, his own considerable professional skills — and no little intuition — James A. Brussel blazed a trail that day for future crime investigation. Yet superlatively accurate though his resultant psychological profile proved to be, the technique was not enough in itself to change traditional law enforcement procedures. It left obvious, inherent problems still to overcome. Chief among them was that too much responsibility rested on the professional judgement of the consultant. Had Dr Brussel been mistaken the police search for the Mad Bomber might well have been further delayed,

*George Metesky did not stand trial for the bombings. Instead he was declared unfit to plead, and was confined in an institution for the criminally insane for the rest of his life. Ironically, as assistant commissioner for New York State's mental health department, Dr Brussel was one of his official visitors.

perhaps irrevocably misdirected. Some sort of safety net was needed. But where to look for it? Simply to increase the number of professional consultants was clearly not the answer.

Even the most experienced of mental health consultants are liable to submit opposing views when jointly asked to profile some unknown, violent offender. A classic example was provided during the 'Boston Strangler' investigation in the 1960s. On that occasion Dr Brussel was invited to serve on the distinguished medical-psychiatric advisory committee which included six such professional consultants. In the event there was a wide divergence of opinion among them, and the eventual committee report – which found there were *two* Boston Stranglers, one a homosexual – proved to be completely inaccurate (see Albert DeSalvo, pp. 206–18.)

That said, the concept of investigating violent crime by behavioural analysis was clearly a viable one, given the right formula; and the challenge was taken up in the early 1970s by FBI agents from the Behavioural Science Unit at Quantico (see pp. 76–9). The essential difference in approach was that instead of attempting to identify an individual offender via a combination of mental health diagnosis and statistical probability, the FBI agents proposed to use their professional analysis of the crime scene (drawing on police reports, autopsy findings and photographic evidence, in addition to statistical probability), to profile the *type* of criminal responsible. The type of violent offender they had in mind was every bit as difficult to apprehend as any Mad Bomber. Their concern was the sex killers, some of whom were undoubtedly responsible for the ever-growing number of apparently motiveless murders being committed nationwide: 'motiveless' in the sense that there was no apparent connection between killer and victim.

The first investigation in which the new technique was successfully employed was in 1974. Four FBI agents took part, three of them instructors from Quantico, the fourth a field agent from Montana. Howard D. Teten, an experienced former police officer from California and a gifted, natural profiler who joined the FBI in 1962, was the senior. Within seven years he was appointed an instructor in applied criminology at the old National Police Academy in Washington, DC. In 1972 he moved on to the newly-formed, replacement FBI National Academy at Quantico, where he introduced the practice of informal discussion of bizarre home town murders with each incoming student class. Years earlier Teten had made a point of meeting James Brussel to exchange investigative ideas and techniques with the man who profiled the Mad Bomber with such uncanny accuracy: the classroom talks were simply an extension of the same, mutually-educative process. He was joined at Quantico in 1972 by another far-sighted FBI instructor, Patrick J. Mullany. Mullany, too, was a staunch believer in the classroom exchanges. 'The more we did, the more we realised the possibilities.'

Their opportunity to put theory into practice came soon enough. In June 1973 a seven-year-old girl named Susan Jaeger from Farmington, Michigan, was abducted from a Rocky Mountains campsite in Montana. Sometime in the early hours an intruder slit open her tent with his knife, and overpowered Susan before she could alert her parents, William and Marietta Jaeger, who slept close by. Once the alarm was raised an intensive search failed to reveal any trace of the missing child, or any clue to the identity of her abductor. When the FBI was later called in, the case was referred to Quantico through agent Pete Dunbar, then stationed in Bozeman, Montana.

Combining their own investigative experience with the police report, photographic evidence and Dunbar's local knowledge, Teten, Mullany and a newly-joined instructor named Robert K. Ressler (also destined to become a senior member of the FBI's Behavioural Science Unit) employed the new crime analysis technique to help track down the abductor. They concluded he was a homicidal Peeping Tom who lived in the vicinity of the camp – this was a remote area – and spotted the Jaegers during the course of a periodical, summer's night snoop round the campsite, with Susan Jaeger a victim of opportunity. Statistics pointed to a young, male, white offender (they are almost invariably young men: white because Susan Jaeger was white, and such offences are usually intra-racial). The absence of any clues to his identity, the fact that he carried a knife with him to and from the campsite and made off with his victim without any alarm being raised, indicated an *organised* violent criminal. Sexually motivated murder frequently occurs at an early age, yet this was not the handiwork of some frenzied teenager. This bore the stamp of an older person, perhaps in his twenties. Statistical probability made him a loner, of average or possibly above average intelligence. Gradually the three instructors fitted together each piece of the behavioural jigsaw puzzle. The length of time the girl had been missing without word – and no sign of a ransom demand – persuaded them Susan Jaeger had been murdered. They thought it likely her abductor was that comparatively rare type of sex killer who mutilates his victims after death – sometimes to remove body parts as 'souvenirs' (see pp. 64–9).

Early on in the investigation an informant contacted FBI agent Dunbar with the name of a possible suspect – David Meirhofer, a local, twenty-three-year-old, single man who had served in Vietnam, By chance Dunbar knew Meirhofer, who seemed a quiet, intelligent person. More important, there was no known evidence to connect him with the abduction. Then in January 1974, the charred body of an eighteen-year-old girl was found in nearby woodland. She had known Meirhofer, but avoided his company; otherwise there was no known circumstance to connect him with the crime. Inevitably, however, he became a possible suspect for the second time: but on this occasion David Meirhofer volunteered to undergo both a lie-detector test and interrogation after injection with the so-called 'truth serum' (sodium pentathol) to prove his innocence. He passed both tests so convincingly that Dunbar felt compelled to believe him.

Not so the Quantico profilers. Experience had taught them how some sex killers deliberately seek ways of inserting themselves into an investigation, if only to find out how much the authorities know. As a precaution, they advised Susan Jaeger's parents to keep a tape-recorder by their telephone. On the first anniversary of their daughter's disappearance, an anonymous male caller rang their home in Farmington and boasted to Mrs Jaeger that he was keeping Susan alive, and prisoner. Instead of upbraiding him, Mrs Jaeger responded gently: and by turning the other cheek reduced her anonymous caller to tears. Analysis of the tape identified the voice as Meirhofer's. However, such unsupported identification was then insufficient under Montana law to obtain a warrant to search Meirhofer's apartment, where the profilers believed he kept the 'souvenirs' which would tie him to Susan's murder, and possibly that of the eighteen-year-old.

The answer was supplied by FBI instructor Mullany. He

reasoned that if Mrs Jaeger could reduce David Meirhofer to tears by telephone, a face-to-face meeting might prove even more rewarding. Such a step called for fortitude on the parents' part, but William Jaeger escorted his wife to Montana where she met Meirhofer in his lawyer's office. He appeared totally controlled, and said nothing to incriminate himself. The Jaegers returned home, thinking the plan had failed; but they were wrong. Shortly afterwards they received another phone call – this time from Salt Lake City, Utah, some four hundred miles south of Bozeman – from a man calling himself 'Mr Travis'. He told Mrs Jaeger that *he* was the man who abducted her daughter - but she recognised the voice, and called his bluff. 'Hello, David', she said.

Backed now by Mrs Jaeger's sworn affidavit, FBI agent Dunbar in Bozeman obtained his search warrant. As the Quantico profilers had predicted, he unearthed the 'souvenirs' – body parts, taken from both victims – which proved Meirhofer's guilt. At that, the man who had passed both 'truth tests' so convincingly also confessed to two more unsolved murders (of local boys). Although he was not brought to trial – David Meirhofer hanged himself in his cell – he became the first serial killer to be caught with the aid of the FBI's new investigative technique. It was a breakthrough which, within a decade, was to lead directly to the accurate, *systematic* profiling technique known as the 'Criminal Investigative Analysis Programme', or CIAP – which today forms the NCAVC's main weapon in the fight against these elusive, predatory serial offenders.

Under the stewardship of Howard Teten and Patrick Mullany (both of whom have since left the FBI), new names began to emerge during the 1970s as expert Behavioural Science Unit profilers in their own right. Among them were special agents Robert 'Roy' Hazelwood, now a leading authority on serial violent crime involving sexual assault; Robert Ressler, the then newly-joined instructor who had won his spurs in the pioneer Meirhofer case, and John E. Douglas. John Douglas, a strapping, stylishly-dressed man now in his mid-forties, was recruited into the FBI as a graduate from Wisconsin State University. Like Howard Teten, Douglas showed a natural aptitude for profiling; and within six years, while still in his twenties, he was posted to the crack FBI Behavioural Science Unit at Quantico.

He and Robert Ressler spent long hours of off-duty time in the latter part of the 1970s interviewing convicted sex murderers, thereby amassing a stockpile of common behavioural characteristics to feed back into the ever-expanding criminal profiling programme. In earlier years Teten, Mullany and the giants of the past had been forced to rely too much on personal investigative experience to supplement crime scene analysis, and so focus each new search for the type of offender responsible. Now the newcomers took this hitherto untried 'short cut' (of prison interviews) to build on the infant organised/disorganised findings. They sought subject material in whichever states they happened to be working at the time, and persuaded the interviewees to help solve such riddles as why some killers deliberately hide the bodies of their victims, while others just as deliberately leave them to be found by passers-by whose immediate reaction is to inform the police, and so raise the alarm.

The appalling injuries inflicted by some of the prisoners on their victims was already a matter of medical record. What the FBI agents now sought to discover was what *caused* the offenders to dismember, or 'depersonalise' these victims (beat them until their faces were unrecognisable) — many of them total strangers until the moment of the attack? Had the prisoners themselves been sexually abused as children or adolescents? Were they incapable of normal sex? Did pornography 'turn them on'? What did their bizarre acts of mutilation mean to the killer who 'signed' all his homicides in this way? Why did some offenders torture live victims, and others mutilate them only after death?

All of it was interrogation with intent: the aim was to identify common behavioural characteristics peculiar to certain types of murderer. But they were all 'gut' questions, which needed to be put with rare tact. It was the first time that law enforcement officers had attempted to 'read' every facet of some particularly brutal murder through the eyes of the criminal responsible. Furthermore — as so often occurs in instances of unconventional research — the interviews were 'unofficial'. Had there been any adverse reaction by way of legal complaint, say, or prison incident, the consequences for the pioneer researchers concerned could have been disastrous. Patrick Mullany (who became manager of corporate security with the oil giant, Occidental Petroleum, after leaving the FBI) was quoted in a 1989 newspaper interview as saying that these unofficial interviews 'had the potential to crack back and hurt them badly career-wise'.

Fortunately, none did. The information gained from those early interviews was to prove invaluable, particularly in so-called 'motiveless' murder cases (i.e. where there is no apparent connection between murderer and victim). A convincing early demonstration of its importance in this field was afforded in 1979, during the manhunt in New York City for the killer of schoolteacher Francine Elveson.

Miss Elveson — a tiny four-feet-eleven-inches, twenty-six-year-old Plain Jane who suffered from a slight curvature of the spine — was found naked, badly beaten about the head and face and with her body mutilated, spreadeagled on the roof of the Pelham Parkway Houses apartment building in the Bronx where she lived with her parents. So severe was the physical assault that her jaw and nose were both broken, and the teeth in her head pounded loose. Her nylon stockings were loosely tied round her wrists and ankles, even though no restraint had been needed: she was unconscious, or already dead, when that was done. Her pants had been tugged over her head, hiding her battered features from view. There were toothmarks visible on her thighs and knees.

Using a pen taken from her handbag, her killer had scrawled a challenge to the police on one thigh: '*You can't stop me*'. On her stomach it was four-letter abuse: '*Fuck you*'. Both the pen and the dead teacher's umbrella were found thrust into her vagina, and her comb (also taken from the handbag) wedged in her pubic hair. Her pierced earrings had been removed from the lobes, and placed on either side of her head. Both breasts were mutilated, by cutting off each nipple and placing it back on the chest. There were no deep knife wounds: this suggested the killer had used a small weapon — a penknife, probably — and taken it with him. A pendant which the victim habitually wore, manufactured in the shape of a Jewish good luck sign (Chai), was missing — presumably taken by her assailant. Now the dead woman's limbs were arranged in the shape of the pendant, as if to form a replica.

Francine Elveson was attacked within minutes of leaving her

parents' apartment-house flat shortly after 6.30 a.m. on 12 October 1979. Her body was found on the roof some eight hours later, after she failed to arrive at the school for handicapped children where she taught. The police report showed the attack took place as she made her way downstairs, when she was battered unconscious and carried up to the roof for the ritual that followed. Medical evidence revealed that she had not been raped. The cause of death was strangulation; she had in fact been twice strangled, manually first and then with the strap of her handbag. Lack of forensic evidence — fragments of skin tissue, fibres, etc. — under her fingernails indicated that she had made no attempt to fight off her assailant. Traces of semen were found on her body, but genetic fingerprinting was then unknown,* so that there were no apparent clues to the identity of her murderer.

Because of its bizarre features the case attracted much publicity, but despite intensive police investigation which included questioning some 2,000 people, checking on known sex offenders and patients undergoing treatment in mental hospitals, the search for Miss Elveson's killer became bogged down. Finally in November 1979 the FBI was called in. Even the police investigators thought they were on a hiding to nothing. One experienced murder squad detective was quoted as saying, 'Frankly I didn't see where the FBI could tell us anything, but I figured there was no harm in trying'. Crime scene photographs, together with the police report, autopsy findings, etc., were duly forwarded to the FBI's Behavioural Science Unit for analysis.

Enter special agent John Douglas, to profile the *type* of person responsible — from his desk at Quantico, some three hundred miles away. He knew from the police report that Miss Elveson, who was self-conscious about her size and physical deformity, had no boyfriends. That ruled out a lovers' quarrel. Moreover it was spontaneous choice which led her to leave for work that morning via the stairs, rather than use the elevator. Those two factors meant it was a chance encounter between victim and murderer — yet an encounter with someone who promptly spent a long time on the roof mauling his victim in broad daylight. To John Douglas that meant he was no stranger to the building; he knew its routine well enough to feel

*Genetic fingerprinting (or coding) by analysis of semen, blood, skin tissue, etc. was not discovered until 1984.

92

confident he would not be disturbed during the ritual mutilation murder that ensued.

Again, the fact that he was in the building at that hour suggested someone who might live, or perhaps work there. And Miss Elveson – this shy, almost reclusive young woman who shunned men because of her appearance – had neither screamed nor made any apparent attempt to ward off a man who suddenly lashed out as they passed on the stairs. It had to mean that either he was someone she knew, if only by sight, or who was wearing an identifiable uniform – postman, say, or janitor – whom she believed she had no reason to fear.

The offender left 'mixed' crime scene characteristics, as many sex killers do. He used restraints (organised), yet left the body in full view (disorganised). He 'depersonalised' his victim (disorganised), yet having mutilated her body took the knife with him (organised). On balance, however, John Douglas classified him as a 'disorganised' offender, acting out a fantasy ritual which had probably been inspired earlier by a bondage article and/or sketches in some pornographic magazine. The FBI agent profiled him as white (Francine Elveson was white), male, of roughly her age (say between twenty-five and thirty-five), and of average appearance, i.e. who would not seem in any way out of character in the apartment building environment. Statistics pointed to a school 'dropout' type, possibly now unemployed. Because of the time at which it happened, the crime seemed unlikely to be either drink or drug-related. Francine Elveson's killer was a man who found it difficult to behave naturally with women, and was almost certainly sexually inadequate. (The ritual mutilation provided the gratification he craved – a fact borne out by forensic evidence, which revealed traces of semen on the body.) He was the type of sex offender who would keep a pornography collection, while his sadistic behaviour pointed to one with mental problems.

He left the body in view because he *wanted* it to shock and offend. That decision was part and parcel of his implied challenge to the police, inked on the victim's thigh – 'You can't stop me'. It ws a challenge which John Douglas believed meant he was liable to kill again, should opportunity arise. His profile stressed the importance of the attacker's prior knowledge of the apartment building where the victim lived – and her apparent lack of alarm as they met on the stairs.

Once the answer to these two, connected factors was found, the rest of the puzzle would slot into place.

Armed with the profile, the investigating police re-examined their list of suspects. One man in particular seemed to fit the description like a glove. His name was Carmine Calabro. He was thirty years old, an unmarried, out-of-work actor; an only child, and former high-school dropout with a history of mental illness. He had no girlfriends. He himself did not live in the apartment building where Francine was found murdered, but his father — whom he often visited — lived there and was a near-neighbour of the Elvesons. The problem was that it seemed impossible for Carmine Calabro to be the killer.

The police had interviewed Calabro's father (as they had every other resident in the complex) before calling on the FBI for help. The father told them that his son — who lived elsewhere, and alone — was an in-patient undergoing psychiatric treatment at a local mental hospital, which appeared to rule him out as a possible suspect. Now enquiries were redoubled, and the police discovered that — because security was lax — patients at the hospital concerned were able to absent themselves almost at will. When they learned that Carmine Calabro was absent without permission on the evening before Francine Elveson was murdered, he was arrested — thirteen months after the body had been found.

Carmine Calabro pleded not guilty to the murder at his trial. However, the evidence given by three forensic (dental) experts — whose independent tests showed that impressions from Calabro's teeth matched the bite marks on the dead teacher's thigh — proved conclusive, and he was imprisoned for twenty-five years to life. The police had got their man, but this had been a further, impressive demonstration of the value of the FBI's behavioural analysis technique when the law enforcement agencies are confronted by an apparently motiveless murder. Above all, it had been a virtuoso performance by special agent John Douglas, whose startling accuracy of profiling matched that of the legendary James A. Brussel in the case of the Mad Bomber twenty-two years earlier. Aptly, one of the warmest tributes came from the head of the police task force assigned to the Elveson murder investigtion, Lieutenant Joseph D'Amico. 'They had [Carmine Calabro] so right' he said, 'that I asked the FBI why they hadn't given us his phone number too.'

Official recognition of the importance of the FBI's new investigative technique soon followed. In 1982, the Behavioural Science Unit at Quantico received a grant of 128,000 dollars from the National Institute of Justice to extend the practice of interviewing convicted, incarcerated offenders. More FBI agents — some from outside the Behavioural Science Unit, specially trained for the task — were brought in and a mass survey of convicted, incarcerated murderers was begun. Its objective was to develop and expand the emergent criminal profiling technique: and since the organised/disorganised classification of offenders from crime scene evidence was law enforcement's principal weapon in applying that technique, it was here that the main thrust of the research was directed. The flood of information emanating from these prison interviews helped: *one*, to enumerate common behavioural charcteristics in convicted sex killers (in whose ranks America's serial killers were to be found), and to relate those characteristics directly to crime scene evidence; *two*, to identify significant differences in the crime scene behaviour of organised and disorganised offenders; and *three*, to highlight specific characteristics (sociological, environmental, etc.) which could be used statistically to profile the type of offender responsible for a particular crime.

The FBI lists five categories of murder. They are *felony murder* (committed during the commission of a felony or serious crime, such as armed robbery, hijack, arson, etc.); *suspected felony murder; argument-motivated murder* (as distinct from criminally-motivated homicide, domestic dispute, etc.); murder committed for *'other motives'* (any identifiable motive not included in the first three categories); and murder committed for *'unknown' motives*. Many sex murders may wrongly be included in this last category, since the underlying sexual motivation is often difficult to recognise by any but the trained observer.

The lowest denomination, i.e. the murder of one person in circumstances unrelated to any other murder, is classed as 'single homicide'. Similarly, two victims in the one location and in the course of an otherwise unrelated event is a 'double homicide', and three victims murdered in like circumstances a 'triple homicide'. However, when four or more persons are murdered in one location in an otherwise unrelated event, the classification is upgraded into two categories, 'family' and 'classic' mass murder.

Family mass murder, as the name implies, is the killing of four or more members of one family by another member of that family. The most bizarre case in contemporary American crime history is the alleged murder by John List, a New Jersey insurance salesman and former Sunday-school teacher, of his mother, his wife and their three children in 1971. List disappeared from his eighteen-roomed mansion in Westfield, New Jersey, on the night of 9 November 1971 when – according to the police – he shot dead his entire family with a 9mm automatic pistol. The five murders remained undiscovered for a month. When found, the bodies lay side by side on sleeping bags in the front room, as if in an undertaker's parlour. Their heads were covered, their arms folded across their chests. Four of the victims had been killed by a single shot, behind the left ear. The fifth – the Lists' second son, John, aged fifteen – had ten bullet wounds to the head and body.

A police search of the house then revealed a five-page 'confession' allegedly written by the missing John List Snr. Two days later his car was found, abandoned in a car park at Kennedy airport in neighbouring New York. The contents of the 'confession' were not disclosed, although the police described them as a 'play by play' account of what List had done, and why. Press reports said he was in financial difficulty at the time, and had been siphoning off cash from his mother's account.

Nothing more was heard of List for eighteen years. Whether he was alive or dead was uncertain, but there were indications of careful planning and he was placed on the FBI's wanted list as a federal fugitive. Then in June 1989 a television reconstruction of the New Jersey family mass murder – shown on the top-ranking 'America's Most Wanted' programme – screened two facial likenesses of how John List (by then aged sixty-three) might look after eighteen years on the run. One likeness was a sculpture, the other a robotic, computer-built 'photograph'.

The bust, which proved to be incredibly accurate, brought three hundred telephone calls to the FBI from viewers who identified the person portrayed as 'Robert Clark', an elderly married man then living in a suburb of Richmond, Virginia. When interviewed, 'Robert Clark' (who had married a woman from Denver, Colorado, in 1977) denied he was John List, but was subsequently finger-printed and arrested. Within hours, the family mass murder case took a dramatic new turn. An FBI spokesman announced that the Bureau was reopening its file on the United States' most wanted *hijacker* – a man hitherto known only as 'D.B. Cooper'.

D.B. Cooper was the name given by a man who bought a ticket for a North-West Airlines flight from Portland, Oregon to Mexico on Thanksgiving Day,* 24 November 1971. After the plane was airborne he handed a hijack note to a stewardess, which said he was carrying a live bomb and was taking over the aircraft. The pilot was forced to head north, and landed at Seattle, Washington, where 'D.B. Cooper' demanded and was given 200,000 dollars in twenty-dollar bills and four parachutes. In turn he allowed the other passengers and some of the cabin crew to disembark before ordering the pilot to take off again for Mexico. Once airborne, however, the pilot was forced to level off at 10,000 feet over the snowy Cascade Mountains range south of Seattle, whereupon the hijacker attached one parachute harness to the suitcase containing the ransom money, strapped a second on himself, and baled out, via the tail-section passenger entrance. No trace of 'D.B. Cooper' was found, dead or alive, despite a massive ground search; and the theory that he might have perished during or after descent – this was grizzly bear country – appeared to be strengthened by the discovery nine years later of 5,800 dollars of the ransom money, washed up on the banks of the Columbia River (which marks the border between Washington State and Oregon). Whatever the fate of the resourceful 'D.B. Cooper', John List – alias 'Robert Clark' – left Virginia in handcuffs on 8 June 1989 for Newark, New Jersey, to face charges of family mass murder dating back to 1971. No date for his trial – which could perhaps shed new light on the 'D.B. Cooper' hijack – had been set when this book went to press.

The second category of 'mass murder' – *classic mass murder* – i.e. the killing of four or more (non-family) victims in a

---

*Thanksgiving is a variable date, falling on the fourth Thursday in November.

single location at one time – is a type of homicide which is becoming increasingly frequent worldwide. Charles Whitman, a twenty-five-year-old architectural engineering student at the University of Texas, in Austin, was an early classic mass murderer. In August 1986, after first murdering his wife and mother (by stabbing both to death), he piled a handcart with guns, ammunition, ropes, a radio and supplies of food, barricaded himself in a campus tower at Austin and blazed away at everyone who came into his sights. Within ninety minutes Whitman shot dead sixteen men and women and wounded thirty more, some seriously. Police eventually surrounded the tower and shot him dead.

Classic mass murderers are usually found to be mentally ill men, who unleash their growing hostility to society in an orgy of stabbing or shooting (mostly) random victims. Whitman himself had earlier called on the campus psychiatrist, and spoken of spasmodic 'rages' which caused him to assault his wife and at times threatened to overwhelm him. However, he cancelled a subsequent appointment, saying he 'would work things out himself'. Instead, he ran amok. The post-mortem revealed that he had a brain tumour.

A number of similar classic mass murders have occurred since the Whitman shootings, particularly in Australia and Canada as well as the United States. The most recent, which also took place on a university campus, was at the University of Montreal in December 1989. There Marc Lepine, a single, French-speaking, unemployed young man of twenty-five who himself aspired to become an undergraduate, burst into classrooms brandishing a semi-automatic .22 Storm Ruger rifle. At first some students thought it was a joke. 'You're all a bunch of feminists,' he shouted – but then opened fire selectively on women students, killing fourteen and wounding nine more before taking his own life. Four men students were also wounded in the course of the massacre.

It transpired that Lepine, a dark-haired, heavily bearded man who was obsessed by books and films about war, bore a grudge against all women – whom he blamed for 'a life filled with disappointments'. Police found a letter on him which contained a 'hit list' of fifteen prominent Quebec women, and was filled with complaints that 'feminists . . . have always spoiled my life'. He entered the campus without arousing suspicion by carrying the semi-automatic rifle wrapped in a green refuse bag. He opened fire first in the engineering building cafeteria, killing three girl students. Next he burst into a classroom on the second floor, separated the two sexes at gunpoint and — after ordering the men to leave — fired bursts at the screaming girl students, killing six and wounding several others. 'It was a human hunt, and we were the quarry', said student Françoise Bordelau later. 'I heard the man say "I want the women!"' ' Lepine moved on to shoot dead three women undergraduates working in the computer room, and stalked those who fled through the corridors, firing as he went. Finally he turned the gun on himself.

FBI profilers list two other kinds of multiple murderer — 'spree' and 'serial' killers. A *spree killer* is one who commits murder in two or more locations with no cooling-off period between the homicides — all of which are related in that they form part of a single event. Such events may be of indeterminate length, and involve more than one local police force. On 6 September 1949 Howard Unruh walked through his home town of Camden, New Jersey, firing a 9mm Luger at anyone who crossed his path. In the one deadly twenty-minute event he murdered thirteen chance victims and wounded three more. This was officially classed as a spree killing because the killings were carried out in different areas of the town.

The most notorious spree killer in British criminal history was a twenty-seven-year-old, unmarried man named Michael Ryan. On 19 August 1987 Ryan — who had no previous criminal record — murdered sixteen people and wounded fourteen others in what became known as 'The Hungerford Massacre', and took his own life when cornered by the police. Ryan lived alone with his mother in Hungerford, a market town in rural Berkshire on the ancient Roman road to Bath. He was a fantasist who found difficulty in establishing any kind of normal relationship with women. Instead, he *invented* 'girlfriends'. Male acquaintances (Ryan had no close friends, of either sex) knew him as a loner who bragged about his women friends and even spoke of his former 'wife', who had divorced him for his adultery. He also claimed to be an ex-paratrooper and a trained pilot. None of it was true. Relatives — who had never seen him with a girl — thought him a pleasant, quiet young man who neither drank to excess nor took drugs. Yet all the evidence suggests that a singularly clumsy bid by Ryan to rape at gunpoint a respectable married woman — who had never set eyes on him before, and was out for the day with her children — was the single event which sparked off the 'Hungerford Massacre'.

It may be an indication of the kind of mental hurdle the prospect of sex with a woman presented to Ryan that, on the sunny summer's morning he set out for Savernake Forest — a beauty spot nine miles from Hungerford — he armed and equipped himself like a man marching off to war. He stowed a semi-automatic AK47 Kalashnikov assault rifle, loaded with armour-piercing bullets, and an M1 carbine (as used by US infantry in World War Two and the Korean war) in the boot of his car, and tied a 9mm Beretta pistol to his wrist. He further donned a bullet-proof waistcoat and a 'Rambo'-style headband, and carried full survival kit (groundsheet, filled water bottle, food, spare magazines, etc.) with him. It later emerged that he had been seen at Savernake earlier: the events of 19 August suggest it may have been for reconnaissance.

Sometime that morning Mrs Susan Godfrey, a thirty-three-year-old housewife who lived near Reading and had driven her two children, aged four and two, to Savernake for a picnic treat, became Ryan's first chance victim of the day. He forced her, at gunpoint, to strap her children in the back seat of her car, and made her accompany him into the forest carrying her blue family picnic groundsheet. Mrs Godfrey died shortly afterwards in a hail of bullets fired from the Kalashnikov, presumably as she attempted to flee. She was not sexually assaulted. Ryan apparently panicked and headed back to Hungerford, leaving the children unharmed. He stopped briefly at a service station on the Hungerford-Marlborough road to fill up with petrol. He then aimed a burst from the AK47 at the woman cashier (who knew him by sight) — but she escaped unhurt by diving to the floor, and rang the police. Ryan reached Hungerford ten minutes later and went on the rampage, murdering fifteen people — including his mother, and the first (unarmed) policeman to arrive on the scene — and burned his mother's house to the ground, before holing up in the school he attended as a boy. Rather than surrender to the armed police who then surrounded the building (and tried to talk Ryan into giving himself up) he put the Beretta to his temple and pulled the trigger.

It was this nine-mile drive from Savernake Forest — where he murdered Mrs Godfrey — to the second killing ground at

Hungerford which, by FBI classification, changes Ryan from 'classic mass murderer' into 'spree killer'. This is not to split hairs: such meticulous classification is of major importance to the Quantico criminal analysis programme, which is based on common behavioural characteristics identified in specific types of violent offender.

FBI analysts, for example, define a *serial killer* as a murderer who is involved in three or more separate events, with an emotional cooling-off period between each homicide. As we have previously noted (see pp. 62–4), this cooling-off period is the main trait which distinguishes the serial killer from all other multiple murderers. Other identifiable differences may be found in their choice of victim. Serial killers tend to pre-select a *type* of victim to murder, whereas classic mass murderers and spree killers will both murder whichever human targets happen to present themselves. Similarly the serial killer controls the successive stages of each murder he commits (to a larger or lesser degree, depending whether he is an organised or disorganised offender); while neither the classic mass murderer nor the spree killer is likely to have an opportunity to do so once the law enforcement agency concerned closes in on him.

Again, serial killers rarely commit suicide when apprehended (see pp. 71–5). Yet spree killers frequently take their own lives, even when they cannot fail to be aware that no death sentence awaits them in law. Michael Ryan, ringed by police in Hungerford and unable to escape, was one such example: the death penalty for murder in Britain had been abolished for eleven years at the time of the 'massacre'. Many classic mass murderers also seem not to want to live, once their own compulsive urge to kill has abated. Some, like Marc Lepine, then shoot themselves. Others – Charles Whitman, for example – carry on killing until the law enforcement agency concerned is left with no recourse but to kill *them*; offender behaviour which some regard not as defiance of authority, but as an oblique form of suicide.

Similarly, the specific classification of single homicides – possibly committed in different locations over an indeterminate period and not immediately connected – may enable them to be linked as series murder, either by forensic evidence or crime scene analysis. Another demonstration of the value of homicide classification by behavioural analysis was provided by the

Francine Elveson investigation (pp. 91-4), during which the FBI profile advised the police that the (then unknown) offender was liable to kill again unless apprehended.

Sometimes a serial killer will turn spree killer. Heightened tension is usually the cause, for example during an investigation in which the serial killer is positively identified. As pressure on the offender mounts hourly from police vigilance and media publicity, so the man on the run puts aside the cooling-off period and kills repeatedly, spree-style. Even his motivation for killing may change. Instead of stalking a specific type of victim for sexual gratification, he may murder from sheer desperation — for instance, if he urgently needs to buy time by changing his getaway car and so throw his pursuers off the scent.

This was the scenario which unfolded in 1984 during the nationwide hunt by police and FBI for the most notorious serial-turned-spree-killer in US criminal history, Christopher Bernard Wilder. 'Chris' Wilder was an unmarried, wealthy Australian-born racing driver and entrepreneur who arrived in Miami in 1970, aged twenty-five. He invested in commerce and property and lived in style, with a Cadillac alongside the Porsche racing car at his luxury home in Boynton Beach, an Olympic-size swimming pool, and a speedboat tied up at the quay. An athletic, neatly-dressed man with a beard and moustache, Wilder was also an able photographer; good enough to boast of many a conquest by promising to transform aspiring models into cover-girls for smart fashion magazines.

In 1980, unknown to his friends on the Grand Prix circuit, he was charged with raping two teenagers at Palm Springs, California. It was a case which attracted little publicity. The teenagers said they felt 'dizzy' and were raped by Wilder after he photographed them eating pizzas — which he supplied — ostensibly for an advertising feature. He told the court the girls were willing participants who sued only when they learned he was rich. In the absence of any forensic evidence to support the drug allegations, Wilder was bound over for five years. Then in August 1983, during a brief return visit to Australia where he was alleged to have posed as a professional photographer and agent, Wilder appeared in court in Sydney charged with abducting and raping two fifteen-year-old girls. By then he held dual US and Australian citizenship; and after he had pleaded urgent business in America and with relatives standing bail, the hearing was put back until April 1984.

How many murders he may have committed following his return to Miami is uncertain, since he did not live long enough to stand trial. But in the seven weeks between 26 February and 12 April 1984 Chris Wilder is thought to have attacked and abducted at least eleven women, ten of whom were duped into believing he was a professional photographer. Eight of the ten were either murdered or disappeared — presumed murdered — during the course of a marathon, serial-turned-spree-killer manhunt which started in Florida, moved north to Georgia, headed west through Texas, Oklahoma, Kansas, Colorado and Nevada into California, then swung back east via Indiana, New York, Massachusetts and New Hampshire to within a few miles of the Canadian border, where Wilder — the quarry — was shot dead.

Three of the four victims whose bodies were found had been raped and stabbed to death. The fourth — Wilder's last victim, and oldest of the eleven at thirty-three — was shot dead and dumped in a gravel pit. He hijacked her car in a desperate attempt to shake off his pursuers, and made no attempt to molest her. The fate of the four missing women remains unknown. The three who survived were all abducted, bound hand and foot, gagged with adhesive tape, beaten, raped, sexually abused and tortured by Wilder with an electric prod; one also had her eyelids sealed with superglue. Two of them escaped — one outwitted Wilder, the other was stabbed several times by him and left for dead. Wilder himself freed the third — a sixteen-year-old girl whom he had abducted ten days earlier in Torrance, California. She lived because she developed what is sometimes called the 'Patti Hearst' syndrome (see p. 24) — a shocked condition, in which a kidnap victim may identify with her captor(s) as the only means of saving her life.

Wilder first came to the attention of the Miami police in February 1984 following the disappearance of a Cuban model named Rosario Gonzales. Miss Gonzales, a pretty twenty-year-old who was engaged to be married, vanished from a Grand Prix race meeting in which Wilder competed (he came seventeenth) and where she had taken a part-time job. Wilder was questioned when her fiancé told the police he photographed the missing girl during the meeting. Wilder agreed that he had, but said she had approached him for help in finding work as a model, and insisted they had not met again.

Two weeks later Elizabeth Kenyon, aged twenty-three and a part-time teacher and model, vanished after pulling in at a service station in Coral Gables, Miami, with a male companion who paid for the petrol. Miss Kenyon told the pump attendant (whom she knew) that she was on her way to the airport for a photographic session. Two days later the car was found abandoned at Miami international airport. She was never seen again. When enquiries revealed that Wilder knew and had photographed Elizabeth Kenyon before her disappearance, he was again questioned by the police. He denied meeting her on the day she drove to the airport, and the garage attendant was unable to describe the man he had seen with Miss Kenyon in the car.

This time, however, the investigating police persisted with their enquiries, and discovered that Wilder had twice appeared in court on rape charges, in Palm Springs and Sydney. Two days later, on 20 March 1984, Miami detectives drove to Bainbridge, south Georgia, where a nineteen-year-old woman student had been sexually assaulted by a man answering Wilder's description. Guests in a motel at Bainbridge had broken into a locked bathroom overnight to rescue a screaming, hysterical, naked girl whose hands were tied behind her back and her ankles hobbled by nylon cord. A strip of silver-coloured adhesive tape hung from one corner of her mouth, and she was unable to open her eyes. After treatment in hospital she told the police that a well-dressed, bearded man approached her the previous afternoon in a shopping centre at Tallahassee (in north Florida, five hours' drive from Bainbridge), claiming to be a fashion photographer. He allayed her suspicions by showing her a montage of pictures. As she posed fully-dressed for photographs in nearby public gardens the man hit her, hid her bound and gagged inside a sleeping bag in the boot of his car, and drove to Bainbridge − where he smuggled her into the motel room under cover of darkness.

After submitting her to an ordeal of beating, rape, and torture he eventually allowed her to use the bathroom − with her hands tied behind her back, her ankles hobbled, and (as a further precaution against escape) her eyelids sealed with superglue. Once inside she managed to slide the bolt with one hand, held her face against the corner of a cabinet to tear the sticking plaster from her mouth – and screamed. All her rescuers saw of the man were the rearlights of his car. However, she was able to identify Wilder from photographs carried by the police from Miami, and the manhunt began.

By the time detectives reached Wilder's house at Boynton Beach the bird had flown. Enquiries revealed that he had drawn 50,000 dollars from the bank, and bought an air ticket to Sydney. This proved to be a false trail; Wilder had resold the ticket to add to his cash in hand. His two expensive cars were still in his garage, but the two-tone Chrysler he used to abduct the nineteen-year-student from Tallahassee (one of a fleet of company cars owned by Wilder) was missing. An alert was put out, while frogmen searched the canal flowing past his house for bodies: no trace of Miss Gonzales or Elizabeth Kenyon was found.

Then on 23 March 1984 the body of Terry Diane Walden, a twenty-three-year-old university nursing student who disappeared two days earlier from a shopping centre in Beaumont, Texas, was found floating in a canal on the outskirts of the town. She had been beaten, bound hand and foot, and stabbed to death, gagged with adhesive tape similar to that used to silence Theresa Ferguson (murdered on 18 March) and the unnamed student subsequently kidnapped in Tallahassee. Medical evidence showed that Terry Walden, who was clothed, had been raped. Her orange-coloured Mercury Cougar was missing: Wilder's two-tone company Chrysler was found abandoned in the shopping centre car park. The chase was on again.

On 25 March English-born Suzanne Logan, aged twenty-one and a bride of only nine months, drove her husband to work in Oklahoma City. After calling at a local shopping centre – where she was seen talking to a well-dressed, bearded man – she failed to arrive home. Three days later and three hundred miles away her body was found on the banks of a reservoir near Junction City, Kansas. She too had been beaten, raped and stabbed to death. Silver-coloured plaster still adhered to her mouth, and she was bound hand and foot with nylon cord.

Charges of first-degree murder, kidnapping and rape were filed against Wilder in Kansas, with bail (should he be apprehended) set at two million dollars. FBI assistant director Oliver Revell told a press conference in Washington, DC, that

Wilder's murders represented 'a classic case of sexual, series murders that take place so many miles apart the local authorities cannot readily connect them'. Wilder became one of the FBI's 'Ten Most Wanted' fugitives, and all police forces were asked to keep a lookout for Terry Walden's distinctive Mercury Cougar.

The trail led next to Colorado where Sheryl Bonaventure, a blue-eyed blonde of eighteen who wanted to be a model, vanished from a shopping centre in Grand Junction. She was never seen again. With Wilder heading westward, a trap was set for him in southern California where two Grand Prix meetings were due to take place, at Long Beach and Riverside. However, on 1 April seventeen-year-old Michelle Korfman from Boulder City, Colorado – who modelled clothes for a local department store, and had entered a nationwide, magazine-sponsored 'Miss Teen' beauty competition in Las Vegas, Nevada – was reported missing. Wilder, who arrived in Las Vegas the night before the competition, coolly took a front-row seat and invited entrants seeking a career in modelling to contact him later at Caesar's Palace Hotel. Miss Korfman, whose car was found parked there, has not been seen since.

Wilder missed the trap set for him by only a few miles. Instead of driving to Long Beach for the Grand Prix, he went instead to Torrance (another suburb, to the west of Los Angeles) on 4 April and abducted a sixteen-year-old girl who 'wanted to become a model'. After telephoning a boyfriend to announce that a professional photographer was to pay her one hundred dollars for a photo session, she too disappeared. For a time the trail went cold. Then on 10 April a second sixteen-year-old was reported missing, this time from a shopping centre in Merriville, Indiana.

Two days later – and more than one thousand miles still further east – the second missing girl was seen bleeding profusely as she staggered along a road near Barrington, in upper New York state. A passing motorist (who thought she was an accident victim) drove her to the nearest hospital, where she was found to have multiple knife wounds. After an emergency operation she told the police that a girl of her own age had approached her in Merriville on 10 April, and asked if she would take part in a photographic session. She explained that the photographer required two models for the assignment, and would pay them twenty-five dollars apiece. The Merriville teenager agreed — only to be dragged into a waiting, orange-coloured Mercury Cougar by a man armed with a gun. He gagged the girl with adhesive tape, and sexually assaulted her on the back seat as the other sixteen-year-old drove. The three of them spent that night in a motel at Akron, Ohio, where the girl driver warned the Merriville teenager not to resist Wilder or 'they would both be killed'.

They spent a second night in a motel at Syracuse, New York State, where the Merriville captive was again sexually abused and tortured. Next morning, 12 April, Wilder's picture was shown on television — and as soon as he had shaved off his beard, the trio left Syracuse in a hurry. 'We've got to change cars,' said Wilder. Shortly afterwards he stopped in a wooded area, and promised to release the Merriville girl unharmed if she said nothing to the police to incriminate him. Although she gave her word, Wilder stabbed her repeatedly and left her for dead.

Early that afternoon a lorry driver saw what he thought was a tailor's dummy in a gravel pit near Victor, N.Y. It was in fact the body of a woman named Beth Dodge: she had been shot dead, after leaving work to drive home for lunch in the nearby town of Phelps. At first no-one realised Wilder might be the murderer: Beth Dodge was older than the type of victim he usually targeted, and had not been sexually assaulted. However, all doubts evaporated when the Mercury Cougar was found abandoned twenty miles away — while Beth Dodge's car, a Pontiac Firebird, was missing. This in turn posed a new mystery. The Merriville teenager was alive and safe in hospital: but where was the sixteen-year-old from Torrance, and was she still alive?

In fact Wilder had driven the Torrance girl to the international airport at Boston, Massachusetts, in the Pontiac. On arrival he paid for her airline ticket back to Los Angeles — and handed her five hundred dollars in cash. 'I've got a feeling the end is close,' he told her, prophetically. 'You just go home and forget what's happened.' Unpredictably violent to the end, however, he then drove into Boston and all but succeeded in abducting another young woman, whose car had broken down. It took only seconds for Wilder to force her into the hijacked Pontiac at gunpoint — but he had no opportunity in a Boston street to bind and gag victim number twelve. She escaped by jumping out at the first set of traffic lights, and was later able to identify Wilder from police photographs.

Next day — Friday the 13th (of April 1984) — two New Hampshire state troopers on patrol at Colebrook, eight miles from the Canadian border, spotted the Pontiac at a filling station. Wilder had time only to grab his .357 Magnum revolver from the glove compartment before Trooper Leo Jellison — 6'2" in height and weighing some 250 pounds, or seventeen stone — landed on top of him. Two shots sounded in quick succession. The first bullet passed clean through Wilder's body to enter the trooper's chest, but missed the vital organs. The second shot killed Wilder instantly. In that short, desperate struggle it was not clear if Wilder had tried to kill Trooper Jellison — or himself. Either way, the 5,000-mile chase was over.

The mystery of the 'missing' Torrance teenager was solved the same day when she arrived back in California, and was interviewed by police. She said she did not know why Wilder spared her: she had been raped and tortured like his other victims, and he had threatened to kill her several times. She admitted leading the Merriville sixteen-year-old to the car where Wilder lay in wait, but said she was too terrified of him to disobey his orders.

Although the marathon chase was eventually brought to a successful conclusion, it emphasised the enormity of the task facing individual law enforcement agencies when attempting to track down and apprehend transient violent criminals in a land as vast as the United States. The mounting toll of victims Wilder left behind him served only to underline — yet again — the imperative need in America for a *national* resource centre, staffed and equipped to monitor, advise — and where need be, assist — at every turn in such a fast-developing situation. Fortunately, such plans were already well advanced. Within two months of Wilder's death the essential, first administrative step toward fulfilling that requirement was taken by President Reagan, with the formal establishment of the NCAVC at Quantico on 21 June 1984.

* * *

By then serial murder had been a cause of growing concern in the US for at least three decades. In 1950, Dr Paul de River wrote about the 'lust killers', now recognised as a most dangerous sub-species of serial killer (pp. 64–9). In the early 1960s the thirteen serial murders committed by Albert DeSalvo, the Boston Strangler, reduced the state capital of Massachusetts to near panic. The 1970s were positively a vintage decade in America for notorious serial killers. Among them were Gerald Schaefer, the Florida deputy policeman suspected of twenty-eight murders, Californian schizophrenic Herb Mullin (ten murders), Ed Kemper (ten murders), Texan homosexual Dean Corll (twenty-seven murders), John Gacy, another homosexual, from Chicago (thirty-three murders), 'Hillside Strangler' Kenneth Bianchi and Angelo Buono (nine murders), and Ted Bundy (twenty-three admitted murders, but thought to be 'good for thirty-four'). Small wonder that President Reagan reflected the nation's concern in 1984, by giving the newly-created NCAVC as its primary mission 'the identification and tracking of repeat killers'.

An important factor which added to the widespread fear aroused by 'working' serial killers in the United States in those early years was that no-one knew how many were at large at any given time, or the sum total of lives they claimed each year. On the other hand their crimes were such that they were quite properly reported by the media in full, so that at times the American public must have felt some new plague had come among them. Again, serial killers were not recognised as a distinct species of murderer until agents of the FBI's Behavioural Science Unit first learned to identify and profile them from crime scene analysis. Hitherto such bizarre cases were often recorded as 'sex murders', 'unknown motive' homicides, or simply as 'unsolved'. The reason why many remained unsolved was not lack of effort by the local law enforcement agency involved, but rather the lack of a tested technique to investigate these seemingly motiveless, clue-less murders in a prescribed, systematic manner.

That situation changed once the NCAVC became operational and CIAP (the Criminal Investigative Analysis Programme) was introduced. In a joint survey published in the FBI's *Law Enforcement Bulletin* in December 1986, headed '*Criminal Profiling: A Viable Investigative Tool against Violent Crime*', the authors — special agents John Douglas and Alan Burgess

– made the specific point that: 'Sexual homicides . . . yield much information about the mind and motivation of the killer. A new dimension is provided to the investigator via the profiling technique, particularly in cases where the underlying motive for the crime may be suddenly hidden from even the more experienced detective.'

President Reagan called the offenders 'repeat killers'. Credit for coining the term 'serial killer' is given to FBI special agent Robert Ressler, one of the three Quantico instructors who took part in the test-case Meirhofer investigtion in 1974 (pp. 86–9). In an article in the *New York Times* magazine of 26 October 1986, journalist and author Stephen G. Michaud wrote: 'Mr Ressler started using the term [serial killer] because such an offender's behaviour is so distinctly episodic, like the movie house serials he enjoyed as a boy.' In June 1983, one year before the establishment of the NCAVC, a Senate Judiciary committee debated the impact of serial murder on American society, under a heading that said it all: 'Patterns of murders committed by one person in large numbers with no apparent rhyme, reason or motivation.' The four principal subjects listed for debate were 'Missing and murdered children', 'Sexual exploitation of children', 'Unidentified bodies' and 'Serial killers'. Thus the term passed officially into the American idiom.

When responsibility for leading the campaign to reduce violent crime in the United States was delegated to the Behavioural Science Unit of the FBI in June 1984, the NCAVC had four main programmes to administer. They were research and development (Quantico's traditional 'think tank' role), training, profiling and consultation, and VICAP (the Violent Criminal Apprehension Programme). While these four still form the bedrock of the Centre's programming, their administration is divided between two wings of the Behavioural Science Unit, viz. Instruction and Research (BSIR), and Investigative Support (BSIS). Though the two wings have separate functions, in the long term they are wholly complementary.

BSIR looks to the future. In addition to furthering research and training incoming agents for their new, specialist duties, this wing is responsible for programming law enforcement in the United States in the twenty-first century. BSIS, or the 'operational wing', deals with today's problems. It uses the most modern technology to help reduce the unacceptable levels of violent crime – particularly in the field of serial murder, rape and arson, but also including a variety of other offences ranging from kidnapping, extortion, certain aspects of terrorism (hostage survival, etc.), and tampering with consumer goods – a growth industry in many countries in recent years – to public corruption. Research in all areas is unceasing at the NCAVC. 'PROFILER', the first automated profiling system to be employed in criminal analysis, is already operational. Although there are still some areas in which it cannot match the human analyst – notably the hunch, that intuitive judgement which comes to the human investigator only after years of experience – this computerised system delivers such accurate analyses that Quantico's ten senior analysts use it constantly as a consultant, and apprentice analysts in training. A second expert system is in the pipeline, designed to apprehend the serial rapist and based on information gleaned from mass interviews with convicted offenders.

FBI unit chief John Henry Campbell commands the Behavioural Science Unit at Quantico, and with it the NCAVC. The two wings of the Centre each have their own unit chief, subordinate to John Campbell. BSIS, the 'operational wing', is led by supervisory special agent (SSA) Alan E. Burgess. Alan Burgess – a quiet, confident executive known as 'Smokey' to FBI colleagues – is also Administrator of the NCAVC.* SSA John Douglas, widely acknowledged as the most experienced of modern profilers, is manager of the operational wing's 'cutting edge' – the CIAP, or the Criminal Investigative Analysis Programme. Together, the two men make a powerful crime-fighting team. The programme itself is operated by ten senior analysts, the only ten of their kind in the world.

Under the stewardship of Alan Burgess and John Douglas, these ten men form the aces in the pack at Quantico. They wage their unique, solitary war against serial offenders either from a desk sixty feet underground (the NCAVC is housed in a former nuclear bunker, originally intended for intelligence personnel in the event of an atomic war), or from a plane or car seat; they travel extensively, both in and beyond the United States. They are officially known as 'criminal investigative

---

*Burgess retired from the FBI in 1990. He was succeeded as Unit Chief of the BSIS unit by SSA John E. Douglas.

111

analysts', rather than 'profilers'. Profiling is what they do, but not as before: psychiatrist Dr James Brussel gave the New York city police a genuine 'psychological profile' of Mad Bomber George Metesky in 1957 (pp. 81−6). The FBI analysts at Quantico are not psychiatrists. They are trained investigative agents who draw on police reports, their own murder scene analysis based on photographic, medical and forensic evidence, VICAP data and the automated PROFILER system − plus their years of experience − to compile a systematic analysis of both the type of offender responsible, and the crime itself.

Although the responsibility for listing each component of an analysis rests with the special agent concerned, all at BSIS work on the principle that investigative experience shared is knowledge gained: 'The more minds at work, the better.' Tremendous importance is therefore placed on the daily 'group profiling conferences', where every known detail pertaining to each incoming case goes into the melting-pot of expert, round-table discussion. Other specialist advice, in the fields of pathology, forensic science, sociology, legal problems, etc., is also always available at Quantico. Should further local knowledge be sought, the ten Quantico analysts − each of whom has responsibility for a given area nationwide − are backed by a force of one hundred and ten specially trained FBI agents (known as Field Profile Co-ordinators), stationed throughout the United States. Although the co-ordinators have several duties, special attention is always given to serial murder investigations.

To gauge the extent of the possible workload facing the operational wing at Quantico, one need only examine the violent crime statistics in the US for 1988 − the most recent available when this book went to press. The sum total of all types of homicide for the year − 20,675 − was some 3,000 down on the peak 1980 figure. However, murder represented a mere one per cent of violent crime overall. Nationwide, there was an average rate of one violent crime every twenty seconds, including one 'aggravated assault'* every thirty-five seconds, one robbery a minute, one forcible rape every six minutes, and one murder every twenty-five minutes.

In itself, that total of 20,675 murders was an increase of 3% over the preceding year. Worst hit were the big cities

*Attempted murder is classed as aggravated assault.

(average 4% up). The bigger the population of the city, the greater the rise in the murder rate; those with more than a quarter of a million inhabitants registered increases ranging from 1% to 8%. In New York – the biggest city in the country, the 'Big Apple' – there were 6,530 murders in the 1960s decade: that total more than doubled to 15,569 during the 1970s: the sum total for the 1980s is expected to show a further increase of between 2,000 and 3,000. Much of this rise in the big city murder-rate is undoubtedly drug-related. Dr Thomas Reppetto of the New York Citizens Crime Commission put the blame squarely on gang wars arising from the drugs traffic. 'In 1988,' he said, '40% of the killings were drug-related, as opposed to 20–25% in the early 1980s. A lot of this was the result of wars on the street between different gangs.'

To try to relate serial murder to the overall violent crime figures is more complicated. The FBI's uniform crime rate for 1988 breaks down types of homicide by percentage as follows: argument-motivated (i.e. non-criminally motivated) 34.3%; calculating all percentages on the sum total of 20,675 homicides, this represented some 7,300 murders and the biggest single category. Felony and felony-related homicide accounted for a further 20.2% (say 4,200 victims), and 'miscellaneous' (any identifiable motive not covered by the above classifications) 18.9%, or 3,800 victims. A total of 26.6% (approximately 5,200 murders, the second biggest category) were classed as 'unknown' motive.

The 1988 figures also showed that, on average nationwide, 70% (or 14,480) of all murders committed in the United States were solved by the law enforcement agencies. The 30% unsolved represented 6,200 homicides: and somewhere among that number must lie the bulk of all unidentified serial murders committed during the year. The problem facing the NCAVC is, in what proportion? Even the obvious-seeming clues may be misleading. According to the uniform-crime rate returns, 12% of all homicide victims in 1988 (say 2,480) were murdered by strangers. By no means all 'stranger' murders, however, are committed by serial killers. For lack of evidence to the contrary, a percentage of felony-related and miscellaneous homicides will inevitably have been included among the sum total of 6,200 'unsolved' cases. Likely examples would be the habitual offender – facing certain long-term imprisonment if apprehended – who kills when murder presents his only opportunity to escape unidentified. Similarly, 'first-timers' may kill unintentionally and flee in panic. In a country such as the United States, where one violent crime was committed every twenty seconds on average during 1988, such 'stranger murders' could conceivably add up to a formidable total over twelve months. As the nineteenth-century Scottish author Thomas Carlyle once observed, 'You might do anything with figures'.

When we were commissioned to write this book, we were aware that some observers in the US — the country worst affected — believed that serial murder claimed thousands of lives there each year, possibly 5,000 or more. It so happens that we have both lived and worked in America, and Colin continues to visit the US regularly and the average sum total of 20,000 murders of all kinds each year — compared with today's 700 or so in Britain — occasioned no surprise. What was intriguing, however, was the remarkable apparent disparity in the two *serial* murder rates. If these unofficial estimates were accurate, they represented a ratio not of thirty to one (as with the overall homicide total), but of thousands to one.

In Britain, where Jack the Ripper sent shivers down every spine more than one hundred years ago, the serial killer remains a rarity. One can count the number to emerge over the past three or four decades on the fingers of both hands: Christie (hanged in July 1953), Brady and Hindley (sentenced to life imprisonment in 1966), Sutcliffe (jailed for a minimum thirty years, 1981), Nilsen (sentenced to life imprisonment in 1983), Erskine (jailed for a record minimum of forty years, in January 1988), and Duffy (sentenced to a minimum thirty years imprisonment, one month later). One has to think long and hard to recall many others.

One instance apart,* serial killers are a twentieth-century phenomenon in the United States. Among the more notorious in the first half of the century were Earle Nelson (p. 12), and Carl Panzram (pp. 16–18). Nelson, who murdered twenty-two women in seventeen months in the late 1920s, employed the simplest of *modus operandi* to maximum effect. He targeted landladies who put 'Room to Let' notices in their front-room

*See Howard Henty Holmes, p. 78.

114

windows (a common practice in the Depression years that followed World War One), waited until the two of them were alone and then raped, strangled and robbed them before moving on. As with Chris Wilder sixty years later, simply to cross from one state into the next virtually ensured temporary respite from pursuit. Carl Panzram was a tough, long-term offender who had been homosexually gang-raped as a young man. He exacted revenge from society by committing twenty murders, mostly homosexual in nature, starting in 1918. In 1930 Panzram, by then thirty-eight years of age, contrived his own execution by murdering a prison guard – a crime which he knew to mean an automatic sentence. In 1934 Albert Fish, a New York painter and decorator, was executed for the murder of a ten-year-old girl whose flesh he cooked and ate. Following his arrest, Fish confessed to four hundred child murders; and while that confession was discounted (p. 70), he was believed to be responsible for 'dozens' of murders. In general however, before World War Two serial murder in the United States was rare in comparison, say, with the gangster killings of the Prohibition era.

Ed Gein, a necrophiliac serial killer and devotee of the wartime Nazi concentration camp medical experimentalists, is thought to have inspired the Alfred Hitchcock thriller 'Psycho' by his macabre deeds in the late 1950s. On one occasion he plundered a Wisconsin graveyard by night for edible body parts, and flayed one corpse to fashion a waistcoat 'souvenir'. Some time later, when police called at his house to question Gein about a missing elderly woman, they discovered the gutted torso of one of his earlier female victims hanging from the beams. Gein, who is believed to have committed nine murders in all, was detained in an institution for the criminally insane. As an old man in his late seventies, he was interviewed by FBI agents – who were conducting their mass survey of known sex murderers for the Criminal Analysis programme.

Serial murder in the United States began to surface in earnest during the 1960s, along with all other forms of violent crime. Albert DeSalvo set the pace early in the decade, with thirteen murders in eighteen months – a reign of terror that the city of Boston is unlikely ever to forget. As we have already shown, he was followed over the years by the likes of Schaefer, Corll, Mullin, Kemper and Bundy, a deadly quintet who between them murdered at least a hundred men and women. One of the most recent of these so-called 'high-scoring' serial killers was Richard Ramirez, alias 'The Night Stalker' — twenty-eight years of age, unmarried, a drifter and satanist from El Paso, Texas.

In the fifteen months between June 1984 and August 1985 the Night Stalker murdered thirteen people and sexually assaulted several others in the suburbs of Los Angeles, terrifying the local communities in the process. His *modus operandi* was to break into houses by night at random, taking whatever opportunity offered by way of sex, robbery and murder. Men were shot or stabbed to death as they slept. The women were beaten, raped and sexually abused, regardless of age: most were then murdered by strangulation, stabbing or shooting. Their children (of both sexes, some as young as six) were either sexually assaulted in their homes or abducted, to be raped or sodomised before being turned loose on the streets, miles away. All Ramirez' attacks were marked by extreme cruelty; on one occasion he gouged a woman's eyes out. He 'signed' some of his murders by sketching in lipstick a pentagram — a five-pointed star, often associated with satanism — at the scene of the crime, either on the victim's body or the wall above.

Ramirez, who had been profiled by the FBI at Quantico, was positively identified from a smudged fingerprint found on a getaway car. In a bid to prevent any more murders, the local law enforcement agencies then issued his photograph to the media. Shortly afterwards, Ramirez was recognised by a grocer's assistant; he ran into the street, but was chased by an angry mob after trying to steal a woman's handbag, overpowered and arrested. In September 1989, after a trial lasting five months, Ramirez was found guilty of thirteen murders and thirty associated felonies (five attempted murders, eleven sexual assaults and fourteen burglaries). When the jury later recommended that he should die in the gas chamber, Ramirez flaunted his satanic beliefs to the media crowding the courtroom. 'Big deal, death comes with the territory,' he jeered. 'See you in Disneyland!' He now awaits the outcome of an appeal.

Perhaps the most graphic illustration of the threat the serial killer poses to society lies in the fact that the Night Stalker's victim count (thirteen murders in fifteen months) is positively 'low-scoring' compared with some. As we have shown (pp. 60–1), the highest known individual tally of serial murders rests with the Ecuadoran peasant Pedro Lopez. After his arrest in 1980, he confessed to murdering 'about' three hundred and fifty young girls in two years. In the United States a half-century earlier, Earle Nelson killed more people more quickly (twenty-two in seventeen months) than did Ramirez; while Albert Fish probably murdered more than Nelson and Ramirez put together. Nor are such numbers exceptional. Since the sharp rise in all types of homicide began to manifest itself in America in the 1960s, serial killers such as John Wayne Gacy (thirty-three victims), Gerald Schaefer (twenty-eight), Dean Corll (twenty-seven) and Ted Bundy (at least twenty-three), etc., have all murdered more people than Ramirez, but over a longer period.

In our view this represented an important field for research in any realistic assessment of the serial killer problem. Broadly speaking, were the unofficial estimates of the numbers killed annually in the United States correct? If they were, why should one country – and that one the leader of the western world, a stable society enjoying an enviable prosperity – suffer such a plague of serial murder, yet the rest of us largely be spared? That the US suffers more homicides annually than any other western nation is a matter of record, and that this should apply pro rata to serial murder would seem only logical. However, while the anti-gun lobby blames the constitutional right to bear arms for much of America's huge annual murder total, there appeared to be no rational explanation for the apparently phenomenal rise in the serial murder rate. Clearly, there was only one oracle to consult on this problem; and in September 1989 – courtesy of the FBI – Donald Seaman became the first author from Britain to be granted access to the National Centre for the Analysis of Violent Crime at Quantico.

The NCAVC is not normally open to the public, and security is impressive. The Centre lies sixty feet underground, directly below the FBI Academy. The academy itself stands in a 600-acre enclave of woodland, encircled by thousands more acres of lowland Virginia countryside – which in turn comprise the great US Marine Corps base at Quantico. Guards in strategically-placed checkpoints monitor all traffic, in and out. The sound of small-arms fire echoes from ranges alongside the road threading through the outer perimeter. Within the FBI enclave, more gunfire sounds from indoor and outdoor ranges; all law enforcement officers selected to undergo an eleven-week training course at the academy are issued with a .38 Police Special. In the Hogan's Alley complex – a ghost town, complete with a bank, shops, service station, cleaner's, fast-food restaurant and cinema (forever showing the programme seen by Public Enemy Number One John Dillinger in Chicago in 1934, immediately before he walked out to his death in a trap sprung by the FBI) – students undergoing specialist training fight every kind of street battle they are likely to encounter in a lifetime of duty. At all times there are enough armed, disciplined men in place here to fight a small war.

Entry to the NCAVC is via the Academy front door, and a foyer of which any five-star hotel would be proud; the one difference being that the 'counter clerk' here wears police uniform, sergeant's stripes, and a .38 on his hip instead of the customary clerical grey. Once signed in and tagged with a badge, visitors are escorted along a corridor and down by elevator to the BSIS wing, a futuristic high-tech beehive of a crime-fighting centre, the only one of its kind in the world. Its business is the analysis of violent crime, not the physical arrest of violent criminals. There are no cells here, no interrogation rooms, no 'Most Wanted' posters; only desks and computers. On arrival visitors are introduced to an NCAVC senior analyst who will act as guide and mentor throughout their stay in this windowless, air-conditioned, subterranean wing which seems a world away from the blue skies and sunshine, and ranks of flowering dogwood, spruce and pine bordering the FBI Academy grounds sixty feet overhead.

Our guide is supervisory special agent Gregg O. McCrary (the 'O' stands for Oliver). SSA McCrary is forty-four years old, married with two children, and was born in New York State. He has been an FBI agent for half his life. Before he joined the elite 'A (for analyst) Team' here at Quantico he was a Field Profiling Co-ordinator, and before that he served in FBI counter-intelligence. He stands some six feet in height, a spare, upright figure with a pale face, carefully trimmed moustache and brown hair flecked with grey. As with all personnel in the NCAVC he is smartly dressed, reflecting the evident high morale. Equally, this is the FBI at work; McCrary's dark blue blazer reveals no hint of the Smith & Wesson 9mm semi-automatic below, fully loaded with twelve rounds in the magazine, plus one (for emergencies) already in the chamber.

No law enforcement officer in the United States carries a gun for show. The handgun is also criminal America's favourite weapon, as the FBI uniform crime report lying on McCrary's desk will testify. It says that during 1988, 45% of all the 20,675 murder victims in the US − 9,300 people − were shot dead with revolvers or pistols, with a further 10% killed by shotguns or rifles. It therefore comes as no great surprise to discover that FBI agent and senior analyst McCrary is a man of many parts. He is also a crack shot and former firearms instructor. In addition, he holds a black belt in the martial art of *shorinji kempo* − a blend of the better known *karate* (punch, kick and block) and *aikido/ju-jitsu* (defensive) techniques. Instructors in this rare martial art travel worldwide from their headquarters in Todatsu, Japan, to ensure that its exacting standards become in no way debased. In McCrary's case this entails two visits (and two gruelling workouts) each year, physical examinations which he describes, with feeling, as a 'most humbling experience'. In his capacity as a martial artist, McCrary was formerly an FBI instructor in defence tactics − and in the field, a 'Special Weapons and Tactics' (SWAT) team leader. A SWAT team is deployed only in high-risk situations.

Visitors start with a brief tour of the Investigative Support wing. The jewel in the NCAVC's technological crown is unquestionably VICAP, the Violent Criminal Apprehension Programme. This unique, multi-million-dollar computer system acts basically as a serial crime databank, with the master computer housed at FBI headquarters in Washington, DC, forty miles away. Its task is to store, collate and analyse all unsolved, homicide-related crimes reported to the NCAVC by law enforcement agencies nationwide, and fed on-line from Quantico via a secure telecommunications network.

When a new case is submitted, the master computer in Washington simultaneously retrieves more than one hundred cases from the appropriate *modus operandi* category, and overnight checks them against all other cases in store for similarities and discrepancies. Once that search is completed, a printed, computerised report is telexed back to Quantico − listing the 'top ten' matching cases in pecking order. This remarkable crime-pattern analysis technique is known as 'Template pattern matching', or more usually 'The Template' by VICAP analysts working in the BSIS, or Investigative Support, wing. It was specifically designed and programmed for VICAP in the mid-1980s by the unsung heroes of the FBI's backroom Technical Division.

As soon as the Template is received at BSIS in Quantico, the VICAP analyst (as distinct from the 'senior analyst', or profiler) determines which if any of the top ten matches are linked with the new case as one series crime. Suppose, say, there are four. After consultation, the VICAP analyst then informs the four law enforcement agencies involved, asks if they want a profile, and puts each in touch with the others so that the least possible time is lost in mounting a co-ordinated attempt to apprehend the offender.

The VICAP system, straightforward in concept yet fraught with problems in development, took *twenty-seven years* to evolve from a germ in one man's mind to operational readiness by 1985. It was the brainchild of Commander Pierce Brooks, retired now but formerly of the Los Angeles Police Department and first manager of the VICAP programme. During the course of two 'unusual' murder investigations in 1958, Brooks – then a homicide detective – became convinced that both unknown killers had murdered before. In those days there was no central source which stored data on the *modus operandi* of transient multiple murderers. Instead Brooks had to search computerised newspaper files and books in the city library for the information he needed: a laborious task which gave rise to his dream of an automated, central, permanently-updated, violent crime databank to serve all America's law enforcement agencies. Gradually his idea won support; and in the 1970s, the US Department of Justice funded a VICAP task force of senior homicide investigators and analysts from more than twenty states to evaluate the Brooks project. They were later joined by men from the FBI's Behavioural Science Unit, where the concept of an American NCAVC was then under examination. As a result, VICAP and the complementary Criminal Analysis Programme were merged into the single crime-fighting system in use today.

The first twelve months following the formal establishment of the NCAVC in June 1984 were employed as a test-bed period for all aspects of the nascent VICAP system: a formidable task.

There were major technological problems to solve, first in designing and programming the unique computer system required, and additionally in dovetailing complementary internal procedures at Quantico. There was also one fundamental difficulty to overcome. VICAP's role is to analyse, not investigate, serial violent crime. The two tasks call for quite different skills when co-operating to solve the same homicide. This meant tabling a comprehensive, dual-purpose crime report designed to cover every type of case — yet which would enable the *analyst* at Quantico to profile the specific type of offender responsible, by using behavioural patterns emanating from the *investigative* feedback.

To no-one's great surprise, many setbacks were encountered. Most important, from the operational point of view, it soon became apparent that fewer crime reports were being returned than had been anticipated, and after six months the entire process was overhauled and simplified. The outcome was a VICAP Crime Analysis Report which has remained unchanged since 1986, a ten-section questionnaire listing: administrative detail (law enforcement agency, county, town, state etc); everything known about victim; ditto offender; description if any of vehicle used; *modus operandi*; condition of victim when found (including use of restraints — gag, handcuffs, bonds, etc., evidence of torture if any, indications of removal of 'souvenir' items, other than clothing); cause of death; forensic evidence; request for profiling (a tick in the required box is sufficient); and details of related cases, if any.

The VICAP form lists the types of crime dealt with by the system, as follows:

1. Solved or unsolved homicides or attempts, especially those that involve an abduction; are apparently random, motiveless, or sexually oriented; or are known or suspected to be part of a series.
2. Missing person, where the circumstances indicate a strong possibility of foul play and the victim is still missing.
3. Unidentified dead bodies, where the manner of death is known or suspected to be homicide.

The report form also reminds investigators that 'Cases where the offender has been arrested or identified should be submitted, so unsolved cases in the VICAP system can be

121

linked to known offenders'. According to SSA McCrary, this reminder is of crucial importance. 'The strength of VICAP – and inversely, its weakness – lies in getting these reports sent to us. The difficulty lies in convincing local investigators, who feel they have enough paperwork to do and enough forms to fill in as it is, that it is to *their* benefit to fill in one more. Because if these reports aren't submitted, and no-one tells us about the crimes, we have no way of *knowing* these serial killers are out there.

'Right now California is about to send us *several thousand* unsolved homicides, cases spread over the last ten years or so which as yet have not been entered in the VICAP system. It's going to mean an awful headache for someone when all this hits us, but the fact remains – the more cases we get, the better job we can do. As a matter of fact attempts are being made to set up legislation, which would make it mandatory to put all unsolved homicides into the VICAP system.'

These crime analysis reports are entered into the master system via the BSIS computer, which stands in its own centre along the corridor. Because it needs controlled atmosphere and humidity to function at maximum efficiency, casual entry to the centre is barred by cypher and key locks. All the visitor sees through the protective screen is a red light, pulsing in the computer's steel face like a great bloodshot eye as it 'talks' to Washington. Crime reports apart, 'Old Red-Eye' is also used for the BSIS Artificial Intelligence System ('AI'), and other in-house tasks such as the PROFILER system. It also has an additional onward link with the National Crime Information Centre (NCIC) in Washington. The NCIC is linked in its turn, by telecommunications network, with all 17,200 police departments and other law enforcement agencies scattered throughout the United States: and entry to this system enables the NCAVC to request 'off-line' checks (for instance, when attempting to monitor the movements of transient serial offenders).

VICAP analyst Kenneth A. Hanfland works from an office close by the BSIS computer centre. As he describes his job this big, cheerful man from Oregon sounds oddly reminiscent of, say, an art expert called in to check on the authenticity of a painting; years of comparing and contrasting Template 'matches' with crime reports have given him rare assurance in assessing the *modus operandi* of specific types of serial killer. After a while the conversation turns to British serial killers:

and VICAP analyst Hanfland and SSA McCrary both hear for the first time of Kenneth Erskine, alias The Stockwell Strangler. They learn that Erskine committed seven murders in fifteen weeks in 1986, targeting old age pensioners exclusively, the majority of whom were sexually assaulted. No further description of Erskine is given, other than to add that he was aged twenty-four and British. Hanfland nods, and asks: 'He's coloured, right?' McCrary agrees — and they *are* right (see p. 48).

The question is, how can any analyst know the offender's race from those bare details? Senior analyst McCrary explains: 'In the FBI we don't go into the race area as such, except in so far as it applies to profiling. Obviously, when the police in any multiracial society are looking for a specific type of offender, it's important for them to know if he's black or white. As it happens, most serial killers are white. No-one knows why, but the statistics show it to be so.

'Most violent crime is intra-racial, i.e. white on white, hispanic on hispanic, and so on. The exception is the black offender, who crosses the racial line more frequently than do other offenders. You told us just now that this strangler in London targeted old folks exclusively, and sexually assaulted most of his victims . . . and it's a statistical fact that sexual assault of the elderly is the only sex crime that blacks commit more often than whites. Again, no-one knows why.'

VICAP analyst Hanfland's next-door neighbour in the underground complex is social psychologist Dr Roland Reboussin. Dr Reboussin — he is a doctor of philosophy — is a bespectacled, middle-aged, civilian member of the Behavioural Science Computer Engineering Services Sub-unit: a boffin. His unique role in the operational wing lies in the administration of PROFILER — the first 'expert system' to profile serial offenders by computer.

Expert systems are part of that domain within the computer sciences known as 'artificial intelligence'. Their function is to employ the computer in given areas, in a way which simulates the processes of *human* intelligence. To achieve this they require a 'knowledge base' — which may consist of up to five hundred rules — to guide the automated system towards its interpretative decisions in whichever field the expert system obtains. This knowledge base is made up of 'artificial intelligence' — i.e. expertise culled from the minds of human experts employed in a variety of areas: commercial, medical and most recently, criminal investigative analysis.

Dr Reboussin refers with genuine pride to the many successful uses of the expert system. 'In the commercial world they are used to search for mineral deposits, to fly and navigate passenger-carrying aircraft, to land NASA's shuttles after their journeys through space, and to serve a host of complex electronic systems . . . One famous example in medicine is *Mycin*, an expert system which diagnoses diseases of the blood.' How does an expert system work? 'Well, take *Mycin*. Each rule in the *Mycin* knowledge base is an "if-then" statement: for example, "If the patient's temperature is over 100F, then an infection may be present". The user, however, never sees the rules. Instead it is the expert system which puts the questions, and uses its knowledge base to diagnose the illness from the information supplied by the user.'

PROFILER employs the same technique in investigative analysis. The artificial information on which its knowledge base is built is similarly a compound of human skills, culled mostly from the NCAVC's related investigative disciplines. Its initial rules were developed by observing the complete investigative analysis process (based on field reports, crime scene evidence, pathology, forensic science, victimology, etc.), performed in a group setting. Individual expert human analysts further checked and adjusted every rule until the first 150 were ready for the prototype PROFILER trials.

In a joint paper entitled *Expert Systems for Law Enforcement* published in August 1989, Dr Reboussin and his fellow author Mr Jerry Cameron, Chief of Police at Fernandina Beach in Florida, explained how the basic system worked. 'Information about the victim and the crime scene is essential to the analysis process.' After stressing that the analysis is designed to profile the *type* of offender responsible, rather than the individual, they continued: 'With detailed information as to age, sex, occupation and daily habits of the victim, the autopsy report, and a specific description of the crime scene, the behaviour of both the victim and the offender during the crime can be reconstructed. The result of this analysis is a description of the (type of) person who committed the crime, which includes physical characteristics (age, sex, and race), behavioural characteristics (whether the offender lives near the scene of the crime, lives alone, or is unemployed), and personality traits and characteristics (the nature of relationships with women, or volatile temper). An intermediate trait would be the nature of the offender's relationship with the victim.'

Now two years old and fully operational, PROFILER provides an accurate computerised profile of the type of offender responsible for serial violent crime. The depth of the profile is limited, as always, by the number of rules programmed into the system; already these have risen to some 270, and this knowledge base is continuously being expanded (see p. 180). Although it is unable as yet to match the human analyst in all areas, PROFILER has already become an efficient working robot member of the 'A Team' at Quantico.

Each of the ten senior analysts has his own computer, which he uses to bring up PROFILER on-screen to compare the various aspects of both human and automated profiles. Should any variance emerge both are re-examined to discover why, so that the difference may be resolved. Dr Reboussin and Police Chief Cameron emphasise that the computerised programme 'will never replace skilled human investigative analysts, nor is it intended to do so . . . Rather, the system will function as an analyst's assistant or consultant in several ways'.

Laymen pose the question: what if there should be a conflict between man and machine? The professionals do not see it that way. McCrary explains: 'The human analyst has the last word in profiling: it is his responsibility. You have to say "I'm doing the profile, tnd this is what it *is* − A, B, C, D and E, right through". Having said that, obviously there may be areas where queries arise. Take a case in which the offender displays mixed characteristics, a frequent occurrence. The human analysis may read simply "mostly disorganised", whereas the computer says "Point 75 disorganised, point 25 organised". Okay, it's confirming in effect what you've said, but has made the point definitively. On other occasions there may be an area where *you* think, "Why doesn't the computer see it this way as strongly as we do?" This time you re-examine both profiles and you realise, "Ah! I'd forgotten that", and adjust accordingly. That, of course, is the great strength of the computer. It never forgets anything.

'Given that, what emerges ultimately is the sole responsibility of the human analyst. We don't actually ask the computer if we're right, for the simple reason that it doesn't have the final say. Now, I feel comfortable profiling. With experience, and enough successes, I guess you become confident in whatever you're doing, that's only natural. But I hope never to feel *over*-confident: I'm aware that I neither know all there is to know about profiling, nor do I know all there is to learn about profiling. Equally, the computer doesn't have the benefit of "experience" – whereas we humans do. So I look on PROFILER as one more tool to use when completing what has to be a carefully thought out, fine-tuning process.'

At the NCAVC there is total belief in the fine-tuning process called CIAP, the Criminal Investigative Analysis Programme, which has successfully wedded human and computerised techniques. 'By the end of this year (1989), we will expect to have dealt with more than seven hundred cases', says McCrary. 'That doesn't mean seven hundred serial murder cases, and in any event not all serial murder cases require profiling. For example, if the law enforcement agency already have a suspect, they don't *need* a profile. But they might still ask us for a "personality assessment".' (A situation in which, without knowing the identity of the suspect, a profiler uses the behavioural analysis technique to answer the question – is the suspect capable of such a crime?) The BSIS wing at Quantico furnished such an assessment in the case of Robert Hansen, the Alaskan big-game hunter and serial killer who stalked his human victims gun in hand as if they were wild animals (see pp. 68–9).

'We may also be asked for specific investigative strategies, and/or interview techniques,' he said. 'At other times we may give on-site assistance during the investigation. Some cases we deal with will be over quickly, others will prove more difficult. All of it is time-consuming, a heavy workload at times. One analyst may find himself involved in fifteen or even twenty cases – and that's pressure. But we're in the young stages of this whole analysis process as yet; and I firmly believe that we're headed in the right direction, and that this is the way to do it.'

We catch a glimpse of the pressure that faces everyone in the 'operational wing' the moment we step inside McCrary's office. A mass of paperwork relating to one more homicide – police report, photographic evidence, pathologist's report, forensic details, and victimology – waits on his desk alongside his computer, telephone, notepad, legal and investigative reference works, *et al*. This new investigation centres on a torso murder, one in which the nude, headless, legless body of an adult white male was discovered – wrapped in a tarpaulin and dumped at a lay-by for truck drivers – on Route 8, south of Torrington in upper Connecticut. The police investigation has encountered problems, and they have submitted a VICAP crime report requesting a profile; a task assigned to SSA McCrary. After studying the relevant documents, discussing every feature of the case at daily group conference, and consulting with various NCAVC resident advisory specialists, McCrary furnished the police with a profile. The 'Template' is still awaited from the master VICAP computer at FBI headquarters in Washington.

Because this is an ongoing case, no details of the profile can be disclosed. We know, however, that it will have listed some twenty or more components, including the age, sex, race, marital status (or equivalent), IQ, school and college grades, and the 'rearing environment' of the type of offender responsible; plus personality traits, life-style, demeanour, appearance and grooming, the kind of job he holds and past employment history, his behaviour during the murder, from Phase One (his meeting with the targeted victim) to Phase Four (disposal of the body, after dismemberment and mutilation); where the offender lives in relation to the body disposal site, his motive for the murder – everything bar his name.

Even so, the early signs indicate that this may prove to be one of the 'more difficult' homicides to solve. Connecticut, where the body was dumped, covers more than 5,000 square miles in area: not nearly as big as Texas, say, or California (or most states), but still the size of Northern Ireland. And if in fact Connecticut turns out to be where the unknown killer lives – one of the profiling decisions McCrary has to make – to track him down is never going to be easy. In this case the task is further complicated by the fact that the murdered man (whom the police have identified as a known homosexual, aged twenty-six, with convictions for both prostitution and burglary) was also transient, and on both counts a 'high risk' victim – a homosexual hitchhiker. He set off on his last hike from Nevada – almost the entire breadth of the United States away – nine days before his body was found, hitching lifts

127

mainly from truck drivers. At what point along the route he was picked up, propositioned, attacked and murdered is uncertain: a vital profiling component, which will have called for a very finely-tuned decision by SSA McCrary.

Every twist and turn in this torso murder analysis would seem to provide seemingly obvious behavioural clues, yet equally evident contradictions. For example: the victim's head and legs are both missing, while the torso has been mutilated by emasculation and removal of the nipples. Even to the untrained observer, it would seem logical to assume that this combined dismemberment and mutilation must have taken hours to perform. In turn this would appear to be a clear indication that the murder was pre-meditated and methodically thought-through, even though the victim was one of opportunity. To execute such a crime successfully would necessitate a secure base, where the offender knows he will be able to work undisturbed during those hours of surgery; and he will need more time afterwards to wash away all traces of his sawbones task – and to hide the incriminating body-parts – before setting out to dispose of the torso.

The place best suited for such a lengthy and potentially risky chore would obviously be the killer's home and/or workplace. As we have shown, one of the profiler's first tasks is to calculate where the offender lives in relation to the scene of the crime. In this case, only the body disposal site is known thus far: in itself a not uncommon feature in homicide investigations. But what is doubly baffling (in behavioural terms) is why the murderer first 'de-personalised' his victim (by severing and retaining the head), only to dump the body in a truckers' lay-by on a main road, thus ensuring it would be found with the least possible delay. Furthermore, why compound the felony, literally, by deliberately leaving the victim's arms (and more importantly, his hands) attached to the torso – as if to *invite* identification by fingerprinting?

There are a number of possible reasons why a lust killer – which is clearly what this offender is – may remove and retain his victim's head. One might be that the murderer is a 'souvenir' collector, a psychopath who stores selected body parts to re-live at will the violent fantasy which first inspired the crime. But that would not explain the apparent behavioural contradiction in first 'de-personalising' the victim, only to ensure his identification at the earliest possible moment. By the same token, no matter why he beheaded his victim it cannot have been to thwart identification. Nor is this apparent contradiction the product of a confused mind. The *modus operandi* shows this to be a meticulously planned murder, patently the work of an 'organised' offender – which points to a causative decision, and one more riddle for the analyst to fathom.

At this moment, the telephone rings to involve McCrary in yet another serial murder enquiry – thus rendering all questions on the torso case superfluous. (The ten senior analysts in the BSIS wing are each allotted a separate national area of responsibility. In normal circumstances, all serial cases reported in that area are automatically assigned to the analyst concerned; while the initial report of each new case will come in one of two ways – mostly from VICAP crime returns, but sometimes through direct calls to the NCAVC.) Today's direct call comes from another state in SSA McCrary's 'area of responsibility' – Rhode Island, Connecticut's eastern neighbour.

The caller identifies himself as a psychiatrist who has been asked to take part in a televised discussion of the triple murder ten days earlier of housewife Mrs Joan Heaton, aged thirty-nine, and her daughters Jennifer, ten, and Melissa, eight, at their home in Metropolitan Drive, Warwick, Rhode Island. All three were found dead from multiple stab wounds, and also suffered severe blows to the head and body, following a break-in. Preliminary medical tests showed no evidence of sexual assault. According to press reports, the police have found no trace of the offender or the murder weapon, despite house-to-house enquiries. Local residents fear that this triple murder is the work of an unknown serial killer – the same person responsible for the unsolved murder, two years earlier (in July 1987) and one street away, in which twenty-seven-year-old Rebecca Spencer, also the mother of two children, was found stabbed to death in her home after a break-in. Can the NCAVC help?

Because of the similarities in the two events, SSA McCrary – who has not received the all-important VICAP crime report – checks out the call. First he rings the FBI's Field Profiling Co-ordinator for the area. That brings welcome news: the co-ordinator has already spoken with the local police, who have requested a profile. Their VICAP report, together with the relevant documentary evidence, will shortly be on its way to the NCAVC. McCrary himself then calls the local Captain of Police to discuss various aspects of the case, and reports the facts in his turn at the BSIS group conference.

Within six days of the initial phone call to McCrary, the police at Warwick, Rhode Island, had their suspect in custody — and a confession to all four murders. In order of events: on receipt of the police report, crime scene evidence, forensic details and VICAP report, analyst McCrary furnished a profile by return of a youthful, black offender who lived within walking distance of the Heaton family home. He said this was the type of offender who came from a domestic background of a weak or absent father-figure and dominant female influence, and would have a police record of 'Peeping Tom' prowling activity. He would also, said McCrary, be the kind of offender who takes and retains souvenirs of his crime. The detectives in Warwick, who from the outset believed the two 'events' to be the work of one murderer, now used the BSIS profile as a screening mechanism.

As soon as they identified a suspect who matched the profile components, McCrary provided an interview strategy. Within hours Craig Price — a burly, coloured, fifteen-year-old high school student standing five feet ten inches tall and weighing two hundred and forty pounds (seventeen stone) — confessed both to the Heaton murders, and that of Rebecca Spencer in 1987. A search warrant was obtained and — as predicted in the profile — a knife, thought to be the murder weapon, and certain other items (believed to be 'souvenirs' but not publicly identified) were recovered.

As well as demonstrating the efficiency both of FBI analysts and the NCAVC's Criminal Investigative Analysis Programme, the Heaton-Spencer serial murder case looks set to make legal history in the United States. When Craig Price appeared before Judge Carmine R. DePetrillo in Kent County Family ('Juvenile') Court on 21 September 1989, he admitted killing Mrs Joan Heaton, her two daughters, and Rebecca Spencer. In an adult court he would have faced charges of first-degree murder. However, because Price was under sixteen at the time all four murders were committed (he was aged thirteen when he knifed Rebecca Spencer), he was charged with 'delinquency, by reason of murder'. The four homicides and two related burglaries were entered as evidence of his 'delinquency'.

Under the existing laws of Rhode Island, no matter how

many murders a child under sixteen may commit, he or she may be detained only until their twenty-first birthday – when they are automatically freed. Furthermore, in no circumstances may any child adjudged to be 'delinquent' be sent to an adult corrective institution. Accordingly, Judge DePetrillo ordered Price to be detained in state training school (for treatment and rehabilitation) until the age of twenty-one. Ironically, twenty-one is the age at which serial killers are reckoned to be entering their prime years as multiple murderers; so the Price case aroused considerable public concern.

Earlier attempts, in 1988 and 1989, to introduce legislation which would enable juveniles charged with a capital offence to be tried in adult court, regardless of their age, were defeated in the Rhode Island General Assembly. However, after the Price Family Court hearing, Representative Jeffrey J. Tietz – chairman of the House of Representatives' Judiciary Committee – said that reform of the state juvenile justice laws would be one of his committee's 'highest priorities' in the next session. Should such legislative reform be proposed, it will almost certainly mean calling FBI Behavioural Science Unit experts at the NCAVC to testify on their research into the bahavioural characteristics of serial killers generally, including their development years and their response – if any – to attempted rehabilitation.

There is increasing international interest in the achievements of the NCAVC during its first five years of operational life. By September 1989 there had already been enquiries about CIAP and its offspring computerised techniques from Australia, Canada, Britain, Norway, West Germany, Italy, the Caribbean, Singapore, Hong Kong, Costa Rica – and Communist China. (The Chinese request for information was put on ice following the Tiananmen Square massacre.) In August 1989 two Australian officers started a ten-months profiling course in the BSIS wing of the NCAVC, the first to be invited from any foreign country. While Donald Seaman was in Quantico an Italian police officer, attending another training course at the FBI Academy, brought with him the documentary evidence relating to the sixteen murders committed to date by 'Il Mostro', the Monster of Florence (pp. 63–4). The police in Florence have since been furnished with a profile.

Under the aegis of the Home Office, British officials have also visited the NCAVC to evaluate the Criminal Investigative

Analysis Programme and other related techniques. Significantly, Douglas Hurd (then Home Secretary) told the Police Superintendents' Association at their Torquay conference in 1989 that the government was considering the establishment in Britain of a national, FBI-style criminal intelligence unit. He said that although the proposed unit would not be given operational powers like the FBI, '. . . we should ask ourselves whether the increasing sophistication of major crime, whether the link between drug trafficking and other crime, make it necessary to bring all criminal intelligence together in a national unit'.

Agents of the Investigative Support wing of the NCAVC have had their setbacks as well as successes in the past five years. By December 1989 the task force investigating the Green River serial murder case in Seattle, Washington, was thought to be on the point of disbandment after five years of continuous enquiry (aided by BSIS profiling and on-site FBI investigative support) at a minimum estimated cost of fifteen million dollars. The Green River case − in terms of victim count the worst known, unsolved, serial murder case in American crime history − involved the deaths or disappearance of some forty-nine women, mostly Seattle prostitutes, between 1982 and 1984. It took its name from the river area in King County, Washington, where the first five victims were found. All five had been strangled. Thereafter as each new victim was discovered, the cause of death was recorded simply as homicidal violence; most were just heaps of bones.

Only one man was arrested and named as a 'viable' suspect during the entire investigation. He was William Jay Stevens II, aged thirty-nine. He ws arrested in June 1989 following a tip-off prompted by the *Manhunt* TV screening of the case. Despite lengthy interrogation, however, no murder charges were filed against him. Finally, in November 1989, the Green River Task Force commander and King County police chief, Robert Evans, declared: 'The guy is a prolific thief and a world-class liar, but after we looked at everything we took' − a reference to a police search of Stevens' quarters − 'and interviewed everybody we could interview, I can't tell you in good conscience I think he's responsible for any murders in

King County.' Whoever murdered the forty-nine Green River victims was thought to have posed as a police officer to lure them to their deaths. Stevens himself was subsequently transferred into custody in Arizona, to await trial on charges arising from the cache of twenty-nine handguns, video films and items of police equipment found during the search of his quarters.

One senior FBI agent who took part in the Green River investigtion was the legendary profiler, SSA John Douglas. It almost killed him. The pressure of too many cases over too many years finally caught up with him in Seattle in 1983, and fellow agents found him in a state of collapse suffering from paralysis of the left side, a temperature of 105, and a pulse rate of 220. Doctors diagnosed viral encephalitis, and rated his chances of survival as slim. Douglas proved them wrong. After two months in hospital, and five more convalescing, he returned to duty. Today he is manager of the Criminal Investigative Analysis Programme in the 'operational wing' of the NCAVC – with his matchless skills as a profiler available at every session of the BSIS daily group conference (see footnote p. 111).

SSA McCrary spoke about the stress that goes hand-in-hand with profiling. 'After reviewing the case material in detail, we often visit the significant sites – by which I mean abduction and/or murder scenes, if known, or the body recovery sites – to familiarise ourselves with the areas in which the killer worked. The end result is the construction of our analysis, including a profile of the type of offender responsible . . . But when you first arrive at the scene of a series of ongoing murders, you enter a pressure-cooker environment. The stress is almost palpable, and it transfers to you all too easily. Even though we're talking about mental effort, it leaves you physically drained: exhausted.'

For McCrary, 1989 ended and 1990 began with a non-stop round of serial murder investigation. Some new cases took him overseas, to the Caribbean and Central America. The majority were in the United States, in his eastern 'area of responsibility'. His busiest spell came in what was intended as a week off in up-state New York, between Christmas and New Year. On 22 December 1989 the Harris family of four – Mr Warren A. 'Tony' Harris, aged thirty-nine, his wife Dolores, forty-one, and their children, Shelby, fifteen and Marc, eleven – were found murdered in their home on Ellis Hollow Road, Ithaca, at the foot of Lake Cayuga. All had been shot in the back of the head with a small-calibre handgun, doused with petrol and set ablaze. Three of them were bound. A VICAP report, requesting a profile, was sent to the NCAVC – and McCrary was assigned to the investigation, aided by Lieutenant John Edward Grant of the New York state police 'special services' unit at divisional headquarters (who had previously undergone training with the Behavioural Science Unit at Quantico).

On 30 December 1989 the *Ithaca Journal* headlined their arrival in a front-page lead story: 'FBI agents called in. "A Team" assigned to Harris murder.' Shortly afterwards – and unknown to the readers – the newly arrived 'A Team', led by SSA McCrary, profiled the type of offender responsible as black, male, aged between the late twenties and early thirties, with a criminal record of burglary and armed robbery. The profile also said he lived in the area, in rented property, possibly with a white woman.

On 7 February 1990, after using the profile as their screening mechanism and carrying arrest and search warrants, New York state police entered a house in Ithaca. The man they hoped to question chose to open fire instead. No police were injured, but the suspect died in an exchange of shots. He was thirty-three years of age, black, and had a criminal record for burglary and armed robbery. A .22 handgun (later identified by ballistic experts as the weapon used to execute the Harris family) was recovered. Subsequent enquiries revealed that the gunman had a common-law relationship with a white woman, a few miles away.

The age of the serial killer is always the most difficult component to gauge when furnishing a profile. In the BSIS wing they take the age of twenty-five as a starting-point, then add or subtract years on the basis of the 'experience' they adjudge to be reflected in the crime scene evidence. The aim is to reduce the profiled age to a span of seven years or less. The problem they face is that their decision has to be calculated from the offender's mental and emotional age as distinct from his chronological age, which may prove to be very different. Because of this possible variant, each profile carries a caution that no suspect should be eliminated on the basis of age alone. (We see a clear example of the age 'variant' in the case of the British serial killer Kenneth Erskine, alias the Stockwell

Strangler. Erskine was twenty-four at the time of his trial in 1988: police revealed later that he had a mental age of only eleven.) FBI analysts take twenty-five as a starting-point because statistics show that incipient serial killers usually — but by no means always — commit their first murder when aged between twenty-five and thirty.

The McCrary-led 'A Team' gave on-site assistance during the holiday period in two other, unrelated serial murder investigations in up-state New York: one at Windsor, the other at Rochester. The Rochester case concerned the unsolved murders of eleven prostitutes — all 'high risk' victims because of the nature of their trade, a factor which makes profiling more than usually difficult. On this occasion the profile said that the unknown killer would return to the scene of the crime (pp. 70–1). He did. Following his arrest by the Rochester police, the astonished offender led his captors to the spot where two of his victims were buried.

Such accurate profiling seems almost uncanny to most outsiders. In fact it is based squarely on the far-sighted, meticulous research which began in the classrooms of the FBI Academy at Quantico, at the persuasion of Howard Teten and his handful of fellow instructors in the early 1970s — and blossomed into the mass survey of thirty-six convicted, incarcerated, sex killers carried out by agents of the FBI, under the aegis of the Behavioural Science Unit, between 1979 and 1983. Among the more meaningful behavioural characteristics which they examined in offenders were their 'rearing environment', their history of physical, sexual and psychological abuse, the influence of violent, sexualised fantasy on their adult lives, their unnatural preference for 'solo sex' (masturbation), and their failure during the critical development years to fulfil their academic promise.

Their rejection of family ties made them self-centred loners. They blamed their own failures on an unjust world, in which their hatred for society flourished naturally. Their response to the physical, psychological and/or sexual abuse they encountered in their formative years was to inflict it on others: first in their fantasy world, and then — as the fantasies grew increasingly violent — on dumb animals and finally, people. Their rejection of normal relationships led to masturbation as an outlet; an unnatural preference stimulated by pornography and 'Peeping Tom' activity and ending, inevitably, in sexual assault. The whole interwoven pattern of unreasoning hatred of society, violent fantasy and sexual immaturity fused eventually into an overwhelming desire to dominate others — by force.

And murder, say the analysts, is the ultimate expression of this 'will to power, or desire to control' (see p. 71).

Four

The Power Syndrome

Serial murder is not about sex; it is about power. Freud once commented that a child would destroy the world if it had the power. In this sense, the mind of the serial killer is that of a child. Fantasy takes precedence over actuality. And the fantasy is about power.

This fact was noted by agent Robert R.Hazelwood, of the FBI Behavioural Science Unit. 'One individual we talked to had a very ritualistic method of operation. For example, he would select six victims in advance. On the evening he would decide to rape one of the victims he would put on his "going-in clothes", as he referred to them: an oversize pair of tennis shoes to confuse the police, baggy nondescript coveralls, a ski mask and work gloves. He would then enter the residence and stand by the victim's bed and count from one to ten in increments of one half. And then he would leap on the victim, rape her, and then immediately leave after tying her up. And when I asked him why he counted to ten, he stated that he was putting off the rape. And I said: "I don't understand." And he said: "Rape is the least enjoyable part of the entire crime." I asked him: "In that case, why didn't you just turn around and leave at that point?" And he stated to me: "Pardon the pun, Mr Hazelwood, but after all I'd gone through to get there, it would have been a crime not to have raped her."

'Now the actual time he spent with the victim was less than two minutes. He told us this was the least enjoyable part of the entire crime. Which substantiates the fact that sexual assault services non-sexual needs — it's power needs, it's anger needs, and the need for *control*.'

This sounds an incredible statement. After all, we know that some rapists spend hours with the victim, raping her again and again. It can only be understood if we remember that 'self-esteem' crime is a fairly recent phenomenon. It springs out of the desire for 'recognition', a craving to 'become known' — or at least, to feel that you *deserve* to become known. When Hazelwood speaks of the need for control, he is not referring simply to control over the victim. This type of criminal has a sense of inadequacy, of inferiority, which produces a burning feeling of resentment. The crime relieves his anger and produces a sense of power, of being 'worthwhile', of being in control *of himself*. As strange as it sounds, such crimes are an attempt to leave behind his immaturity and to grow up. When rape is involved, sex is not the prime objective. The prime objective is to feel himself the *master* — of himself and other people, and to hope that some of this feeling will stay with him.

A case that received nationwide publicity in America in 1985 is perhaps the classic illustration of the power syndrome.

On 19 May 1977 a twenty-year-old girl named Colleen Stan set out to hitchhike from Eugene, Oregon, to Westwood in Northern California, where she intended to help a friend celebrate her birthday. At Red Bluff, a young couple in a blue Dodge offered her a lift; the woman had a baby on her knee, and her husband was a mild, bespectacled individual. Half an hour or so later, in a filling-station restroom, Colleen had an odd intuition that she was in danger and ought to escape; unfortunately she ignored it. When the young couple suggested turning off the main road to look at some ice caves in a national park, Colleen raised no objection. When the car stopped in a lonely place, the man placed a knife to her throat, then handcuffed her hands behind her back. He placed a strap round her head and tightened it under her jaw so she could not open her mouth. Then he bound her, and placed a peculiar wooden box over her head. It had obviously been purpose-made, and when it had been closed it left her in total darkness, hardly able to breathe.

Hours later, the man took her into the cellar of a house, and stripped her naked. His motive was not rape. Instead, he suspended her from the ceiling with leather straps, and whipped her. Then the man and his wife had sexual intercourse beneath her feet. Later, the 'head box' was again clamped round her neck, and she was placed in a large wooden box, about three feet high, and locked in for the night. He also placed a 'prickly object' between her thighs. It was designed to give her an electric shock, but failed to work.

The next day she was chained by her ankles to a rack, and given food. When she showed no appetite, he hung her from the beam again and whipped her until she was unconscious. Later the man made her use a bedpan, which he himself emptied. Then the headbox was clamped on again and she was locked up in the box.

This went on for weeks. When she became dirty and unkempt, he made her climb into the bath. He raised her knees and held her head under water until she began to choke. He did this over and over again, taking snapshots of the naked, choking girl in between. After that, her female jailer tried to comb her hair, then gave up and snipped off the knots and tangles with scissors.

The man's name was Cameron Hooker, and he had been born in 1953. He was a shy, skinny boy who had no close friends. When he left school he went to work as a labourer in a local lumbermill. His only reading was pornography, particularly the kind that dealt with flagellation and bondage. His daydream was to flog nude women who were tied with leather straps. When he was nineteen, he met a plain, shy fifteen-year-old named Janice. She was delighted and grateful to be asked out by this quiet, polite youth who drove his own car and treated her with respect. So far she had fallen in love with boys who had ignored her or treated her badly; in fact, the worse they treated her, the more she adored them. Cameron Hooker was marvellously different. When he explained that he wanted to take her into the woods and hang her up from a tree, she was frightened but compliant. It hurt her wrists, but he was so affectionate when he took her down that she felt it was worth it. In 1975 they married, and she continued to submit to strange demands, which included tying her up, making her wear a rubber gas mask, and choking her until she became unconscious. Finally, he told her of his dream of kidnapping a girl and using her as his 'slave'. Eventually, she agreed. She wanted a baby, and longed to live a normal life; perhaps if Cameron had a 'slave', he would stop wanting to whip and throttle her. It sounds incredible but, as we shall see later, such total compliance of a medium-dominance woman to a high-dominance male is by no means unusual.

That is how it came about that Colleen Stan was kidnapped

on that May afternoon in 1977, and taken to their basement in Oak Street, Red Bluff, where she was to spend the next seven years.

After a month or so, Janice felt she could no longer stand it. The idea of holding someone captive sickened her. What was worse was that the captive was an attractive girl. Even though her husband had agreed that there would be no sex between him and his 'slave', it was obvious that he was deriving from Colleen the same sexual satisfaction that he derived from tying up his wife. Janice decided to weaken the ties with her husband. She went to stay with a sister, and found herself a job in Silicon Valley. She returned every weekend, but this brought about the situation she had been trying to avoid. Left alone with his 'slave' for the whole week, Cameron Hooker gave way to temptation. He made Colleen perform oral sex on him, reasoning that he was not going back on his bargain so long as there was no vaginal intercourse. He also burned her with a heat lamp, administered electric shocks, and throttled her until she blacked out. Six months after the kidnap, he started giving her small tasks, such as shelling walnuts or doing crochet. The Hookers sold the results of her labours in the local flea market.

In January 1981, Hooker discovered an article in an 'underground' newspaper about a company of white slavers who made girls sign a slavery contract, and decided that Colleen should do the same. And on 25 January Colleen was made to sign a long document declaring that she handed herself over, body and soul, to her Master, Michael Powers (alias Cameron Hooker). She had to agree to obey every order cheerfully and instantly, to maintain her body parts in such a way that they should always be open to him — for example, she was never to wear panties, and to make sure that, when in the Master's presence, she always kept her knees apart. Finally, after protest, Colleen signed — and was told that her new name was Kay — or K — Powers.

Now she was allowed to come upstairs and help with household chores, but if Cameron came in and shouted 'Attention', she had to strip off her clothes and stand on tiptoe with her hands above her head. Soon after this, Janice herself suggested to her husband that he should have sex with his slave. Perhaps she would hoping that he would cite his original agreement and refuse; in fact, he promptly brought Colleen up from the basement, spreadeagled her naked on the bed, with a gag in her mouth and her wrists and ankles tied to the corners, then raped her. Janice, meanwhile, rushed off to vomit in the bathroom. After that, Colleen was put back in the box.

A point came when he decided that he would prefer to live in a more secluded place. He gave notice of leaving to his landlord, and bought a trailer on some land beyond the city limits. Nearby ran the Interstate 5 highway — which, in two years time, would earn itself a new and sinister significance as its name became associated with a random serial murderer known as the I.5 killer. Underneath a large waterbed, Hooker constructed a kind of large rabbit hutch, which was to be Colleen's home. Colleen was moved in — blindfolded and handcuffed — one afternoon, and immediately confined in her new quarters.

Now life became a little freer. She was let out for an hour or so every day to perform her ablutions and help with the chores. She made no attempt to escape — Hooker had told her all kinds of horror stories about what happened to 'Company' slaves who tried to run away: having their fingers chopped off one by one was the least of them. To remind her that she was his slave he periodically hung her from the ceiling and flogged her with a whip. He also burned her breasts with lighted matches. There were compensations. In the autumn, Hooker went up into the mountains to cut wood on the land of the company that employed him; he took his slave with him. He made her work; he also made her swim in a pond and run along a dirt road. When she was 'disobedient', he tied her down on a kind of mediaeval rack and 'stretched' her. This excited him so much that he stripped naked and made her perform oral sex. On another occasion he raped her on the 'rack'. Janice was not told of these sexual episodes. Soon after this, the slave was made to drink most of a bottle of wine, then to perform oral sex on Janice; it made her sick.

Early in 1980, after nearly three years of captivity, Colleen was allowed an amazing excursion. She was permitted to dress up in some of Janice's clothes, make up her face, and accompany Janice to a dance. There they met two men and went home with them. Janice vanished into the bedroom with one of them, while Colleen stayed talking to the other. Cameron Hooker apparently suspected nothing, and his wife's liaison continued for the next two months, until it fizzled out. After that, Janice, still unsuspected, had another short affair.

Colleen was also allowed more freedom – she was allowed to go out and jog on her own. Incredibly, she still made no attempt to escape – Hooker had brainwashed her into seeing herself as a well-behaved and loyal slave. As a reward for obedience, she was allowed to write to her sister – without, of course, including a return address – and even, on one occasion, to telephone her family, with Hooker standing beside her monitoring everything she said. She told them she was living with a couple who were 'looking after her'. When they wanted to know more, her Master made her hang up. Soon after that he took her on a visit to his own family, on their ranch outside town. This passed off so well that he decided to take the ultimate risk, and allow her to go and see her own parents, who lived in Riverside, Southern California. In March 1981, he drove her to Sacramento, and ordered her to wait in the car while he went into an office block that belonged to the sinister Company who owned her. When he came back, he told her they had granted permission to visit her family. The visit to Riverside was brief, but went off perfectly. Hooker was introduced as her fiancé Mike, who was on his way to a computer seminar. Colleen Stan spent the night in her father's home, then visited her mother – who lived elsewhere – without divulging where she had been for four years, or why she had failed to keep in touch. The following day, her Master rang her and announced he would be arriving in ten minutes to take her home. Colleen was upset that Hooker had broken his promise to allow her to spend a full weekend with her family, and sulked all the way back to Red Bluff. When they got back, the Master decided that enough was enough. The slave's period of liberty came to an end, and she was put back into the box.

This period lasted another three years, from 1981 until 1984. On one occasion, out of sheer frustration, she kicked out the end of the box and climbed out. She had no thought of running away – the Company would be sure to track her down. Oddly enough, when Hooker came home from work he was not angry, as she expected, but simply repaired the box.

The relationship between Hooker and his wife was becoming increasingly tense – she disliked being tied up and whipped. At one point she left him for a few days and went to stay with her brother. When she came back, she and Cameron had a long, honest talk; she confessed about her two early affairs — her husband seemed indifferent — while he admitted that he had been having sex with Colleen. (This deeply upset Janice.) Then, in an attempt to repair their marriage, they began reading the Bible together. Colleen had already found refuge in the religion of her childhood, and now she joined in the prayer sessions. Cameron, meanwhile, worked on a kind of underground bunker that would be a dungeon for the slave. It was completed in November 1983, and then Colleen was installed. When the winter rains came, howerer, the dungeon began to fill with water, and they had to take her out again and let her back indoors.

Janice and Colleen, whose relationship in the past had often been stormy — Janice was inclined to boss her around — had now become close friends as well as fellow Bible students. Cameron Hooker still flogged his slave — on Company orders — but was also treating her better, giving her more food, and allowing her to babysit with his two daughters. And in May 1984, seven years after her abduction, he sent her out to find a job. She was hired at a local motel as a maid, and proved to be such a hard worker that she soon received promotion. One day, another maid offered her a lift home, and went into the mobile home; she was puzzled when Colleen told her that a small backpack contained everything she possessed. Cameron Hooker came home while Colleen, Janice and the maid were talking, and stared at them with such hostility that the maid felt uncomfortable and left.

Colleen believed implicitly that she was the slave of 'the Company'; she often mentioned it to Janice, and Janice felt increasingly guilty and uncomfortable at having to support her husband's lies. Her new religious faith made it difficult. It became harder still when she and Colleen — with Cameron's permission — began to go to the local church together. Cameron tried to turn the Bible to his own advantage, quoting the passage from Genesis in which Abraham went to bed with his wife's maid Hagar, and suggesting that Janice should take the same liberal attitude towards Colleen. As usual, he finally got his way; he even persuaded Janice to share the bed, and entertain him with lesbian acts with Colleen. Janice was so upset by the new situation that she asked Cameron to strangle her — something he did frequently, but only to the point of unconsciousness. He agreed, but either lost courage, or was suddenly struck by the thought of the inconvenience of disposing of the body; at all events, Janice woke up to find herself still alive.

On 9 August 1984 Janice made her decision. She went to speak to Colleen at work, and told her the truth: that there was no 'Company', that she was not a slave, that Cameron was merely a pervert. Colleen was stunned. Her first reaction was to quit her job. Then she and Janice called on the pastor of their church, and gave him a confused outline of the story. He advised them to leave Hooker. But it was too late in the day for Colleen to take a bus to her family in Riverside. Instead, they picked Cameron up from work as usual, and went back to the mobile home. That night Janice pleaded that she felt ill, and she and Colleen slept on the floor together. As soon as Cameron had gone to work at 5 a.m, they began packing, and fled to the home of Janice's parents. Colleen wired her father to ask him to send her a hundred dollars. The next day she took the bus to southern California. Before she left, she telephoned Cameron to tell him that she knew he had always lied to her, and that she was leaving; he cried. Then Colleen went home to begin a new life.

For Janice, there was no new life. Cameron begged her to go back to him, promising to reform, and she gave in. But she took him to see the pastor, who advised him to burn his pornography and bondage equipment. He said he would. He even kept his promise, and made a bonfire of them in the back yard, but within a short time he began building up his collection of porno magazines again. Meanwhile, back in Riverside, Colleen had told her family about her seven-year ordeal. She rejected the idea of going to the police. She and Janice had talked over the telephone – they kept in touch daily – and Colleen agreed that Cameron deserved another chance. She even talked to Cameron and agreed not to go to the police. With his wife back at home and his former slave in Riverside, he must have felt perfectly safe.

Janice had now found another confidante – a doctor's receptionist. It was to her that, on 7 November 1984, she finally poured out the truth. Her new friend sent her back to talk to the pastor. And the pastor, when he finally heard the whole story, talked her into ringing the police.

What Janice Hooker had to tell them was not simply the

story of Colleen Stan's seven-year ordeal. She had been keeping a more sinister secret. In January 1976, more than a year before Colleen had been abducted, they had offered a lift to a girl in the nearby town of Chico. She told them her name was Marliz Spannhake, and that she was eighteen years old. When the time came to drop her off at her apartment, Cameron had grabbed her and driven off to a lonely spot, where the girl had been tied up, and her head clamped in the 'head box'. Back at home, Hooker stripped off her clothes and hung her from the ceiling. Then, perhaps to stop her screams, he cut her vocal cords with a knife. He tortured her by shooting her in the abdomen with a pellet gun, and finally strangled her. In the early hours of the morning, they drove into the mountains, and Hooker buried Marliz Spannhake in a shallow grave.

The police were able to verify that a girl named Marie Elizabeth Spannhake had vanished one evening in January 1976; but although Janice accompanied them up into the mountains, they were unable to locate the grave. That meant that there was not enough evidence to charge Cameron Hooker with murder. Two detectives flew down to Riverside to interview Colleen Stan, and as they listened to the story of her seven years of torment, they soon realised that they had enough evidence to guarantee Cameron Hooker several years in jail. Hooker was arrested on 18 November 1984.

The trial, which began on 24 September 1985, made nationwide headlines; the 'Sex Slave' case seemed specially designed to sell newspapers. The jurors learned that Hooker was to be tried on sixteen counts, including kidnapping, rape, sodomy, forced oral copulation and penetration with a foreign object. The prosecutor, Christine McGuire, had hoped to be able to introduce the Spannhake murder as corroborative evidence of Hooker's propensity to torture, but had finally agreed to drop it if Hooker would plead guilty to kidnapping. Hooker's attorney, Rolland Papendick, made no attempt to deny that Colleen Stan was abducted against her will, but argred that she had soon been free to leave, and that she had stayed voluntarily. The evidence, he said, showed that Colleen loved Cameron, and had stayed for that reason. His argument was that Janice had regarded Colleen as a rival who would supplant her, and had therefore told her about 'the Company' to get rid of her. Even after her return to Riverside, said Papendick, Colleen had frequently telephoned Cameron

Hooker. And that is why, suspecting that Cameron meant to desert her and move to Riverside, Janice had finally decided to turn him in. In the witness box, Janice admitted that she knew Colleen was in love with Cameron, and that she wanted to have a baby. The jury's sympathy was obviously beginning to waver towards Cameron. But when a doctor described the scars on Colleen's wrists, ankles and thighs – including electric burn marks – and a psychiatrist talked about brainwashing, it began to swing in the other direction. Even so, when the prosecution and defence had presented their closing arguments, the case seemed balanced on a knife edge. On 29 October 1985 the jury retired; on 31 October – Hallowe'en – they filed in to deliver their verdict. Cameron Hooker had been found guilty on ten counts, including kidnapping, rape and torture. On 22 November Judge Clarence B. Knight delivered the sentence. After describing Cameron Hooker as 'the most dangerous psychopath that I have ever dealt with', he sentenced him to several terms of imprisonment amounting to a hundred and four years.

One question remains unanswered – the question that Christine McGuire raises on the last page of her book about the case, *Perfect Victim*: how did Cameron Hooker develop his peculiar taste for torturing women? She has an interesting comment from someone on the case who wished to remain anonymous:

'People like to believe in an Einstein or a Beethoven – geniuses – but they hate to believe in their opposites. A genius is a mutant, something unnatural. But just as some people are born with extra intelligence, others are born without much intelligence or without fingers or limbs or consciences. The human body is phenomenally complex, with trillions of cells, and trillions of things can go wrong. Cameron Hooker is a fluke, an accident of internal wiring. His instincts are simply the opposite of yours and mine.'

Many police officeers who have had to deal with serial killers would concur with that analysis: that however old-fashioned and unsubtle it sounds, some people are simply born bad. Or, to put it less crudely, that some unknown hereditary factors cause some people to be naturally more vicious than others.

But while this is undoubtedly true, the Quantico interviews with thirty-six killers demonstrated that family background plays a crucial role. The interviewers noted a 'high degree of instability' in the family backgrounds, hostile or poor relationship with the father, and physical and/or sexual abuse in childhood or teens. Another study* pointed out that a large proportion of criminals are 'highly sexed' in childhood, and have peeped in through bathroom keyholes on females undressing, or initiated sexual games — sometimes amounting to rape — with girls at school.

Equally important is the fact that, as every psychiatrist knows, sexual perversions seldom appear fully fledged; they sprout, like seeds, from small beginnings. In his book *Sex Perversions and Sex Crimes*, James Melvin Reinhardt cites a typical case of a urophile — a man who liked to sniff and drink women's urine — who began (as a child) simply by being sexually attracted by little girls. One day after he had seen a little girl urinating, he lay down on the ground and sniffed the spot, masturbating at the same time. The taste thus initiated finally developed into an obsession with female urine. We can see clearly that it was merely a matter of association of ideas. Reinhardt goes on to point out that the same thing applies to sadism and masochism: that they are simply a development of 'moral and aesthetic sensitivities that are ordinarily prevalent in a reasonably well socialised man'. He cited the case of a patient whose masochism dated from the day — when he was seven years old — when a maidservant encouraged him to fondle her feet and toes. Then he experienced orgasm while watching a poodle licking the toes of a maid while she was reading. One day he persuaded the maid to allow him to lick her toes, and again experienced an ejaculation. This led to fantasies of being beaten and humiliated by women. If the maid had asked him to bite or scratch her instead of fondling her toes, it is conceivable that he might have developed into a sadist instead.

Fantasy, Reinhardt believes, is the key to the development of sexual perversion. The perversion often has its origin in some casual incident, like the maidservant who enjoyed having her toes fondled. Since the fantasist feels ashamed of his autoerotic

The Criminal Personality by Samuel Yochelson and Stanton Samenow, 3 vols, New York 1976–88.

activities, he tends to avoid too much contact with everyday reality, preferring to spend as much time as possible in the dream world inside his own head, and so fantasy reinforces itself and develops though long sessions of autoerotic daydreaming. The daydreams are often given a direction by pornography. Eventually, a time may come when the dreamer feels the compulsion to burst out of this world of unreality with some act that gives him a sensation of being truly alive. The following case is typical.

In October 1975 Robert Poulin, an eighteen-year-old schoolboy, suddenly went berserk with a shotgun in Ottawa; he entered a classroom at his school and shot seven students, afterwards blowing out his own brains in the corridor. In the room where he lived – in the basement of his parents' home – firemen called to a blaze found the charred naked body of seventeen-year-old schoolgirl Kim Rabat, who had been repeatedly raped and sodomised, then stabbed to death. She was a girl on whom Poulin was known to have a 'crush', and he had spoken to her at the bus stop that morning and persuaded her to go back to his room. A trail of sex magazines running up the stairs revealed that the fire had been intended to burn down the house. Investigators also found his journals, which revealed that he had spent the past two years daydreaming of sex and reading pornography. Seven months before his suicide he had written: 'I thought of committing suicide, but I don't want to die before I have had the pleasure of fucking some girl.' He planned to waylay a girl in a dark alleyway and force her to have sex at gunpoint – he even bought a model gun for that purpose. He also seems to have made a few attempts to waylay a few girls in a local park – at least, he answers the description of a youth who had been exposing himself and attempting sexual assault. Then he saw an advertisement for a blow-up life-size doll, and wrote: 'I no longer think that I will have to rape a girl'. When he bought the doll, it proved to be a disappointment, and he went back to his schemes for rape, culminating in the morning that he spent violating Kim Rabat. He left no record of his feeling after the rape, but it seems safe to assume that he found the reality totally unlike his daydreams.

Why did Poulin, unlike most sexually frustrated young men, turn to rape and murder? The inquest revealed all the essential clues. Poulin had been considered by everyone who knew him a perfectly normal youth, quiet and intelligent. (The book about him – by Christopher Cobb and Bob Avery – is called *Rape of a Normal Mind*.) But there had been a great deal of parental conflict, particularly with his father, an ex-Air-Force pilot with a disciplinary obsession, now a schoolteacher. Poulin felt deep hatred for his family, and had considered killing them all. The fact that he lived alone in a basement that was separate from the rest of the house – and had done so since he was twelve – is a measure of his failure to communicate with the rest of the family (which included three sisters but no brother) or theirs to communicate with him. His father's interests were military, and he wanted Robert to follow suit. In fact, Robert had decided that he wanted to enter the Royal Military College in Kingston when he left school. A few days before the murder, he had been turned down for officer training. This disappointment – and the thought that he would not be able to escape from his family after all – was clearly what motivated the decision to rape and kill. It could be seen as a form of suicide, but, as the investigators finally concluded: 'He was crying out for some sort of recognition: something he had wanted all his life.'

A case that bears many resemblances to that of Robert Poulin – and which occurred two decades earlier – allows us a glimpse of what might have happened to Poulin if he had actually carried out his intention of becoming a serial rapist. In the late 1940s, a young masochist named Harvey Murray Glatman was receiving psychiatric treatment in Sing Sing, where he was serving five years for robbery and attempted rape – he had pointed a toy gun at a girl in Boulder, Colorado, and ordered her to undress. Released in 1951, he set up a TV repair shop in Los Angeles, and became an enthusiastic amateur photographer. For the next six years he remained solitary, daydreaming of tying up girls and raping them. At the age of twelve he had discovered that looping a rope round his neck and half-throttling himself brought on an orgasm. His mother had been deeply concerned – Harvey was very much a mother's boy – but was reassured when a doctor assured her that her son would outgrow it.

On 30 July 1957 Glatman called at the apartment of a young

model who had recently arrived from Florida and looked at her portfolio. His story was that he was a magazine photographer named Johnny Glynn. He was fascinated by a photograph he saw on the wall of a nineteen-year-old model named Judy Ann Dull. She was married, with a fourteen-month-old daughter, but separated from her journalist husband. Glatman finally obtained her telephone number. The following day, he contacted her and asked her to pose for photographs later that afternoon. She was reluctant until he explained that they would have to use her apartment, since his own was being used. Her own home seemed safe enough; but when he arrived that afternoon, he told her that he had managed to borrow a studio from a friend. It was, in fact, his own apartment.

Once there, he told her to take off her dress and put on a skirt and sweater. Then he explained that he had to tie her hands behind her — he was taking a photograph for the cover of a true detective magazine. Dubious but compliant, she allowed him to tie her hands behind her, tie her knees together, and place a gag in her mouth. He took several photographs, then unbuttoned her sweater, pulled down her bra, and removed her skirt. After that he took more photographs. Finally, when she was clad only in panties, he laid her on the floor and started to fondle her. She struggled and protested through the gag. Glatman became impotent if a girl showed signs of having a mind of her own — total passivity was required for his fantasy. He threatened her with a gun until she promised not to resist, then raped her twice. After that, both sat naked on the settee and watched television. Judy promised that if he would let her go she would never tell anyone what had happened. Glatman pretended to agree — he wanted to make her co-operate. He told her that he would drive her out to a lonely place and release her, then he would leave town. Then he drove into the desert near Phoenix, Colorado, and strangled her, after first taking more photographs. He buried her in a shallow grave.

Seven months later, Glatman met twenty-four-year old divorcee Shirley Ann Bridgeford, a mother of two children, through a lonely-hearts club; he was registered as George Williams, a plumber by profession. When he made a date with her over the telephone on 8 March 1958 he told her they were going square-dancing. But when he picked her up at her mother's home in Sun Valley, he told her he would rather take her for a drive in the moonlight. A hundred miles south of Los Angeles he stopped the car and tried to fondle her; when she protested he produced a gun and ordered her into the back seat; there he raped her. Then, in the Anza Borrego desert, he tied her up, took more photographs, and strangled her with a rope. He took her red panties as a keepsake.

Shirley's mother reported her disappearance, but 'George Williams' proved to be as untraceable as 'Johnny Glynn'.

Five months later, he dialled a nude modelling service, and spoke to twenty-four-year-old Ruth Rita Marcado, a strip-tease dancer who also modelled nude. He gave his name as Frank Johnson. When he called on her on 22 July 1958, some instinct made her plead illness and send him away. The following evening he went to her apartment with his automatic pistol, and took her up to her bedroom. There he tied her up and raped her. Then, telling her they were going for a picnic, he marched her down to his car. He drove her out to the desert, where he had killed Shirley Bridgeford, and spent a day taking photographs of her — bound and gagged — and raping her. In between rapes he released her and allowed her to eat. Then he told her he would take her home. On the way, he stopped the car for 'one more shot', tied her up once more, and strangled her with a rope.

Three months later, in September, he tried to persuade another model back to his studio; she found him 'creepy' and declined. She finally contacted a friend named Lorraine Vigil, who was short of money. Glatman called at her house and drove off with her. On a quiet road in a small town called Tustin, he stopped and threatened her with the gun. When he told her he wanted to tie her up, she tried to jump out of the car. He threatened to kill her, but she felt she had nothing to lose, and grabbed for the gun. It went off, frightening them both. She jumped from the car and struggled with him; she even managed to grab the gun and pull the trigger; but it had jammed. They were still struggling when a passing motor-cycle policeman pulled up, and produced his own revolver.

When police searched his apartment, they found the 'bondage' photographs of his three previous victims. Identified in a line-up by witnesses who had seen him, Glatman confessed in full to the three murders. At his trial he asked for the death penalty. The judge agreed, and on 18 August 1959 Glatman died in the San Quentin gas chamber.

There is a sense in which Glatman is the archetypal sex killer — and therefore the archetypal serial killer. He was an ugly little man with a face like a rabbit and ears like jug handles — the kind who never looks anyone straight in the eyes — and from a fairly early age, he must have taken it for granted that no woman would ever gaze at him with adoration. Before his attempt at rape in Boulder, Colorado, he had undoubtedly spent years daydreaming about sex, until the loss of contact with reality that springs from daydreams made it seem an unattainable ideal. Forcible rape seemed the only way of losing his virginity. In fact, the girl screamed, and he was arrested. He broke bail to flee to New York, where he had more success as a stick-up man — always preying on women — until he became known as the 'Phantom Bandit'. Caught breaking and entering, he received five years in Sing Sing. On his release, his mother paid for him to set up a TV repair business. For six more years he indulged in autoerotic daydreams. Apart from his interest in bondage, his sexual desires were normal; he merely wanted to be allowed to explore the body of an attractive girl and then make love to her. He took up photography because it gave him the opportunity to photograph unclothed models in a public studio, but his glimpses of the nude female form only made his celibacy more agonising. At the age of thirty-one — and probably still a virgin — desperation finally overcame Glatman's nervous timidity, and he persuaded Judy Ann Dull back to his apartment. His intention was probably not rape — he realised that this would probably land him in Sing Sing again — but merely to reach a climax of autoeroticism looking at a bound and half-naked girl. But when it came to removing her skirt, nothing mattered but to satisfy a craving that had been tormenting him for almost two decades; whatever it cost, he had to possess her. When he had raped her, and she sat submissively beside him on the settee, watching television, he must have realised that he had burnt his boats. For this delightful but in some ways perfectly ordinary experience he had bartered away the next ten years of his life. Like Robert Poulin after the murder of Kim Rabat, he must have felt like a man who has awakened from a bad dream. If only he could trust her not to go to the police he would undoubtedly have been glad to let her go, but commonsense told him that was unlikely, and that his only chance of escaping the consequences was to kill her. He later described how, when she lay dead, he was consumed by remorse, and begged forgiveness of her dead body. As he drove back to Los Angeles, he knew that what he had done might cost him his life. If the police found his fingerprints in the flat from which he had collected her, they would quickly identify him as New York's 'Phantom Bandit' and trace his present whereabouts — they might even be waiting for him when he got back home. At that point, Harvey Glatman was ready to swear that if he escaped the consequences of this day of insanity, he would live a life that would do credit to a Trappist monk.

As the days and weeks passed, and the police made no headway with the case of the disappearing model, fear and remorse were replaced by memories of a submissive girl who had allowed him to do whatever he liked. Eight months later, the craving to repeat the experience had become overwhelming.

The murder of Shirley Bridgeford again filled him with remorse. This time it might be easier for the police to trace him, since he had joined the lonely-hearts club that had supplied her name. Once more, weeks of anxiety gradually gave way to confidence. Now there was a new fear: the realisation that, sooner or later, he would *have* to do it again. The desire to rape submissive girls had become a compulsion.

He later confessed that the murder of Ruth Rita Marcado was his most traumatic experience so far. In the hours he spent with her — raping her 'four or five times' — he found her so likeable that he was strongly tempted to let her go, but that would have been too dangerous. After her death, he felt far worse than after killing the other two girls.

Only three months later, he was again in the grip of the old compulsion. He realised that the times between rapes was becoming shorter: eight months after Judy Ann Dull, four months after Shirley Bridgeford, now only three months after Ruth Marcado. He was like a man who has fallen into the clutches of a blackmailer, and realises that he will never escape. When the final rape went disastrously wrong, and the door of the police cell clanged behind him, there must have been a certain feeling of relief. Now at least he could no longer give way to the compulsion to which he had become a slave. When the case finally came to trial all desire to escape the consequences of his acts had vanished. Like Carl Panzram, he only wanted to die. This is why he begged his defence lawyer to make sure that he received the death penalty.

To understand Glatman is to understand the basic psychology of the serial killer. The first crime produces fear, revulsion, remorse. But it is also like a dose of an addictive drug. Again and again, serial killers have confessed that they were unable to stop: again and again – from America's first serial murderer H.H.Holmes to the Yorkshire Ripper and Henry Lee Lucas – they have used the same image: that it was if they had fallen into the power of the devil.

In the case of Robert Poulin and Harvey Glatman, the sex was uncomplicated by sadism. In an earlier case, that of Donald Fearn, the power fantasy also involved torture. Fearn, a twenty-three-year-old railway mechanic of Pueblo, Colorado, was fascinated by the practices of a sect of Indians called the Penitentes, whose religious ceremonies involved torture and crucifixion. In August 1941 Fearn's wife became pregnant, and by the following April, when she was in hospital giving birth, he decided to carry out his plan of kidnapping and torturing a girl. On the evening of 22 April 1942, as a pretty seventeen-year-old named Alice Porter walked home from a nursing class, he pulled up alongside her with a gun, and bundled her into his car. A neighbour heard the girl scream, and looked out in time to see a light-coloured Ford sedan disappearing down the street. Fearn drove the girl out to an old one-room ranch building twenty-five miles away, and there raped and tortured her for six hours, binding her with red-hot wires and stabbing her with an awl. Finally he struck her with a hammer, shot her twice through the head, and threw her body down a cistern. Three days later, police located a garage owner, who had been aroused at 4 a.m. on the day after Alice Porter's disappearance, to tow a light-coloured Ford sedan out of the mud. Police went to the spot, and found the abandoned ranch at the top of the nearby hill. A table inside was covered with bloodstains, and on the floor there were scissors, pliers, baling wire and a shoemaker's awl – Fearn's torture kit. In the cistern outside, police found the body of Alice Porter. From the handle of an awl they were able to lift distinct fingerprints, but these failed to match those of any known sexual offender. The police visited every garage in Pueblo, asking if the proprietor had seen a light-coloured, mud-stained sedan. One of them had – it was in the garage at that moment, waiting to be washed. When Donald Fearn walked in to collect it, the police asked him to come to the station for questioning, and took his fingerprints; these matched those found on the awl. When the two sets of prints were placed in front of him, Fearn confessed. 'I always wanted to torture a girl.' He went on to describe how he had waited outside a nursing class every night for weeks and followed the student nurses home; Alice Porter was the one he finally chose as his victim.

On 23 October 1942 Fearn was executed in the gas chamber in Canon City jail.

The Fearn case exhibits an important aspect of the psychology of the sex killer: that the victim is not, in fact, chosen totally 'at random'. Fearn had selected Alice Porter, and followed her around for a week before he killed her – establishing her routine – partly because she lived on a lonely block, but also because she conformed to his fantasy image of the girl he wanted to violate. The fantasy has already determined the type of person to be selected as the victim. In most cases she is selected because she strikes the fantasist as the victim-type; there may be some look of vulnerability about her that excites him. This can again be seen in the case of Cameron Hooker. He apparently murdered the first girl he picked up – Marliz Spannhake – because she screamed and struggled. She was not the 'victim' type. Colleen Stan was. Janice Hooker commented after the case that her husband had picked a victim who was submissive, compliant, and who tended towards destructive relationships. She went on to make the perceptive comment: 'I chose not to be a victim. I hope Colleen makes that choice. Not just to walk out, but to make a total change, to become an unvictim, to take charge'. If Colleen Stan had been that kind of person – an unvictim, the dominant type who 'takes charge' – it is almost certain that Cameron Hooker would not have kidnapped her; he would have recognised her as unsuitable for his purposes, and let her go.

In order to understand a psychopath like Cameron Hooker,

it is also necessary to recognise the importance of Reinhardt's observation that sadism and masochism are simply a development of tendencies that are already present in the reasonably 'well socialised' male. It is not unnatural for a young and healthy male to want to 'fuck some girl', as Robert Poulin put it: *any* girl. The act of penetration brings a sense of triumph, a sudden expansion of self-esteem. The self-esteem of the Casanova-type of male — and most young men would like to emulate Casanova — depends upon 'conquest', as the self-esteem of the hunter depends on the amount of game he can 'bag'. In 1980 in Hanover, West Germany, a plumber named Robert Bilden — who had acquired himself a reputation of being irresistible to women — was tried for a particularly brutal rape. In the spring of that year, he met a pretty nineteen-year-old girl named Tina Schuster, who was shy and intensely prudish. Bilden began assiduously courting her, assuring her that his bad reputation was entirely unmerited. When he had established his good behaviour over a period of many months, she finally consented to go to dinner in his apartment when he told her that his schoolmistress from fifth grade would also be present. The 'schoolmistress' was, in fact, a prostitute named Helga Tallman. After the meal, the prostitute threw herself on the girl and held her down while Bilden removed her clothes; then Helga Tallman subjected her to oral sex, which was intended to excite Tina but in fact made her feel sick. After this Bilden raped her violently — her inner thighs were bruised as she struggled to prevent penetration — and continued to do so for the rest of the night. Bilden and the prostitute also engaged in sex, urging the girl to watch them in the mirror over the bed. As soon as she managed to escape, early the following morning, she rushed to a doctor, who called the police. Bilden was sentenced to five years' imprisonment, Helga Tallman to sixteen months. But the case raises the question: why had Bilden risked jail when he could have spent the night with any number of willing girls? Because, with her innocene and prudishness, Tina Schuster struck him as 'the perfect victim'. The ultimate pleasure was to rape a shy virgin. It produced a far more powerful sense of conquest, of self-esteem, than the seduction of a 'willing' victim.

It must be recognised that this element of 'conquest' is present in all male sexuality. If it were absent, the male would find the female totally undesirable. In 'normal' relationships, protectiveness and affection *outweigh* the desire for 'conquest', but do not replace it; without it, the relationship would be non-sexual. The novelist Thomas Mann remarked that the words of the marriage ceremony 'These twain shall be one flesh' are misleading, for if they were really 'one flesh' they would have no attraction for one another; attraction is based upon 'strangeness', which in turn implies 'forbiddenness'.

In a fantasist like Cameron Hooker — and Hooker, like most fantasists, had been a shy and introverted child — the normal male desire for 'conquest' is raised to a pathological level by fantasy. Reinhardt's chapter on sadism is entitled 'Fantasy Finds a Victim', and includes a typical case in which sadistic fantasy was translated into actuality. In the autumn of 1953, Raymond and Betty Allen set out to drive from Pennsylvania to their new home in San Jose, California, towing an aluminium trailer behind their car. On the morning of 1 December a big, white-haired man struck up a conversation at a gas station; the Allens saw him several times later that day, driving in the same direction. That night, when they were parked at a caravan site in Arizona, Raymond Allen woke up to find a flashlight on his face, and was knocked unconscious by a blow on the chin. When he woke up, he and his wife were tied hand and foot. The white-haired man — Carl J.Folk — demanded money, then drove the car — still towing the trailer — for several miles before he went too close to a ditch and half-overturned it. For the next hour or so, he raped and tortured Betty Allen, burning her with matches and cigarettes, and biting her all over. Allen had to lie there in the next room, listening to her screams. These eventually ceased. Finally Folk went to sleep, and Allen managed to untie his legs. He escaped from the caravan and ran down the road; a car stopped, and the driver untied his hands. Allen went back to his car and took a revolver from under the front seat. In the trailer, Folk was pouring petrol over Betty Allen and her baby. When he went into the next room, he discovered that Raymond Allen was missing. He looked outside, saw Allen, and asked with mild surprise: 'What are you doing there?' Allen then shot him in the stomach. (Five other shots missed.) Betty Allen was dead, strangled with a sheet round her neck.

Folk recovered from his wound, and was found guilty of murder and executed in March 1955. An earlier victim — a seventeen-year-old girl — had been luckier than Betty Allen.

In 1949, she had answered an advertisement for a domestic in an Albuquerque newspaper; the big white-haired man who met her seemed harmless, so she climbed into his car. He drove her to a lonely stretch of road, then ordered her out and tore off her clothes. Then he tied her to a tree, and beat and raped her repeatedly. She noted the number of his car as he drove off, and Folk — the proprietor of a travelling carnival — was arrested. By the time the case was due for trial, the girl had had a mental breakdown and was in hospital. Folk was confined to the same hospital for three years, and was then released to act out his sadistic fantasies with Betty Allen.

If the case of Carl Folk demonstrates the incubation of the sadistic 'power syndrome' in a mentally unbalanced individual, the case of Robert Hansen is an example of how it can develop in an apparently stable one.

In the early 1980s, police in Anchorage, Alaska, took note of the disappearance of a number of 'exotic dancers'. In Anchorage, the temperature is so low that it is impractical for prostitutes to walk the streets. The majority of them solve the problem by working in topless bars, and making appointments with clients for after hours. Few people notice when such a girl vanishes, although bar owners were often puzzled when their dancers failed to show up to collect their pay. And when, in 1980, building workers on Eklutna Road discovered a shallow grave which had been partly excavated by bears, and containing the half-eaten body of a woman, it seemed likely that she might be one of the missing women. Since the state of the body made it impossible to identify, she became known in the records as 'Eklutna Annie'.

Two years later, on 12 September 1982, hunters found another shallow grave on the bank of the Knik River, not far from Anchorage; this time it was possible to identify the body in it as twenty-three-year-old Sherry Morrow, a dancer who had disappeared in the previous November. She had been shot three times, and shell casings near the grave indicated that the weapon had been a high-velocity hunting rifle which fires slugs — a .223 Ruger Mini-14. Here, once again, the investigation reached a dead end since it was impossible to interview every owner of such a rifle. An odd feature of the case was that the clothes found in the grave had no bullet holes, indicating the that the girl had been naked when she was killed.

A year later, on 2 September 1983, another grave was found on the bank of the Knik River; the girl in it had also been shot with a Ruger Mini-14. The victim was identified as Paula Golding, an out-of-work secretary who had found herself a job as an exotic dancer in a topless bar. She had started work on 17 April 1983 and had failed to return eight days later, leaving her pay cheque uncollected. The bar owner commented that he had been reluctant to hire her because she had obviously been a 'nice girl', who was only doing this because she was desperate for money. Again, there were no clues to who might have killed her.

Investigators checking the police files made a discovery that looked like a possible lead. On the previous 13 June a policeman had seen a girl running frantically towards him with a handcuff dangling from one of her wrists. She was a seventeen-year-old prostitute, and a medical examination at police headquarters revealed that she had been tortured. She told of being picked up by a red-haired, pockmarked little man with a bad stutter, who had offered her $200 for oral sex. She had accompanied him back to his home in the well-to-do Muldoon area, and down to the basement. There he had told her to take off her clothes, then snapped a handcuff on her, and shackled her to a support pillar. The tortures that followed during the next hour or so included biting her nipples and thrusting the handle of a hammer into her vagina. Finally, he allowed her to dress. Then he told her that he owned a private plane, and was going to take her to a cabin in the wilderness. The girl knew that he intended to kill her — she knew what he looked like and where he lived. So as they crossed the airfield, she broke away and ran; the man gave up the chase when she reached the street lights.

Her description of the 'John' convinced the police that it was a respectable citizen called Robert Hansen, a married man and the owner of a flourishing bakery business, who had been in Anchorage for seventeen years. Driven out to the Muldoon district, the girl identified the house where she had been tortured; it was Hansen's. She also identified the Piper Super Cub aeroplane that belonged to Hansen. The police learned that Hansen was at present alone in the house — his family were on a trip to Europe.

159

When Hansen was told about the charge, he exploded indignantly. He had spent the whole evening dining with two business acquaintances, and they would verify his alibi. In fact, the two men did this. The girl, Hansen said, was simply trying to 'shake him down'. Since it was her word against that of three of Anchorage's most respectable businessmen, it looked as if the case would have to be dropped.

However, after the discovery of Paula Golding's body three months later, the investigating team decided that the case was worth pursuing. If Hansen had tortured a prostitute, then decided to take her out to the wilderness, he could well be the killer they were seeking.

The investigators decided to contact the NCAVC team in Quantico, Virginia. What they wanted was not a 'profile' of the killer – they already had their suspect – but to know whether Robert Hansen was a viable suspect. What the Alaska authorities were able to tell the Quantico team was that Hansen was a well-known big-game hunter, who had achieved celebrity by bagging a Dall sheep with a crossbow in the Kuskokwim Mountains. The answer was that Hansen was indeed a viable suspect. A big-game hunter might well decide to hunt girls. Since he collected trophies, then it would be likely that he had kept items belonging to his victims. If the police could obtain a search warrant, they might well find their evidence.

What was also clear was that if Hansen knew he was a suspect, he would destroy the evidence; it was therefore necessary to work quickly and secretly. The first step was to try to break his alibi. No doubt his friends had been willing to provide a false alibi because it would cost them nothing. If they could be convinced that it might cost them two years in prison for perjury, they might feel differently. The police approached the public prosecutor and asked him to authorise a grand jury to investigate the charges of torture against the prostitute. Then the businessmen were approached, and told that they would be called to repeat their alibi on oath. It worked; both admitted that they had provided Hansen with an alibi merely to help him out of a difficult situation. They agreed to testify to that effect.

Now Hansen was arrested on a charge of rape and kidnapping. A search warrant enabled the police to enter his home. There they found the Ruger Mini-14 rifle, which a ballistics expert identified as the one that had fired the shells found near the graves. Under the floor in the attic the searchers found more rifles, and items of cheap jewellery and adornment, including a Timex watch. Most important of all, they found an aviation map with twenty asterisks marking various spots. Two of these marked the places where the two bodies had so far been found. Another indicated the place where the unidentified corpse of a woman had been found on the south side of the Kenai Peninsula in August 1980, a crime that had not been linked with the Anchorage killings. The investigators discovered that her name was Joanna Messina, and that she had last been seen alive with a red-headed, pockmarked man who stuttered.

At first Hansen denied all knowledge of the killings, but faced with the evidence against him, he finally decided to confess. The twenty asterisks, he admitted, marked graves of prostitutes. But he had not killed all the women he had taken out to the wilderness. What he wanted was oral sex. If the woman satisfied him, he took her back home. If not, he pointed a gun at her, ordered her to strip naked, and then run. He gave the girl a start, then would stalk her as if hunting a game animal. Sometimes the girl would think she had escaped, and Hansen would allow her to think so — until he once again flushed her out and made her run. Finally, when she was too exhausted to run further, he killed her and buried the body. Killing, he said, was an anticlimax; 'the excitement was in the stalking'.

In court on 28 February 1984 the prosecutor told the judge (a jury was unnecessary since Hansen had pleaded guilty): 'Before you sits a monster, an extreme aberration of a human being. A man who has walked among us for seventeen years, selling us doughbuts [sic], Danish buns, coffee, all with a pleasant smile on his face. That smile concealed crimes that would numb the mind.' Judge Ralph Moody then imposed sentences totalling 461 years.

For the investigating detectives, the most interesting part of Hansen's confession was the explanation of why and how he had become a serial killer. Born in a small rural community — Pocahontas, Iowa — he had been an ugly and unpopular child. His schoolfellows found his combination of a stutter and running acne sores repellent. 'Because I looked and talked like a freak, every time I looked at a girl she would turn away.' He had married, but his wife had left him — he felt that it was because he was ugly. He married again, came to Alaska,

161

and started a successful bakery business — his own father's trade. But marriage could not satisfy his raging sexual obsession, his desire to have a docile girl performing oral sex. Since Anchorage had so many topless bars and strip joints, it was a temptation to satisfy his voyeurism in them; then, sexually excited, he needed to pick up a prostitute. What he craved was oral sex, and many of them were unwilling. Hansen would drive out into the woods, then announce what he wanted; if they refused, he produced a gun.

Since he was by nature frugal, he preferred not to pay them. In fact, it emerged in his confession that he was a lifelong thief, and that this was a result of his meanness. 'I hate to spend money. . .I damn near ejaculate in my pants if I could walk into a store and take something. . .I stole more stuff in this damn town than Carter got little green pills.' Yet his next sentence reveals that it was more than simply meanness that made him steal. 'Giving stuff away, you know, walk out in the parking lot and walk to somebody's car, and throw it in the damn car. But I was taking it. . .I was smarter than people in the damn store. It would give me — uh — the same satisfaction — I don't know if you want to call it that — but I got a lot the same feeling as I did with a prostitute.' The link between stealing and oral sex was 'the forbidden'. This seems to explain why many serial killers — Ted Bundy is another example — begin as habitual thieves.

The murders had started, he said, with Joanna Messina, the woman he had met in a town called Seward. She was living in a tent in the woods with her dog, waiting for a job in a cannery. Hansen had got into conversation with her and taken her out to dinner. Afterwards, they went back to her tent, near a gravel pit, where Hansen hoped she would be prepared to let him stay the night. When they were in bed, she told him she needed money. His natural meanness affronted, he called her a whore and shot her with a .22 pistol; then shot her dog, destroyed the camp, and dumped her body into the gravel pit.

According to Hansen, he was violently sick after the murder. Not long afterwards, he picked up a prostitute and asked her if she would fellate him. She agreed, and they drove out along the Eklutna Road. Then, according to Hansen, she became nervous and ran away; when he gave chase, she drew a knife. He took it from her and stabbed her to death. That was how the unidentified corpse known as 'Eklutna Annie' came to lie in a shallow grave, to be dug up by a hungry bear.

This time, Hansen did not feel nauseated. In fact, he said, when he looked back on the murder, he experienced an odd pleasure. Then he began to fantasise about how enjoyable it would be to hunt down a woman like an animal. . .Like so many other serial killers, Hansen had discovered that murder is addictive.

Over the next three years he drove about sixty prostitutes out into the wilderness and demanded oral sex. If they complied satisfactorily, he drove them back to Anchorage. If not, he forced them to strip at gunpoint, then to flee into the woods. When the hunt was over and the girl lay dead, he buried the body, and made a mark on a map — he even tried to guide officers back to some of the murder sites, but had usually forgotten exactly where they were. Once, when they were hovering over Grouse Lake in a helicopter, he pointed down. 'There's a blonde down there. And over there there's a redhead with the biggest tits you ever saw.'

When Robert Hansen was tried in Anchorage, the death sentence had been abolished in Alaska, but it had still been in existence thirty-four years earlier, when another sadistic killer had been tried there for murder. The case of Harvey Carignan provides some interesting parallels with that of Robert Hansen. On Sunday 31 July 1949, stationed in Anchorage, he went on a drinking spree, and picked up a fifty-seven-year-old woman named Laura Showalter. They walked to a nearby park, but when the soldier tried to remove her underwear in broad daylight, she fought him off. The soldier went into a frenzy, and beat her violently with his fists — so violently that her face was virtually obliterated. Then he tried to rape her. At that moment, a man walked towards them. The soldier looked up and snarled: 'Move on.' The man, assuming that they were engaged in lovemaking, hurried away. The next morning he went past the same spot, and found the woman still lying there. The rape had not been completed.

Six weeks later, on 16 September a soldier tried to rape a girl on a deserted Anchorage street at eleven o'clock in the morning; she succeeded in fighting him off. She described him as tall, and as strong as an ape. Later, the police picked up a man answering to her description — a soldier named Harvey Louis Carignan, born in 1927. Carignan eventually confessed to the murder of Laura Showalter, and was sentenced to death. However, the police had omitted a vital step in the legal proceedings — to charge him with the murder before taking him before a marshal for interrogation — and on appeal, the sentence was overturned. Harvey Carignan might have gone free but for the second rape attempt; for this he was sentenced to fifteen years.

He was paroled in 1960, but his freedom did not last long. Four months later he was arrested for burglary and attempted rape; for this he received five and a half years. Paroled in 1964, he was soon sentenced to another fifteen years for burglary. Good conduct earned him so much remission that he was back on the streets by 1969. This time he made a determined attempt to adjust to 'life on the outside', and found himself a wife in Seattle. The marriage soon failed, and Carignan narrowly avoided another life sentence — he was waiting for his wife with a hammer, but it was his stepdaughter who came down to the basement. He packed up and left. A second marriage in 1972 was slightly more successful; he leased a gas station in Seattle and settled into his wife's home. But after almost twenty years in jail, his sexual daydreams were all of teenage girls. On 1 May 1972 he placed an advertisement in the want-ads column of the Seattle *Times*, offering a job at the Sav Mor Garage. It was answered by a fifteen-year-old girl named Kathy Sue Miller, who wanted a job for the summer vacation. The next day, she went off to meet the owner of the station. It was the last time she was seen alive by her family. Her schoolbooks were found in Everett, twenty-six miles from her home. Harvey Carignan was questioned by police — he had been away for several hours on that day — but he continued to deny meeting Kathy. Her violated body was found on 3 June 1972 among dense undergrowth north of Everett. She had been killed by a tremendous blow from some blunt instrument. There was still no proof that Harvey Carignan had ever met Kathy Miller.

When he became tired of being questioned by the police, Carignan decided to leave town. He drove south to California. Between February 1972 and December 1973, eleven girls were murdered in the Sonoma County area, near San Francisco. Most had been battered to death, one with a crushing blow to the back of the skull, and seven had been raped. Carignan has never been accused of any of these crimes, but they are consistent with his method. Early in 1974 he moved back to his former home, Minneapolis. On 28 June a woman waiting at a bus stop was knocked unconscious by a blow to the back of the head. When she woke up, she was in a pick-up truck with a scowling, bald-headed man. When he tried to place her hand on his flies, she made a grab for the door handle. He seized her by the hair, but it proved to be a wig; the woman fled, leaving it in his hand.

On 9 September 1973 a thirteen-year-old runaway named Jerri Billings was hitchhiking in north-eastern Minneapolis. The pick-up truck that stopped for her was driven by a huge man with a bald head and a receding, ape-like chin. When they had driven a short distance, he unzipped his fly, then grabbed her by the back of the neck and forced her head down to his penis; she was made to perform fellatio on him. Then, still driving fast, he order her to remove her jeans and panties. She thought it was a preliminary to rape, but was mistaken. What he did was to force a hammer handle into her vagina, and move it up and down as though it were a penis. After that he made her fellate him again. When she tried to raise her head, he hit her a blow with the hammer. Soon after this he stopped in a cornfield, and made an attempt to sodomise her. Unable to penetrate, he made her fellate him again, then − amazingly − allowed her to dress and drove her to the nearest town. He ordered her to tell no-one what had happened. She kept her secret for nearly two months, then went to the police. They had no leads on the rapist, and the investigation lost momentum.

In January 1974 Carignan offered help to three Jehovah's Witnesses whose car had broken down. One of them was an attractive twenty-eight-year-old named Eileen Hunley. In May of that year, they began to see a great deal of one another, but by July, she was disillusioned; he drank too much and had a hair-trigger temper. She told him she did not want to see him any more. On 10 August 1974 Eileen Hunley vanished.

A month later, on 8 September two teenage girls, June Lynch and Lisa King, were hitchhiking in Minneapolis when a big middle-aged man stopped to offer them a lift, and offered them money if they would help him bring down a truck from Mora. He turned off into some woods and asked June Lynch to go

165

with him. Lisa King heard her friend scream and ran to see what was the matter. June was lying on the ground, bleeding from the head, and the man had gone. In hospital, it was established that June had been hit on the head with a hammer seven times and was suffering severe concussion.

On 14 September the big man driving a green Chevrolet picked up a nineteen-year-old girl named Gwen Burton, whose car had broken down, and offered to drive home to get tools. When they were outside town, he grabbed her by the neck and forced her to fellate him. After this he ripped off her jeans and underwear, then throttled her. She recovered consciousness to find herself lying on a blanket in a field. The man forced her to commit oral sodomy, then inserted a hammer handle into her vagina, tearing the hymen. After that he punched her in the stomach, knocking the wind out of her, and battered her with the hammer.

When Gwen Burton woke up again, she succeeded in crawling to a road, where a tractor stopped for her. In hospital, her life was saved by immediate surgery — there were fragments of bone in the brain tissue. She recovered eventually, but her health was permanently impaired.

On 18 September 1974 the body of a woman was found in Sherburne County, north of Minneapolis; she had been killed with hammer blows, and her vagina had been lacerated by some hard object, probably a hammer handle. She was eventually identified as Eileen Hunley, missing since August.

A few days later, the man in the green Chevrolet picked up two girls, and offered them twenty-five dollars to help him recover a car. On a lonely road he began to talk about rape, and when one of the girls asked how far they still had to go, he hit her in the mouth. Their abductor had to stop for gas, and the girls managed to escape.

On 20 September an eighteen-year-old girl named Kathy Schultz disappeared from Minneapolis; the following day, her violated body was found by two hunters forty miles north of Minneapolis; she had been killed with hammer blows.

Now, at least, the police had several good descriptions of the man they sought: middle-aged, balding and very big, and driving a green Chevrolet. On 24 September 1974 two policeman on patrol saw a man who answered that description, and watched as he approached a green Chevrolet. When they pulled up behind the car, it drove off at speed; they eventually forced it to move over. The driver identified himself as Harvey Carignan. When four of the attacker's victims unhesitatingly picked him out in a line-up, Harvey Carignan's career of rape and murder was at an end.

On 14 February 1975 Harvey Carignan was tried on charges relating to Gwen Burton, the girl who had been sodomised and left for dead.

The line taken by Carignan's defence was that he was guilty but insane. Carignan himself told the jury that he had picked up Gwen Burton because God had told him to. In fact, he insisted that he frequently held conversations with God, and that it was God who told him to kill. The jurors chose to disbelieve that he was insane, and found him guilty on all counts. Before sentencing, he was tried for the attack on the thirteen-year-old schoolgirl, Jerri Billings. This time, Carignan simply denied that he had ever seen her. Again the jury disbelieved him, and found him guilty. Harvey Carignan was sentenced to sixty years in prison. Even with one third remission for good conduct, this meant that he would serve forty years.

In the following year, Carignan saved the taxpayers the expense of a trial when he pleaded guilty to murdering Kathy Schultz. He unexpectedly pleaded not guilty to murdering Eileen Hunley. Again, the evidence was against him, and he was sentenced to life imprisonment.

After the Gwen Burton trial, Harvey Carignan was sent to St Peter State Hospital for a psychiatric examination. The story he told made it clear that here was yet another classic case of the serial killer syndrome. He had been an illegitimate child and the father – a young doctor – declined to stand by the girl he had made pregnant. Harvey was an undersized, lonely child who wet the bed far beyond the usual age. His mother had been only seventeen at the time of his birth, and she showed little affection for the child who had disrupted her life. 'She was pretty mean,' Carignan told psychiatrists. His mother married when he was four, and bore a second son. Harvey's life became even more lonely and loveless. As the bedwetting became worse, he was sent to live with an aunt and uncle. They soon tired of him and sent him back. When he also began to steal, he was sent to a reform school in Mandan, North Dakota. He was only just twelve years old, and he stayed there until he was eighteen, old enough to join the army.

In order to escape from a life that he found intolerable,

Harvey Carignan became an obsessive reader and daydreamer. He was, in fact, highly intelligent, and in different circumstances, would probably have done well. In spite of his almost permanent scowl, he possessed a great deal of charm; in jail he was a model prisoner, and one of his warders described him as 'a perfect gentleman'.

Perhaps the strangest part of Carignan's account of his childhood is his insistence that he was sexually assaulted by several older women; this, he insisted, was what made him feel defensive and hostile towards women, so that any sign of rejection turned to uncontrollable rage. The psychiatrists were inclined to doubt the truth of the story; but there can be little doubt that Carignan believed it happened. It was his rage at being rejected by an older woman in Anchorage, Alaska, that led to his first murder, and to the death sentence that almost ended his career of murder three decades earlier.

In her book on the case, *The Want-Ad Killer*, Ann Rule comments: 'There is, today, no known treatment that is effective in changing the structure of the antisocial personality. The defect is believed to originate in early childhood, usually before the age of five, and once the child is so damaged, his complete lack of compassion for others only becomes more solidly entrenched as he grows to manhood.'

In Carignan's case, as in that of Cameron Hooker, Robert Poulin, Harvey Glatman, and other killers discussed in this chapter, the frustrated craving for affection turned into a craving for power over the women who denied it. This seems to explain why, although normally sexually potent, Carignan preferred to violate his victims with a hammer handle. Rape with a penis would have seemed close to an act of love-making, and Carignan had no intention of expressing love: only rage, and the desire to obliterate.

While a psychologist would undoubtedly classify Folk, Hansen and Carignan as 'degenerates', none could be described as a psychotic: that is, as clinically insane.

Reinhardt comments: 'While I do not attempt here to draw fine distinctions between "degeneracy" and various forms of psychoses, there is no question in my mind that many sadists, as well as other sexually perverted types, suffer marked psychoses' — in other words, *are* technically insane. Reinhardt is discussing a sadistic pervert named Albert Fish, who was executed in Sing Sing in January 1936. Fish remains the classic example of the psychotic serial killer.

On 28 May 1928 a mild-looking old man called on the family of a doorman named Albert Budd in a basement in Manhattan. He explained he had come in answer to a job advertisement placed in a New York newspaper by Budd's eighteen-year-old son Edward. His name, he said, was Frank Howard, and he owned a farm on Long Island. The old man so charmed the Budds that the following day they allowed him to take their ten-year-old daughter Grace to a party; she left in a white confirmation dress, holding Howard's hand. The Budds never saw Grace again; the address at which the party was supposed to be held proved fictitious, and no farmer by the name of Frank Howard could be traced on Long Island. The kidnap received wide publicity, and the police investigated hundreds of tips. Detective Will King of the Missing Persons Bureau became particularly obsessed with the crime and travelled thousands of miles in search of 'Frank Howard'.

Six years later, the Budds received an unsigned letter that was clearly from the kidnapper. He stated that he had taken Grace Budd to an empty house in Westchester, then left her picking flowers while he went inside and stripped off his clothes; then he leaned out of the upstairs window and called her in. Confronted by this skinny naked man, Grace began to cry and tried to run away; he seized her and strangled her. Then he cut her in half, and took the body back home, where he ate parts of it. 'How sweet her little ass was, roasted in the oven. It took me nine days to eat her entire body. I did not fuck her tho I could of had I wished.' (In fact, Fish was to admit to his attorney that this was untrue.) Finally, he took the bones back to the cottage and buried them in the garden.

With a brilliant piece of detective work, Will King traced the writer — the letter had arrived in an envelope with the inked-out logo of a chauffeurs' benevolent association on the flap. One of the chauffeurs finally admitted that he had taken some of the association's stationery and left it in a room he used to rent on East 52nd Street. This now proved to be rented by a tenant who called himself A.H.Fish, and his handwriting in the boarding house register was identical with that of the letter writer. King kept watch on the room for three weeks before Albert Fish — the mild little old man — returned. He agreed unhesitatingly to go to headquarters for questioning, but at the street door, suddenly lunged at King with a razor in each hand. King disarmed and handcuffed him. Back at police headquarters, Fish made no attempt to deny the murder of Grace Budd. He had gone to her home, he explained, with the intention of killing her brother Edward, but when Grace had sat on his knee during dinner, had decided that he wanted to eat her.

He took the police to the cottage in Westchester, where they unearthed the bones of Grace Budd. Later, under intensive questioning, he admitted to killing about four hundred children since 1910. (The figure has never been confirmed, and a judge involved in the case placed the true figure at sixteen.)

Soon after his arrest, Fish was visited by a psychiatrist named Fredrick Wertham, who would appear for the defence. 'He looked', wrote Wertham, 'like a meek and innocuous little old man, gentle and benevolent, friendly and polite. If you wanted someone to entrust your children to, he would be the one you would choose.' When Fish realised that Wertham really wanted to understand him, he became completely open and forthcoming.

Fish was a strange paradox of a man. His face lit up when he talked of his twelve-year-old grandchild, and he was obviously sincere when he said: 'I love children and was always soft-hearted.' He was also deeply religious, and read his Bible continuously. The answer to the paradox, Wertham soon concluded, was that Fish was insane. He genuinely believed that God told him to murder children.

Albert Hamilton Fish had been born in Washington, DC, in 1870; his father, a riverboat captain, was seventy-five at the time. Various members of the family had mental problems and one suffered from religious mania. One brother was feeble-minded and another an alcoholic. The father had died when Fish was five years old, and he was placed in an orphanage, from which he regularly ran away. On leaving school he was apprenticed to a house painter, and this remained his profession for the rest of his life. Access to other people's homes also gave him access to children. He was twenty-eight when he first married, but his wife eloped with the lodger. Later, there were three more marriages, all bigamous.

Fish talked with complete frankness about his sex life —

he had always enjoyed writing obscene letters, and no doubt confessing to Wertham gave him the same kind of pleasure. Wertham wrote:

'Fish's sexual life was of unparalleled perversity. . .I found no published case that would even nearly compare with his. . .There was no known perversion that he did not practise and practise frequently.

'Sado-masochism directed against children, particularly boys, took the lead in his sexual regressive development. "I have always had a desire to inflict pain on others and to have others inflict pain on me. I always seemed to enjoy anything that hurt. The desire to inflict pain, that is all that is uppermost." Experiences with excreta of every imaginable kind were practised by him, actively and passively. He took bits of cotton wool, saturated them with alcohol, inserted them in his rectum and set fire to them. He also did this to his child victims. Finally, and clearly also on a sexual basis, he developed a craving going back to one of the arch-crimes of humanity — cannibalism.

'I elicited from him a long history of how he preyed on children. In many instances — I stated under oath later "at least a hundred" — he seduced them or bribed them with small sums of money or forced them and attacked them. He often worked in public buildings and had an excuse for spending times in cellars and basements and even garrets. He would put on his painters' overalls over his nude body, and that permitted him to undress in a moment . . .

'Most, if not all, of his victims came from the poorer classes. He told me that he selected coloured children especially, because the authorities didn't pay much attention when they were hurt or missing. For example, he once paid a small coloured girl five dollars regularly to bring him little coloured boys. . .Frequently after a particularly brutal episode he would change his address completely. . .Altogether he roamed over twenty-three states, from New York to Montana. "And I have had children in every state." He also made a habit of writing letters to women, trying to persude them to join him in whipping boys.

'Fish told me that for years he had been sticking needles into his body in the region near his genitals, in the area between the rectum and the scrotum. He told me of doing it to other people too, especially to children. At first, he said, he had only

171

stuck these needles in and pulled them out again. They were needles of assorted sizes, some of them big sail needles. Then he had stuck others in so far that he was unable to get them out, and they stayed there. "They're in there now," he said. "I put them up under the spine. . .I did put one in the scrotum too; but I couldn't stand the pain."

'I checked this strange story on a series of X-rays of his pelvic and abdominal region. They showed plainly twenty-nine needles inside his body. One X-ray of the pelvic region showed twenty-seven. They were easily recognisable as needles. . .Some of them must have been years in his body, for they were eroded to an extent that would have taken at least seven years. Some of the needles were fragmented by this erosion so that only bits of steel remained in the tissue.'

Ih his middle fifties, says Wertham, Fish began to develop psychosis with delusions and hallucinations. (He was fifty-eight when he murdered Grace Budd.) 'At times he identified himself with God and felt that he should sacrifice his own son. He tried to stick needles under his fingernails but could not stand the pain. He made the poignant remark: "If only pain were not so painful!"

'He had visions of Christ and his angels. . .He heard them saying words like "stripes", "rewardeth" and "delighteth". And he connected these words with verses from the Bible and elaborated them delusionally with his sadistic wishes. "Stripes means to lash them, you know."

'He felt driven to torment and kill children. Sometimes he would gag them, tie them up and beat them, although he preferred not to gag them, circumstances permitting, for he liked to hear their cries. He felt that he was ordered by God to castrate little boys. . ."I am not insane. I am just queer." After murdering Grace Budd he had cooked parts of the body with carrots and onions and strips of bacon, and ate them over a period of nine days. During all this time he was in a state of sexual excitement.

'His state of mind while he described these things in minute detail was a peculiar mixture. He spoke in a matter-of-fact way, like a housewife describing her favourite methods of cooking. You had to remind yourself that this was a little girl that he was talking about. But at times his tone of voice and facial expression indicated a kind of satisfaction and ecstatic thrill. However you define the medical and legal borders of sanity, this certainly is beyond that border.'

It became apparent that Fish was a wanted killer who had become known as 'the Brooklyn Vampire', who committed four child murders in 1933 and 1934, luring little girls to a basement, flogging them, then garrotting them with a rope. In 1932, a sixteen-year-old girl had been killed and mutilated near Massapequa, Long Island, where Fish was painting a house. Other murders almost certainly committed by Fish were those of seven-year-old Francis X. McDonnell on Staten Island in 1924, four-year-old Billy Gaffney in Brooklyn in 1927, and eleven-year-old Yetta Abramowitz, who was strangled and mutilated in the Bronx in 1927. (Billy Gaffney's mother subsequently had a series of nervous breakdowns from grief.) Detective Will King, who investigated these murders, was not allowed to introduce them as evidence, since the D.A. was anxious to prove that Fish was sane, and too many murders might throw doubt on this.

To Fish's delight, he was sentenced to death — he remarked with unconscious humour that being electrocuted would be 'the supreme thrill of my life'. When he was on Death Row, the prison chaplain had to ask him not to 'holler and howl' so loud as he masturbated during services. In the execution chamber on 16 January 1936 he mumbled 'I don't know why I'm here' just before the switch was thrown.

Wertham records that he tried hard to get Fish's sentence commuted. 'To execute a sick man is like burning witches', he told the prison governor. He went on to make this important observation — even more relevant today than it was in 1936: 'Science is prediction. The science of psychiatry is advanced enough that with proper examination such a man as Fish can be detected and confined before the perpetration of these outrages, instead of inflicting extreme penalties afterwards. The authorities had this man, but the records show that they paid no attention.' Understandably, the governor was unmoved. Like the D.A, he probably recognised that Fish was legally insane, but felt that it made no difference — that there was no point in burdening society with the keep of such a man. What Wertham had failed to recognise is that the execution of a murderer like Fish actually serves a ritual function. The public wants to see sadistic killers executed, in the same way that children want fairy stories to end with the defeat of the wicked giant. It serves the purpose of exorcising the horror.

In December 1927 twelve-year-old Marion Parker, daughter

of a Los Angeles banker, was kidnapped. When her father went to the appointed spot to pay the ransom, he saw his daughter sitting in a car beside the kidnapper; the man took the money and promised to let Marion out at the end of the street. She proved to be dead, her hands and legs hacked off, her body disembowelled, and her eyelids propped open with wire. A bloodstained suitcase found the next day was traced back to a man named William Edward Hickman, who had a grudge against Marion's father, and he was eventually arrested in Washington State. Psychiatric examination revealed that he was insane, believing that angels had ordered him to kidnap Marion. Yet although his insanity was beyond doubt, so was his ultimate execution; the horror of the crime demanded the ritual exorcism in the death chamber, or at least in a prison cell. The serial killer has no monopoly on irrationality.

What turns a man into a sado-masochist? In the case of Albert Fish, fortunately, we know the answer. In 1875, his father suffered a heart attack in the Pennsylvania Station. Unable to provide for twelve children, Ellen Fish was forced to consign most of them to an orphanage. The five-year-old boy had no idea why he had been suddenly abandoned; he was deeply miserable, and at first ran away repeatedly. Discipline in the St John's Refuge was rigid and severe; the matron made them pray for hours every day and made them memorise chapters from the Bible. The slightest infringement of discipline was punished by flogging, administered by the matron. Fish discovered that he enjoyed being whipped on his naked bottom. His fellow orphans teased him because punishment always gave him an erection. What they did not know was that watching other boys being whipped also produced sexual excitement in him. Since it was a co-educational institution (although the boys and girls were kept strictly segregated outside class) there was naturally a great deal of sex talk. After a while, the young Fish was initiated into masturbation and other sex games. By the time his mother took him away from the orphanage two years later – she had obtained a government job – sado-masochism had been firmly 'imprinted' in the seven-year-old boy. He told Wertham of an occasion when he and some friends had soaked a horse's tail in kerosene and set it on fire.

He was a sickly and introverted child, and a fall from a cherry tree produced concussion; thereafter he suffered severe headaches, dizzy spells and a severe stutter. (It has been pointed out that a large number of serial killers have suffered head injuries in childhood.) He continued to wet the bed for many years, and his companions taunted him about it. Fish's reaction to the jeers was to retreat into a world of daydreams. At about this time he insisted on being called Albert (the name of a dead younger brother) rather than Hamilton because his schoolmates called him Ham and Eggs. He began to suffer from convulsive fits.

The daydreams were often of being beaten or watching others being beaten. When his elder brother Walter came home from the Navy and showed Albert books with pictures of naked men and women, and told him stories of cannibalism which he claimed to have witnessed, more sado-masochistic traits were 'imprinted'. His favourite reading was Poe's story 'The Pit and the Pendulum', with its details of mental torture, and this led him on to study everything he could find about the Spanish Inquisition. He became a devotee of true murder cases, and began carrying newspaper clippings in his pockets until they disintegrated. (He was carrying an account of the Hanover 'butcher' Fritz Haarmann when he was arrested.) Yet at the same time he continued to be a devoted student of the Bible, and to dream of becoming a clergyman. Having become habituated to sexual and religious fantasy from an early age, he saw no contradiction between them.

When he was twelve, Fish began a homosexual relationship with a telegraph boy who excited him by describing what he had seen in brothels. This youth also introduced to Fish peculiar practices such as drinking urine and tasting excreta. By his late teens, Fish was tormented with a violent and permanent sexual appetite that never left him alone. (But this is less unusual than it sounds; the majority of teenagers could tell a similar story.) When he moved to New York at the age of twenty, he quickly became a male prostitute, and spent much of his weekends at public baths where he could watch boys. It was at this time that he began raping small boys. By now the pattern was set, and even a marriage – arranged by his mother – failed to change it. A period in Sing Sing – for embezzlement – virtually ended the marriage, and he returned to homosexuality. After his wife's desertion, he began to show signs of mental disturbance; he heard voices, and on one occasion wrapped himself up in a carpet and explained that he was following the instructions of St John. Then began his period of wandering around the United States and working as a painter and decorator; during this time, he told Wertham, he raped more than a hundred children, mostly boys under six.

When he was twenty-eight, a male lover took him to see the waxworks gallery in a museum; there he was fascinated by a medical display showing the bisection of a penis. He returned to see it many times, and 'imprinting' occurred again, leading to a new obsession with castration. During a relationship with a mentally defective homosexual, Fish tied him up and tried to castrate him. The rush of blood frightened him and he fled. Now he began adding castration to his rapes, on one occasion severing a child's penis with a pair of scissors. He began going to brothels where he could be spanked and whipped. He committed his first murder − of a male homosexual − in Wilmington in 1910. In 1919 he mutilated and tortured to death a mentally retarded boy. From now on, murder also became a part of his pattern of perversion.

Here, then, we are able to study in unusual detail the development of a sado-masochistic obsession. It is impossible to doubt that it began in the St John's Refuge in 1875, when he was first whipped by the matron of the Episcopal Sisterhood. It is possible to say with some degree of confidence that if Fish had not been sent to an orphanage at the age of five, he would never have developed into one of the most remarkable examples of 'polymorphous perversion' in the history of sexual abnormality.

Then why did his fellow orphans never achieve the same dubious notoriety? Presumably because they lacked his intensely introverted temperament, the tendency to brood and daydream about sex and pain. In short, they lacked the ability to retreat so totally into a world of fantasy. It is difficult to avoid the conclusion that what turned Fish into a dangerous pervert was precisely the same tendency to morbid brooding and fantasy that turned Edgar Allan Poe into a writer of genius.

How far does this enable us to understand the serial killer? It enables us, at least, to grasp that there is a link between his abnormality and what we recognise as normality. Fish was turned into a serial killer by a kind of 'hothouse' conditioning that led him to spend most of his childhood brooding about

176

sex. We must bear in mind that he was born in 1870, at a time when sex crime was almost non-existent. By the time of the Jack the Ripper murders, Fish was eighteen – old enough, in theory, to have committed them himself. But he was still living in a world of Victorian morality and Victorian behaviour, where 'dirty books' were still banned – most of the 'obscenity' prosecutions of that period now strike us as incomprehensible – and prostitution regarded with deep disapproval. Fish became a fully-fledged pervert by accident, starting with the accident of being sent to an orphanage at the age of five. If Fish had been alive today, he would have had no difficulty finding material to feed his fantasies, from hard porn magazines to 'snuff videos'. In most large American cities he would have found streets lined with male and female 'hookers' willing to cater to every perversion. It becomes possible to see why, some twenty-five years after the relaxation of the laws governing pornography, serial crime suddenly began to develop into an epidemic.

There is an important basic difference between Albert Fish and the other killers in this chapter. Fish enjoyed pain, and so when he inflicted it on his victims, he felt – in some obscure and muddled way – that he was doing them a favour. The impulse that drove Hooker, Glatman, Fearn, Folk and even Robert Poulin was pure sexual aggression, the will to power. But the development of the obsession followed the same path in all of them, including Fish: fantasy fuelled by frustration. The fantasy, in turn, is subject to 'the law of diminishing returns', so that it becomes distorted and unbalanced. This seems to be one of the few basic rules in the development of sadists and sex killers.

Five

The Jekyll and Hyde Syndrome

It seems self-evident that, if Fish had not been caught, he would have gone on killing indefinitely; but is this obvious 'truth' as incontestable as it seems? A man who does not wish to be caught does not write a letter in a traceable envelope, with the telltale initials merely inked out. It is almost as if he wanted to be caught — or as if, at least, he no longer cared. This seems to be a version of the 'suicide syndrome' discussed in the first chapter. (One third of all murderers commit suicide.)

To recognise the 'suicide syndrome' is also to recognise that sadistic killers are not really a species apart from other human beings. They become suicidal for basically the same reason that anyone else does: because they recognise that their lives are unfulfilled, and are likely to remain so. When the killer recognises clearly that his actions have turned him into a social outcast, a 'monster', the result may be suicide, or some absurd 'mistake' that leads to his arrest. He is, in effect, two people, a Dr Jekyll and Mr Hyde. The 'mistake' is Jekyll's attempt to destroy Hyde.

On 10 December 1945 a maid entering the Chicago apartment of a thirty-year-old ex-Wave named Frances Brown was alarmed to see that the pillow on the bed was bloodstained; in the bathroom she found the woman's naked body draped over the side of the bath. On the wall over the bed, someone had scrawled in lipstick:

> For heavens
> sake catch me
> Before I kill more
> I cannot control myself

Frances Brown was kneeling beside the bath, and she was naked. A pyjama top had been folded loosely round her neck; when this was removed, police discovered a knife driven in with such force that it protruded from the other side of her throat. She had also been shot twice. The body had been carefully washed after death, and wet bloodstained towels lay on the floor.

Four weeks later, on the morning of 7 January 1946, James E. Degnan went into the bedroom of his seven-year-old daughter Suzanne, and saw that she was not in her bed, and that the window was wide open. He called the police, and it was a policeman who found the note on the child's chair; it said she had been kidnapped and demanded $20,000 for her return. Later that afternoon, Suzanne's head was discovered beneath a nearby manhole cover. In another sewer police found the child's left leg. The right leg was found in another sewer, and the torso in a third. The arms were discovered – also in a sewer – some weeks later. The case shocked the nation, but the police seemed to be unable to develop any definite leads.

Six months later, on 26 June 1946, a young man walked into an apartment building in Chicago, and entered the apartment of Mr and Mrs Pera through the open door; Mrs Pera was in the kitchen preparing dinner. A neighbour who had seen the young man enter called to Mrs Pera to ask if she knew a man had walked into her apartment. The young man immediately left, but the neighbour called him to stop. Instead, he ran down the stairs. He pointed a gun at a man who tried to stop him, then ran out of the building. Minutes later, he knocked on the door of a nearby apartment and asked the woman who answered for a glass of water, explaining he felt ill. She sensed something wrong and rang the police. In fact, an off-duty policeman had already seen the fleeing youth, and ran after him. When cornered, the young man fired three shots at the policeman; all missed. As other police answered the call, the burglar and the police grappled on the floor. Then one of the policemen hit him on the head – three times – with a flowerpot, and knocked him unconscious.

The prisoner turned out to be a seventeen-year-old youth named William George Heirens, and he had spent some time in a correctional institution for burglary. When his fingerprints were taken, they were found to match one found on the Degnan ransom note, and another found in the apartment of Frances

Brown. In the prison hospital, Heirens was given the 'truth drug' sodium pentathol, and asked: 'Did you kill Suzanne Degnan?' Heirens answered: 'George cut her up.' At first he insisted that George was a real person, a boy five years his senior whom he met at school. Later, he claimed that George was his own invisible alter-ego. 'He was just a realization of mine, but he seemed real to me.' Heirens also admitted to a third murder, that of a forty-three-year-old widow, Mrs Josephine Ross, who had awakened while he was burgling her apartment on 5 June 1945; Heirens stabbed her through the throat. In addition to this, he had attacked a woman named Evelyn Peterson with an iron bar when she started to wake up during a burglary, then tied her up with lamp cord; he had also fired shots through windows at two women who had been sitting in their rooms with the curtains undrawn.

The story of William Heirens, as it emerged in his confessions, and in interviews with his parents, was almost predictably typical of a serial sex killer. Born on 15 November 1928, he had been a forceps delivery. He was an underweight baby, and cried and vomited a great deal. At the age of seven months he fell down twelve cement steps into the basement and landed on his head; after that he had nightmares about falling. He was three years old when a brother was born, and he was sent away to the home of his grandmother. He was frequently ill as a child, and broke his arm at the age of nine. The family background was far from happy; his mother had two nervous breakdowns accompanied by paralysis, and his father's business failed several times.

Heirens matured very early sexually – he had his first emission at the age of nine. Soon after this, he began stealing women's panties from clotheslines and basement washrooms, and putting them on. (After his arrest, police found forty pairs of pink and blue rayon panties in a box in his grandmother's attic.) He came to think of sex as something 'dirty' and forbidden. This was confirmed when, at the age of thirteen, he walked into the school washroom and found two boys playing sexually with a mentally retarded boy; he refused to join in. Being a good-looking boy, he was attractive to girls; on eight occasions he attempted some form of sex play, touching their breasts or pressing their legs, but this had the effect of upsetting him so much that he cried. There was a deep conflict between his sexual obsession and his rigid Catholic

Harvey Murray Glatman, a Californian strangler and power-motivated serial killer, photographed and raped his female victims before murdering them in lonely desert country. At his trial, Glatman asked the judge to impose the death penalty – a wish that was granted; he died in the San Quentin gas chamber in August 1959.

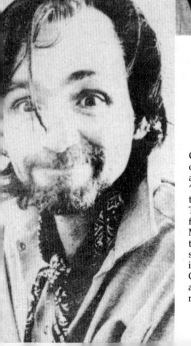

Charles Manson's drug-crazed gang of male and female hippies (known as 'The Family') were convicted of 9 'motiveless' murders – including that of Hollywood film star Sharon Tate (then 8 months pregnant), 4 friends and her houseboy in 1969. Manson and 7 of the gang were sentenced to death in 1972, but these sentences were commuted to life imprisonment a year later when the Californian Supreme Court voted to abolish the death penalty for murder.

In 15 months of random break-in crimes in the mid-1980s, Richard Ramirez – alias 'the Night Stalker', a 28-year-old drifter, Satanist and serial killer from El Paso, Texas – terrified suburban Los Angeles with an orgy of 13 murders plus the shooting, stabbing and sexual abuse of many other victims (children included). When sentenced in September 1989 to die in the gas chamber, he jeered, 'See you in Disneyland.' Ramirez is now on Death Row awaiting an appeal hearing.

George Metesky, alias the 'Mad Bomber' of New York City and on the police wanted list for 17 years, made criminal history in 1957 as the first urban terrorist to be caught with the aid of psychological profiling – thanks to psychiatrist Dr James A. Brussell MD. Metesky, aged 54, was found unfit to plead and spent the rest of his life in an institution for the criminally insane.

Robert Diaz, one of the earliest 'medical' serial killers and a Los Angeles male night nurse who liked to 'play doctor', was found guilty of murdering 12 patients with injections of Lidocaine (a powerful heart drug) 'for his own amusement and entertainment', and sentenced in March 1984 to die in the gas chamber.

This picture shows homosexual serial killer John Wayne Gacy, dressed as a clown at a children's party. When Chicago police raided Gacy's home in 1978, they discovered a trap door which led down to a charnel-house filled with the bodies, bones and decaying remains of many of his victims. All were youths or young men thought to have been homosexually raped and strangled. After confessing to 32 murders Gacy was imprisoned for life in 1980.

In the hot summer nights of 1976 David Berkowitz – aged 23, a tubby, smiling, paranoid schizophrenic who lived alone in a wretchedly furnished room – began shooting couples parked in cars in New York City, killing 6 and wounding 7. In a letter to the police he wrote, 'I am the Son of Sam,' and said he hunted women because they were 'tasty meat'. He was traced a year later via a parking ticket – issued while he made his last attack. After pleading guilty at his trial he was sentenced to 365 years' imprisonment.

Albert DeSalvo, alias the Boston Strangler, reduced the capital city of Massachusetts to panic in the early 1960s by killing 13 women in 18 months – but was never charged with their murder, even though he confessed to the crimes. After plea-bargaining, he was imprisoned for a series of lesser offences (in the hope of obtaining psychiatric treatment) but after six years was himself murdered, in November 1973, by an unknown fellow-prisoner.

Theodore Robert ('Ted') Bundy, possibly the most notorious of all modern US serial killers, was a handsome Peeping Tom who confessed to 23 murders (and is believed to have committed at least 34) before his arrest in Florida in April 1978. He was charged with 3 murders only, complimented by the judge for the way he conducted his own defence – but eventually died in the electric chair in January 1989, after a decade of appeals.

Cameron Hooker, a married man and a psychopath described as 'an accident of internal wiring', kidnapped a 20-year-old hitchhiker in 1977 and kept her captive in his home at Red Bluff, California for 7 years as his 'sex slave'. In 1985 Hooker was sentenced to 104 years' imprisonment on charges of kidnap, rape and torture.

Ed Kemper, a serial killer from a broken home, showed all the 'early warning signs' of violence to come as a child (playing death games with his sister, beheading her dolls and later cutting the family cat into pieces). He grew into a necrophiliac lust killer standing 6ft 9in tall and weighing 300lbs, with a hatred for his dominant mother. Kemper offered lifts to attractive female university students (the type of girl his mother said he could never date), then shot and decapitated them before sexually abusing the headless corpses. Finally, in 1973, then aged 25, he murdered and decapitated his mother and her closest friend and later gave himself up to the police. He was judged legally sane and imprisoned for life for 8 murders.

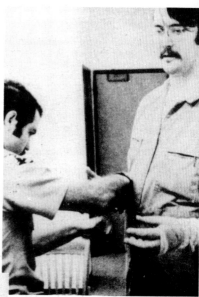

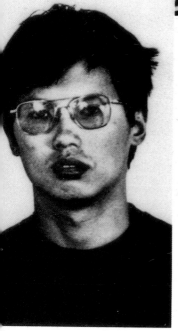

Charles Ng (pronounced 'Ing'), a young Chinese currently serving a 4½-year sentence in Calgary, Canada for armed robbery, is wanted for questioning by the US authorities for his alleged part in a series of sex-slave murders committed in Calaveras County, North California in the mid-1980s. Former US Marine Leonard Lake, Ng's alleged accomplice in the sex-slave murders, committed suicide by swallowing a cyanide pill when arrested by police in San Francisco on an unrelated charge in June 1985.

The Supervisory Special Agents of the FBI's renowned 'A Team'. *From left to right:* John E. Douglas, Unit Chief of the Behavioural Science Unit (Investigative Support Wing); Judson Ray; Larry G. Ankrom; Thomas F. Salp; Alan E. Burgess (former Unit Chief of that wing and Administrator of the National Centre for the Analysis of Violent Crime); Gregg O. McCrary; James A. Wright; Peter Smerick; Stephen R. Mardigian. Missing from the photograph are Alan C. Brantley; Stephen E. Etter; and William Hagmaier III.

upbringing. He found normal sexual stimulation repellent. From the age of thirteen he had been burgling apartments, entering through the window, and experiencing sexual excitement – to the point of emission – as he did so. After this, he lost interest in underwear, and began to experience his sexual fulfilment by entering strange apartments through the window. He often urinated or defecated on the floor. He also began lighting small fires.

He was arrested for the first time in the same year – 1942 – charged with eleven burglaries and suspected of fifty; in many of them he had stolen guns and women's dresses. He was sentenced to probation and sent to a semi-correctional Catholic institution. After a year there he transferred to a Catholic academy, where he proved to be a brilliant student – so much so that he was allowed to skip the freshman year at the University of Chicago. Back in Chicago, the sexual obsession remained as powerful as ever, and led to more burglaries. If he resisted for long, he began to experience violent headaches. On one occasion, he put his clothes in the washroom and threw the key inside in order to make it impossible to go out; halfway through the night, the craving became too strong, and he crawled along the house gutter to retrieve his clothes.

Once inside an apartment, he was in such a state of intense excitement that any interruption would provoke an explosion of violence. This is why he knocked Evelyn Peterson unconscious with an iron bar when she stirred in her sleep. On another occasion he was preparing to enter what he thought was an empty apartment when a woman moved inside; he immediately fired his gun at her, but missed.

None of the victims was raped – the thought of actual sexual intercourse still scared him. Sexual fulfilment came from the 'forbiddenness', the excitement of knowing he was committing a crime. After the ejaculation, he felt miserable; he believed that he was a kind of Jekyll and Hyde. He even invented a name for his Mr Hyde – George. Although he later admitted that the invention of an alter-ego was partly an attempt to fool the psychiatrists, there can be no doubt that he felt that he was periodically 'possessed' by a monster. This is why he scrawled the message in lipstick on the wall after killing Frances Brown. It may also explain why he eventually courted arrest by wandering into a crowded apartment block in the late afternoon and entering a flat in which a married woman was

181

cooking the dinner as she waited for her husband to return from work. Dr Jekyll was turning in Mr Hyde. In July 1946 Heirens was sentenced to three terms of life imprisonment in Joliet penitentiary.

It is clear that, unlike most of the sex killers discussed in the previous chapter, Heirens was young enough to experience deep guilt about what he was doing. The same is true of Heinrich Pommerencke, a German serial killer of the postwar years.

On the morning of 9 June 1959 a tall, slim young man with a girlish complexion entered a tailor's shop in Hornberg, in the Rastatt-Karlsruhe district of West Germany. The tailor, Johann Kohler, was glad to see him, for the youth had ordered some clothes two months earlier, and had failed to collect them. He explained that he was working as a waiter in a hotel in Frankfurt, and pulled out a wad of notes to pay for the clothes. After changing in a cubicle, the customer looked at himself in a mirror and asked if he could leave his old grey suit behind while he went for a haircut. When the young man had gone, the tailor decided to move the suit — as well as a bulging briefcase — to a safer place. As he lifted them, the lid of the briefcase opened, and a sawn-off rifle fell out. It seemed a strange item for a respectable young man to be carrying about, and the tailor decided to notify the police.

The inspector who arrived from the local police station looked through the contents of the briefcase; it proved to contain money, a box of cartridges, some pornographic literature, and half a rail ticket from Karlsruhe to Zingen. These items made the inspector thoughtful. He had already received a report of a robbery at nearby Durlach railway station the previous night, and the burglar had been interrupted by a railway employee. He had pointed a sawn-off rifle at the employee and made his escape. It was obviously possible that the young man, whose name was Heinrich Pommerencke, was the burglar.

The pornography and the railway ticket gave rise to another suspicion. A girl had been raped in Zingen less than two weeks earlier by an intruder who had climbed through her bedroom window, and throttled her into submission. She had seen the rapist in the moonlight, and her description sounded like the owner of the briefcase.

When Pommerencke returned, the inspector asked him to accompany him to the police station. As soon as they were outside, the young man fled like a hare. The inspector chased him on his bicycle, and another passing policeman joined in the chase. Pommerencke was cornered in a fairground and taken in handcuffs to the police station.

Commissioner Heinrich Koch also examined the contents of the briefcase, then accused the young man of the burglary at Durlach. He observed the look of relief that passed briefly over Pommerencke's face, and knew that the inspector was probably right about the rape. In fact, Pommerencke not only admitted the Durlach burglary, but three others in the surrounding area. Two of these had been at Karlsruhe and Rastatt. And Koch was aware that there had also been rape murders in these places. In the previous March, there had been a rape murder in Hornberg itself. But for the time being, Koch decided, he would allow Pommerencke to think that he was only suspected of burglary.

Two weeks later, in police headquarters in Freiburg, Heinrich Pommerencke was identified by the rape victim from Zingen as the man who had entered her bedroom. Pommerencke heatedly denied that he was the rapist. Then a waitress who had been attacked in Karlsruhe — but managed to escape — also identified him as her assailant. When Koch tried a bluff, and told him that blood spots found on his grey suit had been identified as belonging to the same group as three murder victims, Pommerencke finally lost heart and decided to confess.

It was the typical story of a sex criminal. Born in Bentwisch, near Rostock in East Germany, in 1937, Pommerencke had been the child of a broken marriage. He had been an abnormally lonely child, but had been in the grip of a powerful sexual urge from an early age. 'When I was a boy I never had a friend in the world. . .Other men always had girlfriends with them. I wanted girlfriends too, but I never succeeded.' He was shy, clumsy and tongue-tied. At the age of fifteen he began hanging around the local dance hall and made a few clumsy attempts to attack girls. In 1953, at the age of sixteen, he fled to West Germany and found work as a waiter and a handyman. He also served a term in jail for burglary. He always lived alone in rented rooms, read pornography, and daydreamed of sex.

Then, in late February 1959, in Karlsruhe, he went to see a film called *The Ten Commandments*. 'I saw half-naked women dancing around the golden calf. I thought then that many women were evil and did not deserve to live. I knew then I would have to kill.'

When he left the cinema he bought a knife, then followed a pretty waitress down a deserted street. He seized her from behind and threw her to the ground, tearing at her clothes. When he held a knife to her throat, she screamed, and a passing taxi driver heard her. As the taxi approached, Pommerencke fled. His desire was so overpowering that he continued to stalk women. He followed a thirty-four-year-old cleaning woman, Hilda Konther, and attacked her near her home. This time no one heard the scream. The next morning, her body was found lying in some bushes; she had been raped and stabbed to death, and the clothes had been literally torn from her body by a man who was obviously in a sexual frenzy.

On 26 March 1959 he stalked an eighteen-year-old beautician, Karin Walde, in Hornberg; he knocked her unconscious with a heavy stone, then tore off her clothes and raped her. Finally, he killed her, using the stone as a bludgeon.

On 2 June 1959 Pommerencke bought a platform ticket at Freiburg, and slipped on board the Italian Riviera Express. There he waited on the front platform of one of the carriages until he saw a girl go into the toilet. He removed the bulb from the ceiling of the corridor, and as the girl came out, seized her and hurled her out of the open platform door and on to the line. Then he pulled the communication cord and, as the train came to a halt, jumped off and hurried back down the line. He found his victim — twenty-one-year-old teaching student Dagmar Klimek — unconscious beside the tracks, about two miles back. He dragged her into the bushes, tore off her clothes and raped her. Then he stabbed her through the heart. When daylight came, he walked to the village of Ebringen, washed in the fountain, then hitched a lift with a motorist back to Freiburg.

Five days later, on 8 June, he waited near the station at Rastatt. An eighteen-year-old secretary, Rita Walterspacher, came out of the station and turned down a deserted road. As Pommerencke moved swiftly towards her, the girl sensed that she was about to be attacked, and ran away screaming. A woman on the train saw the running girl, and noted that the man who was pursuing her was tall, young and wore a grey suit. As she watched, he flung his arms round the girl and pulled her into some woods at the side of the road. The woman assumed that they were a courting couple playing games, and forgot about it until she heard on the radio of the disappearance of a young girl near Rastatt. Rita Walterspacher's body was found concealed under a pile of branches. She had been strangled, and her clothing torn off her. Her purse was missing from her handbag — Pommerencke made a habit of taking any money he found on his victims.

To the police investigating the case, it was obvious that the murderer was a man in the grip of such sexual frenzy that he would pursue a screaming girl in full view of a train, and drag her into the woods. The similarity in method in all four rape murders convinced them that all were committed by the same man, and that he would go on killing until he was caught. By the time Rita Walterspacher's body was discovered later that day, the rapist was already in custody in the Hornberg police station, having made the absurd mistake of leaving his briefcase containing the sawn-off rifle in a tailor's shop . . .

Like William Heirens, Pommerencke was not cut out to be a serial killer; his crimes produced a powerful inner conflict, deep feelings of guilt. Commissioner Gut, head of the Freiburg murder squad, had speculated that the murderer of Hilda Konther and Karin Walde was a Jekyll and Hyde personality. And Pommerencke admitted after his arrest: 'Everything I did was cruel and bestial. From the bottom of my heart I would like to undo all this.' His incredibly careless act of leaving a gun in a tailor's shop may be interpreted as his own attempt to undo it all. On 22 October 1960 he received a life sentence with hard labour.

The foregoing cases underline a point of fundamental importance for the understanding of the criminal personality: that by definition, *all* criminals are self-divided. The criminal is one who decides to take what he wants from society by force or stealth. In the act of doing this, he has become an 'outsider' — that is, he has placed himself outside society, 'beyond the pale'. But he has no desire to remain outside society; that would amount to psychological suicide. In 1961, two American psychologists, Samuel Yochelson and Stanton Samenow, began a programme to study criminals in St Elizabeth's Hospital, Washington DC. Both were liberals who believed that criminals were really 'victims of society', people with 'deep psychologic problems'. The conclusions they reached dismayed them both. In their book *The Criminal Personality*, they admit that they have found that the chief characteristics of the criminal are weakness, vanity and self-delusion. 'The greatest fear of these criminals was that others would see some weakness in them and they reacted very angrily to being "put down".' That is to say, the urge to self-esteem — to be liked and respected by others — was paramount in them. Men who distinguish themselves in the public eye, from creative geniuses to famous sportsmen, are doing something of which everyone can approve. As the criminal commits a crime, he knows that he is doing something which, if discovered, will turn him into an outcast. So there is a basic conflict between his criminality and his craving to be admired. (In this respect, the Mafia forms an exceptionally interesting subject of sociological study, in its attempt to transform the criminal into an accepted member of society, a 'man of respect'.) A part of him dreams of taking the 'social route' to self-esteem, becoming respected and famous. Another part is in a hurry and is in favour of taking short-cuts. (Every crime is in essence a short-cut.) Robert Poulin, William Heirens and Heinrich Pommerencke developed an exceptionally powerful sex-drive at an early age, when normal fulfilment seemed only a remote possibility. Since most young people are notoriously amoral — a child is more concerned with his own needs than other people's — they found it easy to drift into sex crime. As the personality matures, there is a subconscious recognition that this conflicts with the urge to self-esteem, the desire to be 'recognised'. Jekyll becomes increasingly resentful of the Hyde who is obstructing his evolution. It is arguable that, in Poulin's case, this led to the decision to commit suicide, and, in the case of Heirens and Pommerencke, to the act of carelessness that led to arrest.

We have seen that specific patterns of crime can be identified with specific periods. You would not expect a sadistic sex murder to be committed in, say, 1810 — not because men were less corrupt and degenerate in 1810, but because sexual sadism had not yet emerged in the field of criminal activity. Similarly, the crime of self-esteem seems to be a phenomenon that emerges in the 1960s. It is hard to imagine a murderer of the 1940s saying, like Robert Smith: 'I wanted to become known, to get myself a name.'

Crime — particularly murder — produces the feeling of being 'beyond the pale'. Case after case demonstrates that the 'self-esteem killer' copes with this problem in a manner reminiscent of the Marquis de Sade: by telling himself that, in the war against society, he is in the right and society is in the wrong. This explains why such killers often keep journals. If possible, he finds himself an accomplice — or, in the case of the Manson clan, a group of accomplices — who share his antisocial outlook. If he lacks accomplices, he may choose the rather more dangerous course of taking a 'normal' acquaintance into his confidence. In this way, Dr Jekyll can be propitiated by a kind of intellectual sleight of hand: if a 'normal' person knows about his crimes, then they cannot be truly abnormal, and he himself cannot be 'outside society'.

One of the most characteristic of such cases occurred in America in the late 1950s; although it involved sex crime, the self-esteem element is so obtrusive that the case may be regarded as a kind of watershed or turning point.

On Sunday, 11 January 1959 an old blue Chevrolet forced another car off a lonely country road in Virginia, and a tall, thin young man with staring eyes advanced on it waving a revolver. He ordered the Jackson family — consisting of Carrol Jackson, his wife Mildred, and their two children, Susan, age five, and a baby, Janet — into the boot of his car, and sped off. Carrol Jackson was later found dead in a ditch; underneath him lay Janet, who had also been shot. Two months later, the bodies of Mildred Jackson and Susan were uncovered in Maryland; Mildred Jackson had been strangled with a stocking and Susan battered to death.

Two years earlier, in June 1957, a man with staring eyes had approached a courting couple in a car — an army sergeant and a woman named Margaret Harold — and asked for a lift. On the way he pulled out a gun and demanded money; when Margaret Harold said: 'Don't give it to him', he shot her in the back of the head. The sergeant flung open the door and ran. When police found the car, they also found the body of Margaret Harold lying across the front seat without her dress; a police spokesman described the killer as 'a sexual degenerate'. Near the scene of the crime the police discovered a deserted shack full of pornographic pictures.

Five months after the murders of the Jackson family, in May 1959, the police received an anonymous tip-off that the murderer was a jazz musician named Melvin Rees; but police were unable to trace Rees. Early the following year, a salesman named Glenn Moser went to the police, acknowledged that he was the author of the anonymous tip-off, and told them that he now had the suspect's address: Melvin Rees was working in a music shop in Memphis, Arkansas. Rees was arrested there, and soon after he was identified by the army sergeant as the man who had shot Margaret Harold. A search of the home of Rees's parents uncovered the revolver with which Carrol Jackson had been shot, and a diary describing the abduction of the Jacksons and their murder. 'Caught on a lonely road. . .Drove to a select area and killed the husband and baby. Now the mother and daughter were all mine.' He described forcing Mildred Jackson to perform oral sex, and then raping her repeatedly; the child was also apparently raped. (Full details have never been released.) He concluded: 'I was her master.' The diary also described the sex murders of four more girls in Maryland. Rees was executed in 1961.

Violent sex murders were common enough by the late 1950s. What makes this one unique for its period was Rees's 'Sadeian' attitude of self-justification. On the night before the Jackson killings, Rees had been on a 'benzedrine kick', and in the course of a rambling argument had told Moser: 'You can't say it's wrong to kill. Only individual standards make it right or wrong.' He had also explained that he wanted to experience everything: love, hate, life, death. . .When, after the murders, Moser asked him outright whether he was the killer, Rees disdained to lie; he simply refused to answer, leaving Moser to draw the self-evident conclusion. Rees was an 'intellectual' who, like Moors murderer Ian Brady in the following decade, made the decision to rape and kill on the grounds that 'everything is lawful'. He may therefore be regarded as one of the first examples of the curious modern phenomenon, the 'high IQ killer'. His sexual fantasies involved sadism (Mildred Jackson's death had been long and agonising) and power. In

188

that sense, his crimes anticipate those of the serial killer who was to emerge two decades later.

Unfortunately we know nothing of Rees's background, or what turned him into a serial killer. Yet on the basis of other cases, we can state with a fair degree of confidence that parental affection was lacking in childhood, and that he was a lonely introverted child who was not much liked by his schoolmates. It is difficult, if not impossible, to find a case of a serial killer of whom this is not true.

Rees and Glatman are early examples of the 'power-motivated' criminal, a category that would become so familiar in the 1980s. Germany's version of the Cameron Hooker case came to public attention in May 1984. On 3 May a nineteen-year-old girl named Beate Koch was walking along a country road near the village of Pillnach – not far from Regensburg – when she was attacked by a man who dragged her into the nearest house – his own. She recognised him as a member of the academic community from the University of Regensburg, Dr Ulrich Kochwald, whose field was sexual research. Kochwald was an odd-looking man – six feet four inches tall and very thin, with protruding eyes that were magnified by pebble glasses; the top of his head was bald, but thin blond hair descended from the back and sides to his shoulders. Having threatened to kill her if she didn't stop struggling, Kochwald tore off her clothes, raped her, and beat her with a rope. Then he handcuffed her and forced her down to the basement, where she was surprised to discover that she was not the only prisoner. Another handcuffed girl was confined there – also naked – hanging from a hook in the ceiling. This was twenty-four-year-old Sabine Pauli; she was one of Kochwald's students, and had been flattered when he invited her to lunch one day. After lunch, he had attacked her, raped her, and taken her to the basement, where she had been ever since. Kochwald beat her regularly and treated her as a 'sex slave'. Since her family lived far away, no-one had yet noticed her disappearance.

That night, Beate Koch succeeded in escaping. The two women were close enough together for Beate to lift herself by locking her legs around her companion, and jerking the handcuffs clear of the hook in the ceiling. Sabine urged her not to bother about releasing her, but to leave as quickly as possible. Beate staggered home through the dark, and arrived there covered in mud and scratches. Her parents had notified the police of her disappearance, and a local sergeant had already obtained search warrants for various houses along the road between the villages. Within a short time the sergeant was knocking on Dr Kochwald's door; when Kochwald opened it, the sergeant informed him that he was under arrest, and handcuffed him to a radiator. Then he hurried down to the basement, and freed Sabine Pauli, who was covered with bruises and cigarette burns.

Newspaper publicity caused another of Kochwald's victims to come forward. Her name was Susanne Wagner, and she had lived with Kochwald for some time after the break-up of his marriage. But they had quarrelled a great deal, and on 4 June 1981 she had announced that she was leaving him. Kochwald's reaction was to handcuff her, tear off her clothes, and drag her to the basement, where he had hung her from a hook in the ceiling, then beat her with a rope. He had terrorised her and kept her prisoner for the next year. Sometimes she was handcuffed to the kitchen stove, sometimes to the radiator in Kochwald's bedroom. Later, when he was certain that she was too terrified to try to escape — he told her he would hunt her down and kill her — he even allowed her to go around without handcuffs. He kept her naked, hoping that this would deter her from showing herself in public. On 24 May 1982 she managed to slip her handcuffs by greasing her wrists with soap, and escaped through a window. A passing motorist took her to hospital, but Susanne was so afraid of Kochwald that she had told no-one of her year in captivity.

On 22 May 1986 Ulrich Kochwald was sentenced to five and a half years in jail for kidnapping.

As in the case of Melvin Rees, we know nothing of the psychological background that turned Kochwald into a sadist. But other cases in this chapter would suggest that this unattractive man — noted at the university for the dullness of his lectures — had been an unattractive and lonely child, with a tendency to fantasise. The latter is confirmed by Susanne Wagner, to whom he had confided that he had always dreamed of keeping several women as sex slaves, and that he had once enquired into the possibility of becoming a Mohammedan —

190

so that he could have four wives — but had discovered that in Germany bigamy is illegal, even for Moslems.

We have seen that the Jekyll and Hyde syndrome has many strange variations. The sufferer may attempt to deal with it through a variety of techniques, ranging from intellectual self-justification in the manner of de Sade to making some absurd error that leads to arrest. In a few cases, the 'suicide syndrome' results in actual self-destruction.

On 16 July 1973 a hysterical teenage girl who identified herself as Mary Ellen Jones rushed into a police station in Fort Lauderdale, Florida, and told the police that her boyfriend had been murdered, and that she had been repeatedly raped by the killer. Two days previously, the young couple — who had met only the day before on the local beach — had been offered a lift by a middle-aged man driving a white Dodge van. He had introduced himself as 'Eric', and offered to give them work in his home in south Miami. Once inside the bungalow, the man had threatened them with a gun and told them to undress. Then he ordered them to perform various abnormal sex acts while he took photographs. In order to hold the camera, he had to place the gun beside him. The youth — sixteen-year-old Mark Matson — waited his chance, then hurled himself at their tormentor. He was not quick enough; 'Eric' snatched up the gun and fired three times, hitting the youth in the head, shoulder and chest. Then he dragged the body into the bathroom, and took the girl through a steel-lined door and into a soundproof compartment at the end of his bedroom. There he shackled her to the wall, and raped her repeatedly for twenty-four hours. At the end of that time, when she was expecting to die, he unchained her, telling her: 'I've taken a life, but now I'm going to give you your life.' He drove her back into Fort Lauderdale and released her.

She hurried to the nearest police station. When the police learned she was a runaway, they telephoned her home in Frankfort, Kentucky; the girl's mother told them that she was a pathological liar, and advised them not to believe a word she said. The mother then wired money, and the girl was sent home by plane to Kentucky.

Five days later, on Saturday, 21 July 1973, a housewife in

South Dade County was removing washing from her clothesline when she noticed that her next-door neighbour, Albert Brust, was sitting in a chair on his lawn, oblivious of the falling rain. And when her son mentioned that Brust had been there for the past two days, she rang the Fort Lauderdale police and told them: 'I think there's a dead man in the garden next door.'

An autopsy revealed that Albert Brust, a forty-four-year-old Dade County building inspector, had taken a dose of cyanide in chocolate milk. When the police entered his house, they noticed the unpleasant smell, like rotting meat. It came from the bathroom. When the shower curtain was pulled aside, they found themselves looking at a wall of concrete, from which a little blood was seeping. It had to be demolished piecemeal before it revealed a mutilated body, minus its hands, feet and head. The head had been obscenely placed between the thighs, and the hands and feet were found embedded in the concrete. At that point, the police remembered Mary Ellen Jones's story, and realised that she must have been telling the truth.

A search of the rest of the house made it clear that Albert Brust was a 'sex freak' obsessed with torture. In fact, the room at the end of the bedroom – in which the teenage girl had been raped – had obviously been designed as a torture chamber, with chains hanging from the ceiling, and a variety of whips, cat o' nine tails, belts and padlocks. An item of furniture of peculiar design was apparently a 'Chinese raping stool'. There were also pornographic videos and books, and obscene pictures on the walls. Yet he possessed many gramophone records, and the bookcase contained a wide range of philosophical texts, from Spinoza and Voltaire to Unamuno and William James's *Varieties of Religious Experience*. Brust also owned several volumes of the Marquis de Sade, whose works had been published openly in America in the 1960s.

Investigation into Brust's background revealed that he was a New Yorker, born in 1929. When he was twenty-one, he had been sentenced to a term of from three to ten years in jail for abduction, assault, robbery and grand larceny. In prison he learned carpentry and welding, and taught himself calculus. He became a construction worker for twelve years before moving, in 1972, to Dade County, Florida, where he obtained a position as an inspector of buildings. This ugly, short little man had few friends. He drove a powerful motor cycle, and frequented a local motor-cycle shop, apparently hoping to find sex (he was bisexual). The owner of the shop commented that Brust described himself as a Jekyll and Hyde personality, and that he talked a great deal of sex, suicide and murder. Brust had told him that he had killed someone in New York and disposed of the body in the East River, and that he had once 'concreted' somebody. 'When you first kill someone,' Brust told him, 'it's like breaking the ice. It's an obstacle in the beginning, but after that nothing.'

These remarks led the police to dig up Brust's back garden and to search his house carefully for more signs of 'concreting'. They found nothing.

Like so many 'loners', Brust kept a journal, and it revealed a negative, morbid personality. 'Rape, murder, suicide. These thoughts are constantly with me. . .Of course, this is not mentally 'healthy' – there is no doubt that by present standards I am mentally ill, a hopeless sociopath.' 'My reason tells me that I have nothing to live for. Intellectually, sexually, occupationally, socially – everywhere a dead end. The pain now outweighs the pleasure and every day adds weight to the logic of self-destruction.' 'I need this safety valve, this writing, to keep me straight and calm and determined to bring my – death project – to a successful end.' The 'death project', apparently, was suicide. He suffered, he said, from 'alienation and sexual frustration and creative impotence.' There is a classic statement of the problem of the 'romantic outsider': 'While my books have a tranquilising effect on me, reinforcing the Dr Jekyll side of my personality, it is also true that they paralyse me into inaction. They cause me to think about death, to be fatalistic and pessimistic, prone to suicide.' 'The culprit is my emotions. Once stirred, blind rage tends to take over and I get both homicidal and suicidal.' Brust's philosophy was that man was evil, that government was useless, and that society must be strictly controlled. These views led him to express admiration for Hitler; he also enjoyed talking, in a mock-German accent, about what should be done with Jews.

Brust was irritable, sarcastic and aggressive. 'He thought he was above everyone else,' said one of his acquaintances. 'And the terrible thing was, it was true.' Brust had passed a University of Chicago correspondence course in algebra and analytic geometry; but years of frustration had developed a

193

highly intolerant personality. 'He hated Catholics, cats, dogs – almost everything,' said the motor cycle shop owner. He craved a woman, but was only willing to contemplate a relationship with one who was willing to be his slave. He told a woman psychology student that he had once thought of marrying a blonde female acquaintance, 'big in bosom and bottom', and decidedly dumb, but had changed his mind. Incredibly, it seems probable that, at forty-four, he was still a virgin. 'After work I always get home as soon as possible to enjoy my solitary sanctuary and its music and books and TV. No sex yet, but I'm working on it – slowly, but with determined resolve. I know what I want. I need someone for sex, yes – but not an idiot I have to cater to. Enter the Brustian solution. . .' The 'Brustian solution' was to kidnap a girl and hold her as his slave in the 'torture chamber'. His opportunity came when he saw Mark Matson and Mary Ellen Jones hitchhiking out of Fort Lauderdale; but the orgy that followed left him as unsatisfied as the murder of Kim Rabat had left Robert Poulin – whom, in spite of the twenty-seven-year age difference, Brust resembles in so many ways. 'I have miscalculated', Brust wrote.'. . .I know I can save the situation by a lot of disagreeable work' – he obviously meant recovering Mark Matson's body and burying it in the garden – 'but I see no good reason for going on. What would come next? The whole business is not worth it; life is not worth the trouble after all.' After completing this entry, he poured himself a glass of chocolate milk, added cyanide, and sat down on his lawn to drink it.

In 1987, another 'sex slave' case made headlines across America; this time it had ended in two fatalities. The psychiatric evidence that emerged means that we know a great deal more about Gary Heidnik than about Melvin Rees or Albert Brust. But although a jury found him sane, there can be little doubt that Heidnik was as psychotic as Albert Fish. The case offers an example of yet another stratagem by which the unconscious mind deals with the problems of the Jekyll and Hyde syndrome.

Towards midnight on 24 March 1987 a black prostitute, Josefina Rivera, knocked frantically on the door of her boyfriend's apartment in Philadelphia. Vincent Nelson had not seen her since the previous November, when she had gone out on a rainy evening to 'turn a trick'. Now he was shocked to see how much she had changed in four months; she looked like a concentration-camp victim. He was even more startled by the words she was babbling — his first suspicion was that she was full of drugs. She seemed to be saying that three women were being kept chained up in a basement, and that two more were dead. Nelson finally called the police. The two men who arrived in a squad car were at first equally sceptical; but when she showed them marks around her ankles where she had been manacled, they decided that it might be worth investigating after all. The house in which Josefina alleged she had been held was three blocks away, on a slum street called North Marshall. A thin-faced, bearded man opened the door, and raised his hands when he saw drawn guns. Had they come about his child support payments? he wanted to know. The policeman assured him it was more serious, and took him to headquarters — the Sex Crimes Unit. His name was Gary Michael Heidnik, and he was forty-three years old.

At five o'clock the following morning, police with a search warrant broke down the door at 3520 North Marshall Street — arousing the neighbours — and rushed down to the basement. On a mattress in the middle of the room lay two black women, huddled under blankets; they screamed as the police burst in, but when they realised that the intruders had come to rescue them, they shouted 'We're free!' and kissed their hands. Neither seemed to be embarrassed by the fact that they were naked from the waist down. In a deep hole in the floor — covered over by a board — there was another black woman, this one completely naked, with shackles on her ankles and her wrists handcuffed behind her back.

The story that emerged was appalling and incredible. Josefina Rivera had been the first captive. Heidnik, driving an expensive car, had picked her up towards midnight on 26 November 1986. Josefina was also impressed by the walls of his bedroom, which were papered with five and ten dollar bills. After sex, she began to dress again, but as she did so, Heidnik seized her by the throat and throttled her until she came close to blacking out. When he released her, she gasped that she would do whatever he wanted if he promised not to hurt her. He handcuffed her and took her down to a cold, mildewy basement. There he chained her, fixing around her ankle a clamp of the type used to suspend a car exhaust. The next day, he came down to the basement, and dug a hole in a spot where the concrete had been removed. She was afraid it was her grave, but his manner as he talked reassured her. He told her that what he wanted most in all the world was a large family, and that he intended to capture ten women, keep them in the basement, and make them all pregnant. He explained that he had once had a baby daughter by a black woman – he seemed uninterested in whites – but he had helped her sister to escape from a mental institution. As a result he had been charged with the rape of the sister and sentenced to four years in prison – which was unfair, since the sex had been voluntary. His daughter had been placed in a home. 'Society owes me a wife and family,' he told her – after which he made her perform oral sex on him, then had vaginal sex with her.

Later that day, Josefina succeeded in forcing open the boarded-up window, and screamed as loud as she could, but the run-down neighbourhood was used to screaming women; the only person who paid any attention was Heidnik, and he beat her and threw her down the hole he had dug. Then he left her with the radio playing rock at top volume.

Two days later – on 29 November – Heidnik added another captive to his harem, a woman called Sandra Lindsay, who was black and mildly retarded. She had apparently known Heidnik for years, and had even carried his baby – Heidnik had been furious when she had had an abortion. She told Josefina that she had no idea why her former lover had made her a captive. She also mentioned the astonishing fact that Heidnik was a bishop in his own church.

The following day Heidnik made her write a note to her mother, telling her that she would be in touch; he mailed this from New York.

The basement was cold, permanently lit by a naked bulb, and covered in litter. The daily routine consisted of beatings, rapes, oral sex and a prison diet of oatmeal and bread. No-one in the outside world seemed to know or care where they were. In fact, Sandra's mother had reported to the police that she thought her daughter was being held by a man called Gary Heidnik, but a mentally retarded friend of Heidnik's whom the police questioned mis-spelled the name Heidaike, and when it failed to show up on the police computer – where there were several entries under Heidnik's name – the search was dropped.

One by one, other captives were introduced to the basement. On 22 December it was Lisa Thomas, a black high-school dropout who accepted a lift in Heidnik's Cadillac. On 1 January 1987 Deborah Dudley was added. Heidnik was to regret this — Debbie proved to be more argumentative than the other two, and had to be beaten more often. On 18 January eighteen-year-old Jacqueline Askins, another prostitute, was 'captured'. Her ankles were so small that he had to shackle them with handcuffs. On 23 March he brought his final captive, a twenty-four-year-old prostitute named Agnes Adams; Josefina Rivera — now allowed out of the cellar — had been with him when he picked her up. By then, two of his captives were dead. In February, Sandra Lindsay had been suspended from the ceiling by her hands for a week as a punishment for trying to escape from the hole. On 7 February she died of exhaustion. On 18 March Heidnik filled the pit with water, made three women — exempting Josefina — climb into it, then tortured them with shocks from a bare electric wire. It touched Deborah Dudley's chain and killed her.

By that time, most of Sandra Lindsay's body had been put through a meat grinder, and her head cooked in a saucepan. Three days after her death, neighbours complained of the stench of cooking meat. The policeman who investigated the complaint accepted Heidnik's assurance that he had merely burnt his dinner. He did not ask to look into the cooking pot on the stove.

In an attempt to make his captives deaf — so they could not hear him — Heidnik had pushed a screwdriver into their ears and twisted it round, damaging the eardrums. Josefina Rivera was the only one who was not subjected to this treatment. She had gained Heidnik's trust by 'snitching' on the others when they plotted to escape, and beating them under Heidnik's orders. (She was not the only one; Heidnik forced them all to beat one another.) She was often taken out to fast-food restaurants, and for rides in his Cadillac and Rolls-Royce. On 24 March she finally persuaded him that it was time to go and see her family. He trusted her, and dropped her off at the spot where he had picked her up four months earlier. She lost no time in rushing to the apartment of her boyfriend; by the next morning Heidnik was in custody. The sergeant who had arrested him had found a human forearm in the freezer. A few days later, Josefina led police to the body of Deborah Dudley, buried in a shallow grave in a wood in New Jersey.

Any police officer with a knowledge of serial killers would have been able to predict certain elements in the early history of Gary Michael Heidnik, as it emerged during his psychiatric examination that he hated his father — probably his mother too, that his childhood had been loveless and lonely, that he had been ridiculed by other children, that he was shy, and that much of his childhood had been spent in a world of fantasy. All this would have been correct. In fact, he was an object of ridicule because of the shape of his head: he was called 'football head', and this was due to the fact that, at an early age, he had fallen out of a tree on to the crown of his head. (As already remarked, there seems to be a remarkably high incidence of childhood head injuries among serial killers.) After that, said his brother Terry, he had experienced a personality change.

Gary Heidnik had been born in November 1943, son of a toolmaker in Cleveland, Ohio. His mother was of Creole descent, and was a heavy drinker. The result was that Heidnik's parents separated when he was two. Ellen Heidnik would commit suicide in 1970 when dying of cancer. The father, Michael Heidnik, soon remarried, and the stepmother did not take to her new children. The father showed them little affection; he was a stern disciplinarian. Gary was a bedwetter — another characteristic that the Quantico research unit found to be typical of serial killers — and his father would hang the soaking sheet out of Gary's bedroom window for everyone to see. This is perhaps one reason why Gary loked forward to becoming a soldier. He attended a military academy in Virginia before — at the age of eighteen — he joined the army.

From an early age Gary Heidnik had been fascinated by high finance — perhaps because his childhood fantasies involved becoming a millionaire. He read the financial pages as other children read comics, and when the opportunity finally presented itself, showed himself to be a skilful operator in the stockmarket. He never became a millionaire, but at the time of his arrest he had more than half a million dollars.

In the army Heidnik saved his money and became a 'loan shark'. He lost $5,000 when he was suddenly sent out to Germany. Here he was beset by the the mental problems that were to plague him for the rest of his life. He suffered from dizzy spells and headaches. This may have been due to the head injury as a child, or to the fact that, like so many of the flower children of the sixties, he had been taking hallucinogenic drugs. Doctors prescribed Stelazine, a major tranquilliser with powerful effects. In January 1963, when he was nineteen, the army decided that he was a schizophrenic personality and granted him an honourable discharge.

Back in the US, he went to Philadelphia and began training as a psychiatric nurse; he also gained credits in a number of subjects at the University of Pennsylvania, including marketing. (His IQ was 130, about 30 above average.) Attempts at settling with his mother, then his father, were failures. His father wanted to get him permanently out of his life, and broke with him (as he had done with Gary's brother Terry). From then on he was in and out of mental hospitals — a total of twenty-one times. He also attempted suicide thirteen times. (His brother Terry also had mental problems and was suicidal.) He took many overdoses, drove his motor cycle head on into a truck, and drank down a ground-up light bulb.

In the spring of 1971 he drove to the west coast on a sudden impulse and, as he stood on the sea shore, had a revelation from God: to start a church. While still under psychiatric treatment he joined the United Church of Ministers of God and founded his own congregation in Philadelphia. His aim, he says, was to care for the mentally and physically handicapped. In this he was undoubtedly sincere. Although his church did not take up collections, it went in for fund-raising activities such as bingo and loan-sharking. In 1975, Heidnik was able to open an account with the stockbrokers Merrill Lynch, in the name of his church, with $1,500. With skilful investment, it made him a rich man.

In 1976 Heidnik had his first brush with the law. A man to whom he was renting an apartment tried to climb into a locked basement to switch on the electricity, which Heidnik had turned off. Heidnik was waiting for him with a gun, and fired; the man turned his head and was only grazed. For reasons that are unclear, the charge of assault with a deadly weapon was dismissed.

By March 1978 Heidnik was a father; the mother of the child was a mentally retarded black woman named Anjeanette Davidson. She had a thirty-four-year-old sister named Alberta, who was in a mental institution near Harrisburg. On 7 May

1978 Heidnik and Anjeanette went to see Alberta and took her on an outing. When they failed to return her, police searched the house where Heidnik was living, and found Alberta hiding in a basement. Medical examination revealed that she had recently had sexual intercourse, and gonorrheal infection in her throat revealed that she had recently been subjected to oral sex. Heidnik was arrested and charged with unlawful imprisonment and deviate sexuality. He was sentenced to four years' imprisonment, most of which was spent in a mental ward. At least one of the guards concluded that he was faking when, after years of 'mutism', he met an old friend and began chatting normally. Heidnik would later tell Josefina Rivera that if he was caught, he would be able to fake insanity.

Heidnik's house was always full of women; he seemed to be sexually insatiable. There were many regular girlfriends; one of them told how Heidnik would insist on having three-in-a-bed sex. He also had a taste for mentally retarded black women – many drawn from his congregation.

In 1983 Heidnik decided that he wanted an oriental wife having heard, no doubt, that oriental girls are trained to obey their husbands in all things. A matrimonial agency found him a Filipino girl named Betty Disto. In September 1983 she flew from Manila to Philadelphia; they were married within three days. A week later she came in from a shopping trip and found her husband in bed with three black women. Heidnik assured her that all American males did it. From then on he often brought home mentally retarded black women for sex. He often made her watch, after which she was ordered to cook for him. He also forced her to submit to sodomy. She left him in January 1986. A court ordered him to pay her $135 a week.

In November of that year, Heidnik decided it was time to inaugurate his plan for a harem, and kidnapped Josefina Rivera . . .

When the story of Heidnik's arrest broke on 26 March 1987 newspaper headlines declared: MAN HELD IN TORTURE KILLINGS, MADMAN'S SEX ORGY WITH CHAINED WOMEN, and WOMEN CHAINED IN HORROR DUNGEON. No-one realised at the time that the description 'madman' was literally true, and that Heidnik was as psychotic as Albert Fish. When the information on Heidnik's background emerged, it was inevitable that his defence would be one of insanity, and when Heidnik's trial opened in May 1978, this is the course his attorney, Charles Peruto Jnr, chose. Even as he did so, Peruto must have realised that the jury would be unlikely to accept it: that in a case involving rape and torture, a sentence of detention in a criminal lunatic asylum would be regarded as a disappointing anticlimax. One psychiatrist, Dr Clancy McKenzie, argued that the birth of Heidnik's brother Terry when he was seventeen months old had caused a trauma that meant that a part of his brain had failed to mature beyond seventeen months, and that it was this infantile part that had kidnapped and raped women. Judge Lynne Abraham was openly sceptical of this explantion. Nevertheless, McKenzie's theory of why Heidnik kidnapped six women was highly plausible: that after his wife left him, he was determined that no woman should ever leave him again. When the prosecutor Charles Gallagher asked whether it was possible to fake schizophrenia, McKenzie replied indignantly that it would be impossible to fake it with *him*. His impatience is understandable; he was aware that no amount of psychiatric evidence would convince the jury that Heidnik did not deserve the death sentence.

He was right. On 1 July 1988 Gary Heidnik was found guilty on eighteen counts, including two of first-degree murder. The following day, he was sentenced to death. When someone telephoned Heidnik's father, asking if he wanted to know what the verdict was, he replied: 'I'm not interested.'

Heidnik's life story seems to be typical of the serial killer: the hostile father, the broken home, the head injury, the lonely and introverted childhood, the abnormally powerful sex drive. We can also see that one of his basic problems was self-esteem. His preference for black, semi-retarded women reveals an inferiority complex; he feels he lacks the qualifications for approaching middle-class white girls; if he had found himself in bed with such a girl, he might well have become impotent. In order to be potent, he must feel that the partner is thoroughly 'below' him, little more than a sex slave.

From the psychiatric point of view, the revelation on the Pacific coast was one of the most interesting events in Heidnik's life. It can be seen as a cry from the unconscious mind, a demand that he should find some way to develop self-esteem.

201

Becoming a bishop in his own church was the answer; it offered him an established position in the community, and an abundance of sexual partners. His subsequent success as a stock-market speculator confirmed that new position. In a mentally stable person, all this success would have brought about a personality transformation; but Heidnik's psychoses were too deep-rooted for that. To feel wholly secure, he needed to be a family man as well as a bishop. At first his Filipino wife seemed to offer the solution; but it was essential that, like the wife of some oriental potentate, she should accept the rest of the harem. When she refused to do so and left him, the whole structure of self-esteem was suddenly threatened. The solution was something that the sane part of him knew to be criminal: to kidnap women and keep them as sex slaves. But how could a bishop be a criminal? This is tantamount to asking the question: how can Dr Jekyll co-exist with Mr Hyde? Heidnik's response was the same as that of Albert Fish: collapse into a delusional state in which anything he did was justified by some divine command. From then on, he could kidnap, rape and torture with total moral self-approval.

Then was the jury mistaken to decide that he was sane? Not entirely, for Heidnik had undoubtedly learned to use his mentally unstable state as a weapon of survival. Like Albert Brust, he knew he was mentally ill, and was cunning enough to use it to his advantage. We can observe the same mechanism in Heinrich Pommerencke. The craving for sexual satisfaction had produced powerful sexual tensions, but 'Dr Jekyll' was too strong to allow Mr Hyde to commit rape. The catalyst was an American biblical epic, *The Ten Commandments*. When he saw the half-naked women dancing around the golden calf, Pommerencke suddenly decided that women are the source of all the world's troubles, and that he would be justified in committing a sex crime. Did he really believe anything so illogical? The answer to that question depends on what we mean by belief. *The Ten Commandments* provided the excuse he required to overcome his scruples about murder and rape. Most 'conversion' is of a similar nature. A system of belief offers a release of tensions and a design for living. Some beliefs may be regarded as more or less realistic – such as the belief in political freedom. Others – Nazism is an obvious example – are little more than an excuse for the release of negative emotion. Pommerencke accepted the 'revelation' that women are evil as an excuse to release his sexual tensions; he had entered into a state of 'voluntary delusion' — but Dr Jekyll was not wholly deceived, and the 'mistake' that led to Pommerencke's arrest suggests that he was fighting back.

Gary Heidnik went one step further: the craving for mental and social stability also led to the belief that women are evil and deserve to be treated as slaves; but the 'conversion' was so complete that Dr Jekyll was not only overruled but consigned to oblivion in some remote Siberia of Heidnik's mind.

The Heidnik case suggests the conclusion that in most murders that involve inhuman sadism — Fish is another obvious example — the criminal is technically insane: that is, suffering from delusions that disguise what he is doing from himself. This conclusion is supported by a case that occurred in Italy during the period when Heidnik was kidnapping his 'sex slaves'.

Beginning in February 1985, middle-aged prostitutes in the Turin area were abducted and tortured, then murdered; the bodies were dumped in ditches. The killers cut off fingers and toes and made numerous cuts and burns all over the victim's body. The third and fourth victims — who vanished from a village festival — had been suspended by the wrists and whipped to death. The fifth victim had been tortured for two days before her death. The sixth and seventh were mutilated in a manner reminiscent of Jack the Ripper. On 28 June 1957 a handsome young man in a sports car picked up a thirty-six-year-old prostitute on the highway from Turin to Piacenza. She was considerably younger than most of the victims (whose ages had ranged from mid-forties to mid-sixties), and it may have been this realisation that made the driver decide to dispose of her without further ado; he stopped the car and shot her through the head, then dumped the body in a cemetery. A few miles further on he was halted by police making a routine check on cars, and their suspicious were aroused by his nervousness; then one of them noticed blood on the passenger seat and a gun sticking out of a bag on the back seat. Giancarlo Guidice, a thirty-four-year-old lorry-driver from Turin, immediately confessed to the murder of Maria Rosa, and led the police back to her body. A search of his apartment revealed an elaborate torture kit of handcuffs, knives, scissors and other instruments. Fingerprints of three of the murdered women were also found in his apartment. Psychiatrists concluded that Guidice was driven by an overwhelming rage against older women — a rage that almost certainly had its origin in his relationship with his mother. Psychiatric examination also revealed that he was incurably insane, and in March 1989 he was confined in an institution for criminal psychotics. Police and forensic scientists who had studied the corpses had already concluded that they were dealing with a madman.

Even clinical insanity is not the ultimate stratagem of the unconscious mind when faced with intolerable conflict. There is a still more bizarre extreme known as multiple personality, in which Robert Louis Stevenson's division into Jekyll and Hyde becomes a psychological reality. One of the most bizarre cases of this type on record is that of the rapist Billy Milligan.

During a three-week period in October 1977, three girls were kidnapped from the campus of Ohio State University in Columbus, driven out to remote spots in the countryside, then raped. Each was also made to cash cheques and hand over the money. The victims went through mugshots at police headquarters, and quickly identified their assailant as a twenty-two-year-old ex-convict named William Stanley Milligan; but even as the police were on their way to arrest him, Milligan was telephoning his local police station to give himself up. When arrested, he stared in front of him in a strange, trance-like manner, and appeared to grasp very little of what was happening; the police, understandably, thought he was merely being unco-operative.

In prison, Milligan attempted suicide by banging his head against a wall. By now it was obvious that he was not malingering, and a doctor diagnosed acute schizophrenia. When a psychiatrist went to see him in his cell, he denied that he was Billy, and explained that his name was David. Asked where Billy was, he pointed to his chest and said: 'He's sleeping. In here.' David stated that he was eight years old. The following day, Billy identified himself in a cockney accent as Christopher, aged 13. He mentioned that he had a three-year-old sister named Christine, also British. The next day it was sixteen-year-old Tommy, a painter and electronics expert. Then came Danny, a fourteen-year-old boy who had once been buried alive. After this it was Arthur, a cool, controlled twenty-two-year-old Englishman who spoke fluent Arabic, and who seemed to be a kind of ringmaster of this circus of personalities. He told the psychologist that the robberies had been committed by a Serbo-Croat personality called Ragen, but added that Ragen had not committed the rapes. A psychiatrist who went to the prison convinced that he was about to confront a faker left several hours later shaken and totally convinced that he was dealing with a genuine case of 'MPD' – multiple personality disorder.

Multiple personalities have been known to doctors since the early nineteenth century. One of the first, Mary Renolds of Pennsylvania, woke up one morning in 1811 with a totally blank memory: she had to be taught everything, like a baby. Five weeks later, the original Mary came back. For the next decade or so, the two Marys shuttled in and out of the body until, in middle life, they eventually fused together. There have been many famous cases since then – two of the most recent being those of Christine Sizemore, documented in the book *The Three Faces of Eve*, and 'Sybil', a girl with fourteen personalities, described in the book *Sybil* by Flora Rheta Schreiber. Most 'multiples' have had highly traumatic childhood experiences, and it is now widely believed that the most important common factor is sexual assault by an adult – often a parent – in childhood.

This, according to Billy Milligan, explained how he had originally began to split into sub-personalities: at the age of eight, he had been frequently sodomised and beaten by his stepfather, Chalmer Milligan, who also used to beat Billy's mother. In order not to hear his mother's screams, Billy closed his eyes and became a deaf child called Shawn. Soon several other personalities – including the physically powerful Ragen – were also sharing the body. When he attempted suicide – by throwing himself off the school roof at the age of fourteen – the 'others' took over, and put Billy to sleep. He remained asleep until his arrest eight years later.

Unfortunately, some of the twenty-two personalities who were sharing the body were criminals; one of them, Kevin, committed a robbery that landed 'Billy' in jail. It was also

Kevin, in association with a nineteen-year-old lesbian called Adalana — yet another of the Milligan menagerie — who abducted the girls. Adalana raped them, and Ragen robbed them. When Danny woke up in the body and realised that something terrible had happened, it was he who rang the police to give 'himself' up. In fact, the police had by then identified the rapist, and were already on their way to arrest him. After psychiatrists had diagnosed Billy Milligan as a multiple personality, he was sentenced to detention in a mental hospital, and the psychiatric treatment to fuse his multiple personalities ended.

Many mysteries remain. If the various personalities of Billy Milligan were all fragments created by his unconscious mind, how is it that one of them could speak fluent Arabic and another Serbo-Croat? Whatever the solution, it seems clear that Billy Milligan displayed a far more severe form of the self-division than can be seen in so many psychotic killers, from Albert Fish to Gary Heidnik.

The sadist is a retarded personality, trapped at an infantile stage of development by a tendency to live in a world of fantasy; his sense of reality is as weak as that of a child, and this is why he is capable of treating other human beings as if they were mere objects. We can see, for example, that the realisation of Cameron Hooker's daydream of possessing a 'sex slave' had the effect of transforming him into something more like a socially normal human being. The sadistic murder represents a muddled quest for fulfilment: sexual fulfilment and fulfilment of the urge to self-esteem. In a few rare cases, such as that of Hooker, it actually achieves its object. The most striking of these occurred in Boston in the 1960s.

Between June 1962 and January 1964 the city of Boston, Massachusetts was terrorised by a series of murders that achieved worldwide publicity. The unknown killer, who strangled and sexually abused his victims, became known as the Boston Strangler. The first six victims were elderly women, whose ages ranged from fifty-five to eighty-five.

On 4 June 1962 fifty-five-year-old Anna Slesers was found in her apartment in the Back Bay area of Boston. She had been knocked unconscious with a blunt instrument — later determined to be a lead weight — and then strangled. The body, clad only in an open housecoat, was lying on its back with the legs apart. No semen was found in the vagina, but she had evidently been sexually assaulted with some hard object such as a soda bottle. The apartment had been ransacked.

Two weeks later, on 30 June, sixty-eight-year-old Nina Nichols failed to call back a friend after a telephone conversation had been interrupted by a ring at the doorbell. The friend asked the janitor to check her apartment. Nina Nichols was lying on the bedroom floor, strangled with a stocking, her legs open in a rape position. Her killer had also bitten her. Medical examination revealed that she had been sexually assaulted with a wine bottle after death. There was semen on her thighs, but not in the vagina.

Two days later, on Monday 2 July, neighbours of a sixty-five-year-old retired nurse named Helen Blake, who lived in Lynn, north of Boston, became anxious at not having seen her for two days, and sent for the police. Helen Blake was lying face downwards on her bed, a stocking knotted around her throat. Again, there was dried semen on her thighs but not in the vagina. Mrs Blake had apparently been killed on the previous Saturday, the same day as Nina Nichols.

On 21 August Mrs Ida Irga, seventy-five, was found dead in her apartment. Death was due to manual strangulation, after which a pillow case had been tied round her neck. She had been sexually assaulted with some hard object, and bitten. It was estimated that she had been dead for two days.

The last of the elderly victims was sixty-seven-year-old Jane Sullivan, another nurse. She was found in a kneeling position in the bathtub, her face in six inches of water. She was a powerful Irishwoman, and had evidently put up a tremendous fight — her assailant must have been very strong to overpower her. Two stockings were knotted around her neck. She had been killed on the day after Ida Irga, but the body was not found for more than a week; consequently it was impossible to determine whether she had been raped, but she had been sexually assaulted with a broom handle.

Boston was in a state of hysteria, but as weeks went by without further stranglings, it slowly subsided. A hot summer was succeeded by a very cold winter. In the early evening of 5 December 1962 two girls rang the doorbell of the apartment they shared with a twenty-year-old black girl, Sophie Clark, and were surprised when she failed to answer. They let themselves in, and found Sophie lying on the floor; she was naked and in the rape position. She had been strangled with nylon stockings knotted round her neck. Medical examination established that she had been raped, and a semen stain on the carpet beside the body indicated that her killer had later masturbated over her. This was the first case in which rape was unquestionably established, and it led to the speculation that her killer was a second Boston Strangler, one who preferred young girls.

Three weeks later, on the last day of 1962, a businessman stopped his car outside the apartment of his secretary at 515 Park Drive and blew his horn. When she failed to come down, he assumed that she had already left, but when he found that she was not at the office, he rang the superintendant of her apartment building to ask him to check on her apartment. Patricia Bissette, twenty-three, was lying in bed, covered with the bedclothes. She had been strangled with stockings, and medical examination established that she had been raped.

On 18 February 1963 a German girl named Gertrude Gruen survived an attack by the Strangler. A powerfully built man with a beaky nose, about five feet eight inches tall, knocked on her door and told her he had been sent to do work in her apartment. She was suffering from a virus, and only allowed him in after some argument. The man removed his coat and told her that she was pretty enough to be a model. Then he told her she had dust on the back of her dressing gown; she turned, and he hooked a powerful arm round her neck. She fought frantically, and sank her teeth into his hand until they bit to the bone. The man pushed her away, and as she began to scream, he ran out of the apartment.

The police were excited when the girl reported the attack — and then frustrated when they discovered that the shock had wiped all traces of the Strangler's face from her memory.

A month later, on 9 March 1963, the Strangler killed another elderly victim. Sixty-nine-year-old Mrs Mary Brown lived in Lawrence, an industrial town twenty-five miles from Boston. The fact that her breasts had been exposed and a fork stuck in one of them should have suggested that she had been murdered by the 'Phantom' (as the press had now labelled the killer). However, because her skull had been beaten to a pulp with a piece of brass piping, she was not recognised as a Strangler victim – it was assumed that she had disturbed a burglar. In fact, she had been manually throttled.

The next victim was also nontypical. On 9 May 1963 a friend of twenty-three-year-old graduate student Beverly Sams was puzzled when she failed to answer the telephone, and borrowed a key from the building supervisor. Beverly had been stabbed in the throat, and a stocking knotted around her neck. She was naked, and her legs spreadeagled and tied to the bed supports. Medical examination revealed that she had been raped.

Four months later, on 8, September friends of a fifty-eight-year-old divorcee, Evelyn Corbin, wondered why she failed to keep a lunch appointment and let themselves into her flat. Evelyn Corbin was lying almost naked on the bed, nylon stockings knotted around her throat and her panties rammed into her mouth. There was semen in her vagina and in her mouth.

On 23 November 1963, the day President Kennedy was assassinated, the Strangler killed his next victim in Lawrence. She was Joanne Graff, a Sunday-school teacher. She had been strangled with stockings and raped.

The final victim was strangled on 4 January 1964. She was nineteen-year-old Mary Sullivan, who was found by room-mates when they came back from work. She was sitting on the bed, her buttocks on the pillow, her back against the headboard. Her knees had been parted, and a broom handle inserted into her vagina. Semen was running from the corner of her mouth. A card saying 'Happy New Year' had been propped against her foot. The killer had placed her body in a position where it would be seen as soon as anyone opened the door.

The murders ceased; but a rapist who became known as The Green Man – because he wore green clothes – began operating over a wide area that included Massachusetts, Connecticut, New Hampshire and Rhode Island. On one occasion he raped four women in a single day. He gained entrance to the apartment – sometimes forcing the lock with a strip of plastic – and often threatened the victim with a knife. When she was stripped, he would caress her with his hands and mouth; then, if he judged she wanted him to, he 'raped' her. (He was later to insist that the 'Green Man' had never raped an unwilling woman.) He was never physically violent, and had even been known to apologise before he left.

On the morning of 27 October 1964 a young married woman was dozing in bed after her husband had gone to work when a man entered the bedroom. He was dressed in green trousers, a green shirt, and wore green sunglasses, and he insisted that he was a detective. After seizing her by the throat he threatened her with a knife. He tore off her nightclothes, stuffed a pair of panties into her mouth, and tied her wrists and ankles to the bedposts. Then he kissed and bit her from head to foot, finally ejaculating on her stomach. His sexual appetite was obviously enormous; he continued to abuse her sexually for a great deal longer before he seemed satisfied. Then, after apologising, he left. The girl called the police immediately, and went on to descrbe her assailant in such detail that a police artist was able to make a sketch of his face. As one of the detectives was studying it, he commented: 'This looks like the Measuring Man.' The 'Measuring Man' had been a harmless crank named Albert DeSalvo, who had been arrested in 1960 for talking his way into girls' apartments claiming to represent a modelling agency. If the girl indicated that she might be interested in modelling, he would take her measurements with a tape measure. After that he would thank her politely and leave. The aspiring model would never hear from him again, and it was this that made some of them so indignant that they reported him. The police were baffled, since there seemed to be no obvious motive – although some girls admitted that they had allowed him to raise their skirts to measure from the hip to the knee. On a few occasions, he had allowed himself an intimate caress; but if the girl protested, he immediately apologised. One girl, as he crouched with his hand on her panties, had said: 'I'd better get these clothes off or you won't get the right measurements', and stripped. On this occasion, as on a number of others, the 'Measuring Man' had ended up in bed with the girl.

On 17 March 1960 a police patrol that had been set up to trap the 'Measuring Man' saw a man acting suspiciously in a backyard in Cambridge, Mass., and arrested him. Girls identified him as the 'Measuring Man', and he finally admitted it – claiming that he did it as a kind of lark, in order to make himself feel superior to college-educated girls. In May 1961 DeSalvo was sentenced to serve two years in the Middlesex

County House of Correction. He served eleven months before being released. He had told a probation officer that he thought there was something wrong with him — that he seemed to be wildly oversexed, so that he needed intercourse six or more times a day. No-one suggested that he needed to see a psychiatrist.

Albert DeSalvo had clearly graduated from caressing girls as he measured them to rape. He was arrested on 5 November 1964 and identified by some of his victims. On 4 February 1965 he was committed to the Bridgewater State Hospital, a mental institution in Massachusetts.

Bridgewater had — and still has — many sexual psychopaths in residence, and many spoke freely about their exploits, particularly in the group therapy sessions. Albert DeSalvo was not reticent about his own sexual prowess, which was apparently considerable. He described how, in the summer of 1948, when he was seventeen, he had worked as a dishwasher in a Cape Cod motel, and spent much time swimming and sunbathing on the beach. There were many college girls there, and they found the powerfully-built youth attractive. Word of DeSalvo's amazing sexual prowess soon spread. 'They would even come up to the motel sometimes looking for me and some nights we would spend the whole night doing it down on the beach, stopping for a while, then doing it again . . .'

Possibly because he encountered a certain scepticism — he had a reputation as a boaster — DeSalvo began hinting that he had done far more serious things than raping a few women. Only one of his ward-mates took him seriously: a murderer called George Nassar. At first, Nassar also thought DeSalvo was merely boasting — particularly when he confided that he was the Boston Strangler. What finally convinced him was DeSalvo's detailed knowledge of the crimes. 'He knows more about them stranglings than the cops.'

Nassar knew there was a large reward for the Boston Strangler, and he spoke to his attorney, F.Lee Bailey, who had achieved fame when he obtained freedom for Dr Sam Sheppard, accused of murdering his wife. Bailey was also sceptical — there are endless fake confessions to almost every widely publicised murder — but when he went to see DeSalvo on 4 March 1965, he soon realised that this sounded authentic. DeSalvo was not a man of high intelligence — although bright and articulate — and it seemed unlikely that he could have read and memorised newspaper accounts of the murders. He even mentioned a murder that no-one knew about – an old lady of eighty or so who had died of a heart attack as he grabbed her. In fact, DeSalvo's account enabled the police to identify her as eighty-five-year-old Mary Mullens who had been found dead in her Boston apartment two weeks after the murder of Anna Slesers, the first Strangler victim. DeSalvo's descriptions of other murder scenes made it clear that he knew details that had never been published. Most important of all, he knew exactly what the Strangler had done to various victims. This information had been deliberately suppressed, giving rise to all kind of wild rumours of torture and perversion. DeSalvo knew, for example, precisely what position Mary Sullivan – the last victim – had been left in, and that she had a broom handle inserted into her vagina; and he was able to describe in precise detail the rooms of most of the victims.

There were some odd complications. Several witnesses who had seen a man entering apartment buildings where stranglings had taken place failed to identify DeSalvo as the man. And two women who had seen the Strangler – including Gertrude Gruen, the German girl who had fought him off – not only failed to identify DeSalvo, but identified George Nassar as the strangler. Yet DeSalvo's incredibly detailed knowledge of the crimes finally convinced most of those involved with the case that he alone was the Boston Strangler.

In the long run, all this proved irrelevant. Albert DeSalvo stood trial for the Green Man rapes, and in 1967 was sentenced to permanent detention in the Walpole State Prison, where he could receive psychiatric treatment. On 26 November 1973 DeSalvo was found dead in his cell, stabbed through the heart. No motive was ever established, and whoever was responsible was never caught.

In January 1964, while the Boston Strangler was still at large, the assistant attorney general of Massachusetts, John S. Bottomly, decided to set up a committee of psychiatrists to attempt to establish some kind of 'psychological profile' of the killer. One of the psychiatrists who served on that committee was Dr James A.Brussel, the man who had been so successful in describing New York's 'Mad Bomber' (see pp. 81–6). When he attended his first meeting, Brussel discovered that there was a sharp division of opinion within the committee. One group believed that there were two stranglers, one of whom killed old women, and the other young girls; the other group thought there was only one strangler.

It was at his second meeting of the committee — in April 1965 — that Brussel was hit by a sudden 'hunch' as he listened to a psychiatrist pointing out that in some cases, semen was found in the vagina, while in others, it was found on the breasts, thighs, or even on the carpet. When it came to his turn to speak, Brussel outlined the theory that had suddenly come to him 'in a flash'.

'I think we're dealing with one man. The apparent differences in M.O., I believe, result from changes that have been going on in this man. Over the two-year period during which he has been committing these murders, he had gone through a series of upheavals . . .'

The first five victims, said Brussel, were elderly women, and there was no semen in the vaginas. They had been manipulated in other ways — 'a type of sexual molestation that might be expected of a small boy, not a man'. A boy gets over his sexual obsession with his mother, and transfers his interest to girls of his own age. 'The Strangler. . .achieved this transfer — achieved emotional puberty — in a matter of months.' Now he wanted to achieve orgasm inside younger women. And with the final victim, Mary Sullivan, the semen was in her mouth and over her breasts; a broom had been inserted in the vagina. The Strangler was making a gesture of triumph and of defiance: 'I throw my sex in your face.'

This man, said Brussel, was a physically powerful individual, probably in his late twenties or early thirties, the time the paranoid reaction reaches its peak. He hazarded a guess that the Strangler's nationality was Italian or Spanish, since garrotting is a method used by bandits in both countries.

Brussel's final 'guesses' were startlingly to the point. He believed that the Strangler had stopped killing because he had worked it out of his system. He had, in effect, grown up. And he would finally be caught because he would be unable to resist talking about his crimes and his new-found maturity.

The rest of the committee was polite but sceptical. But one year later, Brussel was proved correct when DeSalvo began admitting to George Nassar that he was the Boston Strangler.

In 1966, Brussel went to Boston to interview DeSalvo. He had been half-expecting a misshapen monster, and was surprised to be greeted by a good-looking, polite young man with a magnificent head of dark hair. (Brussel had even foretold that the Strangler would have well-tended hair, since he was obsessed by the impression he made on women.) Brussel found him charming, and soon realised how DeSalvo had talked his way into so many apartments; he seemed a thoroughly nice young man. Then what had turned him into a murderer? As usual, it proved to be the family and childhood background. DeSalvo's father was the worst kind of brute. He beat his wife and children mercilessly – on one occasion he broke his wife's fingers one by one. He beat one son with a hosepipe so badly – for knocking over a box of fruit – that the boy was not allowed on the beach all summer because he was covered in black and yellow bruises. He often brought a prostitute home and had sex with her in front of the children. Their mother was also less than satisfactory. She was indifferent and self-preoccupied, and had no time for the children. As a child Albert had been a 'loner', his only real friend a dog that lived in a junkyard. He developed sadistic compulsions at an early age. He and a playmate called Billy used to place a dog and cat in two compartments of an orange crate and starve them for days, then pull out the partition, and watch as the cat scratched out the dog's eyes. But, like so many psychopaths (Albert Fish and Gary Heidnik, for example) he could display considerable charm and make himself liked.

The real key to DeSalvo was sex. From an early age he was insatiable, 'walking around with a rail on most of the time, ready to take on any broad or fag come along, or to watch some broad and masturbate. . .thinking about sex a lot, more than anything, and needing it so much all the time. If only somebody could've seen it then and told me it was not normal, even sick. . .' DeSalvo is here exaggerating; a large proportion of healthy young males go around in much the same state. DeSalvo's environment offered a great deal of sexual stimulus. He participated in sex games with his brothers and sisters when he was five or six years old. At the age of eight he performed oral sex on a girl at school, and was soon persuading girls to do the same for him. Albert DeSalvo was turned into a sexual psychopath by the same kind of 'hothouse environment' that had nurtured Albert Fish. Combined with the lack of moral restraint that resulted from his family background, his tremendous sex urge soon led him to rape – his own estimation was that he had raped or assaulted almost two thousand women. During the course of the Green Man attacks, he raped four women in a single day, and even then tried to pick up a fifth. This was something that Brussel had failed to recognise. The Strangler had not been 'searching for his potency' – he had always been potent. During his teens, a woman neighbour had asked him if it was true that he had a permanent erection, and when he modestly admitted it, invited him into her apartment. 'She went down on her knees and blowed me and I come almost right off and she said: "Oh, now you went and come and what am I going to have to get screwed with?", and I said: "Don't worry, I'll have a hard on again in a few minutes".' When he left her, she was exhausted, but he was still unsatisfied. It was not potency DeSalvo was searching for, but emotional stability.

Yet Brussel was undoubtedly correct about the main thing: that DeSalvo's murders were part of an attempt to grow up. The murders of elderly women were acts of revenge against the mother who had rejected him; but the murder of the young black girl Sophie Clark signalled a change. When he knocked on her door DeSalvo had no idea that she would be so young – he was looking for elderly women, like his mother. Her white dress and black stockings excited him. He talked his way into her apartment by claiming to be a workman sent to carry out repairs – the method he invariably used – then, when she turned her back, hooked his arm round her neck and squeezed until she was unconscious. After that he raped her, then strangled her. The experience taught him that he preferred young girls to older women, and caused the change in his method.

Yet from the beginning, DeSalvo suffered from the same problem as so many sex killers: self-division. A month before he killed Anna Slesers – the first victim – DeSalvo talked his way into the apartment of an attractive Swedish girl, claiming that he had been sent to repair the ceiling. 'She was laughing and she was very nice. An attractive, kind woman.' In the bathroom she turned her back on him, and DeSalvo hooked his powerful forearm round her neck. As he began to squeeze, he saw her face in the bathroom mirror, 'the look of awful fear and pain.' 'And I see myself, the look on my own face. . .and I can't do it. I take my arm away.' The girl asked him what he was going to do, and he admitted that he was going to rape her and possibly kill her. 'I tell you now that I was ashamed — I began to cry.' He fell on his knees in front of her and said: 'Oh God, what was I doing? I am a good Catholic man with a wife and children. I don't know what to do . . . Please call the police.' The girl told him to go home. 'She was a kind person and she was trying to be good to me. But how much better it would have been if she had called the police right then and there.' The episode is an interesting confirmation of a theory advanced by Brussel to his fellow committee members: that the Strangler only attacked women who turned their backs on him, because it seemed a form of 'rejection'.

After killing Sophie Clark, he came very close to sparing his next victim, Patricia Bissette. 'She was very nice to me, she treated me like a man — I thought of doing it to her and I talked myself out of it.' She offered him coffee, and when he offered to go out and get some doughnuts, told him she had food there. 'Then it was as good as over. I didn't want it to happen but then I knew that it would.' After he had throttled her into unconsciousness and was raping her, 'I want to say that all the time I was doing this, I was thinking about how nice she had been to me and it was making me feel bad. She had treated me right, and I was doing this thing to her . . .'

At other times, Mr Hyde took over — as in his next murder, that of Mary Brown in Lawrence. This murder was not, at the time, recognised as one of the Strangler's crimes, because its ferocity seemed untypical. DeSalvo described how he had knocked on the door and explained to the grey-haired lady who answered that he had come to paint the kitchen. She let him in without question. In his pocket, DeSalvo had a piece of brass pipe that he had found in the hallway. 'As she walked to the kitchen, her back was to me. I hit her right on the back of the head with the pipe . . . this was terrible, and I don't like talking about it. She went down and I ripped her things open, showing her busts . . . she was unconscious and bleeding . . . I don't know why but then I hit her again on the head with the pipe. I kept on hitting and hitting her with the pipe . . . this is like out of this world . . . this is unbelievable . . . oh, it was terrible . . . because her head felt like it was all gone . . . terrible . . . then I took this fork and stuck it into her right bust.' As in so many other cases, DeSalvo was unable to say why he did it. (Similarly, he had been unable to explain why he rifled the apartments after committing the murders: he was not looking for anything specific and apparently took nothing.) What he failed to recognise was that, like so many other serial killers, he had been taken over — literally possessed — by a sadistic compulsion, the sheer joy of destruction. Yet even as he did it, he continued to feel 'This is terrible.'

DeSalvo never suceeded in overcoming his feeling of guilt. He intimidated the tenth victim, twenty-three-year-old Beverly Sams, with a knife; she made him promise not to rape her, because she was afraid of pregnancy. When he had her lying on the bed, DeSalvo decided to gag her. 'Then I thought that I wouldn't want a broad like that, with her stupid ideas to see me, so I tied a blindfold over her eyes.' When she recovered consciousness and discovered that he was raping her, she called him an animal. This enraged him enough to make him stab her. When he could kill like this — giving rein to his resentment — he experienced no guilt.

The last victim, Mary Sullivan, tried to reason with him, to talk him out of rape. Her words struck home. 'I recall thinking at the time, yes, she is right, I don't have to do these things any more now . . . I heard what this girl is saying and it stayed with me.' At the time he was angry, and hit her several times. As he tied her up and prepared to rape her, he realised 'I would never be able to do it again'. After raping her, he strangled her manually, while she struggled to get up. 'This is what I don't like to talk about. This is killing me even to talk about.' After death, her face looked 'surprised and even disappointed with the way I had treated her'. Then DeSalvo propped her up against the head of the bed, straddled her chest, and masturbated so that the sperm would strike her face. 'She is sitting there with the stuff on her nose and mouth and chin. I am not in control of myself. I know that something awful has been done, that the whole world of human beings are shocked and will be even more shocked.' He went into the kitchen and fetched a broom, then inserted it into her vagina, 'not so far as to hurt her . . . you say it is funny that I worry about hurting her when she is already dead, but that is the truth . . . I do not want to hurt her'. And, after leaving the apartment; 'as far as I was concerned it wasn't me. I can't explain it to you any other way.' When Brussel later pressed him to explain why Mary Sullivan was his final victim, he admitted that she had reminded him of his daughter. Dr Jekyll was back in control.

That he would now remain in control was demonstrated in a sensational manner. In February 1967, a month after being sentenced to life imprisonment, DeSalvo and two more inmates escaped from the Bridgewater mental institution. The city of Boston was plunged into panic. Interviewed by the press, Brussel was unconcerned. He pointed out that DeSalvo had left a note behind, apologising for taking unauthorised leave, and explaining that he was only doing so to draw attention to the fact that he was receiving no psychiatric treatment. He promised that he would harm nobody. Brussel stated that he was sure DeSalvo would honour his promise. In fact, DeSalvo gave himself up after only thirty-six hours. His protest failed in its purpose – he was transferred to the virtually escape-proof Walpole Prison, but still failed to receive any psychiatric treatment.

At least Brussel had proved his point. The Boston Strangler had raped and murdered his way to a kind of maturity.

Six

Folie à Deux

Soon after midnight on Sunday 2 November 1980 a young couple emerged from a restaurant in Sacramento, California, and walked towards their car. They had spent the evening at a Founder's Day dance in the restaurant, and were wearing formal evening dress. On their way through the car park, they were accosted by a pretty blonde girl whose swollen stomach suggested an advanced stage of pregnancy. As they stopped politely to find out what she wanted, the girl pointed an automatic pistol at them, and ordered them to climb into the back seat of an Oldsmobile. The front passenger seat was occupied by a big man with a sullen expression.

At that moment, a student who happened to know the young couple – and who was in the mood for a practical joke – decided to climb into the driver's seat of the Oldsmobile, as if about to drive away. His position prevented him from seeing the gun in the hand of the sullen-faced man, but a glance at the face of his friends told him something was wrong. A moment later, he was startled when the pretty blonde screamed: 'What the fuck are you doing in my car?' and slapped his face. As he watched her drive away with a squeal of tyres, Andy Beal had the presence of mind to concentrate on the numberplate of the speeding car, and to write it down on a piece of paper. Then he hurried to the nearest telephone and rang the police. When the registration number was fed into the motor vehicle computer it revealed that the car was registered to twenty-four-year-old Charlene Williams, with an address in Sacramento.

The abducted couple were twenty-two-year-old Craig Miller and Beth Sowers, twenty-one, and when, the next morning, the police went to call on Charlene Williams at the home of her parents, Chuck and Mercedes, they were still missing. The attractive girl who opened the door to the policemen acknowl-

219

edged that she was the owner of the Oldsmobile, but denied any knowledge of the kidnapping. She explained that she had been drunk the night before, and that her memory was hazy. But she insisted that she had spent the evening alone. It was after they had left Charlene Williams that the officers learned that Craig Miller had been found in adjoining Eldorado County; he was lying face down, with three bullets in the back of his head. By the time the police returned to Charlene's residence, the Oldsmobile had gone, and so had Charlene. As the police looked into her background, they soon had reason to believe that she had been accompanied by her thirty-four-year-old 'husband' Gerald Armand Gallego, who had a lengthy record which included three years in jail for armed robbery.

The couple had left in a hurry, and so were unprepared for a long flight. Two weeks later, Charlene contacted her parents and asked them to wire five hundred dollars. When she went to collect it at a Western Union office in Omaha, Nebraska, police were waiting for her. Her 'husband' was also taken into custody. Five days later, on 22 November 1980, the body of Beth Sowers was found in a field in Placer County. Her evening gown was badly torn, and she had been shot three times in the back of the head. Medical examination revealed that she had been raped.

By the time Gerald Gallego was in custody, the Sacramento police had learned a great deal about him, and it suggested that he was a multiple sex killer. Heredity may have played some part in his makeup — his father had been executed for three murders in 1955, at the age of twenty-eight. Gerald was unaware of this when he had his first encounters with the law, at the age of ten. When he was thirteen, he was sentenced to a period in a youth penal facility for having sexual relations with a seven-year-old girl. He married at the age of eighteen, and his first wife bore him a daughter, Sally Jo. By the time he was thirty-two he had been married seven times. He had also been committing incest with his daughter since she was eight. Then, when she was fourteen, he sodomised her and raped her girlfriend. The teenagers went to the Butte County police, and Gallego was forced to flee.

By this time — 1978 — Gallego had already known Charlene for a year. A quiet, shy girl, she was the only daughter of a wealthy Sacramento businessman, and had led a pampered existence. At college she had become acquainted with drugs and sex and, by the time she was twenty-one, she had been married and divorced twice. She had met Gerald Gallego on a blind date, and was fascinated by his air of macho brutality, and his need for violence during sex. They lived together for a while, then married in 1978. (In fact they were not legally married, since Gallego had omitted to get a divorce from a previous wife.) Charlene was not only aware of his criminal record, but of his intense fantasy life. Gallego confided that his greatest desire was for the 'perfect sex slave' — preferably a teenage virgin — whom he could hold captive and order to fulfil his demands, which included oral sex and sodomy. As Charlene later confessed, she had agreed to help him in his quest.

On 11 September 1978 they had driven to a shopping mall in Sacramento, and Charlene had accosted two young girls, Rhonda Scheffler, seventeen, and her sixteen-year-old friend Kippi Vaught. She lured them back to the Oldsmobile with the suggestion that they might like to smoke some marijuana. Once there, they were forced into the back of the van — which had been fitted with a mattress — and Gallego was able to put into operation his fantasy of rape, while Charlene sat in the front of the van. The girls were then driven to a site fifteen miles east of Sacramento, where both were 'executed' with three bullets in the head, and their bodies dumped.

Gerald and Charlene Gallego soon became highly efficient killers. The next victims, nine months later, were a fourteen- and a fifteen-year-old girl, Kaye Colley and Brenda Judd, picked up at the annual county fair in Reno on 24 June 1979; their bodies have never been found, although according to Charlene Gallego they are in a shallow grave near Lovelock, Nevada.

Ten months later, on 24 April 1980, two seventeen-year-olds, Stacy Ann Redican and Karen Chipman-Twiggs, were abducted from a Sacramento shopping mall; their decomposed bodies were found near Lovelock, Nevada, in July 1980. They had been killed by hammer blows to the skull.

Linda Teresa Aguilar was five months pregnant when she disappeared somewhere between Port Orford, Oregon, and nearby Gold Beach on 6 June 1980, less than three months after the two previous victims had vanished. Her body was found three weeks later in a grave nine miles south of Gold Beach; she was bound with a nylon rope, and beaten with a blunt instrument; sand in her windpipe revealed that she had been buried alive.

Five weeks later, on 17 July 1980, a thirty-four-year-old Sacramento waitress, Virginia Mochel, vanished after she walked out of the tavern where she worked. Police learned that she had been talking to a married couple in the tavern: a man who was drunk and boisterous, and a pretty but subdued girl. Her naked body was discovered in October near Sacramento, the hands tied behind her with fishing line.

It was in the following month that Gerald and Charlene Gallego waited in the car park outside the Carousel restaurant in Sacramento, and Gallego saw a pretty girl in evening dress whom he decided he wanted to possess. Beth Sowers was with her fiance, Craig Miller, but that made no difference. Charlene forced them into the van at gunpoint, Miller was despatched a few miles away, then Beth Sowers was taken back to Gallego's apartment and dragged into the bedroom. In the next room, Charlene Gallego listened to her cries and pleas as she was made to cater to Gallego's perverted sexual demands. Then the crying girl was dragged out of the bedroom and thrown back into the van, to be taken to her place of execution. After that, Charlene dropped Gallego off at his flat, and went back to the home of her parents, where she lived. The next morning the police arrived – the prompt action of the student who had taken her registration number had finally put an end to the killing spree.

Gallego proved to be a difficult prisoner; he had always had a reputation for aggression, and during his previous jail term had told a prison counsellor: 'The only thing that interests me is killing God.' Now, at the arraignment, he leapt to his feet and screamed at reporters: 'Get the hell out of here! We're not funny people. We're not animals.' He fought violently, overturning tables and chairs, before he was subdued.

Charlene Gallego was at first unco-operative, but was eventually persuaded to enter into plea-bargaining in exchange for testifying against her 'husband'. Her story made it clear that she had also been Gallego's 'sex slave'; she explained that she needed the emotional security he provided. This is why she felt she had to comply with his demand for help in kidnapping more 'sex slaves'. Her husband, she said, had pursued his aim of the 'perfect love slave' obsessively, even rating his victims on their performances.

On 21 June 1983 Gallego was sentenced to die by lethal injection. In accordance with her plea bargain, Charlene Gallego received sixteen years in jail.

Before the 1960s, cases of 'duo' sex murder in which one of the participants was a woman were unknown. The reason is obvious; more than any other criminal, the sex criminal tends to work alone and to take no-one else into his confidence. A 1980 FBI report on lust killers states: 'The disorganised asocial lust murderer exhibits primary characteristics of social aversion. This individual prefers his own company to that of others and would be typified as a loner.' This applies to most sex killers from Jack the Ripper to Heinrich Pommerencke. Such men may even be married – like the Düsseldorf murderer Peter Kürten or the Boston Strangler – but their wives seldom suspect that their husbands are sex killers. The very idea of a wife helping her husband to rape another woman seems absurd. So why is it that such cases began to appear in the 1960s, and that their number has continued to increase? It can hardly be unrelated to the fact that the 1960s also saw the emergence of the 'self-esteem' killer. In fact, as the Gallego case makes clear, 'duo' sex crimes *are* crimes of self-esteem. As agent Robert Hazelwood observed: 'Sexual assault services non-sexual needs – power needs.' This is not invariably true – or at least, it used not to be true. Robert Poulin's craving for a woman was simply a desire to lose his virginity, to 'fuck some girl'; the same is true of Heinrich Pommerencke. They were like starving men who steal food. The archetypal sex criminal was described by the Austrian novelist Robert Musil in *The Man Without Qualities* (1930–43). Moosbrugger is arresting for stabbing a prostitute to death. Musil writes:

'As a boy, Moosbrugger had been a poverty-stricken wretch, a shepherd-lad in a hamlet so small that it did not even have a village street; and he was so poor that he never spoke to a girl. Girls were something that he could only look at . . . Now one must imagine just what that means. Something that one craves for, just as naturally as one craves for bread or water, is only there to be looked at. After a time one's desire for it becomes unnatural. It climbs over a stile, becoming visible right up to the knees . . . '

This describes the typical sex criminal of the first half of the twentieth century; he craves sex as he craves bread and water. (It shows keen insight on Musil's part to make Moosbrugger a travelling journeyman; it has already been observed in an earlier chapter that a large number of sex killers have been tramps and vagrants.) As the last remnants of Victorianism gradually melt away, 'it' ceases to be visible only up to the knees; it wanders around on beaches in bikinis; underwear advertisements show it in a state of undress that hints at bedrooms; magazines like *Playboy* show it naked in seductive poses. This is why the desire of a Moosbrugger — or Pommerencke or Poulin — finally becomes 'unnatural'.

The new type of sex killer who began to appear in the 1960s was not driven by mere desire, but by self-assertion. In 1973, the police of Veracruz, Mexico, finally caught a sex murderer who had been preying on courting couples since 1968. He was thirty-one year old José Solano Marcelino, and he had made a habit of shooting the man, then raping the girl. 'When I had the luck to find only one car, I'd sneak up on the pair inside. I was always armed with a gun, and my face was masked by one of my wife's stockings . . . When I pointed the gun at them I could see, and enjoyed, the fear of death in their eyes. I liked it so much to see the male squirm, and the woman frightened and crying, that I'd make my threats last for a long time. When I could see that the panic was driving the couple to the brink of madness, I'd shoot the man. Then I'd take the woman. If she tried to give me trouble by fighting or screaming, I'd bang her over the head with the gun and tie her up. I never wanted to have sex with an unconscious woman, and so when they fainted, I waited before I had a session with them.' Asked why he killed the men he explained: 'I guess I sacrificed them because I got a kick out of it, like I did out of tormenting them before I put them out of their misery. And then later it gave an added tang to sexing their women.'

Marcelino had been arrested on suspicion of being the lover's lane rapist in March 1969, but an emotional appeal from his lawyer, who described him as a loving husband who adored his children, had led to his release. While the police continued to keep him under surveillance, he ceased the attacks. In 1970, he began again, until he had killed or seriously wounded more than a dozen men. The women were raped repeatedly, then tortured. 'I'd prick them here and there with my knife, and squeeze and pinch to make them quiver with fear. It made me feel good to see the women suffer, and the fear and horror in their eyes fed something in me that was sometimes even more pleasurable than having sex with them.'

Finally, he crept up on a couple who were picnicking, and hit the man — Gregorio Sanchez Luna — with a stone, then shot him dead. After that he made the girl, Maria Josefina Martinez, strip and drag the body into the bushes. Then, from five in the afternoon until three the following morning, he raped her and played 'torture games'. Finally, sated, he drove off. After he had left, she made her way to the highway and contacted the police. Since Marcelino had failed to wear his stocking mask — for the first time — she was able to give the police an accurate description, which they instantly recognised as the man they had held four years earlier. He was arrested in a dawn raid, and immediately identified by his victim. Sentenced to forty years in jail, the rapist remarked: 'Well, if that's the way it is, that's the way it is. But I *did* have one hell of a time for five years.'

Gerald Gallego's attitude towards women was also sadistic and manipulative. They were there for his pleasure and his use. Most women quickly came to recognise this lack of give and take, and declined to co-operate — hence Gallego's seven marriages in fourteen years. But Charlene Gallego was masochistic and eager to be manipulated. Her only desire was to serve her master; it was a kind of religious conversion. If Gallego's condition for continuing the relationship was that she should help other women to their deaths. It only proved that her husband was thrillingly unlike other men. Gallego's pleasure lay in dominating, hers in being dominated.

The importance of 'dominance' — the 'pecking order' — in animal behaviour has been recognised only in fairly recent times. It was first noticed in flocks of domestic fowl — in which dominant individuals tend to peck subordinate ones. Only then was it slowly recognised that *all* animals, including human beings, have a 'pecking order', a kind of chain in which everyone is more dominant or subordinate than someone else. In groups such as lions, gorillas or rats, dominance is usually established by aggressive encounters, but once one of the animals has won the fight, all aggression usually evaporates, and the loser shows submissive behaviour from then on. The other challengers seem to acquire a sense of social responsibility, and he (or she) passes beyond the range of quarrels. The same phenomenon can often be seen in politicians who have been promoted to prime minister or president; a very mediocre party hack often develops genuine leadership qualities. This helps to explain that fundamental human craving for power, and why those who have acquired power cling to it so tightly. Supreme power places one above the 'rat-race'.

One of the most exciting observations about 'dominance' was made during the Korean war. Attempting to understand why there had been so few escapes of American prisoners, observers discovered that the Chinese had made use of an interesting technique. They had watched the prisoners carefully to establish which of them were 'dominant'; then they had taken these dominant prisoners, and placed them under heavy guard. As soon as the 'leaders' had been removed, the other prisoners became more or less inert, and could be left almost without guards.

The most interesting observation was that the number of 'dominant' prisoners was always the same: one in twenty, or five per cent. In fact, the explorer Stanley had known about this 'dominant five per cent' at the turn of the century. Bernard Shaw once asked him how many people in his party could take over the leadership if Stanley himself was ill; Stanley replied: 'One in twenty.' Shaw asked if that was exact or approximate; Stanley replied: 'Exact.'

Observations of zoologists like Lorenz and Tinbergen indicated that this applies to all animal species: five per cent are 'dominant'. A psychologist named John Calhoun made an equally interesting observation: that when rats are overcrowded, the dominant five per cent becomes a criminal five per cent. Overcrowded rats express their dominance in behaviour in completely uncharacteristic of rats in natural conditions: for example, in rape and cannibalism. Some animals – like Sika deer – simply die of stress when overcrowded. Human beings seem to have a far higher resistance to stress than any other animal; they tend to react to overcrowding – like the rats – by developing criminal behaviour. It is significant that no serial killer has so far emerged from a socially privileged background; the majority were brought up in overcrowded slums. The zoologist Desmond Morris remarked that cities are 'human zoos', and added: 'Under normal conditions, in their natural habitats, wild animals do not mutilate themselves, masturbate, attack their offspring, develop stomach ulcers, become fetishists, suffer from obesity, form homosexual pair-bonds, or commit murder. Among city dwellers . . . all these things occur.' The conclusion to be drawn may be that the 'crime explosion' will continue until such time as the population explosion has been brought under control.

Overcrowded slums have always existed, and, of course, crime has always existed in overcrowded slums. Why should they produce sadistic sex killers in the second half of the twentieth century? The answer to this question has already emerged in earlier chapters. In societies with a high level of poverty, theft is the commonest form of crime. In more 'successful' societies, sex crime makes its appearance, as overcrowding in slums produces the 'criminal rat' syndrome, with the dominant five per cent expressing their dominance through rape. In 'affluent societies', where a higher level of education means that all levels of society begin to glimpse the possibility of wealth and achievement, the craving for 'upward mobility' becomes as urgent as the craving for sexual fulfilment, and 'self-esteem' crime makes its appearance. (It may or may not be significant that self-esteem murder made its appearance at a time when the pop star had become a well-established phenomenon, so that every underprivileged teenager could begin to glimpse the possibility of wealth and fame.) In the second half of the eighteenth century, thinkers like Rousseau and Tom Paine stated the fundamental principle that all men have a right to freedom; in the second half of the twentieth century, there is a powerful unstated assumption that all men have a right to fame and celebrity.

Abraham Maslow — who was the first to describe the 'hierarchy of needs' — also made an important observation about 'dominance'. He had become curious about the subject after observing the behaviour of monkeys in the Bronx zoo. They seemed to engage in almost constant sex — something that has been observed among many animals in captivity; but what puzzled Maslow was that the sex often seemed 'abnormal' — males would mount other males, and sometimes females would even mount males. It slowly dawned on him that this was because sex was a form of 'dominance behaviour'; what was happening was that the more dominant animals were asserting themselves by mounting the less dominant animals. (Robert Ardrey has pointed out that under natural conditions 'sex is a sideshow in the world of animals'; it only assumes exaggerated importance in captivity – another observation that may help to explain the rise in sex crime.)

Maslow also observed that if a new monkey is added to a group of monkeys, the newcomer would often get beaten up, the attack often being led by a previously non-dominant monkey. He noted that the previously non-dominant monkey would often behave with extreme ferocity, as if making up for its previously inferior status. Here again we glimpse a parallel with the sadistic behaviour of many 'self-esteem' criminals.

Perhaps his most interesting observations concerned dominance in women. In 1936, Maslow began a series of Kinsey-type interviews with college women – he preferred women to men as interviewees because they were capable of greater frankness; male answers tended to be distorted by self-esteem. His findings, stated in a paper of 1939 (and another three years later) was that female sexuality is related to dominance. The higher-dominance females went in for more promiscuity, lesbian relations, masturbation and sexual experimentation (fellatio, sodomy, etc.).

What surprised him was that he discovered that his subjects tended to fall into three groups: high dominance, medium dominance and low dominance. A medium-dominance woman might have a high rating for sex drive, but her sexual experience was usually limited; she tended to be a 'one-man woman'. A low-dominance woman (and these were difficult to get into the study group) was inclined to feel that sex was strictly for child-bearing, and one low-dominance woman who was sterile refused her husband sex even though she had a high sex drive. (It is important to note that all three groups could have a high sex drive, but that the *amount* of sex they indulged in depended on how dominant they were.) Medium-dominance women had a romantic attitude to sex; they liked to be wooed with lights and flowers and soft music, and they liked the kind of male who would be a 'good provider' – someone who was stable rather than exciting. Low-dominance women seemed to feel that sex was rather disgusting. Most of them thought that the male sexual organ was ugly, while high-dominance women thought it beautiful.

The really significant observation that emerged from the study was that the women tended to prefer males who were slightly more dominant than themselves, *but* within their own dominance group. Low-dominance females preferred the kind of man who would admire them from a distance for years without pressing his suit. They found medium- and high-dominance males rather frightening. Medium-dominance women found high-dominance males frightening. High-dominance women like the kind of man who would sweep them off their feet, and in lovemaking hurl them on a bed and take them with a certain amount of force. One highly dominant woman spent years looking for a male who was even more dominant than herself, and failed to find him. When finally she discovered a man of slightly superior dominance, she married him and remained faithful; but she enjoyed picking fights that would make him violent and end in virtual rape – an experience she found immensely exciting. One high-dominance woman who could have an orgasm virtually by looking at a man admitted to not having orgasms with two lovers because they were too weak. 'I just couldn't give in to them.'

When writing his biography of Abraham Maslow in the early 1970s, Colin Wilson was struck by the fact that this dominance relation seems to explain many crime partnerships – for example, the Leopold and Loeb murder case (mentioned in Chapter One), in which two Chicago students from wealthy families committed various crimes – ending in murder – for 'kicks'. Most commentators on the case remain content with the dubious explanation that they wanted to prove that they were 'supermen'; but the master-slave relationship between Richard Loeb and Nathan Leopold makes us aware of what really happened. Loeb's ego – his self-esteem – was nourished by his 'slave'; but it was not enough to express this self-esteem merely by dominating Leopold (who, in any case, wanted to be 'used). Like any juvenile delinquent, Loeb had to express it by 'defying society', committing petty crimes for pleasure rather than gain. It was this craving to *express* his dominance through 'defiance' that led to the scheme to kidnap and murder a child. Without his 'slave', Loeb would almost certainly never have become a killer.

The most significant observation about the case is that Leopold and Loeb belonged to two different dominance groups: Loeb was 'high-dominance', Leopold medium. This, according to Maslow, seldom happens in ordinary human pair-bondings. To begin with, the high-dominance person is seldom sexually interested in people outside his own dominance group. He may cheerfully sleep with medium- or low-dominance women, but he is incapable of taking any *personal* interest in them. If, in fact, he consents to relations with a person outside his dominance group − out of loneliness and frustration − the resultant boost to his ego can amount to a kind of intoxication. In a well-adjusted person, this would usually lead to an increase in self-confidence. In a person whose dominance has been suppressed − as in Maslow's 'previously inferior monkeys' − the result may be criminal behaviour, which could be interpreted as a kind of chest-beating to demonstrate triumph.

In some cases, the relationship between a high-dominance and a medium-dominance person may amount to a kind of hypnosis. In November 1899, a New York lawyer named Albert T. Patrick knocked on the door of the Madison Avenue apartment of William Rice, a wealthy retired businessman in his eighties. The man who opened the door was Rice's valet, Charles Jones, and Patrick lost no time in trying to persuade Jones to betray his employer, and furnish some evidence that could be used in a lawsuit against Rice. Jones, who was the old man's only friend, refused with horror, but there was something about the beady eyes and dominant gaze of Albert T. Patrick that fascinated him, and when Patrick returned a few days later, he allowed himself to be persuaded, and agreed to forge a letter in which his employer apparently agreed to abandon the lawsuit. When Patrick learned from Jones that Rice had left his fortune of three million dollars to a college in Texas, he persuaded Jones to co-operate in a scheme to forge a new will, leaving the fortune to Patrick. The next step was to poison Rice with indigestion pills laced with mercury. When these failed to bring about the desired result, Jones was ordered to kill the old man with chloroform. By now he was so completely under Patrick's domination that he complied. As soon as the old man was dead, Patrick hurried to the bank with a forged cheque for $25,000, but Jones had accidentally made out the cheque to 'Abert' T. Patrick, and when the teller noticed this, the scheme began to go wrong. The bank manager demanded to speak to Mr Rice on the telephone and Jones had to admit that the old man was dead. Soon after this, Jones and Patrick found themselves in adjoining cells. Patrick now handed Jones a sharp knife and said: 'The jig's up. It's no use. You go first and I'll follow.' Jones was so completely under Patrick's spell that he cut his throat without pausing to reflect that it would be impossible for Patrick to get the knife back . . . In fact, Jones recovered, and turned state's evidence. Patrick was sentenced to death, but was finally pardoned and released.

Almost half a century later, in 1947, Raymond Fernandez, a petty crook with a toupee and gold teeth who specialised in seducing and swindling lonely middle-aged women, met an overweight nurse named Martha Beck through a lonely-hearts club. Fernandez had become a crook after a serious head injury that caused a total personality change. (We have already noted how many serial killers have suffered head injuries.) His first sight of Martha was a shock — she weighed fourteen stone — but she seems to have possessed a certain wistful charm. Once in bed, they discovered that they were soul-mates, and their sex life became a non-stop orgy. When Martha learned how Fernandez made a living, she proposed to join him — posing as his sister — adding only one refinement: that they should murder the women after he had seduced and robbed them. (In fact, Fernandez may have poisoned a widow named Jane Thompson in the year before he met Martha, but this has never been established — her death was certified as being due to acute gastro-enteritis.) In the course of a year they murdered at least three women, the last being a forty-one-year-old mother and her twenty-month-old daughter. Suspicious neighbours called the police, who soon discovered two freshly cemented graves in the cellar. Tried in New York, they were both electrocuted on 7 March 1951, Martha having some difficulty squeezing into the electric chair. Wenzell Brown's book on the case, *The Lonely Hearts Murders*, makes it clear that Martha was the dominant one of the pair, while Fernandez was weak, vain and easygoing. Both had had the unhappy childhood that seems so typical of mass murderers. Martha's obesity made her feel a 'freak', and because she was pathetically eager to please, she allowed men to fondle her intimately while still a child. Fernandez was a sickly and puny little boy whose highly dominant father despised him; he spent his childhood wrapped in daydreams. When he and three other teenagers were caught stealing chickens, the fathers of the other boys agreed to act as guarantors and they were released; the father of Raymond Fernandez refused to co-operate and he went to prison. Even after the head injury that changed his personality, he never displayed any sadism towards the women he swindled. It seems to have been the partnership with Martha that turned him into 'America's most hated killer'.

Perhaps the clearest example of the influence of the dominance syndrome on criminality is England's Moors Murder case.

Between July 1963 and October 1965, Ian Brady and his mistress Myra Hindley collaborated on five child murders. They were finally arrested because they tried to involve Myra's brother-in-law, David Smith, in one of the murders, and he went to the police.

Ian Brady, who was twenty-seven at the time of his arrest, was a typical social misfit. The illegitimate son of a Glasgow waitress, he was brought up in a slum area of Clydeside. Until the age of eleven he seems to have been a good student; then he was sent to a 'posh' school, together with a number of other re-housed slum boys, and began to develop a resentment towards the better-off pupils. From then on he took to petty crime; his first appearance in court was at the age of thirteen, on a charge of housebreaking. He had served four years on probation for more burglaries when he moved to Manchester to live with his mother and a new stepfather in 1954. As a result of another theft he was sentenced to a year in Borstal. Back in Manchester, he went back on the dole. It was a dull life in a small house, and he seems to have been glad to get a job as a stock clerk at Millwards, a chemical firm, when he was twenty-one.

It was at this point that he became fascinated by the Nazis and began collecting books about them. They fed his fantasies of power. So did his discovery of the ideas of the Marquis de Sade, with his philosophy of total selfishness and his daydreams of torture. It becomes clear in retrospect that Brady always had a streak of sadism. A childhood friend later described how he had dropped a cat into a deep hole in a graveyard and sealed it up with a stone. When the friend moved the stone to check on his story, the cat escaped.

For Brady, the Nazis represented salvation from mediocrity and boredom, while de Sade justified his feeling that most people are contemptible. Brady particularly liked the idea that society is corrupt, and that God is a lie invented by priests to keep the poor in a state of subjugation. Stifled by ennui, seething with resentment, Brady was like a bomb that is ready to explode by the time he was twenty-three.

It was at this time that a new typist came to work in the office. Eighteen-year-old Myra Hindley was a normal girl from a normal family background, a Catholic convert who loved animals and children, and favoured blonde hair-styles and bright lipstick. She had been engaged, but broken it off because she found the boy immature. Brady had the sullen look of a delinquent Elvis Presley, and within weeks, Myra was in love. Brady ignored her, probably regarding her as a typical working-class moron. Her diary records: 'I hope he loves me and will marry me some day.' When he burst into profanity after losing a bet she was deeply shocked. It was almost a year later, at the firm's Christmas party in 1961, that he offered to walk her home, and asked her out that evening. When he took her home, she declined to allow him into the house — she lived with her grandmother — but a week later, after another evening out, she surrendered her virginity on her gran's settee. After that, he spent every Saturday night with her.

Myra found her lover marvellously exciting and sophisticated. He wore black shirts, read 'intellectual' books, and was learning German. He introduced her to German wine, and she travelled as a pillion passenger on his motorbike. He talked to her about the Nazis, and liked to call her Myra Hess (a combination of a famous pianist and Hitler's deputy). He also introduced her to the ideas of the Marquis de Sade, and set out converting her to atheism, pointing out the discrepancies in the gospels — it did not take long to demolish her faith. He also talked to her a great deal about his favourite novel, *Compulsion* by Meyer Levin, a fictionalised account of the Leopold and Loeb murder case.

It was in July 1963 — according to her later confession — that he first began to talk to her about committing 'the perfect murder', and suggesting that she should help him. In her 'confession' (to Chief Superintendent Peter Topping) she alleges that Brady blackmailed her by threatening to harm her grandmother, and by showing her some pornographic photographs of her that he had taken on an occasion when he had slipped a drug into her wine. The photographs certainly exist — thirty of them — some showing them engaged in sexual intercourse and wearing hoods. (These were taken with a time-lapse camera.) Emlyn Williams, who saw them, states that some show keen pleasure on their faces, which would seem to dispose of Myra's claim that they were taken when she was unconscious. Whether or not she was telling the truth about blackmail, it seems clear that Brady could have persuaded her to do anything anyway.

In her confession to Chief Inspector Peter Topping (published in 1989 in his book *Topping*), she described how, on 12 July 1963, she and Brady set out on their first 'murder hunt'. By now Myra Hindley owned a broken-down van. She was sent ahead in the van, with Brady following behind on his motorbike. Her job was to pick up a girl and offer her a lift. The first child they saw was Myra's next-door neighbour, so she drove past her. The second was sixteen-year-old Pauline Reade, who was on her way to a dance. Myra offered her a lift, and she accepted. In the van, Myra explained that she was on her way to Saddleworth Moor to look for a glove she had lost at a picnic. If Pauline would like to come and help her search, she would give her a pile of records in the back of the van. Pauline was delighted to accept.

Once on the moor, Brady arrived on his motorbike, and was introduced as Myra's boyfriend. Then Brady and Pauline went off to look for the glove. (Since it was July it was still daylight.) By the time Brady returned to the car, it was dark. He led Myra to the spot where Pauline Reade's body was lying. Her throat had been cut, and her clothes were in disarray; Myra accepted that Brady had raped her. That, after all, had been the whole point of the murder. Together they buried the body, using a spade they had brought with them. Brady told her that at one point Pauline was struggling so much that he had thought of calling for her to hold the girl's hands — clearly, he had no doubt that she would co-operate. On the way home, they passed Pauline's mother and brother, apparently searching for her. Back at home, Brady burned his bloodstained shoes and trousers.

In an open letter to the press in January 1990, Brady was to contradict Myra Hindley's account; he insisted that injuries to the nose and forehead of Pauline Reade had been inflicted by her, and that she had also committed some form of lesbian assault on Pauline Reade. According to Brady, Myra participated actively and willingly in the murders.

Five months later, Brady was ready for another murder. On Saturday 23 November 1963 they hired a car — the van had been sold — and drove to nearby Ashton market. There, according to Myra, Brady got into conversation with a twelve-year-old boy, John Kilbride, and told him that, 'If Jack would help them look for a missing glove, he would give him a bottle of sherry he had won in the raffle'. Because Myra was present, John Kilbride accompanied them without suspicion. They drove up to Saddleworth Moor, and the boy unsuspectingly accompanied Brady into the darkness. Myra Hindley claims that she drove around for a while, and that when she came back and flashed her lights, Brady came out of the darkness and told her that he had already buried the body. He also mentioned taking the boy's trousers down and giving him a slap on the buttocks. In fact, Myra said, she was fairly certain that he had raped John Kilbride. He had explained that he had strangled him because the knife he had was too blunt to cut his throat.

In June the following year — in 1964 — Brady told her he was 'ready to do another one'. (Like all serial killers he had a 'cooling-off period' — in this case about six months.) According to Myra, he told her that committing a murder gave him a feeling of power. By now they had their own car, a Mini. On 16 June 1964 she stopped her car and asked a twelve-year-old boy, Keith Bennett, if he would help her load some boxes from an off-licence; like John Kilbride, Keith Bennett climbed in unsuspectingly. The murder was almost a carbon copy of the previous one; Keith Bennett was strangled and buried on Saddleworth Moor. Brady admitted this time that he had raped him, and added: 'What does it matter?' Keith Bennett's body has never been found.

On Boxing Day 1965 Brady and Hindley picked up a ten-year-old girl, Lesley Ann Downey, at a fairground at Ancoats. Myra Hindley had taken her grandmother to visit an uncle. They took the child back to the house, and Brady switched on a tape recorder. Myra claims she was in the kitchen with the dogs when she heard the child screaming. Brady was ordering her to take off her coat and squeezing her by the back of the neck. Then Lesley's hands were tied with a handkerchief and Brady set up the camera and a bright light. The child was ordered to undress, and Brady then made her assume various pornographic poses while he filmed her. At this point, Myra claims she was ordered to go and run a bath; she stayed in the bathroom until the water became cold. When she went back into the bedroom, Lesley had been strangled, and there was blood on her thighs – from which Myra realised that she had been raped. At eight o'clock that evening they took the body up to Saddleworth Moor and buried it.

In his open letter to the press in January 1990, Ian Brady denied that Myra had played no active part in the murder of Lesley Ann Downey. 'She insisted upon killing Lesley Ann Downey with her own hands, using a two-foot length of silk cord, which she later used to enjoy toying with in public, in the secret knowledge of what it had been used for.'

In October 1965, Brady decided it was time for another murder. He had also decided that he needed another partner in crime, and that Myra's seventeen-year-old brother-in-law, David Smith, was the obvious choice. Smith had already been in trouble with the law. He seemed unable to hold down a job. His wife was pregnant for the second time, and they had just been given an eviction notice. So Smith listened with interest when Brady suggested a hold-up at an Electricity Board showroom. On 6 October Smith came to the house hoping to borrow some money, but they were all broke. Brady suggested: 'We'll have to roll a queer.' An hour later, Brady picked up a seventeen-year-old homosexual, Edward Evans, and invited him back to the house in Hattersley. Back at the flat, Myra went off to fetch David Smith. They had only just returned when there was a crash from the living room. Brady was rolling on the floor, grappling with Evans. Then he seized an axe and struck him repeatedly: 'Everywhere was one complete pool of blood.' When Evans lay still, Brady strangled him. Then he handed the bloodstained hatchet to Smith, saying 'Feel the weight of that'. His motive was obviously to get Smith's fingerprints on the haft. Together, they mopped up the blood and wrapped up the body in polythene. Then Smith went home, promising to return the next day to help dispose of the body. But Brady had miscalculated. Smith might feel in theory that 'people are like maggots, small, blind and worthless', but the fact of murder was too much for him. When he arrived home he was violently sick, and told his wife what had happened.

Together they decided to phone the police, creeping downstairs armed with a screwdriver and carving-knife in case Brady was waiting for them. The following morning, a man dressed as a baker's roundsman knocked at Brady's door, and when Myra opened it, identified himself as a police officer. Evans's body was found in the spare bedroom. Forensic examination revealed dog hair on his underclothes – the hair of Myra Hindley's dog – indicating that he and Brady had engaged in sex, probably while Myra was fetching David Smith.

Hidden in the spine of a prayer book police found a cloakroom ticket, which led them to Manchester Central Station. In two suitcases they discovered pornographic photos, tapes and books on sex and torture; the photographs included those of Lesley Ann Downey, with a tape recording of her voice pleading for mercy. A twelve-year-old girl, Patricia Hodges, who had occasionally accompanied Brady and Hindley to the moors, took the police to Hollin Brown Knoll, and there the body of Lesley Ann Downey was dug up. John Kilbride's grave was located through a photograph that showed Hindley crouching on it with a dog. (When later told that her dog had died while in the hands of the police, she made the classic remark: 'They're nothing but bloody murderers.') Pauline Reade's body was not found until 1987, as a result of Myra Hindley's confession to Topping. Brady helped in the search on the moor and as we know, the body of Keith Bennett has never been recovered.

Brady's defence was that Evans had been killed unintentionally, in the course of a struggle, when he and Smith tried to rob him. Lesley Ann Downey, he claimed, had been brought to the house by Smith to pose for pornographic pictures, for which she had been paid ten shillings. (His original story was that she had been brought to the house by two men.) After the session, she left the house with Smith. He flatly denied knowing anything about any of the other murders, but the tape recording of Lesley Ann Downey's screams and pleas for mercy made it clear that Brady and Hindley were responsible for her death. Both were sentenced to life imprisonment.

Perhaps the most interesting point to emerge from Myra Hindley's confession was that Brady 'didn't show a lot of interest in her sexually', but for the first few times they had normal sexual intercourse. There were times when he just wanted her to relieve him, and on a couple of occasions he had forced her to have anal sex with him, which she described as being 'dreadfully painful'. On other occasions he liked her to insert a candle in his anus while he relieved himself. Nothing could demonstrate more clearly the lack of enthusiasm of the high-dominance male for the medium-dominance female. Sexual excitement must involve a sense of conquest, and this girl had been a pushover. To enjoy sex he has to 'use' her. The first time was satisfactory because she found it painful. Sodomy was no doubt enjoyable for the same reason. He has no desire to give her pleasure; she, as the 'slave', must give him pleasure – by masturbating him or inserting a candle in his anus while he masturbated himself (the ultimate indignity) – while receiving none herself. All this made no difference. She said she could not stress strongly enough how totally obsessed and besotted she was with Brady. After he finally invited her out and she became in her own words 'a Saturday night stand', she would spend the week in a fever of anxiety waiting for Saturday night to come round again. She said she could not explain the infatuation, but it stemmed partly from the fact that Brady was so different from anybody else she had met. 'Within months he had convinced me there was no God at all: he could have told me that the earth was flat, the moon was made of green cheese and the sun rose in the west, I would have believed him, such was his power of persuasion, his softly convincing means of speech which fascinated me, because I could never fully comprehend, only browse at the odd sentence here and there, believing it to be gospel truth.'

She goes to the heart of Brady's psychological motivation when she says: 'He wanted to get rich and become "a somebody" – not just do a nine-to-five job working for somebody else.' This was the source of that curious and irrational resentment that seems so typical of the criminal – anger at feeling that life had cast him for the role of a nobody. In his 1990 'confession', Brady explained obscurely that he saw the murders 'as products of an existentialist philosophy, in tandem with the spiritualism of Death itself'. What *is* clear is that, like Panzram, Brady felt that somebody deserved to suffer for his own miseries. Topping remarks: 'On one occasion when I was with him he told me that he did not believe in God, that it was a nonsense to believe in a deity. But he said that after the killing of John Kilbride, he looked up into the sky, shook his fist and said "Take that, you bastard!"' We may recall that Gallego had told a prison counsellor: 'The only thing I really care about is killing God.' The phrasing here is interesting. It is obviously impossible to 'kill' God. All that *is* possible is to 'defy' God, to try to get revenge on God, as William Hickman tried to get revenge on Perry Parker by kidnapping and killing his daughter Marian. Gallego's resentment was so fierce that the word 'defy' seemed inadequate; he had to speak of 'killing' God, because killing was his ultimate way of expressing resentment. This is the vital key to the self-esteem killer: the desire to 'get back' at somebody. The artist Paul Gauguin said: 'Life being what it is, one dreams of revenge.'

One of the first recorded cases of a wife acting as a procurer for her husband's rape victims occurred in 1963 in Lansing, Michigan. On 4 July twenty-year-old Lloyd Higdon and his wife picked up the fourteen-year-old daughter of a neighbour and offered to take her for a drive. Instead she was tied up and taken to Higdon's house; there she was ordered to undress and, when she protested, told that if she refused she would be sold into white slavery and never see her parents again. The girl removed her own clothes and made no resistance to rape. She was then driven home and told never to mention it. Unable to conceal her state of shock, she finally told her parents. Higdon was arrested, but since intercourse had taken place with her consent, a court decided to regard it as statutory rape, and he was sentenced to a term of between four to fifteen years. He was out two years later. On the afternoon of 17 July 1967 he and his live-in girlfriend, Lucille Brumit, aged twenty-nine, picked up thirteen-year-old Roxanne Sandbrook in Lansing; the girl already knew Higdon, who lived only three streets away. She was driven to a rubbish dump near Jackson, Michigan, where Higdon tried to rape her; when she resisted, he strangled her. Her body was found on the dump a month later, in an advanced state of decomposition. Interviews with the dead girl's friends revealed that she often babysat for the next-door neighbour of a known sex offender, Lloyd Higdon — who happened to be serving a term in the local jail for violating his parole and leaving the area. Questioned separately, Higdon and Lucille Brumit finally admitted to the abduction of Roxanne Sandbrook. Higdon pleaded guilty to murder, and received life imprisonment.

Since that time there have been many similar cases, in some of which it becomes clear that the woman played an active part in the rape and murder. In 1968 Mrs Joyce Ballard of Chatham, Kent, admitted to enticing a twelve-year-old girl into her flat so that her husband, Robert Ballard, could assault her. Ballard, who was obsessed by books on torture and witchcraft, tied up the girl, cut open her veins, and stabbed her; then — probably appalled by what he had done — he committed suicide. Joyce Ballard was sentenced to three years in prison.

A case that took place in Western Australia in 1986 may be cited as another typical example. On Monday 6 November a half-naked teenage girl ran into a shopping centre in Fremantle begging for help; she later told police that she had been dragged into a car the previous evening by a man and a woman and taken to a house where she was chained to the bed and raped repeatedly. On Monday afternoon the couple left her unchained in the bedroom, and she succeeded in escaping through a window. The police went immediately to the house in Moorhouse Street, Willagee, where the girl had been held, and arrested David and Catherine Birnie, both thirty-five years old. Questioned by detectives from Perth's Major Crimes Squad, they quickly admitted murdering and burying four other girls in four weeks, and led the police to the graves. In the Glen Eagle Forest, thirty-four miles south of Perth, police discovered three naked bodies in shallow graves, and another on the edge of a pine forest near Wanneroo, fifty miles north of Perth. They were identified as twenty-two-year-old Mary Neilson, a psychology student at the University of Western Australia, Noelene Patterson, thirty-one, an airline hostess, Denise Keren Brown, twenty-one, a computer operator, and a fifteen-year-old schoolgirl, Susannah Candy. The women had vanished between 6 October and 5 November 1986 — the last victim, Denise Brown, was murdered earlier on the same day that the teenage girl was abducted and raped.

It soon became clear that Catherine Birnie had played an active part in the murders. She had taken photographs of the corpses, one of which showed her husband in an act of intercourse, and had helped him to kill the women. The victims were abducted — two of them while hitchhiking — and taken to the Birnies' house, where they were chained up in a bedroom and repeatedly raped. Mary Neilson had gone to the Birnies' house to buy car tyres. (Birnie worked in a car-wrecking yard.) She had been held at knifepoint and chained to the bed; Catherine Birnie watched while her husband raped her. Then she was taken to the Glen Eagle National Park, where she was raped again. She was begging for her life as Birnie garrotted her with a nylon cord. After this, both Birnies mutilated the body to prevent it from swelling in its shallow grave.

On 20 October fifteen-year-old Susannah Candy was picked up while hitchhiking. She was held prisoner and raped for several days. During this time she was made to write two letters to her parents, explaining that she was safe and well. She was finally strangled by Catherine Birnie.

Noelline Patterson had been abducted after her car had run out of petrol; the Birnies had helped to push it to a service station, after which she was forced into their car at knifepoint. According to a workmate of Birnie's, the couple already knew Noelline Patterson, and had helped to wallpaper her home. During the three days she was kept prisoner, Birnie showed so much interest in her that Catherine Birnie became violently jealous. It was she who finally insisted that Noelline should be killed. Birnie gave her a heavy dose of sleeping tablets, and strangled her while she was unconscious. (When she showed the police Noelline's grave in the Glen Eagle Forest, Catherine Birnie spat on it.)

Denise Brown was also hitchhiking when the Birnies abducted her at knifepoint on 4 November. She was taken to the house at Willagee, chained to the bed and raped over a two-day period. Then she was taken to a pine plantation near Wanneroo; Birnie raped her again, and stabbed her twice while doing so. He failed to kill her, and Catherine Birnie handed her husband a bigger knife, with which he stabbed her in the neck; but even in her grave, the victim tried to sit up. Birnie had to fracture her skull with blows from the back of the axe before she could be buried. Three days later, they abducted the seventeen-year-old girl whose escape led to their arrest.

The Birnies were also suspected of being involved in three earlier disappearances of women; but it has been pointed out that this seems unlikely, since they confessed so readily to the four later murders. The pattern of the murders suggests that the abduction of Mary Neilson was unplanned — that Birnie decided to rape her when she came to the house to buy tyres, and that having experienced the pleasure of possessing a 'sex slave', he went on to abduct the other four girls. Case after case of this kind indicates how quickly sex crime becomes an addictive obsession.

Because the Birnies pleaded guilty, little evidence about the crimes, or about the psychology of the killers, emerged in court. Newspaper reporters tried to make up for this by interviewing their relations and acquaintances. Birnie's twenty-one-year-old brother James — who had himself been in prison for sex offences — stated that his brother was a violent and romantic man, a complex and contradictory character who often gave his women flowers and chocolates, but who owned a huge pornographic video collection and needed sex six times a day. During a temporary break-up with his wife, Bernie had forced his brother to permit sodomy. As a twenty-first birthday present, James was allowed to make love to his brother's wife.

David Birnie was the oldest of five children; the family had broken up when he was ten, and the children had been placed in institutions. Birnie's mother told reporters she had not seen him in years. The father, a laundry worker, had died the previous year.

Catherine Birnie had also had a lonely and miserable childhood; after her mother's death she had been sent to live with her grandparents in Perth. 'People who knew her well said she rarely laughed and had few pleasures. She never had a playmate and other children were not allowed in her grandparents' house.' Her grandmother died in front of the child in the throes of an epileptic fit.

She had known David Birnie since childhood. When she became pregnant at sixteen, she and Birnie teamed up and went on a crime rampage, breaking into shops and factories. They were caught and convicted, but Birnie escaped and they committed another string of burglaries. Again, both were convicted. When she was released, Catherine Birnie became a domestic help, and married the son of the house; they had six children. Birnie, in the meantime, had an unsuccessful marriage, and became a jockey; his employment terminated when he tried to attack a woman sexually wearing nothing but a stocking mask. After sixteen years of marriage, Catherine met Birnie again and began an affair with him. Two years later, she left her husband, walking out without warning, and went to live with Birnie. A psychologist who examined her after her arrest said that he had never seen anyone so emotionally dependent on another person.

Birnie's counsel read a statement in which Birnie said he was extremely sorry for what he had done, and was pleading guilty to spare the victim's families the ordeal of a trial. 'He does not wish to present any defence of insanity. "I knew and understood what I was doing and I knew it was wrong."'

Their trial, on 3 March 1987, lasted only thirty minutes, and both Birnies were sentenced to life imprisonment.

There is an obvious difference between the Birnie case and the Moors Murders. Although Myra Hindley was brought up in the home of her grandmother, she had an emotionally secure childhood, and was a well-adjusted teenager. Yet both women became criminals as a result of becoming emotionally dependent on a man with criminal tendencies. Both participated willingly in abductions which they knew would lead to rape and murder. Myra Hindley claimed to have taken no active part in the rapes and murders (although Brady was later to deny this and insist she had participated in both); Catherine Birnie watched with pleasure and even strangled one of the victims. Yet it seems clear that neither woman would have become involved in crime except under the influence of a high-dominance male. If we consider again the case of Patty Hearst and the 'Symbionese Liberation Army', it is hard to avoid the conclusion that 'brainwashing' may be a far more frequent phenomenon than is generally realised.

On 20 June 1955 a fourteen-year-old girl, Patty Ann Cook, was sunbathing on an inflated mattress in her backyard in Rome, Georgia, when a green pick-up truck stopped, and the driver asked directions. Then he asked her if she would like a lift to the swimming pool, and she accepted eagerly. A neighbour saw them drive off. Instead of taking her to the pool, Willie Cochran, an ex-convict in his middle thirties, drove on to a remote logging road, dragged her from the vehicle, and raped her. After that he shot her through the head, and dropped her in the river, weighted down with a big monkey wrench. After the girl's disappearance, Cochran came under suspicion because he was a known sex offender, and drove a green pick-up truck. Under police questioning, he involved himself in contradictions, and finally confessed to the murder. Cochran was electrocuted in August 1955. The case is made memorable by a remark made by the judge, J.H. Paschall: 'The male sexual urge has a strength out of all proportion to any useful purpose that it serves.' The comment could stand as an epigraph to the history of sex crime.

While it would be a mistake to assume that all serial killers are riven by the kind of resentment that motivated Brady and Gallego, there can be no doubt that all are driven by a sexual urge that 'has a strength out of all proportion to any useful purpose that it serves'. We have seen that the combination of a high-dominance, highly sexed male with a medium-dominance and emotionally dependent female can lead to strange examples of partnership in sex crime. Another widely publicised case of the seventies demonstrates how a combination of a high- and a medium-dominance male can produce the same effect.

In the four months between 18 October 1977 and 17 February 1978 the naked bodies of ten girls were dumped on hillsides in the Los Angeles area. Newspapers christened the killer 'the Hillside Strangler'. In fact, it was known to the police from an early stage that two men were involved; sperm inside the dead women revealed that one of the rapists was a 'secretor' (one whose blood group can be determined from his bodily fluids) and one a non-secretor.

The first victim was a black prostitute named Yolanda Washington, who operated around Hollywood Boulevard. Her naked corpse was found in the Forest Lawn cemetery near Ventura Freeway; she had been strangled with a piece of cloth. Two weeks later, on 1 November 1977, fifteen-year-old Judy Miller, a runaway, was found in the town of La Crescenta, not far from the Los Angeles suburb of Glendale. She had been raped vaginally and anally, then strangled, and marks on her wrists and ankles, and in the area of her mouth, indicated that she had been bound with adhesive tape. It was not until the last weeks of November, around Thanksgiving, that the police realised that they had an epidemic of sex murders on their hands; seven more strangled corpses were found, tossed casually on hillsides or by the road, as if thrown from a car. The youngest victims were two schoolgirls, aged twelve and fourteen; the oldest was a twenty-eight-year-old scientology student, Jane King. The last victim of the Thanksgiving 'spree' was eighteen-year-old Lauren Wagner, and burn marks on her palms suggested that she had been tortured before death.

Los Angeles has about seven murders a day, but this number of sex murders in a few weeks was something of a record. Women became afraid to go out alone at night, and shops ran out of tear gas and Mace (similar to CS gas). By the time Lauren Wagner's body was discovered, Los Angeles was in a state of panic.

In this case, at least, they had an important clue. Lauren Wagner had been abducted as she climbed out of her car in front of her parents' home. A neighbour had looked out of her window to see why her dog was barking, and had heard Lauren shout: 'You won't get away with this.' She had then seen two men force the girl into a big dark sedan with a white top, and drive away. The woman had seen the men clearly; the elder of the two had bushy hair and was 'Latin-looking', while the younger one was taller, and had acne scars on his neck. The following day, her telephone rang, and a voice with a New York accent told her she had better keep quiet or she was as good as dead.

If the police had grasped the significance of this phone call they could have terminated the career of the Hillside Stranglers forthwith, for the only way a man could have obtained a telephone number without knowing the name of the subscriber was through some friend at the telephone exchange. A check with the Los Angeles exchange would have revealed the identity of one of the stranglers . . .

There would be two more victims. One was a seventeen-year-old prostitute named Kimberley Diane Martin; on 15 December 1977 her naked body was found sprawled on a vacant lot near City Hall. A man had telephoned a call-girl agency the evening before and requested a blonde in black underwear to be sent to the Tamarind Apartment building in Hollywood; Kimberley Martin was despatched, and disappeared.

On 17 February 1978 someone reported seeing an orange car halfway down a cliff on the Angeles Crest Highway. The boot proved to contain another naked body, that of twenty-year-old Cindy Hudspeth, a student and part-time waitress; she had been raped and sodomised by two men. After this, the Hillside murders ceased.

Almost a year later, on 12 January 1979, the police chief of Bellingham, a small coastal town in Washington State, was

245

notified that two students, Karen Mandic and Diane Wilder, were missing. On the previous evening, Karen Mandic had told her boyfriend that she had been offered $100 by a security supervisor named Ken Bianchi to do a 'house-sitting' job — to spend an evening in an empty house while its security alarm was repaired.

Bianchi was a personable young man from Los Angeles, and he had been in Bellingham since the previous May. He was known to be an affectionate husband and father, and a conscientious worker; it seemed unlikely that he had anything to do with the disappearance of the two girls. In fact, he denied knowing them. Later that day, the bodies of the girls were found in the rear seat of Karen Mandic's car, parked in a cul-de-sac.

Kenneth Bianchi was immediately picked up. His air of bewilderment seemed so genuine that the police were convinced they had the wrong man. His common-law wife Kelli Boyd, who had recently borne his child, was equally certain that Bianchi was incapable of murder. When Bianchi's home was searched, and the police found stolen property in his basement, it became apparent that he was not as honest as everyone had assumed. Medical evidence left no doubt that he was the murderer. Both girls had semen stains on their underwear; so did Bianchi. Diane Wilder had been menstruating, and Bianchi had menstrual stains on his underwear. On the stairs leading down to the basement of the empty house, police found a pubic hair identical to Bianchi's. Carpet fibres on the clothes of the dead girls corresponded to the carpet in the basement of the house. What had happened became clear. Bianchi had offered Karen Mandic the 'house-sitting job'. When she had arrived, he made some excuse to take her in alone — probably to turn on the electricity. As she preceded him to the basement, he strangled her with a ligature — the angle of the marks on her throat showed that the killer was standing above and behind her. Then he went out and got Diane Wilder. When both girls were dead he had completed some kind of sexual assault — no semen was found inside them — then placed them in Karen's car and driven it away. Both girls had been sworn to silence about the house-sitting job, 'for security reasons', and he had no idea that Diane had told her boyfriend where she was going.

When Sergeant Frank Salerno, a detective on the Hillside Strangler case, heard of Bianchi's arrest, he hurried to

Bellingham. Bianchi sounded like the tall, acne-scarred young man seen outside Lauren Wagner's home, and his cousin Angelo Buono, who lived in Glendale, Los Angeles, sounded exactly like the other — the bushy-haired, Latin-looking man. Buono was a highly unsavoury character. He had been married four times, but all his wives had left him because of his brutality — when one of them had refused him sex, he had sodomised her in front of the children. He had also been a pimp, forcing girls into white slavery — and Bianchi had been his partner. He was an obvious suspect as the second Hillside Strangler.

At this point a strange and interesting development occurred. Bianchi's lawyer had been impressed by his apparent sincerity in denying that he knew anything about the murders; so was a psychiatric social worker. They sent for Professor John G. Watkins of the University of Montana, and suggested to him that Bianchi might be suffering from the same problem as Billy Milligan (see p.204) — multiple personality. Watkins placed Bianchi under hypnosis, and within minutes, Bianchi was speaking in a strange, low voice, and introducing himself as someone called Steve. Steve seemed be an unpleasant, violent character with a sneering laugh, and he declared that he hated 'Ken' and had done his best to 'fix him'. Then he described how, one evening in 1977, Ken Bianchi had walked into his cousin's home, and found Angelo murdering a girl. Steve had then taken over Ken's body, and become Buono's willing accomplice in the Hillside Stranglings . . .

Suddenly, it began to look as if there was no chance of convicting either Bianchi or Buono for the murders. If Bianchi was 'insane', then he could not be convicted, and he could not testify against his cousin in court. Another psychiatrist, Ralph B. Allison, the author of a classic on multiple personality called *Minds in Many Pieces*, also interviewed Bianchi and agreed that he was a genuine 'MPD'. Soon after the arrests, there was even a book written about the case, *The Hillside Strangler* by Ted Schwarz, which accepted that Bianchi was a multiple personality.

At this point, the prosecution decided to call in their own expert, Dr Martin T. Orne. A simple experiment quickly convinced Orne that Bianchi was faking. Good hypnotic subjects can be made to hallucinate the presence of another person. Orne hypnotised Bianchi and told him that his lawyer, Dean Brett, was sitting in an empty chair. Bianchi immediately did something that Orne had never seen before in a hypnotised subject — leaned forward and shook the invisible lawyer warmly by the hand. In Orne's experience, a truly hypnotised person never tries to touch the hallucination. Orne also felt that Bianchi overplayed the situation, saying 'Surely you can see him?' A subject who genuinely 'saw' his lawyer would assume that everyone else did too. Bianchi was clearly faking hypnosis. Was he also faking multiple personality?

Again, an experiment provided the answer. Orne dropped a hint that most 'multiples' have at least three personalities. The next time he was under hypnosis, Bianchi immediately produced another personality, a frightened child named Billy. It now seemed virtually certain that Bianchi was malingering.

It was the police who proved it beyond all doubt. Allison had asked 'Steve' if he had a last name, and Steve had mumbled 'Walker'. Salerno had seen the name Steve Walker in Bianchi's papers. It proved to be the name of a graduate in psychology from California State University. One of Bianchi's dreams had been to become a psychiatrist, but he had possessed no qualifications. He had overcome this with a little confidence trickery. He had placed an advertisement in a Los Angeles newspaper offering a job to a graduate in psychology. Thomas Steven Walker had answered the advertisement, and sent Bianchi some of his academic papers. He never saw them again. Bianchi used Walker's name — and papers — to obtain a diploma from California State University, requesting that the name should not be filled in because he wanted to have it specially engraved. When he received it, Bianchi simply filled in his own name, and set himself up as a psychological counsellor.

The fact that there was a real Steve Walker, and that Bianchi knew of his existence, finally left no doubt whatever that Bianchi was malingering. At a sanity hearing in October 1979, Orne's opinion carried the day; Bianchi was judged sane and able to stand trial. Now he realised that he might go to the electric chair for the Hillside Stranglings in Los Angeles, Bianchi hastened to plead guilty to the two Bellingham murders, and to engage in plea-bargaining: to plead guilty to the Bellingham murders and to five of the Hillside Stranglings for a life sentence with a possibility of eventual parole, in exchange for testifying against his cousin Angelo Buono. The plea of guilty made the expense of a full-scale trial unnecessary, and on 21 October Kenneth Bianchi was sentenced to life imprisonment. He sobbed convincingly, and professed deep remorse.

He was flown to Los Angeles, where his cousin had been arrested, but the case was still far from over. Incredibly, the Los Angeles prosecutor's office decided that since the chief witness against Buono was his cousin, and that Bianchi was clearly unreliable – if not insane – it might be best to save the cost of a trial by dropping all murder charges against Buono. This extraordinary decision was fortunately overturned by Judge Ronald M. George, who decreed that Buono should stand trial anyway.

Even in prison, Bianchi made strenuous efforts to persuade various women to supply him with alibis, and one of them actually agreed to claim that he was with her on the night of one of the murders; at the last minute, conscience prevailed and she changed her mind.

There was still another strange development to come. In June 1980, Bianchi received a letter from a woman signing herself Veronica Lynn Compton, who asked him if he would be willing to co-operate on a play about a female mass murderer who injects semen into the sex organs of her victims to deceive the police into thinking the killer was a male. When Veronica Compton came to see him in prison, Bianchi became distinctly interested. She proved to be a glamorous brunette who was obviously slightly unbalanced. She was fascinated by murder, and together they fantasised about how pleasant it would be to go on a violent crime spree, cut off the private parts of their victims, and preserve them in embalming fluid. Soon afterwards, they were exchanging love letters. Bianchi now suggested that he should prove her love by putting into operation the scheme she had devised for her play: that she should murder a woman in Bellingham and inject her with sperm through a syringe, so that it would appear that the strangler was still at large. The infatuated Veronica agreed. Bianchi provided the sperm by masturbating into the finger of a rubber glove, and smuggling it to her in the spine of a book. Veronica flew to Bellingham and registered at a motel called the Shangri-la. In a nearby bar she got into conversation with a young woman called Kim Breed, and after several drinks, asked her if she would drive her back to her motel. At the Shangri-la, Kim Breed agreed to come in for a final quick drink. In the motel room, Veronica vanished into the toilet, then came out armed with a length of cord; she tiptoed up behind the unsuspecting girl and threw the cord round her neck. Kim Breed was something of an athlete; she managed to throw her attacker over her head. As Veronica Compton lay, winded, on the carpet, Miss Breed fled. When she returned to the motel with a male friend, her attacker had checked out and was on her way back to Los Angeles.

It proved easy to trace her through her airline reservation. Veronica Compton was arrested, and in due course, the 'copycat slayer', as the newspapers labelled her, received life imprisonment for attempted murder.

The trial of Angelo Buono, which began in November 1981 and ended in November 1983, was the longest murder trial in American history. When it came to Bianchi's turn to testify, it was obvious that he had no intention of standing by his plea-bargaining agreement; he was vague and contradictory. When Judge George pointed out that he could be returned to Washington's Walla Walla – a notoriously tough jail – he became marginally more co-operative. Bianchi spent five months on the stand, and the murders were described in appalling detail. Buono was finally found guilty of seven of them. Since his cousin had already escaped with life imprisonment, the jury recommended that he should not be sentenced to death. Buono received a life sentence with no possibility of parole. Bianchi was returned to Walla Walla to serve out his sentence. In 1989, he married a 'pen pal', Shirlee J. Book, whom he met for the first time the day before the wedding.

Through the detailed evidence given by Bianchi, it slowly became clear what had turned the cousins into serial sex killers. Angelo Buono, born in New York in October 1935, had been in trouble with the police from the age of fourteen, and spent time in reformatories. He married for the first time at the age of twenty, but his brutality – and his penchant for sodomy – led to divorce; three more unsuccessful marriages followed. In 1975, Buono set up his own car-body repair shop in Glendale, and became known as an excellent upholsterer – one of his customers was Frank Sinatra. In spite of a certain brutal coarseness, he was always attractive to women, and liked to seduce under-age girls. His cousin Kenneth Bianchi joined him in Los Angeles in 1976.

Kenneth Alessio Bianchi was born in May 1951, the child of a Rochester (N.Y.) prostitute who gave him up at birth; he was adopted at the age of three months. (Zoologists have pointed out that the most important 'imprinting' occurs in the first weeks of a baby's life; if a child receives no affection during this time, it remains permanently incapable of any deep relationship, and may become a psychopath.) He proved to be a bright, intelligent child, but a compulsive and pointless liar. Unlike his highly dominant cousin Angelo, Bianchi was a weak-willed person whose chief craving was to be regarded as a 'somebody', and he would lie and deceive indefinitely to this end. When rejected by girlfriends, he had a tendency to turn violent. He was also a habitual thief. Unable to hold down a regular job, and turned down by the police force as obviously unsuitable, he decided to move to Los Angeles at the age of twenty-four.

He moved in with his cousin Angelo, and was deeply impressed by the way the older man bedded teenagers and induced them to perform oral sex. He applied to join the Los Angeles and the Glendale police, but both turned him down. It was then that he decided to set up as a psychiatrist, and placed the advertisement that brought a reply from graduate Steven Walker.

After a few months, Buono became bored with his weak-willed cousin and asked him to move out. Bianchi found a room in an apartment block and obtained a job with a real-estate company, which he soon lost when marijuana was found in his desk drawer. Armed with his forged graduation certificate, he rented an office and set up as a psychiatrist, but patients failed to materialise. It was then that Buono made the suggestion that they should become pimps. Bianchi met a sixteen-year-old girl named Sabra Hannan at a party, and offered her a job as a photographic model. When she moved into Bianchi's house, she was raped, beaten, and forced into prostitution. So was a fifteen-year-old runaway named Becky Spears, who was subjected to sodomy so frequently that she had to wear a tampon in her rectum. These were only a few of Buono's 'stable' of women.

Problems arose in August 1976 when a Los Angeles lawyer rang and asked for a girl to be sent over. Becky Spears looked so obviously miserable that he asked her how she became a prostitute; when she told him her story he was so horrified that he bought her a plane ticket and put her on the next plane home to Phoenix. Buono was enraged when Becky failed to return and made threatening phone calls. The lawyer countered by sending an enormous Hell's Angel to see him, backed by a number of equally muscular friends. When Buono — who was working inside a car — ignored his callers, the Hell's Angel reached in through the window, lifted Buono out by his shirtfront, and asked: 'Do I have your attention, Mr Buono?' After that the lawyer received no more threatening phone calls.

This episode was almost certainly crucial in turning Buono into a serial killer. An intensely 'macho' male, he was undoubtedly outraged by the humiliation; in the curiously illogical manner of criminals, he looked around for someone on whom he could lay the blame, and his anger turned against women in general and prostitutes in particular. Soon after, his pride received another affront. From an experienced professional prostitute, Bianchi and Buono had purchased a list of clients who liked to have girls sent to their houses. When he tried to use it, Buono discovered that he had been swindled: it was a list of men who wanted to visit a prostitute on her own premises. The woman who had sold him the list was nowhere to be found. She had been accompanied by a black prostitute named Yolanda Washington, who worked on Hollywood Boulevard. On 16 October 1977 Bianchi and Buono picked up Yolanda Washington, and both raped her before Bianchi strangled her in the back of the car. She was the first victim of the Hillside Stranglers.

The experience of killing a woman satisfied some sadistic compulsion in both of them. On 31 October 1977 they picked up a fifteen-year-old prostitute named Judy Miller and took her back to Buono's house at 703 East Colorado. There she was undressed, and taken into the bedroom by Buono. After he had finished with her, Bianchi sodomised her. Then they strangled her, suffocating her at the same time with a plastic supermarket bag. The murder was totally unnecessary since the girl would have been glad to accept a few dollars.

The next victim was an out-of-work dancer named Lissa Kastin. They stopped her and identified themselves as policemen — a method they used in most cases — then took her back to Buono's house. There she was handcuffed and her clothes cut off with scissors. Both men were repelled by her hairy legs; so Bianchi raped her with a root beer bottle, then strangled her, while Buono sat on her legs shouting 'Die, cunt, die!' (Buono invariably referred to women as 'cunts'.) Bianchi enjoyed strangling her, and allowed her to lose consciousness and revive several times before killing her.

A few days later, Bianchi fell into conversation with an attractive Scientology student, Jane King, at a bus stop. When Buono drove up and offered him a lift home, the girl also accepted. Back in Buono's home they were delighted to find that her pubis was shaven. Because she struggled when being raped, they decided that she needed a lesson. A plastic bag was placed over her head while Bianchi sodomised her, and she was allowed to suffocate to death as he came to a climax.

The shaven pubis gave them the idea that it would be exciting to rape a child. On 13 November they approached two schoolgirls, fourteen-year-old Dollie Cepeda and Sonja Johnson, twelve, and identified themselves as policemen. The girls had just been shoplifting, and made no objection when asked to accompany the 'policemen'. In Buono's house, both were raped, then Sonja was murdered in the bedroom. When Buono came back for Dollie, she asked: 'Where's Sonja?', and Buono told her: 'You'll be seeing her soon.'

When Bianchi had been living in the apartment building in Hollywood, he had been enraged when an art student next door spurned his advances. So Bianchi and Buono called on twenty-year-old Kristina Weckler and Bianchi told her he was now a policeman, and that someone had crashed into her Volkswagen outside. She accompanied them down to see, and was hustled into their car and taken back to Buono's house, where Bianchi obtained his revenge for the earlier snub. They decided to try to kill her by a new method – injecting her with cleaning fluid – but when this failed, they piped coal gas into a plastic bag over her head, strangling her at the same time.

On 28 November 1977 they saw an attractive red-headed girl climbing into her car, and decided to follow her. Lauren Wagner was having an affair with a married man, and had just spent the afternoon in his bed. The two 'policemen' told her they were arresting her as she pulled up in front of her parents' home, and she was dragged, struggling, into their car. A dog barked, and a neighbour saw what was happening, but failed to grasp its implications. At Buono's house, Lauren Wagner pretended to enjoy being raped, hoping that they would allow her to live. They tried to kill her by attaching live electric wires to her palms, but these only caused burns; they were finally forced to strangle her. The next day, Buono obtained the telephone number of the house where the dog had barked by ringing a friend on the exchange, then made the threatening phone call.

In December, the prostitute Kimberley Martin was summoned by telephone to the Tamarind Apartments, where Bianchi lived, then taken back to Buono's where she was raped and murdered. Both men agreed she was no good in bed.

The final Hillside killing was virtually an accident. On 16 February 1978 a girl named Cindy Hudspeth came to Buono's garage to see about new mats for her car. Bianchi arrived at the same time. The opportunity seemed too good to miss. The girl was spreadeagled naked on the bed and raped for two hours. Then she was strangled, and her body packed into the boot of her Datsun, which was pushed off a cliff on a scenic route. Bianchi had noted the spot some time before when he had been fellated there by a teenage girl.

Buono was becoming increasingly irritated by his cousin's irresponsibility, and was anxious to break with him. So when Bianchi's girlfriend, Kelli Boyd, decided to leave him and go back to her parents in Bellingham, Buono encouraged Bianchi to follow her. Bianchi took his advice in May 1978. He could see that his cousin wanted to be rid of him, and it rankled. He felt like a rejected mistress. This seems to be the reason that, in January 1979, he decided to prove that he was capable of committing murder without Buono's help. He chose as his victim Karen Mandic, a girl with whom he had worked in a big store. When he learned she was living with a friend, he told her to bring the friend too, but Karen Mandic failed to keep her promise to tell no one where she was going, and Kenneth Bianchi found himself under arrest. In prison, he sent a cautiously worded letter to Buono, indicating that he had no intention of 'snitching'. Buono's response was a carefully worded phone call threatening violence to Bianchi's family if he changed his mind. It was Buono's biggest mistake. Bianchi would almost certainly have been glad to remain silent if he felt he was protecting his hero. Buono's response turned hero-worship to hostility, and Bianchi decided to forget loyalty and concentrate on saving his own skin by inventing a criminal alter-ego. That scheme came very close to succeeding; but when it failed, Bianchi had thrown away his last defence.

Back in Buono's presence, in the courtroom in Los Angeles, the old hero-worship seems to have reasserted itself, and he decided to go back on his word to help put Buono behind bars. In the event, it made no difference.

Is it possible that Bianchi was a genuine multiple personality? Judge George criticised psychiatrist John D. Watkins, who first diagnosed Bianchi as an MPD, for 'incredible naiveté'. Watkins himself remains unrepentant, commenting: 'The Kenneth personality . . . *always* smoked filter-tip cigarettes and held them between first and second fingers, palm towards the face. The Steve personality always tore the filters off and held the cigarette between the thumb and first finger, palm away from the face. Bianchi still continues to show the same alternation now in prison, although the law is no longer interested in his true diagnosis.'*

Yet two pieces of evidence contradict this view. When asked by his employer in Bellingham if he knew Karen Mandic, Bianchi insisted that he had 'never heard of her'. Yet he had made her acquaintance that summer when both had worked for the same department store. Unless his alter-ego 'Steve' was in charge during the whole of his time at the store – in which case 'Ken' would have been puzzled by long periods of amnesia – this must have been a lie.

Again, 'Steve' told Dr Watkins that he had first become involved in murder when 'Ken' had walked in on Angelo Buono and found him killing a girl. His more detailed confession makes it clear that this is untrue; the first murder (Yolanda Washington) and all subsequent ones involved them both.

Most multiple personalities – probably all – have experienced severe traumas in childhood, often involving sexual abuse and brutal beatings; investigations into Bianchi's childhood background revealed none of this; it was normal and affectionate. His allegations of ill treatment by his mother – made to the psychiatrists – proved to be untrue.

What may be of more significance is that soon after his arrest in Bellingham, Bianchi saw the television film *Sybil*, based on the case study by Flora Rheta Schreiber, about a girl with fourteen personalities. It was after this that Bianchi's social worker began to suspect him of being a 'multiple'.

*Quoted in *Open to Suggestion, The Uses and Abuses of Hypnosis*, by Robert Temple, 1989, p. 394.

Dr Allison later retracted his view that Bianchi was a 'multiple'; he explained that he had since become a prison psychiatrist, and was shocked to discover that criminals were habitual and obsessive liars, capable of offering as many as half a dozen differing and incompatible views of the same event. Altogether, there seems to be little doubt that Bianchi was faking multiple-personality disorder.

From the point of view of the study of serial killers, one of the major points to emerge from the case is that the murders were not primarily sex crimes. Three of the victims were prostitutes, and a fourth had expressed her intention of becoming one. In these instances, rape was obviously unnecessary; the real motive for the crime was satisfaction of the sadistic sense of power that came from torture and murder. The case is an interesting illustration of Hazelwood's remark that sex crime can service 'non-sexual needs' such as power and anger.

In his book on the Hillside Stranglers *Two of a Kind*, Darcy O'Brien mentions that while Veronica Compton was in prison she entered into a romantic correspondence with another serial killer, the 'Sunset Slayer' Douglas Clark, and that Clark sent her a photograph of a body he had decapitated. It seems clear from her behaviour – her playwriting activities and her attempt at a 'copycat crime' – that Veronica Compton belonged to Maslow's high-dominance group. Her attempts to enter into relationships with mass murderers may be interpreted in the light of Maslow's observation that even high-dominance women seem to require a male who is of slightly higher dominance. In fact, the case of the Sunset Slayer illustrates such a bizarre relationship.

On 9 August 1980 the headless body of a man was found in a car park on a street in Van Nuys, a Los Angeles suburb; he had been shot and stabbed to death. A check with the licensing department revealed that the car belonged to a man called Jack Murray, and that his home was not far from the place where he was found. Searching the house, the police found evidence that, until a few months ago, he had lived with a nurse called Carol Bundy. She had now apparently moved in with a man named Douglas Clark. The name struck a chord in the minds of the investigating officers. A few days earlier, an unknown man had telephoned the police to tell them that several recent murders of prostitutes had been committed by a boilermaker named Douglas Clark; but it was only one of many tips. On the other hand, one of the murders being investigated involved the decapitation of a Sunset hooker named Exxie Wilson. Her headless body, together with that of her room-mate Karen Jones, had been found on 24 June 1980 in the area of Studio City and Burbank. Both had been shot. Exxie Wilson's head had been found in a box dumped in a driveway in Burbank. The hair had been washed and the face had been made-up like a Barbie doll; the mouth contained traces of sperm. It seemed an unusual coincidence that Douglas Clark's girlfriend should also be associated with a case of decapitation . . .

Carol Bundy, a good-looking but overweight woman of thirty-seven, was arrested, and under police questioning she stated that Jack Murray had been murdered by her new lover, Douglas Clark. However, Carol Bundy's nursing supervisor had a different story to tell: that Carol had admitted to her that *she* had killed Jack Murray; her reason was that Murray was threatening to tell the police that Clark was 'the Sunset Slayer'. It seemed likely that Murray was the man who had made the phone call about Clark.

Clark himself was now arrested — a handsome, bespectacled man in his mid-thirties. His story was that he had merely agreed to help Carol Bundy dispose of Murray's head after she had killed him. (The head was never found.) He alleged that Carol Bundy had blackmailed him into helping her by threatening to show the police a photograph of himself having sex with an eleven-year-old girl.

Clark insisted that Carol Bundy and her ex-lover Jack Murray were murderers of six prostitutes in the Hollywood area. He also admitted that he had been wearing women's underwear since he was a child, and that his sexual tastes were 'kinky'. When police found two guns at his place of work, and a bullet fired from one of them matched a bullet found in Exxie Wilson's head, it began to seem likely that Clark himself was the man who had been killing prostitutes by shooting them in the head.

The story that now emerged as Clark and Bundy tried to implicate one another startled even the Hollywood police officers, accustomed to cases involving sexual perversion. Clark, it seemed, was a necrophile, one who enjoys having sexual intercourse with dead bodies. He cruised along Sunset Boulevard until he had found a prostitute who was willing to perform oral sex on him — most Hollywood prostitutes being willing to oblige for a sum of thirty to forty dollars. If the fellatio was successful and he reached orgasm, the girl was usually allowed to go free. If it was unsuccessful, he shot her through the head, then undressed her — keeping her underwear as a masturbation fetish — and had intercourse with the body. Finally, the victims were dumped off freeway ramps or in remote canyons.

Clark finally admitted that he had been responsible for a stabbing that he had taken place on 2 April 1980. He had picked up a young prostitute outside a Sunset Boulevard supermarket and requested oral sex. While she was engaged in fellatio, he pulled out a knife and stabbed her repeatedly in the back, the head and chest. In spite of this — and an attempt to throttle her — she managed to open the door of the estate car and fell out; Clark quickly drove away. The girl later recovered.

The bullets linked Clark to at least six murders over a period of four months. The first had occurred on 2 March 1980 when the body of a teenage girl had been found in the Saugus-Newhall area of Los Angeles County; she had been shot to death with a small-calibre pistol. The last was discovered on 30 June 1980: the naked body of a seventeen-year-old runaway named Marnette Comer was found in a ravine near Sylmar, in the San Fernando valley; she had been shot four times through the head, and her stomach had been slit open. (Clark later admitted that this was to hasten decomposition.) On 11 June, two teenage girls had disappeared after a party: fifteen year old Gina Marano and her stepsister Cynthia Chandler. Their bodies were found the next day, dumped in the same manner as the Hillside Strangler victims, off a freeway. They had been shot through the head, after which their bodies had been sexually abused.

Four days later, a friend of Cynthia Chandler received a phone call from a man who identified himself as 'Detective Clark', and told her that the two girls were dead. On 22 June the same man called again, to describe in detail how the girls had been killed and then raped. The caller declared that he had seen the girl to whom he was speaking at the party where he had picked up Gina and Cynthia, 'and now I want to do the same to you'. He told her he was having an orgasm while he was talking to her. The girl was to identify the voice as that of Douglas Clark. It emerged later that, after killing the stepsisters, Clark had gone back home to fetch Carol Bundy, so she could share in his pleasure; but she was not at home.

Later that same day, Clark went back to the room of Exxie Wilson, a prostitute from Little Rock, Arkansas, and shot her through the head. After he had decapitated her, Karen Jones returned home. Clark was about to get into his car after placing the head in the boot; he pursued Karen down the street and shot her. Then he went home and placed the head in the refrigerator. Carol Bundy described how he had taken it with him into the shower and used it for oral sex. According to Carol, she then washed the hair and made up the face as an act of bravado. 'We had a lot of fun with her.' She admitted that it was she who had dumped the head, in its cardboard box, in the driveway in Burbank.

It emerged that Carol Bundy had talked to her ex-lover, Jack Murray, about her new paramour's murders, and it was Murray's threat to tip off the police that led her to shoot him and cut off his head. (Bullets found in his body came from her gun.) This in turn led to her arrest, and to that of Douglas Clark.

Carol Bundy told the police that she and Clark had come together because they wanted to co-operate on crimes. He treated her badly, she said, and although he was 'extremely good in bed', he was not very interested in normal sex. It had to be 'kinky', and he preferred teenage girls. One of his fantasies was to cut a girl's throat and have sex with her as she bled to death. The furthest he had gone in this direction was to stab the young prostitute as she fellated him.

At Clark's trial in October 1982, his lawyer argued that he was insane, while Clark himself insisted — without much hope of convincing the jury — that he had played no part in the crimes. On 28 January 1983 Clark was convicted of killing six girls and sentenced to die in the gas chamber. Carol Bundy had originally planned to plead guilty but insane, but at her trial in May 1983 she changed this to a plea of guilty; she was sentenced to life imprisonment.

Seven

The Roman Emperor Syndrome

Cases like the Moors Murders, Gallego, Birnie, and the Sunset Slayer, make the reader aware that something very strange is happening to our society. Douglas Clark told the jury: 'I don't march to the same drummer you do. If we were all like me, Sodom and Gomorrah might look a nice place to stay.' It might seem fair comment to say that killers like Clark, Heidnik, Gallego, Birnie, and Brady are a sign that our world is rushing down a Gadarene slope into decadence and ruin. Yet such a verdict might be premature. There is nothing in the career of any modern serial killer that could not be paralleled by equally horrifying events from the past – from the lives of Tiberius, Caligula, Tamerlaine, Ivan the Terrible, Vlad the Impaler, Gilles de Rais, Countess Elizabeth Bathory and dozens of others. The historian John Addington Symonds, in a section on 'The Blood-madness of Tyrants' in his *Renaissance in Italy*, suggests that it might be explained in medical terms, 'a portentous secretion of black bile producing the melancholy which led him [Ibrahim ibn Ahmet] to atrocious crimes'. We can see that this explanation simply fails to go to the heart of the matter. Tyrants become cruel because they are unaccustomed to contradiction, and the least opposition to their ideas fills them with a genuine conviction that the objector deserves to die a painful death. They do not see it as a matter of cruelty, but of righteous anger and just punishment.

In the past, only two groups of men were in a position to behave in this way: men in authority (which includes men like Gilles de Rais whose wealth seemed to place them beyond the law) and men who regarded themselves as 'outside society' – bandits and outlaws. The latter were often involved in incidents of hair-raising cruelty – as can be seen, for example, in *A Hangman's Diary* by the sixteenth-century Nuremberg executioner Franz Schmidt, who describes robbers disembowelling pregnant women, while others forced a wife to eat fried eggs off the corpse of her husband. In both cases — tyrants and outlaws — the brutality seems to spring from a sense of being *outside* or above society and the law. This feeling, as we can see, was shared by Ian Brady, Gerald Gallego and Douglas Clark. 'I don't march to the same drummer you do.'

What seems to have happened is that the advance of civilisation has raised the general level of comfort so that large numbers now have a security that was unknown even in the nineteenth century. The trouble is that leisure and comfort also produce boredom, a desire for sensation, which explains why an increasing number of criminals have come to behave like Caligula or Gilles de Rais, and to regard their victims as 'throwaways'. Melvin Rees, Ian Brady, Gerald Gallego, Douglas Clark, are modern examples of what might be called the 'Roman emperor syndrome'.

As to Clark's strange sexual perversions, we only have to read the first general textbook on the subject — Krafft-Ebing's *Psychopathia Sexualis*, published in 1886 — to see that this was just as common in the nineteenth century, and that many of the perversions were even more bizarre than Clark's. It tended to be a well-kept secret, known only to a few doctors and police officers. After the 'swinging sixties' had made pornography more generally available — particularly hard-core videos — it was inevitable that a small number of addicts should decide to experiment in rape and murder. *For the sexual criminal, the most important step is the one that bridges the gap between fantasy and actuality*. After that, rape or murder becomes a habit. Perhaps the surprising thing is that so few pornography addicts take that step.

The sexual criminal who best illustrates this descent into violence is also perhaps the most notorious of modern serial killers. Theodore Bundy developed into a Peeping Tom as a result of catching an accidental glimpse of a girl undressing through a lighted upstairs window. From then on, he began to prowl the streets of Seattle at night, looking for bedroom windows to spy through. 'He approached it almost like a

261

project,' according to his biographers Stephen G. Michaud and Hugh Aynesworth, 'throwing himself into it, literally, for years'. Then, 'like an addiction, the need for a more powerful experience was coming over him'. He made clumsy attempts to disable women's cars, but since these were parked in the university district, they usually found help without any difficulty. Bundy regarded this as a kind of game, a flirtation with danger; 'but the habit grew perceptibly more insistent, just as Ted had become a bolder and bolder thief over the years'. One evening in the summer of 1973, after drinking heavily, Bundy saw a woman leaving a bar and walking up a dark side street. He found a heavy piece of wood in a vacant lot, and stalked her. 'There was really no control at this point.' 'The situation is novel,' said Bundy (speaking of himself in the third person), 'because while he may have toyed around with fantasies before, and made several abortive attempts to act out a fantasy, it never had reached the point where actually he was confronted with harming another individual.' Nevertheless, he got ahead of the girl and lay in wait for her, but before she reached the point where he was hiding, she stopped and went into a house. Bundy told his interviewers: 'The revelation of the experience and the frenzied desire that seized him really seemed to usher in a new dimension to that part of him that was obsessed with violence and women.' (Like so many other serial killers, Bundy saw himself as a dual-personality, a Jekyll and Hyde; he referred to Mr Hyde as 'the Hunchback'.) 'What he had done terrified him, purely terrified him. Full of remorse and remonstrating with himself for the suicidal nature of that activity' — Bundy also recognised murder as a form of suicide — 'he quickly sobered up. He was horrified by the recognition that he had the capacity to do such a thing.'

Nevertheless the craving to watch girls undressing was too strong to be resisted. One night he was peering through a basement window at a girl preparing for bed when he discovered that the door had been left open. He sneaked into her room and leapt on her, but when she screamed, he fled. 'Then he was seized with the same kind of disgust and repulsion and fear and wonder at why he was allowing himself to attempt such extraordinary violence.' He was so upset that he gave up his voyeuristic activities for three months; but on 4 January 1974 he again crept into a basement after he had watched a girl undressing. He wrenched a metal bar from the bed frame and struck her repeatedly on the head. Then, apparently finding himself impotent, he rammed the bar into her vagina. The girl recovered after a week in a coma. It took Bundy a month to recover from the trauma of what he had done. Next time he carried his fantasy through to the end. On 31 January 1974 he entered a students' lodging house and tried bedroom doors until he found one that was unlocked. It was that of twenty-one-year-old Lynda Ann Healy. This time he seized her by the throat and ordered her to remain silent. Then, either at knifepoint or gunpoint — it never became clear which — he forced her to dress, then bound and gagged her, and made her walk out of the house with him. He drove her out to Taylor Mountain, twenty miles from Seattle, then spent hours acting out his sexual fantasies. The interviewers asked him whether there had been any conversation with his victim. 'There'd be some. Since this girl in front of him represented not a person, but again the image, or something desirable, the last thing we would expect him to want to do would be to personalise this person.' Finally, he bludgeoned her to death and left the body on the mountain. Lynda Ann Healy would be the first of four girls he raped and murdered in the same place.

Perhaps the most frightening thing about Bundy's account of himself is the description of how he descended into sex murder by a series of almost infinitesimal steps. Any normal male might experience sexual excitement at a casual glimpse of a woman taking off her clothes near a lighted window. Any normal male might return to a place where he knew he could watch a girl undressing. Any normal male might become increasingly obsessed by watching girls undress until he had turned it into a 'project'. At what point *would* the normal male draw the line? Possibly at actually harming another human being — but then, Bundy also drew the line there, until his craving pushed him the inevitable step further . . .

In the months following the murder of Lynda Ann Healy, Bundy's compulsion increased. Four more girls — Donna Gail Manson, Susan Rancourt, Roberta Parks and Brenda Ball — were abducted, raped and murdered in the same way. On 14 July 1974 he abducted two girls on the same day — Janice Ott and Denise Naslund — from Lake Sammamish Park. Both were approached by a good-looking young man with his arm in a sling, who asked for help in lifting a boat on to the luggage rack of his car. People sitting near Janice Ott heard him introduce himself as Ted, and heard her ask him to sit down and talk for a while before she went off to help him. Bundy abducted her at gunpoint, took her to an empty house, and raped her. Then he went back to the park, picked up his second victim, and took her back to the same house, raping her in front of Janice Ott. Finally he killed them both and dumped their bodies in undergrowth a few miles away.

In September 1974 Bundy moved to Salt Lake City to study law. If he wished to remain uncaught it would obviously have been sensible to stop killing girls, since if he used the same *modus operandi* in two places, it would be a great deal easier to track him down. (In fact, Bundy's name already appeared on a list of police suspects – two women had named him as the possible killer – but since the list comprised 3,500 names, he was only one of many.) But he would have been unable to stop, even if he wanted to: the 'hunchback' was now in full control. So in Salt Lake City five more girls were abducted and raped between October 1974 and January 1975. One girl escaped. Seventeen-year-old Carol DaRonch was in a supermarket complex on 8 November 1974 when a good-looking young man approached her and identified himself as a detective. He told her that her car had been broken into, and lured her into his own car – a Volkswagen – on the pretext of taking her to the police station. Then he snapped a handcuff on one of her wrists and pointed a gun at her head. The girl grabbed for the door handle and fell out of the car; the man was following her, holding an iron bar, when the headlights of an oncoming car illuminated them both; Bundy leapt into his car and drove off. Later that same evening, he abducted another seventeen-year-old, Debbie Kent, from a school concert, and murdered her.

On a Saturday night in August 1985, a policeman in a patrol car was startled when a Volkswagen pulled out from the pavement and drove off at top speed. The policeman followed and finally made the car pull over. Its driver was Ted Bundy, and handcuffs and burgling tools were found in the trunk. By now, the crime computer in Seattle had reduced the list of suspects to ten, and Bundy's name was at number seven. When Salt Lake City police realised that Bundy was from Seattle, they made him stand in a line-up in the Hall of Justice. Carol DaRonch and two other witnesses identified him as the abductor of 8 November. On 27 December 1976 Bundy was found guilty of aggravated kidnapping and sentenced to between one and fifteen years in prison.

By now police were also gathering evidence to link him with the disappearance of a twenty-three-year-old nurse, Caryn Campbell, from a holiday hotel in Colorado. In January Bundy escaped from the Colorado courthouse, but was recaptured within days. The following December he escaped again by unscrewing a light fitment, and this time succeeded in making his way to Tallahassee, Florida, where he rented a room in a student hostel. Now, with everything to lose, he was still unable to resist the compulsion to murder. On the night of 15 January 1978 he entered a student rooming house on the university campus and attacked four girls in quick succession with a wooden club. One was strangled with her tights and raped; another died on her way to hospital; the other two were to recover. An hour and a half later, still unsatisfied, he broke into another rooming house and clubbed another girl unconscious; he was disturbed by the girl's next-door neighbour, and fled. Bundy returned to the anonymity of his student rooming house, where he was known as Chris Hagen.

A month later, on 9 February 1978, he abducted a twelve-year-old schoolgirl, Kimberley Leach, from the Lake City Junior High School; she was his youngest victim. Her body was found two months later in an abandoned shack. By this time, Bundy had been arrested — again by a policeman in a patrol car who was puzzled by his erratic driving.

At his trial in Florida, Bundy maintained his innocence, insisting that it was pure coincidence that he had been in the areas where sixteen girls had been raped and murdered. Teeth marks on the buttocks of one of his victims were demonstrated by a dental expert to be Bundy's own, and he was found guilty and sentenced to death. (Bundy had insisted on conducting his own defence, and rejecting the plea-bargaining that might have saved his life.) Before his electrocution on 24 January 1989, he had confessed to another seven murders, bringing the total to twenty-three, and was obviously prepared to confess to more when time ran out. Police remain convinced that the total could amount to as many as forty.

Bundy differs from most serial killers in one basic respect: his childhood was apparently normal and happy. Nevertheless, his background was far from 'normal'. Theodore Robert

Bundy was an illegitimate child, born in November 1946 to a respectable and religious young secretary, Louise Cowell, in a home for unmarried mothers in Philadelphia; his mother has always refused to disclose the father's identity. The child was left alone for several weeks before being taken to the home of his grandfather, a market gardener, and that initial period without parental affection may account for his later inability to form close relationships. His grandfather was a despotic and violent man who often beat up his wife, although he doted on the baby (who was explained to neighbours as an adopted child). When his mother decided to move to Tacoma (Washington state) when the baby was four, Ted was miserable at losing the only 'father' he had ever known. Louise Cowell married an ex-navy cook, John Bundy, but the child never formed any close relationship with his stepfather, finding him boring and uncultured.

As a schoolboy Bundy was an incorrigible fantasist, daydreaming of being adopted by the cowboy star Roy Rogers, and trying, at one point, to persuade his mother to allow him to be adopted by an uncle who was a professor of music. He soon became a thief and habitual liar. He also became an excellent skier, but he had stolen much of the equipment on which he learned. He experienced a basic drive to 'be somebody', to be famous, but a streak of self-pity, the feeling that the world was against him, prevented him from making the kind of effort that might have led to success.

Although good-looking, the young Bundy was also shy and introverted − it was not until his early twenties that he lost his virginity while sleeping off a drunken evening on a friend's settee, when the lady of the house came and 'raped' him.

The ultimate key to Bundy − and probably to the majority of serial killers − is obviously his immensely powerful sex drive. From an early age he was a compulsive masturbator; he fantasised about necrophilia, and later became a devotee of hard porn. His long-term girlfriend told how he liked to tie her up with stockings before sex; but such acts could not satisfy his desire − like some legendary caliph − for sexual variety and for total control of his partner. He later admitted that he often strangled the victim during the sexual act; vaginas were stuffed with twigs and dirt and one victim was sodomised with an aerosol can.

Perhaps the most important single factor in turning Bundy

into a serial killer was a relationship with a fellow student named Stephanie Brooks. Bundy fell in love with her in his late teens; she was beautiful, sophisticated and came of a wealthy family. To impress her he went to Stanford University to study Chinese; but he was lonely, emotionally immature, and his grades were poor. 'I found myself thinking of standards of success that I didn't seem to be living up to.' Stephanie wearied of his immaturity and dropped him. He was shattered and deeply resentful. His brother later commented: 'Stephanie screwed him up . . . I'd never seen him like this before.' One consequence of the emotional upset was that Bundy returned to thieving on a regular basis; he began shoplifting and stealing for 'thrills'. On one occasion he even stole a large potted plant from someone's garden, and drove off with it sticking through the open roof of his car.

He formed a relationship with a young divorcee, Meg Anders, and became a full-time volunteer for the black republican candidate for governor. He also found a job working for the Crime Commission and Department of Justice Planning – other males in the office envied his confidence, charm and good looks. When Stephanie Brooks met him again seven years after dropping him, she was so impressed by the new and high-powered Ted that she agreed to marry him – they spent Christmas of 1973 together. Bundy's object, however, was not to win her back but to get his revenge for the earlier humiliation. When, in the new year, she rang him to ask why he had not contacted her since their weekend together, he said coldly: 'I have no idea what you're talking about,' and hung up on her. Then, as if his 'revenge' had somehow broken an inner dam and inspired him with a sense of ruthless power and confidence, he committed his first murder.

The vital clue to Bundy lies in a comment made by his friend Ann Rule, a Seattle journalist, in her book *The Stranger Beside Me*. She remarks that he became violently upset if he telephoned Meg Anders – his long-time girlfriend in Seattle – from Salt Lake City, and got no reply. 'Strangely, while he was being continually unfaithful himself, he expected – demanded – that she be totally loyal to him.' This is one of the basic characteristics of a type of person who has been labelled 'the Right Man' or 'the Violent Man'.

The insight came to the science-fiction writer A.E. van Vogt in 1954, when he was preparing to write a novel about a Chinese prison camp run by an authoritarian dictator figure. It struck van Vogt that what dictators seem to have in common is a total and irrational conviction of their own 'rightness', and of the stupidity and wrong-headedness of anyone who opposes them. It is, in fact, the 'Roman emperor' syndrome noted at the beginning of this chapter. All children regard themselves as the centre of the universe; but if they maintain this attitude beyond early childhood, we regard them as thoroughly obnoxious. Emperors like Caligula and Nero maintained the attitude into adulthood — because no-one had the courage to gainsay them — and their cruelties were less the result of sadism than of total self-centredness.

The 'Roman emperor' syndrome arises out of the natural need of all human beings for some degree of self-esteem and self-confidence. Self-confidence means the ability to stick to our own aims and beliefs in the face of opposition. It is as necessary to nursery schoolchildren as to millionaire businessmen. Once most of us have established what we regard as a comfortable degree of self-confidence — that is, adequate to our everyday needs — we turn our attention to other matters: schoolwork, making a living, etc. For various reasons, some people fail to achieve this 'comfortable' level, perhaps because some early trauma has permanently undermined them, perhaps because they are surrounded by people whose respect they totally fail to win. Low-dominance people are inclined to accept their rather poor self-image; high-dominance people may develop a lifelong craving for the respect of others.

Again, some of these people may develop into 'achievers' — even such dubious achievers as Hitler and Stalin. Others may simply become remarkable for the size of their egos. Others become boasters and liars. Van Vogt noted that a certain percentage of these people achieve a sense of security in a peculiar manner: they marry, produce a family, and then behave exactly like a dictator, treating their wife and children as their subjects. Not even the slightest hint of contradiction is allowed. The personality of such a man (or woman) is totally non-flexible. In no circumstances will he ever admit that he is in the wrong, or has made a mistake. If evidence that he is in the wrong is placed so firmly under his nose that he can no longer ignore it, he is likely to explode into violence. This is why van Vogt christened him 'the Violent Man' or 'the Right Man'.

Van Vogt began by studying newspaper accounts of divorce proceedings, and noting how often husbands could treat their wives — and children — with appalling irrationality, flying into a rage at the least sign of opposition, and yet expecting to be allowed to do exactly as they liked. One such man, a commercial traveller, had an endless series of affairs (these being an important prop to his self-esteem), yet would knock his wife down if she so much as smiled at another man. Oddly enough, most such men seem to their colleagues at work to be perfectly normal; the Right Man never tries to indulge his power fantasies with his superiors or equals.

He is, of course, living in a kind of sand castle, and it can be destroyed if his wife has the courage to kick it down — that is, to leave him. Van Vogt noted that in such cases — when the 'worm turned' — the husband would often experience total psychological collapse, sometimes resulting in suicide. His security is built upon a fabric of self-delusion, and he has become skilled in refusing to face this fact. If it is no longer possible to avoid facing it, he feels that the foundation of his life has been swept away.

Bundy was good-looking and intelligent; but he was a late developer, and early frustrations and disappointments seem to have convinced him that he was a 'loser'. This may be deduced from his compulsive thieving — potential 'winners' are too concerned with their future to risk being labelled a criminal. Bundy's stealing became a compulsion after Stephanie Brooks had 'dumped' him; it obviously contained mildly suicidal elements, the feeling that 'Nothing matters any more'. In spite of his intelligence he was a poor student, and his grades were usually Bs. The tide began to turn when he worked for the Justice Department and the Republican candidate, but by that time he was already a compulsive Peeping Tom. 'Revenge' on Stephanie Brooks also came too late; it only served to rationalise his feeling that all women were bitches and deserved to be raped. The Right Man can justify any action that he wants to take, no matter how immoral. Most of the cases van Vogt observed involved Right Men 'cheating' compulsively on their wives. Bundy went several steps further and became a compulsive rapist and killer as he had become a compulsive thief.

As soon as we understand this curious mechanism of self-deception, we can see that it seems to apply to most serial killers. Angelo Buono was another 'Right Man', a man who was capable of sodomising his wife in front of the children to 'teach her a lesson'. When one of his prostitutes ran away, it was the kind of 'desertion' that all Right Men fear. When his threatening phone calls led to humiliation at the hands of an outsize Hell's Angel, all his outraged self-esteem became directed — with typical irrationality — against women. Murdering women and dumping them like trash on hillsides restored his macho self-image. There was no reason to chant 'Die, cunt, die' as he sat on Lissa Kastin's legs and watched Bianchi strangling her; she had never done anything to merit his hatred. But the Right Man was murdering and humiliating *all* women.

Similarly, the Right Man syndrome can be seen to be the key to Cameron Hooker, Melvin Rees, Harvey Carignan, Gary Heidnik, Gerald Gallego, David Birnie, Douglas Clark and Ian Brady. Heidnik's collapse into insanity when his Filipino wife walked out on him is typical of the Violent Man. So is Heinrich Pommerencke's sudden decision that all women deserved to die. The same applies to cases of *folie à deux*, like the Moors Murder case. For Ian Brady, Myra Hindley was the equivalent of the Right Man's family — a kind of little dictator state, which enables him to indulge his power fantasies. When the sense of power-starvation is so overwhelming, the appetite increases with feeding, the starved ego swells like a balloon.

It should now be clear that the Right Man syndrome is a form of mild insanity, allied to that of a madman who believes he is Napoleon. It cannot be described as true insanity because it does not involve psychotic delusions. (Fish, for example, was not a Right Man; he was genuinely insane.) Gary Heidnik occupies a blurred space between the Right Man syndrome and genuine psychosis; it is almost impossible to say how far he was insane, and how far he was merely suffering from the Right Man's delusions of power and grandeur. The Right Man syndrome, in its most primitive form, is simply a desire to behave like a spoilt child, to punish those who refuse to do what the child demands. Robert Hansen and Douglas Clark are examples of this stage: they only killed girls who failed to bring them to orgasm.

It is easy to understand the development of the syndrome. There is nobody in the world who does not want 'his own way'. Most of us learn to make realistic adjustments to not getting our own way. This is obviously easier for someone whose life is fairly stable. Children with serious problems – difficult parents, broken homes, traumatic frustrations – tend to react to disappointments with an out-of-proportion sense of misery and defeat. They compensate by fantasy, and perhaps (like Bundy) by lying and stealing. These reactions have an identical root; both are attempts to take what the world refuses to give freely. If this 'naughty boy' aspect goes unpunished (as with Bundy) it can develop into a kind of self-indulgence that strikes us as insane, but which is actually a calculated and conscious form of wickedness.

This type of serial killer is epitomised by Dean Corll, the homosexual mass murderer of the 1970s. Corll, like most serial killers, had a difficult childhood, with a father 'who did not like children', and the parents eventually divorced. Meanwhile, Dean (born 1939) had become a mother's boy. His mother started a candy company which was to provide her sons with a living. In 1968, on the advice of a psychic, she moved away from Houson, and left Dean, who was then in his late twenties, on his own. Life was easy; he smoked pot, sniffed glue – although he had a heart condition – and made advances to young boys. When he turned thirty, he became thin-skinned and secretive about his age. His former friends noticed that he became moody; he preferred the companionship of a number of teenage juvenile delinquents. These included Elmer Wayne Henley, a child of a broken home, and David Brooks. The latter, a convicted thief and something of a sadist, had on one occasion been knocked unconscious by Corll, tied to a bed, and repeatedly sodomised; nevertheless, he and Corll remained friends. He had introduced Henley to Corll. With the aid of his two friends, Corll began luring teenage boys to the house, then raping and killing them, often after various forms of torture, such as biting the genitals.

The first killing took place in 1970, when Corll murdered

271

a hitchhiking student named Jeffrey Konen. Most of the other victims came from the run-down Heights area of Houston. Corll's usual method was to wait until they were unconscious from glue-sniffing, then to chain them to a board and sodomise them, sometimes for days, before strangling them with a rope. In December 1970 he murdered two boys – James Glass, fourteen, and Danny Yates, fifteen – at the same time. Two brothers – Donald and Jerry Waldrop – were killed in January 1971. Between 1970 and 1973, Corll murdered twenty-nine boys, with the aid of Brooks and Henley. (Brooks seemed to enjoy causing pain, and on one occasion, shot a boy after inserting the barrel of the revolver up his nose.) Most of the bodies were buried in a rented boatshed, wrapped in plastic sheeting. The youngest victim was a nine-year-old boy who lived in a shop opposite Corll's apartment.

The end came on the morning of 8 August 1973. Henley had arrived at a glue-sniffing party with another youth and a fifteen-year-old girl. Corll was furious about the girl – 'You've spoilt it all' – and Henley woke up to find himself tied and handcuffed, and the vindictive Corll standing over him with a gun. 'I'll teach you a lesson.' Finally, by offering to help rape and torture the other two, Henley succeeded in persuading Corll to release him. The two semiconscious teenagers were then undressed and chained up. Henley tried to rape the girl, but failed. Corll was in the process of raping the youth when Henley said: 'Why don't you let me take the chick outa here? She don't want to see that.' When Corll ignored him, Henley grabbed the gun and ordered him to stop; Corll taunted him: 'Go on, kill me.' Henley fired repeatedly, and Corll collapsed. Henley then rang the police and informed them: 'I've just killed a man.' When the police arrived, Henley told them the story of the attempted rapes and the shooting, and added that Corll had boasted of having killed other boys and burying them in a boatshed. In the boatshed in south Houston, police uncovered seventeen bodies, then Henley led them to sites where another ten were buried. Henley's estimate was that Corll had murdered thirty-one boys.

Henley's knowledge of the burial sites made it clear that he was not as innocent as he pretended; eventually, both he and David Brooks were sentenced to life imprisonment.

One of the most widely published photographs of Corll, as an adult, shows him clutching a teddy bear. Jack Olsen's book on the case, *The Man With the Candy*, makes it clear that Corll never grew up. The murders were simply the expression of a kind of 'spoiltness', a desire to have his own way.

The same also seems to be true of another widely publicised case of mass murder in the 1970s. Between 1976 and his arrest in December 1978, John Wayne Gacy, a Chicago building contractor, killed thirty-two boys in the course of sexual attacks. Gacy's childhood – he was born in 1932 – was in many ways similar to Corll's, with a harsh father and a protective mother. He was a lifelong petty thief. Like Corll, he also suffered from a heart condition. In childhood, he had been struck on the head by a swing, which caused a bloodclot on the brain, undetected for several years. He married a girl whose parents owned a fried-chicken business in Waterloo, Iowa, and – again like Corll – became a successful businessman. (Maslow would point out that this indicates that both belong to the 'dominant five per cent'.) He was also known as a liar and a boaster. His marriage came to an end when Gacy was imprisoned for sexually molesting a teenager (although Gacy always claimed he had been framed). Out of jail, he married a second time and set up in business as a building contractor. He was successful (although notoriously mean), and was soon regarded as a pillar of the local community – he was even photographed shaking hands with First Lady Rosalynn Carter, the wife of President Jimmy Carter. His own wife found his violent tempers a strain, and they divorced.

In 1975, while he was still married, one of his teenage employees vanished; it was after this that his wife noticed an unpleasant smell in the house. After their separation in the following year, Gacy made a habit of picking up teenage homosexuals, or luring teenagers to his house 'on business', handcuffing them, and then committing sodomy. They were finally strangled, and the bodies disposed of, usually in the crawl space under the house.

In March 1978, a twenty-seven-year-old named Jeffrey Rignall accepted an invitation to smoke pot in Gacy's Oldsmobile. Gacy clapped a chloroform-soaked rag over his face, and when Rignall woke up he was being sodomised in Gacy's home. Gacy raped him repeatedly and flogged him with a whip; finally, he chloroformed him again and left him in a park. In hospital, Rignall discovered that he had sustained permanent liver damage from the chloroform. Since the police were unable to help, he set about trying to track down the rapist himself, sitting near freeway entrances looking for black Oldsmobiles. Eventually he saw Gacy, followed him, and noted down his number. Although Gacy was arrested, the evidence against him seemed poor.

On 11 December 1978 Gacy invited a fifteen-year-old boy, Robert Piest, to his house to talk about a summer job. When the youth failed to return, police tracked down the building contractor who had offered him the job, and questioned him at his home in Des Plaines. Alerted by the odour, they investigated the crawl space and found fifteen bodies and parts of others. When Gacy had run out of space, he had started dumping bodies in the river.

Gacy's story was that he was a 'dissociated' personality, and that the murders were committed by an evil part of himself called Jack. In court, one youth described how Gacy had pulled him up, posing as a police officer, then handcuffed him at gunpoint. Back in Gacy's home, he was sodomised, after which Gacy made an attempt to drown him in the bath; but Gacy changed his mind and raped him again. Then, after holding his head under water until he became unconscious, Gary urinated on him, then played Russian roulette with a gun which turned out to contain only a blank. Finally, Gacy released him, warning him that the police would not believe his story. Gacy proved to be right. The jury who tried him believed a psychiatrist who told them that Gacy was suffering from a narcissistic personality disorder that did not amount to insanity, and on 13 March 1980 John Wayne Gacy was sentenced to life imprisonment.

In cases like these, it seems clear that the answer should not be sought in psychological diagnoses so much as in weakness and self-indulgence. Although Gacy's biographer Tim Cahill tries hard to make a case for Gacy as a doom-haunted necrophile (he once worked in a morgue), the psychological evidence shows that both he and Corll were childish and undisciplined personalities in the grip of total selfishness.

The same probably applies to the only British example of a homosexual serial killer, Dennis Nilsen. Between December 1978 and February 1983, Nilsen murdered fifteen young men whom he had lured to his flat in north London, and got rid of the bodies by dissecting them, boiling the pieces, and disposing of them in various ways — even leaving them in plastic bags for the dustbin men to collect. On 8 February 1983 a drains maintenance engineer called at a house in Muswell Hill to examine a blocked drain; he found that it contained decaying flesh that looked human. When Dennis Nilsen, a thirty-seven-year-old employment officer, returned home, he was questioned by the police, and immediately pointed to a wardrobe; inside were two plastic bags containing two severed heads and a skull.

Nilsen insisted that there was no sexual motive in the crimes, but this is hard to believe. The son of a drunken father and a puritanical mother, he had the kind of lonely childhood that seems typical of serial killers. His troubles began, according to Nilsen, when he was seven years old, and was taken by his mother to see the corpse of his grandfather — to whom he had been deeply attached. A necrophiliac obsession began to develop. After twelve years as an army cook, and a period in London as a policeman and security guard, he obtained work in a job centre in Soho and began living with a man. It was after this man left in 1977 that Nilsen began to invite young males — picked up in pubs — back to his flat, get them drunk, then strangle them.

Nilsen's biographer Brian Masters accepted Nilsen's curious explanation that he was killing out of loneliness — the book is entitled *Killing for Company* — and that having a corpse around the flat gave him a sense of companionship; but since Nilsen admitted that he was a necrophile, this explanation is hard to accept. What *is* quite clear from Masters' book is that Nilsen was a man of high dominance; Masters went to see him in prison and reported that Nilsen behaved as if interviewing him for a job. One of his acquaintances reported: 'The only off-putting thing about him was his eyes. They can stare you out, and not many people can stare me out.' Others found his immense loquacity tiresome; Nilsen regarded himself as an intellectual, and had a high opinion of himself. This seems to be the most probable explanation of why he turned to murder. When the man with whom he was living, David Gallichan, announced that he was leaving — he had been offered a job in the country — he was surprised when Nilsen's reaction was a cold and highly controlled rage. 'It was as though I had insulted him, and he wanted me to go immediately.' This is, of course, the reaction of a Right Man on being abandoned by someone whom he has been accustomed to dominate; the whole foundation of his insecure self-esteem is shaken. This may also explain why, since his arrest and life imprisonment, Nilsen seems to have taken a certain pride in being 'Britain's biggest mass murderer'.

One final important fact must be taken into account: that Nilsen, like Ted Bundy, was an extremely heavy drinker. He met his victims in pubs, then brought them back home to consume large quantities of vodka. Alcohol had the same effect on Nilsen and Bundy that drugs had on Dean Corll and on the Manson clan, creating a sense of unreality, a kind of moral vacuum without inhibitions. In this vacuum, murder meant very little.

Perhaps the most basic characteristic of the serial killer is one that he shares with most other criminals: a tendency to an irrational self-pity that can produce an explosion of violence. In that sense, Paul John Knowles may be regarded not merely as the archetypal serial killer but as the archetypal criminal.

Knowles, who was born in 1946, had spent an average of six months of every year in jail since he was nineteen, mostly for car thefts and burglaries. In Florida's Raiford Penitentiary in 1972 he began to study astrology, and started corresponding with a divorcee named Angela Covic, whom he had contacted through an astrology magazine. She flew to Florida, was impressed by the gaunt good looks of the tall red-headed convict, and agreed to marry him. She hired a lawyer to work on his parole, and when he was released on 14 May 1972, Knowles hastened to San Francisco to claim his bride. She soon had second thoughts; a psychic had told her that she was mixed up with a very dangerous man. Knowles stayed at her mother's apartment, but after four days Angela Covic told him she had decided to return to her husband, and gave him his air ticket back to Florida. We have seen that, when the Violent Man is rejected by a woman, the result is an explosion of rage and self-pity that contains a suicidal component. Knowles conformed to type; he later claimed that he went out on to the streets of San Francisco and killed three people at random.

Back in his home town of Jacksonville, Florida, on 26 July 1974 Knowles got into a fight in a bar and was locked up for the night. He escaped, broke into the home of a sixty-five-year-old teacher, Alice Curtis, and stole her money and her car. He rammed a gag too far down her throat and she suffocated. A few days later, as he parked the stolen car, he noticed two children looking at him as if they recognised him – their mother was, in fact, a friend of his family. He forced them into the car and drove away. The bodies of seven-year-old Mylette Anderson and her eleven-year-old sister Lillian were later found in a swamp.

What followed was a totally unmotivated murder rampage, as if Knowles had simply decided to kill as many people as he could before he was caught. The following day, 2 August 1974, in Atlantic Beach, Florida, he broke into the home of Marjorie Howie, forty-nine, and strangled her with a stocking; he stole her television set. A few days later he strangled and raped a teenage runaway who hitched a lift with him. On 23 August he strangled Kathie Pierce in Musella, Georgia, while her three-year-old son looked on; Knowles left the child unharmed. On 3 September near Lima, Ohio, he had several drinks with an accounts executive named William Bates, and later strangled him, driving off in the dead man's white Impala. After driving to California, Seattle and Utah (using Bates's credit cards) he forced his way into a caravan in Ely, Nevada, on 18 September 1974, and shot to death an elderly couple, Emmett and Lois Johnson. On 21 September he strangled and raped forty-two-year-old Mrs Charlynn Hicks, who had stopped to admire the view beside the road near Sequin, Texas. On 23 September, in Birmingham, Alabama, he met an attractive woman named Ann Dawson, who owned a beauty shop, and they travelled around together for the next six days, living off her money; she was murdered on 29 September. For the next sixteen days he drove around without apparently committing any further murders; but on 16 October he rang the doorbell of a house in Marlborough, Connecticut; it was answered by sixteen-year-old Dawn White, who was expecting a friend. Knowles forced her up to the bedroom and raped her; when her mother, Karen White, returned home, he raped

277

her too, then strangled them both with silk stockings, leaving with a tape recorder and Dawn White's collection of rock records. Two days later, he knocked on the door of fifty-three year old Doris Hovey in Woodford, Virginia, and told her he needed a gun and would not harm her; she gave him a rifle belonging to her husband, and he shot her through the head and left, leaving the rifle beside her body.

In Key West, Florida, he picked up two hitchhikers, intending to kill them, but was stopped by a policeman for pulling up on a kerb; when the policeman asked to see his documents, Knowles expected to be arrested; but the officer failed to check that he was the owner of the car, and let him drive away.

On 2 November Knowles picked up two hitchhikers, Edward Hilliard and Debbie Griffin; Hilliard's body was later discovered in woods near Macon, Georgia; the girl's body was never found.

On 6 November, in a gay bar in Macon, he met a man named Carswell Carr and went home with him. Later that evening, Carr's fifteen-year-old daughter Mandy heard shouting and went downstairs, to find Knowles standing over the body of her father, who was tied up. It emerged later that Carr had died of a heart attack; Knowles had been torturing him by stabbing him all over with a pair of scissors. He then raped Mandy Carr — or attempted it (no sperm was found in the vagina) and strangled her with a stocking. The bodies were found when Carr's wife, a night nurse, returned home.

The following day, in a Holiday Inn in downtown Atlanta, Knowles saw an attractive redhead in the bar — a British journalist named Sandy Fawkes. She went for a meal with him and they ended up in her bedroom, but he proved impotent, in spite of all her efforts. He had introduced himself to her as Daryl Golden, son of a New Mexico restaurant owner, and the two of them got on well enough for her to accept his offer to drive her to Miami. On the way there, he hinted that he was on the run for some serious crime — or crimes — and told her that he had a premonition that he was going to be killed some time soon. He also told her that he had tape-recorded his confession, and left it with his lawyer in Miami, Sheldon Yavitz. In another motel, he finally succeeded in entering her, after first practising cunnilingus and masturbating

278

himself into a state of excitement. Even so, he failed to achieve orgasm; she concluded that he was incapable of it.

Long before they separated — after a mere six days together — she was anxious to get rid of him. She had sensed the underlying violence, self-pity, lack of discipline. He pressed hard for another night together; she firmly refused, insisting that it would only make the parting more difficult. He waited outside her Miami motel half the night, while she deliberately stayed away; finally, he gave up and left.

The following day, she was asked to go to the police station, and there for the first time realised what kind of a man she had been travelling with. On the morning after their separation 'Daryl Golden' had driven to the house of some journalists to whom he had been introduced four days earlier, and offered to drive Susan Mackenzie to the hairdresser. Instead, he took the wrong turning, and told her that he wanted to have sex with her, and would not hurt her if she complied. When he stopped the car and pointed a gun at her, she succeeded in jumping out and waved frantically at a passing car. Knowles drove off. Later, alerted to the attempted rape, a squad car tried to stop Knowles, but he pointed a shotgun at the policeman and drove off.

Knowles knew that he had to get rid of the stolen car. In West Palm Beach, he forced his way into a house, and took a girl named Barbara Tucker hostage, driving off in her Volkswagen, leaving her sister (in a wheelchair) and six-year-old child unharmed. He held Barbara Tucker captive in a motel in Fort Pierce for a night and day, then finally left her tied up and drove off in her car.

The following day, Patrolman Charles F. Campbell flagged down the Volkswagen — now with altered licence plates — and found himself looking down the barrel of a shotgun. He was taken captive and driven off, handcuffed, in his own patrol car. The brakes were poor so, using the police siren, Knowles forced another car — driven by businessman John Meyer — off the road, then drove off in Meyer's car, with Meyer and the patrolman in the back. In Pulaski County, Georgia, Knowles took them into a wood, handcuffed them to a tree, and shot both in the back of the head.

Soon after, he saw a police roadblock ahead, and drove on through it, losing control and crashing into a tree. He ran into the woods, and a vast manhunt began, involving two hundred police, tracker dogs and helicopters. In fact, Knowles was arrested by a courageous civilian, who saw him from a house, and he gave himself up quietly.

The day after his appearance in court, as he was being transferred to a maximum-security prison, Knowles unpicked his handcuffs and made a grab for the sheriff's gun; FBI agent Ron Angel shot him dead. Knowles had been responsible for at least eighteen murders, possibly as many as twenty-four.

Sandy Fawkes had seen Knowles in court, and was overwhelmed by a sense of his 'evil power'. She had no doubt that he now had what he had always wanted: he was famous at last. 'And enjoying his notoriety. The papers were filled with pictures of his appearance at Midgeville and accounts of his behaviour. The streets had been lined with people. Sightseers had hung over the sides of balconies to catch a glimpse of Knowles, manacled and in leg irons, dressed in a brilliant orange jumpsuit. He had loved it: the local co-eds four-deep on the sidewalks, the courtroom packed with reporters, friends, Mandy's school chums and relatives of the Carr family. It was an event, he was the centre of it and he smiled at everyone. No wonder he had laughed like a hyena at his capture; he was having his hour of glory, not in the hereafter as he had predicted, but in the here-and-now. The daily stories of the women in his life had turned him into a Casanova killer, a folk villain, Dillinger and Jesse James rolled into one. He was already being referred to as the most heinous killer in history.'

So at last Knowles had achieved the aim of most serial killers: 'to become known.' He was quoted in a local newspaper as saying that he was 'the only successful member of his family'.

Yet the central mystery remains, the mystery with which we are confronted again and again in dealing with serial killers. Sandy Fawkes describes him as charming and intelligent. She also describes how, as they watched a group of picnickers, with a man swinging his small child around, he watched with a 'tender smile'. 'He seemed to be so ordinary and yet so lost, as if he knew that scene would never be his, he could not join, would always be separate.' When she asked him if he had many friends he replied: 'I find it difficult to get close to many people,' and she adds: 'The impression was one of rejection, a history of failure to relate.' Their curious sexual relations seem to illustrate the same point — his need to masturbate before he could generate the excitement to achieve penetration.

280

The odd thing that emerges from her book *Killing Time* is that, in many ways, Knowles was obviously a normal, decent human being, capable of playing his role as a 'social animal' rather better than most people. Yet the man who killed two small children because he thought they had recognised him, who shot so many other people without compunction, was — in the precise sense of the word — a wild animal rather than a human being, a creature like a tiger or a mad dog. What could cause such a transformation? Most of us can instinctively understand it, but it is difficult to capture in words. Like so many other criminals, he was trapped in a sense of being unlucky, but then, so are a vast number of human beings who never break the law. We know nothing of what made Knowles into the kind of person, although the reason obviously lies in his family background. (He told Sandy Fawkes that he disliked his father.) What we can sense is that he somehow exaggerated his problems, his 'failure to relate'. When he went to San Francisco from prison in Florida, he was hoping to become 'normal'. Rejection by the woman he had hoped to marry produced the response that 'rejection' always causes in Right Men: a kind of suicidal violence. He went on a rampage of murder, like a naughty child who tries to make his parents feel sorry for punishing him. His own high dominance also made him capable of raping and murdering women without guilt or regret: the high-dominance male can generate little personal feeling for medium- or low-dominance females — they are merely objects to be used. Sandy Fawkes was different, a female within his own dominance group with whom he could have formed a permanent relationship, but, like his bride-to-be in San Francisco, she also sensed his lack of discipline, the low bursting-point that would have made him a liability as a husband. It was after he felt that she had also rejected him that he reverted to his old habit of violence; the attempt to rape Susan Mackenzie was probably an attempt to make her 'feel sorry' for her rejection.

Here once again, we feel instinctively that it was all somehow pointless, that Knowles was acting on unnecessarily pessimistic assumptions. The judge who sentenced Ted Bundy to death evidently felt the same. 'Take care of yourself, young man. I say that to you sincerely. It's a tragedy to this court to see such a total waste of humanity. You're a bright young man. You'd have made a good lawyer. I'd have loved to have you practise in front of me. I bear you no animosity, believe me. You went the wrong way, partner. Take care of yourself.' This was a recognition that, as a high-dominance male, Bundy might have been capable of considerable achievement. Bundy's downfall was his sexual obsession, the craving to prove his 'superiority' by using and discarding women like cigarettes. Knowles was not primarily concerned with sex, but — like Carl Panzram — with 'getting his own back' on society. But as Joyce Cary's Gulley Jimson once remarked, 'You never get your own back — it's always moved on.'

In speaking of the Right Man, Van Vogt used the interesting phrase: 'He makes the decision to be out of control.' Our first response to this is the feeling that he has phrased it badly; surely he means 'the decision to lose control' or 'to go out of control'. But Van Vogt is making an important point. Knowles's decision was not simply to lose control. He recognises that control, discipline, constructive effort, amounts to a *state of being*, and he make a conscious choice of the opposite state. He *decides* to have a low bursting-point.

Such a decision is not only irrational; it is self-destructive. Once they can actually *see* the negative consequences of their conduct, 'mad dog' killers like Panzram and Knowles are intelligent enough to recognise this. By that time it is too late.

'Realise that most Right Men deserve some sympathy,' says van Vogt, 'for they are struggling with an almost unbelievable inner horror.' At first sight, this is perhaps the strangest remark in van Vogt's account of the Violent Man. 'Unbelievable inner horror.' Is he not overstating the case?

To realise why this is not so, we need to understand that members of the 'dominant five per cent' need success as much as they need food and drink. It is difficult to imagine anything more frustrating than a dominant male (or female) stuck in a position that allows absolutely no expression of that dominance. A few people of this type 'sublimate' their dominance into creativity, and become writers or artists or musicians; they may even achieve the success they crave in this way. Many simply remain frustrated and develop ulcers. A certain percentage retreat into a kind of fantasy world in which they are anonymous geniuses or heroes, men whose greatness is simply not recognised by their fellows. Van Vogt comments that such men are 'idealists', meaning that they live in their own mental world and prefer to ignore aspects of reality that conflict with it. When reality administers hard knocks, they go through a crisis of self-justification, and usually end up more certain than ever that they are right and the world is wrong. Typical of this strange, lonely fantasy was the card displayed in the cab of the Yorkshire Ripper: 'In this truck is a man whose latent genius, if unleashed, would rock the nation, whose dynamic energy would overpower those around him. Better let him sleep.' In fact, Peter Sutcliffe had been a shy, lonely child who had developed into a shy, lonely adult. It is also typical that Sutcliffe's violent attacks began after he suspected that his future wife was being unfaithful to him; the superman fantasy was being undermined, and he had to *do* something about it before it collapsed and buried him in its ruins. Yet, as van Vogt goes on to observe: 'If they give way to the impulse to hit or choke, they are losing the battle, and are on the way to the ultimate disaster . . . of their subjective universe of self-justification.' He was, of course, thinking about the 'normal' Right Man, not the Right Man who has surrendered completely to the urge to hit or choke, and become a serial killer.

What happens to such men? We have seen that the first stage is that they become subject to the 'Jekyll and Hyde syndrome', where the sane and non-violent part struggles against the 'hunchback'. Like Bundy, they may be horrified by what they have done and swear never to do it again; but the hunchback has become stronger through being indulged, and they are soon using their talent for self-justification to excuse murder: life is cruel, the law of existence is survival of the fittest, society is rotten and deserves what it gets . . .

As soon as we become aware of the 'Right Man pattern', we can see it again and again in cases of serial killers, even those who, at first sight, seem to be basically motivated by sex. In April 1980 a Colombian man was arrested in Ambato, Ecuador, when he tried to abduct an eleven-year-old Indian girl from the market place. A few days earlier, the rain-swollen river had overflowed its banks and revealed the bodies of four missing girls; ever since then, police had been looking for a multiple sex killer. The prisoner, thirty-one-year-old Pedro Alonzo Lopez, denied that he had anything to do with the murders. A pastor who posed as a fellow prisoner finally extracted a confession; soon, Lopez had told police that he had killed about three hundred and sixty girls, and was leading them to some of the burial sites.

Lopez later told the story of his life to American journalist Ron Laytner. The seventh son of a prostitute in Tolima, Colombia — with twelve brothers and sisters — he was thrown out of the house by his mother at the age of eight for sexually fondling one of his sisters. Kindly neighbours took him in, but the next day his mother took him to the edge of town and left him. He took a day to find his way home, laughing at his success. The next day his mother took him on a bus to another town and left him there. That night, a man found the crying child and promised to be a father to him; in fact he took him to an empty building and raped him.

In Bogotá, where he was begging, a visiting American family sent him to a school for orphans, but a woman schoolteacher tried to seduce him when he was twelve, and he ran away after stealing money.

At the age of eighteen, in prison for stealing a car, he was grabbed by four male prisoners and raped. He swore revenge. It took two weeks to manufacture a knife; then he lured the rapists, one by one, into a dark cell and killed three of them; the fourth stumbled on the bodies and fled, screaming, from the cell. Two years were added to his prison sentence — the murders were looked on as self-defence.

Once out of prison, he began abducting and raping very young girls, preferably under the age of twelve. He would then kill them and bury the bodies. They were mostly Indians, and no-one paid much attention to their disappearance. The Ayacucho Indians caught him carrying off a nine-year-old girl and, after torturing him, prepared to bury him alive. An American missionary intervened and took the bound rapist in her jeep to the nearest Peruvian police outpost. The police were not interested, and sent back across the border into Colombia, where he continued to murder girls — his total was by this time around a hundred. He returned to Ecuador for, as he explained, its girls are more gentle and trusting than those of Colombia. His method was always the same — to walk around markets until he saw a girl with 'a certain look of innocence and beauty'. He would follow the girl, if necessary for days, until her mother left her alone. Then he would approach her and tell her that he had a present for her mother. He would lead her by the hand to the outskirts of the town, then rape and kill her. He hoped one day to rape a white child, attracted by their fair hair, but tourists tended to keep an eye on their children.

In April 1980, the man who had become known as 'the Monster of the Andes' used his usual technique to lure away the eleven-year-old daughter of Carlina Ramon Poveda; but the frantic mother caught up with her daughter, walking hand in hand with her abductor. She denounced him shrilly, and when he called her a dirty Indian, summoned some Indian men to come and help her; they held Lopez down until the police arrived.

In the murders of the three men who raped him, we see the typical response of a Right Man to humiliation. When Lopez was making his complaints to journalist Ron Laytner, he declared: 'I cannot see the sky. This is wrong, for I am the Man of the Century. I will be famous in history.' Like Knowles, he felt he had finally achieved 'success'. Asked to explain how he justified his murders, he told Laytner: 'The arrival of life is divine. It comes through the act of sex. And so if an innocent person dies in the act of sex, it is also divine. That person will find heaven without suffering in this world.' It sounded curiously like Panzram's explanation that he was 'doing people good' by murdering them, since life was so vile that to kill someone was to do him a favour . . . The Right Man lives in a strange universe of fantasy and self-justification, and the serial killer 'punishes' society through murder.

By one of those grisly coincidences that are so frequent in the world of murder, a second 'Monster of the Andes' was operating in Ecuador within five years of the arrest of Lopez. He was Daniel Camargo Barbosa and, like Lopez, he came from Colombia. In 1985 he was serving a life sentence in Colombia for rape and murder, but succeeded in escaping into Ecuador. During 1986, he raped and murdered seventy-two women and girls in the area of the port of Guayaquil. He was arrested in Quito when a policeman noticed bloodstains on his clothing. A slightly built man of fifty-seven, with a great deal of natural charm, he seemed an unlikely mass murderer. Like so many serial killers, he was avid for 'recognition'; he began to boast about his murders, and willingly led detectives to the sites of fifty bodies. He even appeared on television, and when asked whether he had accomplices, replied proudly: 'No, I did it all myself.' Asked why he had committed his crimes, he explained: 'When one has been the victim of traumatic experiences in childhood, one grows up with the mental conditions for committing these acts', a reply that indicates that, like so many serial killers, he possessed a relatively high I.Q. Like Lopez, he was sentenced to sixteen years in prison, the maximum possible under Ecuadorian law.

Henry Lee Lucas might be regarded as the American equivalent of Pedro Alonzo Lopez, at least as far as the number of his victims is concerned: he has confessed to three hundred and sixty murders. A rather mild-looking character, who has become deeply religious since he was sentenced to death, he seems at first an altogether less obvious example of a Violent Man; but, as the evidence makes plain, appearances can be deceptive.

Born in 1937 in Blacksburg, Virginia, Lucas was the son of a prostitute and a railway worker who had lost both legs in an accident. His mother seems to have detested the child and treated him with sadistic cruelty, once causing brain damage when she struck him on the head with a piece of wood. His teacher, who often gave him hot meals, described him as one of the most impoverished and desperate hill children she had ever met. An accident led to the loss of one eye, so that he had to have it replaced with a glass one. By the age of fifteen he had become a juvenile delinquent, and was sent to a reformatory for breaking and entering. 'I started stealing as soon as I could run fast.' He had also by this time committed his first murder, attempting to rape a seventeen-year-old girl at a bus stop and strangling her when she resisted. In January 1960, he murdered his mother during the course of a quarrel, slashing at her with a knife. (He claims that he had no idea that she was dead, and that her death was due to a heart attack.) He was sentenced to forty years in prison, where he made several suicide attempts. He was recommended for parole after ten years. In fact, he seems to have felt secure in prison and wanted to stay there; when paroled, he told the board that he would kill again. On the day he left prison, he kept his word, raping and killing a woman in Jackson. The murder remained unsolved until he eventually confessed to it.

There followed an unsuccessful marriage, which lasted only a short time. In Carbondale, Pennsylvania, he met another drifter, Ottis Toole, a homosexual with a penchant for cannibalism. The two teamed up and, according to Lucas's biographer Max Call, 'left a bloody trail through Michigan, Ohio, Indiana, Illinois and Wisconsin'. Call claims that they kept the head of one murder victim in the trunk of the car for two days. 'I was bitter at the world,' Lucas claimed. 'I hated everything.' 'Killing someone is just like walking outdoors. If I wanted a victim I'd just go to get one.'

Ottis Toole's parents liked Lucas enough to appoint him the guardian of their two youngest children, Becky Powell, nine, and her younger brother Frank. A year or two later, she left her Florida home with Lucas and her brother Ottis, and became Lucas's mistress. She was present during a number of his killings, and even helped to bury the bodies. (Lucas claimed that it was his care in disposing of the bodies that prevented the law from catching up with him for so long.) When Becky was thirteen she was caught and sent to a juvenile detention centre in Florida; with the help of Lucas and her brother she escaped, and the three of them went on another killing spree. Lucas claims that he was also a contract killer for an organisation called 'Hand of Death', but this part of his story is, to say the least, unverified. What *is* certain is that in 1982 he was paid to look after an eighty-eight-year-old woman named Kate – 'Granny' – Rich, and that he was to murder her later. Before then, he and Becky had become members of a fundamentalist sect called House of Prayer in Stoneberg, Texas, and lived and worked there for several weeks. Under the influence of the religious teaching, Becky decided she wanted to go back to Florida and finish her sentence in the reformatory. Lucas wanted her to stay, but finally agreed. On the way to Florida they quarrelled, and when Becky suddenly slapped his face, he stabbed her to death. He dismembered the body and buried it. As far as Lucas was concerned, the murder of Becky was the beginning of the end.

Back in Texas at the House of Prayer, he took Kate Rich for a long drive and both drank cans of beer. A quarrel developed, or Lucas became angry at her questions about Becky; he stabbed her to death, raped the body, and hid it in a culvert.

Lucas was the chief suspect in Granny Rich's disappearance,

but there was no evidence against him. In June 1983 his friend Reuben Moore, head of the House of Prayer, reported to the police that Lucas owned a gun, a felony for an ex-convict. He was arrested and in prison underwent a religious conversion that led him to confess to murdering Becky and Kate Rich. He also confessed to a total of three hundred and sixty murders.

In fact, many of these admissions proved to be false, but several *were* verified by the investigators: a recent figure is 199 murders in twenty-seven states – including the rape and murder of the woman in Jackson, of a West Virginia police officer, and of an unknown female hitchhiker known simply as 'orange socks'. Lucas was eventually sentenced to death for eleven murders; his accomplice Ottis Toole also received a death sentence.

Sheriff Jim Boutwell of Williamson County, Texas, who came to know Lucas well in prison, noted in 1985: 'Henry Lee Lucas is helping write a new chapter in the history of law enforcement . . . Henry's confessions, and the subsequent investigations, have exposed the mobility of crime in the United States.' In fact, it was the Lucas case more than any other that made America aware of the existence of the mobile serial killer.

Since Lucas was a masochist, a man who apparently enjoyed being dominated by women, it may seem doubtful that he should be classified as a 'Right Man', but many points in his confession confirm it. From the murder, at the age of fifteen, Lucas killed those who resisted him. Lucas was a high-dominance, highly sexed male, with an extremely low bursting-point. 'Sex is one of my downfalls. I get sex any way I can get it. If I have to force somebody to do it, I do. If I don't, I don't. I rape them; I've done that. I've killed animals to have sex with them . . . ' He also admitted that he had skinned animals alive during his teens.

Asked about the problems of interrogating Lucas, Sheriff Boutwell replied: 'You don't interrogate him . . . You talk with him just as a conversation. The good/bad guy role that officers traditionally use with suspects wouldn't work with him . . . If at any time you indicate you disbelieve him . . . you'll ruin your credibility with him.' Boutwell describes a case in which a police officer had driven three thousand miles to interview Lucas and, even though he had been warned against it, called Lucas a liar within the first two minutes. His journey was wasted; Lucas immediately refused to hold any further conversation. This is, of course, the behaviour of a Right Man, a man who refuses, in any circumstances, to admit that he could be wrong or a liar. Boutwell also commented on Lucas's high I.Q. and remarked that successfully interrogating him depended upon an appeal to his ego. Lucas was allowed all kinds of privileges — as much coffee as he liked (he was a coffee addict) and endless cigarettes. Asked by the interviewer whether this was not 'babying' him, Boutwell again emphasised that this was the only way to get Lucas to co-operate — to take care that he felt he was not just an ordinary prisoner.

The murder of Becky Powell seems to have been a watershed for Lucas. It is obvious — from his confession — that he loved her in a way he had never loved anyone; she was at once his wife, mistress and daughter, the only person who had ever accepted him without criticism, who regarded him as a kind of god — the kind of ego-balm that the Right Man craves above all else. Yet, because of that fatal tendency to explode under pressure, he killed her. Now he was not only on his own, but deprived of his one reason for living. The murder of Granny Rich — one of the few people who had treated him with kindness — may have been a masochistic gesture of defiance and despair, like shaking his fist at the sky.

One thing becomes very clear from the study of serial killers: that defiance and despair are part of the syndrome. The psychologist Joel Norris, the author of *Serial Killers: The Growing Menace*, writes of a killer who had 'reached the final stage of the serial murderer syndrome: he realised that he had come to a dead end with nothing but his own misery to show for it'.

Norris is writing about Leonard Lake, perhaps the most horrific serial killer of the 1980s. He earns this gruesome distinction by a kind of ruthlessness and sadism that seem to belong in the pages of a horror comic.

The murders — of at least twenty-five people — came to light in the summer of 1985. On the afternoon of Sunday 2 June an assistant at a hardware store, South City Lumber, in San Francisco, observed a slight, bespectacled youth walking out of the store with a $75 vice for which he had not paid, and called a policeman. The man — who was obviously Asiatic

— was putting the vice in the boot of a car, and when the policeman approached he immediately ran away. An older, bearded man, explained that his companion thought he had already paid for it. The policeman pointed at a hold-all in the car boot. 'What's in there?' 'I don't know. It belongs to him . . . ' The bearded man opened the hold-all, and revealed a .22 automatic pistol with a silencer. Since this was against the law in California, the policeman told the man that he would have to accompany him to headquarters.

There the man offered his driving licence for identification; it was in the name of Robin Scott Stapley. The policeman said he would have to do a computer check, and that the suspect would then have to post bond before he could be released. The man asked if he could have a glass of water, and when one was provided put a plastic capsule into his mouth, swallowed and drank it down; seconds later, he slumped forward. His interrogators at first assumed he had suffered a heart attack; but in hospital it was discovered that he had taken a cyanide capsule. Four days later, he died.

Meanwhile, the computer check had revealed that he was not Robin Stapley; the latter was a twenty-six-year-old who had been missing for months. A further check revealed that, soon after Stapley had been reported missing, his pick-up truck and trailer had been in a minor accident in San Francisco. The slight, Chinese youth who had been driving said he took full responsibility for the accident, and that there was no need to report it, but the driver whose goods vehicle had been grazed had to report it under his company's rules. The pick-up truck then proved to belong to the missing Robin Stapley. By this time, the Chinese youth and the truck had vanished.

The car the two men had been driving proved to be registered in the name of Paul Cosner. Cosner had also been reported missing. He had told his girlfriend that he had sold the car to a 'weird-looking man' who would pay cash, and had driven off to deliver it; no-one had seen him since. When forensic experts examined the car, they discovered two bullet holes, two spent bullets, and some bloodstains.

In the pockets of the man who had died from cyanide poisoning police found bills made out to 'Charles Gunnar', with an address near Wisleyville, in Calaveras County, 150 miles north-east of San Francisco. The sheriff there, Claude Ballard, was able to tell the investigators that Gunnar owned a small ranch, and that he lived with a young Chinese named Charles Ng (pronounced Ing). In fact, Ballard had already been checking on the two men. They had been advertising various things for sale, such as television sets, videos and articles of furniture, and Ballard had suspected they might be stolen. However, checks on serial numbers had come to nothing. What was more ominous was that Gunnar had offered for sale furniture belonging to a young couple, Lonnie Bond and Brenda O'Connor, explaining that they had moved to Los Angeles and had given him the furniture to pay a debt. No-one had heard from them since. At a nearby camp site, another couple had simply vanished, leaving behind their tent and a coffee pot boiling on the stove.

By now, a check on the dead man's fingerprints had revealed that he had a criminal record — for burglary and grand larceny in Mendocino County — and had jumped bail there. His real name was Leonard Lake.

The ranch house, in Blue Mountain Road, proved to be a two-bedroom bungalow set in three acres of land. The sight of the master bedroom increased the forebodings of the detectives; hooks in the ceiling and walls, and chains and shackles found in a box, suggested that it might be some kind of torture chamber. A wardrobe proved to contain many women's undergarments and some filmy nightgowns. On the hillside at the back of the house there were burnt bones that looked ominously human. In a cinderblock bunker cut into the hillside they discovered more hooks and chains, and walls covered with pictures of girls posing in their lingerie. What was disturbing about this was that the backdrop of many of these showed a forest scene mural that covered one of the walls; they had obviously been taken in the same room. The expression on some of the faces suggested that the girls were not enjoying it.

The grimmest piece of evidence was a filing cabinet full of videotapes. The police slipped one of these — labelled 'M Ladies, Kathy/Brenda' — into the recorder, and found themselves looking at a frightened girl handcuffed to a chair, with a young Chinese — Charles Ng — holding a knife beside her. Then a large, balding man with a beard enters the frame, takes off the handcuffs, shackles her ankles, and orders her to undress. She does so reluctantly, hesitating before removing her knickers. The bearded man tells her: 'You'll wash for us, clean for us, fuck for us.' After this, she is made to go into the shower with the Chinese. A later scene showed her strapped naked to a bed, while the bearded man tells her that her boyfriend Mike is dead.

Two five-hundred-page journals — in Lake's handwriting — left no doubt what had been happening. His fantasy was to have women as sex slaves, but he was willing to go a great deal further than Cameron Hooker or Gary Heidnik. One couple — Brenda O'Connor, her boyfriend Lonnie Bond, and their two-year-old baby — had been invited to the house for dinner; the man and baby had been killed, and Brenda O'Connor had been handcuffed in the chair, while Ng cut off her clothes. On the video she asks: 'Why do you guys do this?', and he tells her: 'We don't like you. Do you want me to put it in writing?' 'Don't cut my bra off.' 'Nothing is yours now.' 'Give my baby back to me. I'll do anything you want.' 'You're going to do anything we want anyway.' Lake's journal commented: 'The perfect woman is totally controlled. A woman who does exactly what she is told to do and nothing else. There is no sexual problem with a submissive woman. There are no frustrations — only pleasure and contentment.'

Other videos showed the girls being raped and murdered; there were also snapshots of dead bodies, and bags of human bones that seemed to have been boiled.

By now police had dug up four bodies from a trench at the back of the house, two of them blacks. Ng had been seen driving to the ranch with two black men, yet was known to hate blacks and Hispanics. He had also taken various transients to work at the 'ranch'; now it began to look as if some of them may never have left. Another person who had disappeared was Lake's younger brother Donald, who had failed to return after a visit to his brother in an earlier 'survivalist compound' in Humboldt County. Two months before Lake's arrest, a San Francisco couple, Harvey and Deborah Dubs, together with their sixteen-month-old son, had vanished from their San Francisco apartment, and the detective who had looked into their disappearance had been told that a young Chinese-looking man had been seen moving out their furniture; by coincidence, the same officer was now working on the Lake case . . .

Ng was now one of the most wanted men in America, but had not been seen since his disappearance. A few days later, a San Francisco gun dealer who had been repairing an automatic pistol belonging to Ng notified the police that Ng had telephoned him from Chicago asking if he could send him the gun by post. When the gun dealer had explained that it would be illegal to send handguns across state lines, Ng had cursed him and hung up.

On Saturday 6 July 1985, five weeks after Lake's capture, a security guard in a department store in Calgary, Alberta, saw a young Chinese slipping food under his jacket. When challenged, the thief drew a pistol, and as they grappled he fired, wounding the guard in the hand. The man ran away at top speed, but was intercepted by other guards. It became obvious that he had some training in Japanese martial arts, but he was eventually overpowered. Identification documents revealed that he was Charles Ng. A Canadian court sentenced Ng to four and a half years in prison for armed robbery, but resisted the demand that he should then be extradited to California, on the grounds that California still had a death penalty.

FBI agents looking into Ng's background learned that he was the son of a wealthy Hong Kong family. Born in 1961, Ng had been educated at a private school in north Yorkshire, from which he had been expelled for theft. Although Ng was never short of money, he was a lifelong kleptomaniac. He had lived for a while in Preston, Lancashire, then his parents sent him to San Francisco to complete his education. At the age of eighteen, Ng had been involved in a hit-and-run accident, and to escape a jail sentence, joined the marines. At Kaneoke Air Base on Oahu in Hawaii, he was arrested for thefts of weapons amounting to more than eleven thousand dollars. He escaped and made his way back to San Francisco, where he met Lake, and became his close companion; they were later arrested on burglary charges in Mendocino County, where Ng was identified as an army deserter. Convicted on the Hawaii arms theft charges, he spent some time in the Federal Prison at Fort Leavenworth, Kansas. When paroled, he found a job as a warehouseman in San Francisco, and took an apartment there. He spent much of his time at Lake's 'ranch' at Wisleyville. Comments by Ng's attorney made it clear that Ng liked to think of himself as an anti-social 'outsider'; he boasted of placing cyanide in the salt cellars at the Hawaii air base, dropping heat tabs into mail boxes, and of 'assassinating' a man in California.

FBI agents flew to Calgary to question him. Ng's story was that he knew about Lake's murders, but had taken no part in them. Ng described how Lake had killed car dealer Paul Cosner, whose car he was driving when arrested, and also how Lake had killed two employees of a removal company, one of whom was burnt to death.

Leonard Lake, born in 1946 in San Francisco, had an even more disturbing history. He had been in the marines in Vietnam, but had been discharged as having psychiatric problems. Joel Norris's investigation into Lake's background revealed a classic picture of a child rejected by both parents at an early age, and raised by his grandmother, a strict disciplinarian. Both his father and mother came from a family of alcoholics. The grandfather, also an alcoholic, was a violent type who subjected the child to a kind of military discipline. His younger brother Donald, his mother's favourite, was an epileptic who had experienced a serious head injury; he practised sadistic cruelty to animals and tried to rape both his sisters. Lake protected the sisters 'in return for sexual favours' – from an early age he had displayed sexual obsession that seems to characterise the serial killer. He took nude photographs of his sisters and cousins, and later became a maker of pornographic movies starring his wife. His fantasies were of the same type as Cameron Hooker's – total domination over women.

Lake shared another characteristic of so many serial killers: he lived in a world of fantasy – boasting, for example, of daring exploits in Vietnam when, in fact, he had never seen combat. Like so many Right Men, he was skilful in hiding his abnormality, teaching grade school, working as a volunteer fire-fighter, and donating time to a company that provided free insulation in old people's homes. Like the boy-killer John Gacy, he seemed an exemplary citizen; but his outlook was deeply pessimistic. He believed that World War Three would break out at any moment, and this is why he had built the bunker – stocked with food – at the ranch. Like other 'survivalists', he often dressed in combat fatigues, and talked of living off the land. Once out of the marines, his behaviour had become increasingly odd. In his original 'survivalist compound' in Mother Lode, Humboldt County, the police found maps of the area with crosses marking 'buried treasure' – almost certainly bodies. It was there that he had murdered his best friend from the marines, Charles Gunnar, and assumed his identity. After being forced to flee from the earlier compound because of burglary charges, he had moved to Wisleyville. A marriage to a girl called Cricket Balazs had broken up, but she had continued to act as a fence for stolen credit cards and other items. Lake seems to have loved her — at least he said so in a last note scrawled as he was dying — but he nevertheless clung to the paranoid notion that women were responsible for all his problems.

In his journal, Lake describes himself 'with death in my pocket and fantasy in my soul'. He daydreamed of a more heroic and violent era — Vikings and Norse sagas — and of having chained girls as sex slaves (the 'cells' in his bunker were built for them). According to Norris, the later journals show increasing disillusionment. 'His dreams of success had eluded him; he admitted to himself that his boasts about heroic deeds in Vietnam were all delusions, and the increasing number of victims he was burying in the trench behind his bunker only added to his unhappiness. By the time he was arrested in San Francisco, Lake had reached the final stage of the serial murderer syndrome: he realised that he had come to a dead end with nothing but his own misery to show for it.'

What has happened, we can see, is that Lake has gone one step beyond most Right Men: instead of merely fantasising about being a lone 'outsider', an outcast from a materialistic society, he translated his fantasies into reality, acting with a casual ruthlessness that is rarely seen even among serial killers, murdering men — even babies — so that he could lay his hands on women and turn them into sex slaves. But when fantasy is brought into contact with reality, it is bound to melt away. Our sense of our own humanity depends on feeling ourselves to be members of society, on having at least a few close relations with other human beings. To kill men — one of them his own brother and another his best friend — and rape and torture women, was bound to cause a sense of revolt in the part of him that still had a capacity for human warmth. He was systematically raping his own humanity. The published extracts from the tapes suggest that Lake and Ng were still sufficiently human to be aware of this. (For example, they tell Kathy Allen — who had gone there looking for her boyfriend Mike Carrol — that they intend to keep her prisoner for a month then let her go; but since she was their prisoner, they had no practical reason to try and spare her feelings.)

What Leonard Lake did was to act out the fantasies of the Marquis de Sade — who, as we have seen, might be regarded as the patron saint of serial killers. What he proved was the basic incompatibility between these fantasies and our human nature. Even hangmen have to feel that they are useful members of society. Even Nazi torturers had to tell themselves that they were serving a cause. To behave like Haroun Al Raschid or Ivan the Terrible is to commit mental suicide. If Lake had chosen to bluff it out in the San Francisco police station, sticking to his story that he was Robin Stapley, he might well have walked out a free man. Yet his journals reveal that he had ceased to be a free man many months before. The time to end a meaningless existence had arrived, and Lake became his own executioner.

Eight

Into the Future

The question remains: why is it that serial killers have appeared at this particular point in history? One psychiatrist, discussing Leonard Lake — who was born in 1946, the same year as Ted Bundy — suggests that an unusual number of males were born in the year after the war and that, statistically speaking, a proportion of them were bound to become killers. Others have pointed out that many serial killers have been sexually abused in childhood, and suggested that an increase in the sexual abuse of children has led to the rise of the serial killer. In *Compulsive Killers* (1986) Elliot Leyton has produced a 'social' theory of serial killers. He points out that the fifteenth-century multiple murderer Gilles de Rais — who raped and killed at least fifty children in his château at Machecoul — lived in an era when the established order in France was striving to reassert itself against the assaults of peasants and merchants. Gilles was obsessed by the excesses of Tiberius and Caligula, and strove to emulate their lifestyles. His crimes, Leyton suggests, were a personalised expression of this aggressive attitude of his class — his victims were all children of peasants. In our own time, he suggests, serial killers have been members of the working class or lower middle class, struggling with a sense of alienation and frustration. For them, murder is a form of class assertion.

There is certainly some truth in this notion; so far there have been no upper-class — or even upper-middle-class — serial killers. The reason for this may be the one suggested in Chapter Seven: that serial murder may be a human expression of the 'overcrowded rat syndrome', and that upper- and middle-class children are unlikely to suffer from overcrowding.

The overcrowded rat theory suggests that the reasons for the appearance of serial murder are primarily social, and this tends to be confirmed by the study of sex crime. As we have

297

seen, sex crime — in our modern sense of the word — was virtually unknown in the eighteenth century; it made its appearance in the second half of the nineteenth century, and was undoubtedly linked to 'Victorian' attitudes towards sex; that is, to the fact that sex was unmentionable in respectable society, and therefore 'forbidden'.

To understand the crimes of killers like Bundy, Gallego and Lake, we also have to recognise that, in another respect, human attitudes towards sex have hardly changed in many thousands of years. From the *Iliad* to the *Morte D'Arthur*, the image of woman has been much the same: the archetypal heroine is gentle, modest, decorous, virtuous and free from vanity. While sexually desirable, she is uninterested in sex, and only grants it to the male who has proved himself 'worthy' of her. As far as most males are concerned, she is essentially 'forbidden'. If she shows preference for one of her many wooers, the others experience agonising jealousy because their goddess has rejected them. Helen's elopement with Paris, like Queen Guinevere's infidelity with Lancelot, seems doubly shocking because we feel her to be the embodiment of all the female virtues.

The twentieth century has seen a gradual 'emancipation' of 'our attitudes towards sex. From Wells's *Ann Veronica*, through *Ulysses* and *Lady Chatterley's Lover*, to Huxley's *Brave New World*, modern writers have assured us that perfectly nice girls can enjoy copulation and even commit adultery. We nowadays accept that when a girl refers to her 'boyfriend', she usually means the man she sleeps with, and that a girl who has had many lovers is not necessarily a harlot. Yet while the conscious mind has adjusted to this new state of affairs, our instincts continued to harbour the old 'forbidden' female archetype, modest, gentle and virtuous. So in spite of enormous changes in our sexual attitudes, modern man's reaction to a pretty girl is in most respects exactly like that of the troubadours or the knights of the Round Table: she is an unknown country, a sovereign state, that he would love to be allowed to explore. *Brave New World* remains mildly titillating because its apparently 'nice' young ladies discuss the men they have slept with openly without any sense of guilt. We feel the same sense of shock that we would experience if Jane Austen's heroines talked openly about their adulteries.

In other words, so as far as sex is concerned, 'modernity' is only a superficial overlay; but there *is* a field in which change has been genuine and profound: that of political freedom. We are living in the first era in which, for a large proportion of the globe, the Rights of Man have become a reality. They have been discussed and analysed for more than two centuries; but the truth is that political freedom means very little without economic freedom; a desperately poor man is, by definition, one of the oppressed, whether he lives under democracy or dictatorship. It is only in the second half of the twentieth century that welfare states have been able to offer the majority of their citizens some degree of security from starvation. The result is that 'rights' that were once theoretical have finally become an actuality. Every tramp knows that the police have no right to arrest him without good reason; every schoolboy knows that a schoolmaster who loses his temper and hits him runs the risk of dismissal. It is no longer necessary to be wealthy or influential to ensure impartial treatment at the hands of the law.

The negative side of the coin − and it may be a small price to pay − is an increase in the kind of boredom and apathy that were once regarded as diseases of the rich, and in the self-pity and resentment that flourish in such fertile soil. We have seen that the beginning of the thought process that leads to crime involves looking around for someone on whom we can *lay the blame*. In that respect there is a basic similarity between the psychology of Charles Manson and his drug-addict disciples and terrorist organisations like the Japanese Red Army faction, the Baader-Meinhof gang and the Symbionese Liberation Army. When we learn that Ian Brady shook his fist at the sky after one of his murders, that Gerald Gallego declared 'his only desire was to kill God', and that Leonard Lake took pride in declaring himself an atheist, we can begin to understand how the logic of resentment can lead to total rejection of 'conscience', as it looks for an ultimate scapegoat.

It was towards the end of the eighteenth century that political philosophers began to argue that most men are poor because the social system is unjust. Karl Marx went a step further and declared that the poor have the *right* to seize their neighbour's wealth, for if the neighbour was honest he would not be wealthy. By the end of the nineteenth century, Marxism had begun to achieve a certain academic respectability. Nowadays, there are hundreds of academics in 'capitalist' universities all over the world who make no secret of their Marxist affiliations.

The sexual revolution took longer to gather momentum, as we have seen, because when a society is economically deprived, sex is a secondary issue. Once a society is affluent, sex becomes one of the major issues. It is important to understand that the *attitude* that seems typical of sex criminals is also shared by many 'respectable' members of society, including its leading intellectuals. H.G. Wells was well known in London as a tireless adulterer who kept photographs of his mistresses on the mantelpiece; his wife was expected to accept his need for affaires. Bertrand Russell was a lifelong seducer who was pursuing teenage students well into his seventies, when his virility began to fail. The theologian Paul Tillich was a pornography addict who was still seducing female students in his eighth decade. A recent biography of the Catholic artist Eric Gill reveals that he practised a lifelong promiscuity, which included incest with his sisters and daughters, as well as bestiality and a passion for adolescent girls. In the various artistic communities that he formed, he demanded the *droit de seigneur* over all the attractive women, and became intensely jealous if they allowed themselves to be seduced by other males. The painter Augustus John shared Gill's enthusiasm for incest (as becomes clear from Michael Holroyd's biography), and also his attitude of *droit de seigneur* over women in his immediate entourage. (It may or may not be relevant that John was a mediocre artist until he dived into the sea and knocked himself unconscious on a rock; after his recovery, he became a major artist.)

How can intelligent men justify this kind of self-indulgence? The answer is that they have no difficulty whatsoever. Wells's argument was that in order to evolve as a writer he needed to evolve as a human being, and that it would be impossible to evolve as a human being if he went around in a state of permanent sexual frustration. His affaires, he claimed, filled him with creative energy and a sense of the wonder of the universe. His wife was expected to accept this or agree to a separation; she seems to have accepted it, but lived a lonely and unsatisfying existence, dying of abdominal cancer in 1927. (Augustus John's wife committed suicide.)

Wells was a member of a privileged class, an intellectual elite, and he demanded sexual freedom as a right of his class. As we have seen, the slow increase in personal liberty in the twentieth century means that the 'privileged class' has expanded until it includes most dominant and intelligent males. If Melvin Rees or Ted Bundy or Leonard Lake had been called upon to present a reasoned defence of their crimes, they would all have sounded much like H.G. Wells. The main difference, they would have argued, is that Wells, as a famous writer, had a queue of young ladies eager to share his bed. They, as intelligent nobodies, were forced to take a short cut. But since they all believed that 'only individual standards make murder right or wrong', and that nature intended us all to be predators, they had no hesitation in risking life and liberty in the name of individual self-development. They would also have gone on to argue, with the self-justification that never fails the Right Man, that the blame should be placed squarely on modern society, with its endless sexual stimulation — from soft-porn magazines on every newsstand to the obligatory bedroom scene in every film. Man surely has a right to get rid of his frustrations?

There has been, so far, no sexual equivalent of Karl Marx to argue that women have no right to withhold their bodies from sexually frustrated males, and ought to be raped. Yet this obviously describes the attitude of Rees, Bundy, Gallego, and most of the other serial killers in this volume. Every rapist could be regarded as an advocate of the 'propaganda of the deed'. And the 'elitist argument' summarised above is sound in at least one respect: that if the level of sexual stimulation in a society continues to rise, an increasing number of highly-sexed dominant males will cross the threshold into rape. As suggested elsewhere, 'when there is underlying social frustration, it is the criminal who provides a measure of that tension. If a new and horrifying type of crime occurs, a type that has never been known before, it should not be regarded as some freak occurrence, any more than the outbreak of a new disease should be dismissed as a medical oddity.' Criminals might be compared with the rats who die first in a plague.*

The rise of sexual fetishism provides an interesting example of the mechanism. The word was invented by the nineteenth-century psychologist Alfred Binet, who pointed out that if early sexual excitement is associated with some object, such as a woman's hair or shoes, it may become 'imprinted', so that the same object continues to produce excitement, just as the ringing

*A Criminal History of Mankind, page 605, Colin Wilson, 1984.

of a bell made Pavlov's dogs salivate. In fact, one of the earliest cases of fetishism on record dates from April 1790, when London was terrorised by a man who, in the words of the chronicler Archenholtz, committed 'nameless crimes, the possibility of whose existence no legislator has ever dreamt of'. These nameless crimes amounted to creeping up behind fashionably dressed women and slashing at their clothing with a sharp knife, which occasionally caused painful wounds; it was also alleged that he would hold out a nosegay to young ladies, and as they bent to sniff it, would jab them in the face with a 'sharp pointed instrument' hidden among the flowers. 'The Monster' apparently became obsessed with the pretty daughter of a tavern keeper, Anne Porter, and followed her in St James's Park, making obscene suggestions. On the night of 18 January 1790, when she was returning from a ball with her two sisters, he came up behind her, and she felt a blow on her right buttock. Indoors, she discovered that she had a nine-inch knife wound which was four inches deep in the centre. Six months later, out walking with a gentleman named Coleman, she recognised the 'Monster' in the street. Coleman followed the man to a nearby house, accused him of being the attacker, and made a kind of 'citizen's arrest'. The man denied being the 'Monster', but Anne Porter fainted when she saw him. He proved to be a slightly built man named Renwick Williams, a maker of artificial flowers. At his trial, Williams insisted that it was a case of mistaken identity; and offered an alibi. The jury chose to disbelieve him, and he was sentenced to six years in prison for 'damaging clothes'. During the months he was attacking women, Williams created a reign of terror: rewards were offered and walls covered in posters describing his activities. The prosecuting counsel talked of 'a scene that is so new in the annals of humanity, a scene so inexplicable, so unnatural, that one might have regarded it, out of respect for human nature, as impossible . . . ' 'The Monster' clearly created a profound sense of psychological shock amongst his contemporaries, of the kind produced a century later by the Jack the Ripper murders.

A century later still, another bizarre precedent was created by the behaviour of a sexual deviate who became known in California as the Panty Bandit; he would hold up underwear shops or beauty parlours in the Los Angeles area, order a woman to remove her panties and/or tights, and then masturbate with the garment draped over his face before snatching money from the till. Police were accustomed to dealing with nuisances who stole underwear from clotheslines or frequented laundromats in search of soiled panties, but had never encountered a man who would masturbate in front of a crowd of customers and then make off with the underwear. In the summer of 1988, the 'Panty Bandit' was nominated Public Enemy Number One in California. His activities revealed that he was at least disinclined to use his gun. In one shop, he ordered a woman to masturbate him; she made a grab for his gun, and he punched her in the face and ran away. On 23 October 1988 a shop assistant succeeded in notifying the police shortly after the bandit had left, and a man driving a Honda Civic was caught after a chase. He was thirty-three-year-old Bruce Lyons, and in his car the police found a box full of stolen underwear. Lyons was sentenced to fifteen years in prison. The severity of the sentence reflects a recognition of how easily the Panty Bandit could have progressed to rape and murder.

In the two centuries that separate Renwick Williams from Bruce Lyons, it is clear that extraordinary social changes have taken place – changes that would have been incomprehensible to Dr Johnson, but which would have been perfectly understood by his contemporary the Marquis de Sade. Sade lived in an atmosphere of unreality, a world of dreams inside his own head. He was one of the privileged few who could afford that indulgence. Two centuries later, an affluent society had created conditions that could spawn potential de Sades by the thousand.

We are now also in a position to understand what has happened since the days of Renwick Williams – how, in the increased prosperity of the nineteenth century, the age of economic crime gave way slowly to the age of sex crime, and how this in turn is being displaced by an age of crimes that 'service' the craving for self-esteem, the will to power. Rees, Bundy, Hooker, Lake, Heidnik, simply refused to accept that they were not Haroun Al Raschid and could do whatever they liked. Bundy admitted that, at any point during his crimes, he could have stopped himself if he had wanted to; he simply had no desire to stop. He had decided that he had a *right* to kill, just as a thief decides that he has a right to steal.

But exactly how great *is* the problem of the serial killer? In

Serial Killers: The Growing Menace, Joel Norris estimates that in America there may be as many as five hundred at large at any given time; other estimates vary — Elliott Leyton guesses a hundred. An altogether more balanced estimate was provided by FBI agent Gregg McCrary. Asked about the number of serial killers, he said:

'There were six thousand or more unsolved murders last year (1988), and the bulk of the serial killer victims will undoubtedly be somewhere in that number. (But) the unofficial estimates of three hundred, four hundred or five hundred even, do not seem to me to be reasonable . . . There's less than a hundred out there — in my view less than fifty. *My* estimate is between thirty and fifty. Working on that figure, and using as a guide our experience of many serial killers averaging ten or less victims apiece at the time of their apprehension — there will be exceptions, of course — an estimate of a few hundred serial murders per year (in the US) would probably be most accurate.'

About the success rate, he commented: 'Again this is very difficult to calculate. We reckon to "identify" between thirteen and fifteen serial killers each year. By "identifying" I mean identify as *working*, not as individuals: and of those we reckon that half — seven say — will be caught and brought to trial with the help of CIAP profiling. Now seven doesn't tell you the full story. Take the Bundy case, for example. Bundy was charged with just three murders, the three he committed in Florida. But he admitted to twenty-three, and a lot of law enforcement guys think he was good for half as many again, around thirty-four murders. Now we profiled Bundy. OK, he was arrested under another name for driving a stolen car, but he was identified in custody as Bundy — and executed twelve years later, still for only three murders. But how many murders do you claim in the "success rate" — in other words, in this arrest and conviction of a man in which profiling played a part? Was it three murders, twenty-three or thirty-four? So "success rate" is not accountable in the most meaningful sense — i.e. the number of *murders* cleaned up with the aid of profiling.'

Between three hundred and five hundred murders a year sound an alarming total, but it is a long way short of the four or five thousand that has been suggested. These figures makes it clear that America is not full of maniacal serial killers who wander around and kill hundreds of people over the course of years. Most of them, as we have seen, commit their crimes over a fairly brief period and in a restricted area. The mobile serial killer is the exception, and the VICAP computer means that the chance of catching him has been enormously increased. Compared with the most frequent type of murder — domestic killings — the number of victims of serial murder remains relatively small. It is interesting to note that in the decade from 1979 to 1989 — the period during which most of the serial killers in this book committed their crimes — the American murder rate remained stable at around 20,000 a year. To imply that serial murder is 'a growing menace' comparable to AIDS is clearly something of an exaggeration.

What *was* clear, even as early as the 1960s, was that 'motiveless murder' constituted a new and baffling type of crime. Sex crime, as we have seen, was difficult to solve because in most cases there was only a casual connection between the criminal and the victim. Nevertheless, police were often able to catch serial rapists because a certain pattern was discernible in their crimes. In 1973, two rapists in Houston, Texas, made a habit of abducting girls who were getting into their cars late at night, driving them to a remote spot, then subjecting them to hours of sexual humiliation before leaving them naked. After forty rapes and two murders, the police decided to 'stake out' every car park in Houston, using vast numbers of men, including civilian volunteers. On the second night of the stake-out, when the rapists tried to abduct another girl, police heard her scream, and the men were arrested before they could escape. Michael Ohern, twenty, and Howard Braden, nineteen, both received sentences of life imprisonment without possibility of parole. It was a laborious way of catching rapists, but it worked. When, on the other hand, a killer who became known as 'Zodiac' committed five murders and severely wounded two more victims in the San Francisco Bay area in the late 1960s, a vast police operation failed to trap him because the killings were motiveless and random; his identify remains unknown.

We have seen how the major breakthrough occurred in the mid-1970s, with the setting up of the Behavioral Science Unit at the FBI Academy in Quantico, Virginia, with a grant of $128,000 from the National Institute of Justice. The oldest and most experienced of its agents was Howard Teten, who taught a course in applied criminology; he seemed to have a natural talent for 'profiling' criminals. On one occasion he was able to solve a case over the telephone — the multiple stabbing of

305

a girl in California. From the frenzy of the attack, Teten judged that it was a sudden impulsive act, and that it sounded like a teenager, a 'social isolate', who would be weighed down by guilt and ready to confess. He advised the police to look in the neighbourhood where the girl was killed. In fact, when a policeman knocked on a door and was confronted with a skinny teenager, the boy blurted out: 'You got me.'

We have also seen how, when the police of Platte City, Missouri, were confronted with the sex murder of a schoolgirl, Julie Wittmeyer, in 1977, the Behavioral Science Unit was able to 'profile' the killer so accurately that the investigators were immediately able to identify him in their list of suspects. In the case of the Anchorage killer Robert Hansen, FBI agent Glenn Flothe describes how he telephoned the Unit. 'I started to tell the guy from the FBI about Hansen and he goes, 'No, no, no – tell me about the crimes and let me tell you about the guy'. After describing the crimes, the agent told him that the killer probably was a respected member of the community, and probably stuttered. 'He basically outlined Robert Hansen.' Psychological profiling has raised the old-fashioned 'hunch' to the level of a science. In the FBI handbook *Sexual Homicide: Its Patterns and Motives*, it is estimated that psychological profiling has 'helped focus the investigation in 77 per cent of those cases in which the suspects were subsequently identified' – a highly satisfying success rate.

Equally important in the investigation of serial murder has been the use of computers. It was the case of Henry Lee Lucas, in 1983, that made state police forces aware of the need for co-operation; Lucas himself told Sheriff Jim Boutwell that he realised he owed his immunity to lack of co-operation between states. Computerisation of fingerprinting has also been a major advance. Los Angeles computerised its fingerprints in 1985, and within the first three minutes of the operation of the new system, it identified a fingerprint lifted from a stolen car as that of a twenty-five-year-old drifter, Richard Ramirez – thus giving an identity to the unknown serial killer so far known only as the 'Night Stalker'; Ramirez was later sentenced to death for thirteen murders. Perhaps the most exciting advance of recent years has been the development of 'DNA fingerprinting' – the discovery, made by Dr Alec Jeffreys in 1985, that the DNA molecules contained in every single cell of our bodies are almost as individual as a fingerprint, so that a rapist can be identified from his semen, a fragment of skin beneath a victim's nails, or even a single hair. It meant that virtually every rapist could be identified from some trace of evidence left on the victim. Since 1985, the number of 'random' sex criminals who have been caught through genetic fingerprinting has continued to increase dramatically, demonstrating that genetic fingerprinting is probably the most important innovation in crime detection since the original discovery of fingerprint classification in the 1890s.

What this book has tried to demonstrate is that the serial killer is a virtually inevitable product of the evolution of our society. What is happening today could be compared with what happened in Europe in the eighteenth century, when the soaring population rate in the large cities* combined with the introduction of a new cheap drink called gin to produce an unparalleled crime explosion. Cities like London and Paris became vast pestilence-infected slums, and the 'overcrowded rat' syndrome proceeded to operate on the human population. In fact, in these two cities the crime explosion was brought under control with remarkable ease by a new and efficient police force. As the Industrial Revolution brought more overcrowding – between 1800 and 1900 the population more than doubled – the age of economic crime gave way to the age of sex crime. In the mid-twentieth century, the age of sex crime merged into a new age of self-esteem crime; and there was an important difference. Any medium-dominance male might commit rape if he happened to be drunk and sexually frustrated. As far as we can see, self-esteem crimes are always committed by members of the 'dominant five per cent' – and, moreover, by the type van Vogt called Right Men. (There may be examples of serial killers who are not Right Men or members of the dominant five per cent, but not one has been encountered in this study.) The attitude of the dominant male towards women is always predatory, especially towards non-dominant women. In Hermann Hesse's novel *Steppenwolf* – about a lonely 'outsider' – a poem written by the hero captures this attitude perfectly:

*Between 1750 and 1800 the population of Europe rose from 147 million to 187 million.

The lovely creature I would so treasure,
And feast myself deep on her tender thigh,
I would drink of her red blood full measure,
Then howl till the night went by.

In the late nineteenth century there were just as many frustrated, high-dominance working-class males in the world, but poor education and the gap between social classes kept them 'in their place'. By the mid-twentieth century increasing literacy and the erosion of class barriers meant that increasing numbers of these males were able to articulate their resentment. Some of these had the kind of traumatic childhood that seems typical of serial killers — lonely, physically abused, unwanted by parents, accident-prone (often suffering head injuries) and obsessed by sexual fantasies — and the result was bound to be, sooner or later, a sex-crime explosion. This is what we have witnessed in the last four decades of the twentieth century, and there seems no reason to assume that the early decades of the twenty-first century will show any improvement — on the contrary, it seems inevitable that Europe will follow America into the age of serial murder. Joel Norris speaks optimistically about the development of 'profiles that could lead to the development of a diagnostic or prediction instrument'; but although we have seen how psychological profiling can be used to trap serial killers, it seems unlikely that it will ever enable psychiatrists to recognise them in time to prevent them from becoming killers. The best we can hope is that social changes will eventually remove the conditions that incubate the type.

What this means, unfortunately, is that there is no simple short-term solution to the problem of the serial killer, any more than there has ever been a simple solution to the problem of crime and violence. The long-term solution, for our descendants of the twenty-first century, would be to attack the basic causes: 'overcrowded rat' syndrome, child abuse, social frustration. We have seen that, so far, all serial killers have emerged from the same social group — the working class or lower middle class — and in that case, the theoretical solution would be to improve social conditions until some of the worst features have disappeared. Theoretically, a Utopian society with a low birth rate, ample living space and a high general level of prosperity should cease to produce serial killers. However, until we have learned to control the population explosion, such a society is obviously no more than a pleasant daydream.

Nevertheless, it is worth recalling the story of how the eighteenth century crime explosion in England was brought under control by the novelist Henry Fielding. When Fielding became a magistrate in 1748, at the age of forty-one, London was swarming with footpads and robber gangs, and the roads were infested with highwaymen. With no police force except part-time parish constables, the London criminal had never known any organised opposition. Fielding suggested to Parliament that it should vote him six hundred pounds to try to stop the crime wave and the money was granted. He next organised a group of parish constables, all of who knew the most notorious thieves by sight. Victims of robberies were urged to hurry to Fielding's house in Bow Street, from which 'thief-takers' would set out in hot pursuit. (This is why they became known as Bow Street Runners.) Fielding describes his satisfaction as newspaper reports of robberies diminished day by day, until eventually they ceased altogether. As the roads surrounding London were patrolled by heavily armed constables on horseback, burglars and highwaymen who were accustomed to immunity hastened to move elsewhere. In putting a stop to London's crime wave, Fielding used only half the six hundred pounds.

The lesson – known to every police officer – is that in controlling crime, prevention is better than cure, or at least more immediately effective. In this respect, the advances in crime detection that have occurred since the 1970s are even more impressive then those of the Bow Street Runners. In 1986 special agent Roger Depue, then head of the FBI Behavioral Science Instruction and Research Unit and Administrator of the NCAVC, expressed the new sense of optimism when he declared: 'The concerted efforts of the US Congress, the Department of Justice and Federal, State and local justice agencies to bring violent crime under control *have* made a difference in America. They have contributed to slowing the downward spiral, and increasing the risk for the violent offender. The NCAVC was born out of these national efforts and represents the new feeling in America. We are not only going to fight back – we are going to win.'

Appendix

Since this book was written, more than two years ago, there has been an explosion of interest in the subject of murder in general, and serial killers in particular. The latter is largely due to the success of the Thomas Harris film *Silence of the Lambs*, a study of a serial killer. But even this cannot explain the flood of full-length books on specific cases, and the immense success of the British part work *Murder Casebook*. After all, true detective magazines have ben around since the 1920s, but their sales have always been modest. Now, suddenly, their editors are finding it worthwhile to issue paperback anthologies, with titles like *Bizarre Murders*, *Cult Killers* and *Torture Killers*.

One interesting clue may lie in an accidental discovery I made when talking to the proprietor of a 'true crime' bookshop in Melbourne; *a large proprtion of the customers are teenage girls*. Half a century ago, the same teenagers would have been reading adventure comics and 'true romances'. Now, it seems, they experience a craving to read something that is closer to the harsh realities of life.

The reason is obvious. They live in a world with more violence than ever before. In her book, *The Dead Girl*, an American co-ed named Melanie Thernstrom describes the impact made on her by the disappearance of her best friend, Roberta Lee, whose body was found weeks later in a shallow grave. It was discovered eventually that the killer was her boyfriend, but in the meantime, all the girls in the area experienced an appalling feeling of vulnerability. The point is underlined by the fact that, while the search was still going on, another of Melanie Thernstrom's acquaintances was stabbed to death when she resisted a rapist. When violence comes as close as this, it is impossible to ignore it as something that happens to other people, or to those who somehow 'deserve' it. The book was obviously written to get the trauma out of her system. And it seems clear that the basic motivation that leads teenagers – particularly girls – to read about murder, is fundamentally similar; it is a desire to come to grips with a bogey man.

How far anybody *has* come to grips with it – including myself and Donald Seaman – is a different matter. In July 1991, Milwaukee police entered the flat of 31-year-old Jeffrey Dahmer, and found seven skulls and four heads, dozens of body parts and hundreds of photographs of victims taken in various stages of dismemberment. Dahmer, a homosexual who killed black males, confessed to seventeen murders. His gruesome compulsion to dismember bodies brings to mind the case of Dennis Nilsen (Chapter 7). Nilsen, asked to comment about *The Silence of the Lambs*, remarked that the depiction of the intellectual killer Hannibal Lecter is a 'fraudulent fiction'. 'He is shown as a potent figure, which is pure myth', Nilsen told his biographer Brian Masters, '. . . it's not like that at all. My offences arose from a feeling of inadequacy, not potency. I never had any power in my life.'

But these attempts to understand serial killers in terms of potency, weakness, and depth psychology may be complicating something that is essentially simple. The three books that have been published on Henry Lee Lucas (Chapter 7) make it clear that his claim to have committed dozens – possibly hundreds – of murders is basically accurate. They also make it very clear that Lucas killed because his *sexual needs* involved killing, and that it all began at the age of ten, when his mother's lover introduced him to necrophilia – slitting the throat of a calf and having sex with the carcass. From then on, Lucas could achieve full sexual satisfaction only with a corpse. He even violated the corpse of his mistress Becky Powell after killing her. The crimes of Henry Lee Lucas are a simple case of 'imprinting'.

In August 1991, an ex-marine named Donald Evans was arrested in Louisiana on suspicion of kidnapping a ten-year-old girl. He confessed to killing Beatrice Routh, then went on to confess to sixty more killings in seventeen states. Although newspaper reports described Evans as a 'religious fanatic' (he had been a Sunday school teacher), his initial confession makes it clear that the motive was simply rape, not some obscure religious urge.

This point has emerged even more clearly since the publication, in 1991, of *Killer Fiction* by Gerald Schaefer. Schaefer has only a brief mention in *Serial Killers* because he was convicted, in 1973, for the murder of two girls, although suspected of many more. In 1989, an ex-girlfriend of Schaefer's, Sondra London, wrote him a letter, and received a reply. Schaefer began sending her his writings from prison, which Sondra London edited and published privately. *Killer Fiction* begins by stating that Schaefer has been connected to 34 murders, besides the killings for which he was convicted. Then Schaefer himself states: 'I was falsely accused of killing 34 women; I was framed by corrupt men.' But the stories themselves are detailed sadistic fantasies about killing women. The opening story describes picking up a waitress who is an amateur prostitute. In her room, the writer watches her relieve herself on the lavatory, after which she performs fellatio on him. Then, as she leaves the room, he loops a stocking round her neck and strangles her. ' "Suzie's going bye-bye now," I whispered. Her answer was a sputtering fart. With her eyes she asked me, "Why?" "Because," I hissed; and the life went out of her.' Four more stories repeat the same basic theme, except that in some of them the girl is tortured and the sex takes place after death. The book is illustrated with Schaefer's own drawings of women in their underwear hanging from gallows.

It seems odd for Schaefer to insist on his innocence, yet publish five stories that leave no possible doubt that he is guilty. But this is not untypical of the behaviour of serial killers. Ted Bundy kept protesting his innocence, yet gave a series of interviews in which he left no doubt that he was a killer. What is clear is that, like Lucas, Schaefer and Bundy have been 'imprinted' with a powerful compulsion to commit sexual acts on unwilling victims, and that this need is precisely like an alcoholic's craving for booze, or a drug addict's for a fix. To look for deeper motives is usually beside the point.

We can see the same curious irrationality in the case of John Wayne Gacy

311

(Chapter 7). Writer Jeffrey Smalldon corresponded with Gacy in prison, and sent him a copy of *An Encyclopedia of Modern Murder*, by myself and Donald Seaman. Gacy replied at some length, explaining that 'It would take three pages to explain all the errors', and describing my account as 'total garbage'. 'I am not defending myself,' he explains, 'just telling you a fact. I get a kick out of reading how so many people can change my whole life around and yet they have never met me.' (Quoted in *Human Nature Stained*)

My brief account contains, as far as I know, only one factual inaccuracy: the statement that Gacy was sentenced to life imprisonment (when he was actually sentenced to death). But Gacy's protests are basically the same as those quoted by Tim Cahill in his book *Buried Dreams*: that people just don't understand him, and that this somehow means that he is not guilty of the murder of 33 boys. He obviously feels that '*tout comprendre est tout pardonner*'. Two commercial videos of interviews with Charles Manson in gaol reveal that his attitude is much the same. Because people do not understand his philosophy of revolt against a 'corrupt society', he cannot really be held responsible for the murders he inspired.

But then, to actually listen to Manson on tape suddenly makes it obvious that all his arguments are irrelevant, for we are not dealing with a normal, rational human being, capable of objective argument. Underlying everything Manson says is an immense self-opinionatedness, a total certainty that he is right and that other people are wrong, which means that his interview is little more than a rambling monologue. The sense of contact with other people, which forms part of our normal human discourse, is missing.

This, I suspect, is the basic key to the mind of the serial killer. He suffers from a kind of tunnel vision which means that, much more than most of us, he is trapped inside his own head. We are shocked by the suffering he causes to his victims and their relatives, and cannot understand how he can be unaware that he is doing wrong. The answer is that, in a certain sense, he is like a sleepwalker, or a man in a hypnotic trance. Someone has disconnected one of the terminals of the battery that should connect him to other people.

In writing my part of *The Serial Killers* (Chapters 1, 4, 5, 6, 7 & 8), the case that produced in me the strongest sense of 'disconnection' was that of Gerald Gallego (Chapter 6). It seemed incredible that a man *and* a woman could kidnap nine girls – most of them in pairs – and then, after rape and murder, toss away their bodies like used condoms. In the Moors case, its nearest British equivalent, Ian Brady was driven by resentment, sadism and an obsession with Nazism. Gallego, apparently, killed merely to satisfy an itch in the loins. A recent book on the case, *Venom in the Blood*, by Eric van Hoffmann, reveals that it was more complex than that. According to Hoffman, Charlene Williams was a bisexual nymphomaniac. Her sex life with Gallego was satisfactory enough until, in 1978, Gallego brought home a sixteen-year-old go-go dancer, who shared their bed for a night and was sodomised by Gallego. The next day Gallego returned unexpectedly from work to find Charlene and the girl engaged in sex with a dildo. He threw the girl out and beat Charlene; from then on, he lost his appetite for Charlene. But when, on his daughter's fourteenth birthday, Gallego had sex with both her and her girlfriend, it was clear to Charlene (who was present) that he was not impotent. At this point, according to Hoffman, Charlene suggested the idea of kidnapping and murder. In each case, the victims were forced to have sex with Charlene as well as Gallego. Charlene liked to bite one of the girls as the other brought her to a climax with oral sex, in one case virtually biting off a nipple. Hoffman's account makes it clear that Charlene was the driving force behind the murders. As absurd as it sounds, Gallego emerges at the end of the book as *her* victim.

This certainly makes more sense than the other book on the case, *All His Father's Sins* by Ray Biondi and Walt Hecox, in which Charlene is presented as the pliable victim. Once again we become aware that one of the basic keys to the mind of the serial killer is a kind of 'spoiltness' that leads to a total inability to identify with other human beings. In this case, it seems clear that it was the spoilt rich girl who was trapped in total self-centredness, while the working class Gallego, for all his faults, was more normal and realistic.

Does not Charlene's involvement contradict the view, suggested in Chapter 7, that all serial killers are working class? In fact, as far as I can see, there is no psychological law that dictates that a middle- or upper-class person would be incapable of being a serial killer. The fact that all serial killers have had working-class backgrounds only proves that childhood misery and poverty can produce the kind of resentment that leads to serial murder. But the fifteenth-century child murderer Gilles de Rais was spoilt and wealthy, and there seems to be no reason why a modern Gilles should be an impossibility.

Fortunately, at the time of writing, no such person has emerged. When I came across the case of the New Jersey 'torso killer' Richard Cottingham, I was at first inclined to believe that he was an exception. Cottingham, a computer operator who workded for an insurance company, was arrested in May 1980 after screams from a motel room alerted the manager that somethnig was wrong. Cottingham had been torturing a prostitute for several hours, and fairly certainly intended to kill her, as he had killed half a dozen other women. Cottingham's method was to pick up a woman, take her to a bar and slip a drug into her drink, then take her to a motel and rape and torture her. Some victims were allowed to go; others were strangled and mutilated.

Cottingham was the son of an insurance salesman who was brought up in a suburban home, and had attended high school before he married and became a computer programmer. But Ron Leith's book, *The Prostitute Murders*, reveals that he was born in the Bronx and spoke with a Bronx accent. He spent the first ten years of his life in the area, before the family moved to New Jersey. His father was absent from home most of the time, and Cottingham, an only child, found it difficult to make friends at school. Nothing is known of the psychological causes of his passion to humiliate and torture women, but it seems clear that Cottingham is another example of the working-class serial killer.

Cottingham's most obvious characteristic was a high degree of conceit. Like so many serial killers, he seems to have had no doubt that he was the cleverest person in the courtroom. Ron Leith, who was in court, comments that it was Cottingham himself who cemented the state's case, giving an implausibly intricate alibi, and lecturing the judge on the strange world of prostitution. 'His arrogance seemed limitless.'

This, then, seems to the common denominator of serial killers — egoism combined with a kind of tunnel vision. But then, we have all known people like that — people who obviously believe that they are the most fascinating person in the world, and who regard it as natural to begin every sentence with 'I'. There must always have been such people. Then why is it that, in our own time, a percentage of them have turned into serial killers?

It is difficult to pinpoint a precise answer. But we can begin to grasp it if we ask: what would strike a Rip Van Winkle, who had fallen asleep in 1950, and woken up in the 1990s? Not just a faster pace of life, not just the increasing violence, but, surely, the extraordinary increase in frankness about sex and violence. We talk about it more openly, and that is more significant than the violence itself. It is worth remembering that the case of necrophile Ed Gein, which inspired *The Silence of the Lambs*, happened in the 1950s, while the crimes of Albert Fish and Carl Panzram took place in the 1930s. Rom Landau, writing in his autobiography *Seven* about the 1920s in Berlin, remarks: 'Hardly a month passed without some terrible murder becoming known. In many cases ordinary criminal instincts were combined with sexual perversion, typical of the day.' He goes on to cite a number of serial killers — Kürten, Grossman, Haarmann — and concludes: 'Indeed, human nature could assume no lower forms.' Yet, as we read about the Berlin of those days in Christopher Isherwood's *Goodbye to Berlin*, or see it in a film like *Cabaret*, we experience — or are supposed to experience — a certain nostalgia.

In fact, the most obvious difference between Germany in the 1920s and modern America or Europe lies in the communications industry. As Marshall McLuhan remarked, the world has become a 'global village'. Radio was a rarity in the 1920s. In the 1990s, every teenager is accustomed to references on television to Aids, to the use of condoms, and to perverisons like sodomy and fellatio. There is no point in deploring this. The same communications industry is responsible for the Open University, and for Mozart and Handel operas being shown at peak viewing time. The best we can do is to try to be intelligent and adaptable.

To conclude, I would like to refer to the case of Julie Wittmeyer, which is mentioned in Chapter 8. On 2 September 1977, a fourteen-year-old schoolgirl named Julie Wittmeyer failed to return to her home in Platte City, Kansas, after school. Her clothing was found in a field some days later, and her naked and mutilated body the following day. These were the early days of the Quantico Behavioral Science Unit, but a Platte City FBI agent decided to send them the details of the case. Within three weeks, the Unit had sent back a report that commented that the killer almost certainly knew Julie Wittmeyer, that he was probably a sexually frustrated 'loner', who might be regarded by his contemporaries as 'strange', and who might also be below average intelligence. When he saw the report, Police Chief Marion Beeler commented: 'Sure as shootin', that's him.' The description fitted a seventeen-year-old suspect — one of many — named Mark Sager, who looked far bigger than his years, and who was known to talk endlessly about sex. Sager was promptly arrested; at his trial, he was found guilty of the murder and sentenced to ten years. It was one of the Behavioral Science Unit's first triumphs. Since that time, psychological profiling has solved hundreds more such cases. That, at least, can be regarded as an undeniable bonus for contemporary society.

Colin Wilson

Bibliography

All His Father's Sins (The Gallego Case), Ray Biondi and Walt Hecox, Prima Publishing Co., 1988.

Federal Bureau of Investigation: *Criminal Investigation*.

Analysis/Sexual Homicide, 1985 (Law Enforcement Bulletins, 1980, 1985, 1986).

The Boston Strangler, Gerold Frank, New American Library, 1966.

Before I Kill More (The Heirens Case), Lucy Freeman, Award Books, 1955.

The Trial of Brady and Hindley, edited by Jonathan Goodman, David and Charles, 1973.

Killing for Company (Nilsen), Brian Masters, Jonathan Cape, 1985.

The Nilsen File, Brian McConnel and Douglas Bence, Futura Macdonald, London 1983.

Serial Killers: The Growing Menace, Joel Norris, Doubleday, New York, 1988.

Killer, A Journal of Murder (the Autobiography of Carl Panzram), edited by James E. Gaddis and James O. Long, Macmillans, New York, 1970.

Sexual Homicide, Patterns and Motives, Robert K. Ressler, Ann W. Burgess and John E. Douglas, Lexington Books, 1988.

The Want-Ad Killer (Carignan), Ann Rule, New American Library.

The Stranger Beside Me (Bundy), Ann Rule, W.W. Norton and Co., New York, 1980.

Encyclopaedia of Murder, Colin Wilson and Pat Pitman, Arthur Barker, 1961.

Encyclopaedia of Modern Murder, Colin Wilson and Donald Seaman, Arthur Barker, 1983, and Pan Books, 1989.

Written in Blood, A History of Forensic Detection, Colin Wilson, Equation Books, 1989.

Jack the Ripper: Summing Up and Verdict, Colin Wilson and Robin Odell, Bantam Books, 1987.

Human Nature Stained, Colin Wilson, Pauper's Press, 1991.

The Existential Study of Modern Murder, Jeffrey Smalldon, Pauper's Press, 1991.

Index

316